Stress and Tension Control 3

Stress Management

Stress and Tension Control 3

Stress Management

Edited by

F. J. McGuigan

Institute for Stress Management
United States International University
San Diego, California

Wesley E. Sime

Biofeedback and Stress Management
University of Nebraska
Lincoln, Nebraska

and

J. Macdonald Wallace

Health Education Consultant
Formerly of the West London Institute of Higher Education
London, England

PLENUM PRESS · NEW YORK AND LONDON

Library of Congress Cataloging in Publication Data

International Conference of the International Stress and Tension Control Society (3rd: 1989: University of Edinburgh)
Stress and tension control 3: stress management / edited by F. J. McGuigan, Wesley E. Sime, and J. Macdonald Wallace.
p. cm.
"Proceedings of the Third International Conference of the International Stress and Tension Control Society, held August 30–September 3, 1988, at the University of Edinburgh, Scotland"—T.p. verso.
Includes bibliographical references.
ISBN 978-1-4615-7917-5 ISBN 978-1-4615-7915-1 (eBook)
DOI 10.1007/978-1-4615-7915-1
1. Stress management—Congresses. I. McGuigan, F. J. (Frank J.), 1924– II. Sime, Wesley E. III. Wallace, J. Macdonald. IV. Title. V. Title: Stress and tension control three.
[DNLM: 1. Occupational Diseases—congresses. 2. Relaxation Technics—congresses. 3. Stress, Psychological—etiology—congresses. 4. Stress, Psychological—physiopathology—congresses. 5. Stress, Psychological—prevention & control—congresses. WM 172 I61s 1989]
RA785.I58 1989
155.9'042—dc20
DNLM/DLC 89-16248
for Library of Congress CIP

Proceedings of the Third International Conference of the International Stress and Tension Control Society, held August 30–September 3, 1988, at the University of Edinburgh, Edinburgh, Scotland

Softcover reprint of the hardcover 1st edition 1989

Division of Plenum Publishing Corporation
233 Spring Street, New York, N.Y. 10013

PREFACE

These are the proceedings of the Third International Interdisciplinary Conference on Stress and Tension Control, sponsored by the International Stress and Tension-Control Society held at the University of Edinburgh, Scotland from August 30-September 3, 1988.

The Society celebrated the 15th year of its existence. It was founded in 1974 as the American Association for the Advancement of Tension-Control which held annual meetings in Chicago through 1979. Recognizing the multi-national interest in stress and tension control, the association changed its name and scope accordingly. The original American Association was founded and nurtured for many years by Dr. and Mrs. Edmund Jacobson and Professor F. J. McGuigan.

The proceedings of the first international conference in London were also published by Plenum Publishing Company (*Stress and Tension Control*, McGuigan, Sime and Wallace, 1980), as were those of the second international conference which was held at the University of Sussex in Brighton, England (McGuigan, Sime and Wallace, 1984). These and the publication of the proceedings from 1974 reflect the interest in stress and tension control that has grown steadily throughout the past decades, as also does the publication of numerous other books related to Stress Management.

These proceedings are offered for the purpose of advancing the knowledge base of Stress Management for the many diverse circumstances that can cause stress related disorders. The contributions herein are typical of the research and technological practice that are being conducted in the field of Stress Management throughout the world. Our society seeks to continue its efforts to raise the methodological standards in order to increase the quality of research and add to our storehouse of sound knowledge in the field of Stress Management.

Throughout the pages of this volume the editors note that there was only moderate editing of the papers so that they retain the character created by the authors. Modification was necessary in some cases to improve comprehension since English was not the native language for some of the authors. Nor was it possible to carefully edit such matters as citations, references, quotations and statistical analyses, so that they remain the responsibility of the authors.

We want to express our appreciation to Phyllis Blocki for her excellent technical and typing assistance in the production of this book. We are especially grateful to

Kathy Raymer for her valuable assistance in editing the manuscripts for content and readability and in organizing the section topics of the book. The United States International University, the University of Nebraska and the University of Edinburgh are gratefully acknowledged for their support in providing facilities, clerical support and faculty contributions in the voluminous task of organizing and conducting the project from the early planning in 1984 to completion in 1989.

CONTENTS

RELAXATION THERAPY

VARIED APPROACHES IN BEHAVIORAL MEDICINE

STRESS AND COPING STRATEGIES AMONG PROFESSIONALS IN HEALTH CARE AND HUMAN SERVICES

STRESS-COPING STRATEGIES IN BUSINESS AND INDUSTRY

STRESS AND RELAXATION IN EDUCATION

STRESS RESPONSES AMONG MOTHERS DURING PREGNANCY, IN LABOR AND WITH INFANTS

THE PHYSIOLOGY OF STRESS

RELAXATION THERAPY

MANAGING INTERNAL COGNITIVE AND EXTERNAL ENVIRONMENTAL STRESSES THROUGH PROGRESSIVE RELAXATION[1]

F. J. McGuigan

Institute for Stress Management
United States International University
San Diego, CA

Stresses of life come from the external and from the internal environments. External environmental stresses have been variously specified and include problems that develop in social and inter-personal relations, the work place, and such specific circumstances as driving in traffic. Cognitive (mental) stresses may be generated by internal stimuli that are not directly triggered by external events. For instance, frightening thoughts may be evoked as patterns if covert responses occur when we lie quietly at rest or during sleep.

REACTIONS TO STRESSFUL EVENTS

The reactions to both externally and internally generated stresses are the same. They are the primitive ones of tensing the entire set of skeletal muscles as one rises (overtly or covertly) on the balls of the feet in the startle reaction pattern, hunching forward to prepare ourselves to meet an emergency by fight or flight. It is with the skeletal muscles that we immediately prepare ourselves for action. Numerous ensuing complex events throughout the body then follow, including the activation of the autonomic nervous system and the ensuing secretion of adrenaline and other chemical substances to maintain the emergency state. But the tensing of the skeletal muscles constitutes the critical controlling components of this reflexive reaction to danger. This state of heightened bodily tension, like a bullet ready to be fired, facilitates our adaptation by leading us on the attack or retreat. If we are reacting to a truck coming at us, the startle pattern that we assume is overt and obvious. Subtle threats to our well being, such as disturbing messages received on the phone, usually result in more subdued startle reactions. Still, there are heightened muscular tension states that are covert and thus not visible to others with the naked eye. Cognitively related stresses are usually of this covert kind, as for instance when we contract our muscles in the process of having a perplexing thought or worry.

---

[1]Presidential Address at the Third International Conference of the International Stress and Tension-Control Society, Edinburgh, Scotland, 1988.

Tensing to these externally and internally generated stresses is normal and adaptive. Once we have met and solved the problem, we can (and should) relax again. But if we do not relax relatively quickly, and if we sustain the muscular tensing for long periods, the risk of stress-related disorders increases dramatically. For example, chronic over-tension patterns may be described as "bracing" either in parts or all of the body, often in maladaptive positions as in Figure 1. For comparison, the individual is differentially relaxed in Figure 2. If the over-tension pattern as in Figure 1 is sufficiently prolonged, and if one does not learn to differentially relax as in Figure 2, a pathological condition of some system of the body will eventually develop.

STRESS-TENSION DISORDERS

In an approximate sense, the pathophysiology of stress-tension disorders falls within the traditional categories of *psychiatric* and *psychosomatic disorders*. The psychiatric disorders include anxiety reactions, phobias, insomnia and depressions. Psychosomatic disorders include those of the gastrointestinal tract (e.g., ulcers, colitis, spastic esophagus, hemorrhoids), of the cardiovascular system (high blood pressure, cardiac disorders), bruxism, and pain (headaches, and various pains of the body such as in the lower back).

A representation of the physiological events that produce these psychosomatic disorders, is presented in Figure 3. Chronic over-tension of the skeletal (striated) muscles overdrives the central nervous system which in turn, for example, overdrives the cardiovascular and gastrointestinal systems. The functional relationships among chronic over-tension and psychosomatic disorders has been well documented, especially by the classic work of Jacobson (1929). The appropriate therapy is to reverse the process by teaching the patient to systematically relax the striated musculature. If the habit patterns can be reversed, successful treatment of these disorders can be achieved. In some cases, however, the over-tension in conjunction with other factors, often results in permanent damage so that many such disorders are not reversible.

The same therapy is appropriate for some psychiatric disorders, though this might not be apparent at first glance. To understand how we can relax away some psychiatric disorders we first need to understand how cognitive processes occur.

HOW MENTAL EVENTS ARE GENERATED

Extensive research has established the importance of both muscular and brain events during cognition--they are the principal components of neuromuscular circuits that reverberate as we internally process information (McGuigan, 1978). Cognitive processes, both normal and abnormal, by our model, are immediately generated when information is transmitted in neuromuscular circuits that selectively interact throughout the body (McGuigan 1978, 1981, 1984; McGuigan & Dollins, 1989).

We can think of most cognitive processes--"dreams," "thoughts," "hallucinations," "images," "anxieties," "depressions," etc.--as having three components: *speech imagery*, which involves contraction of the speech musculature in conjunction with processes in the linguistic regions of the brain; *visual imagery*,which involves activities of the eyes and eye musculature in conjunction with events in the visual regions of the brain; and *somatic imagery* involving differential reactions throughout the body, depending on the nature of the somatic cognition, in conjunction with events in somaesthetic regions of the brain. Indeed, several hundred empirical psychophysiological investigations summarized in McGuigan (1978) document that the entire body is active during any

Figure 1. Excessive, unnecessary tension may be observed in the left arm and hand pressing against the desk, in the right hand where the pen is gripped excessively tight, and in the neck and shoulders (which is known as the "business person's hunch").

Figure 2. A differentially relaxed individual. In contrast to the excessive tension pattern exhibited in Figure 1, compare the well relaxed left arm and hand resting lightly on the table, the right hand holding the pen with only optimal tension, and the absence of the "business person's hunch."

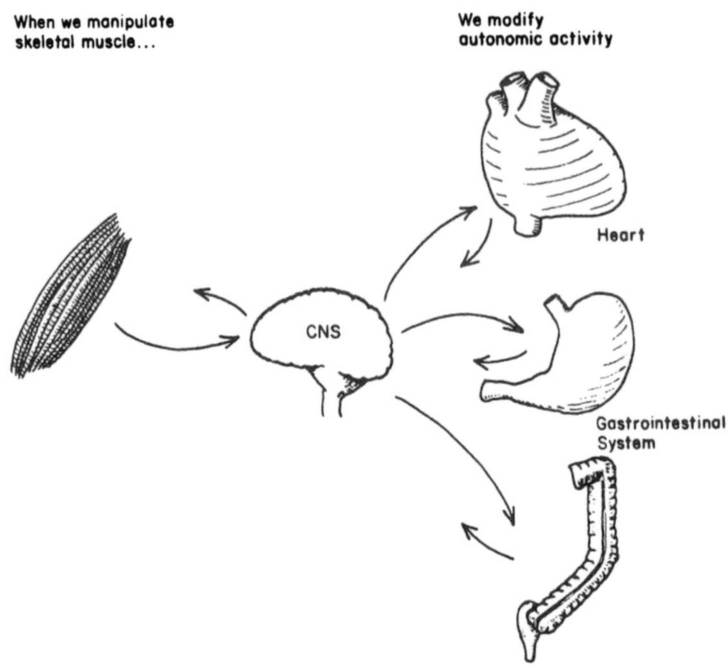

Figure 3. A model of the functional relationships among the skeletal musculature and other bodily systems. As muscular tension increases, activity of the central nervous system increases. In turn, there is heightened activity of various autonomic functions, such as those of the cardiovascular and gastrointestinal systems that if chronic become pathological. The effective therapy is to reverse the process by relaxation of the skeletal musculature which produces a tranquil state throughout the body. The smooth muscle in the gastrointestinal system, for example, then can relax which is therapeutic for spastic colon and other disorders.

kind of cognitive process, the cognitive activity usually involving all three of these kinds of imagery.

CONTROL OF UNWANTED MENTAL EVENTS

Given that cognitive processes are generated by the intricate interaction of the various sets of striated muscles with selected regions of the brain, the control of these cognitive events comes through manipulation of the various neuromuscular circuits. The only way we can directly intervene into these neuromuscular circuits through normal means (thus excluding medical interventions such as using tranquilizers) is by the striated muscles. We exercise self-control by means of our striated muscles, which is why a classical synonym for them is the "voluntary" muscles. As pointed out in the last century by Alexander Bain, the voluntary muscles are the "instruments of the will" (McGuigan, 1981). This principle has been extensively and successfully applied in the clinical research of Jacobson. As far back as the 1920's he started reporting his successes in muscular control therapy for a variety of psychiatric disorders (Jacobson, 1929).

In therapy, the patient first learns to gain control over all of the muscles of the body. Then the patient learns to relax the relevant striated muscles and thereby gains the ability to bring the neuromuscular circuits that generate the maladaptive cognitive processes into a state of tranquility. In short, one can relax away the maladaptive cognitive events by relaxing the striated muscles that control them.

The principle for controlling appropriate psychosomatic and psychiatric disorders is thus straightforward. It is the basic physiological maxim that these disorders can often be alleviated or eliminated merely by relaxing the controlling muscles. Consider the behavior of a typical neurotic, for instance. The neurotic often manifests tensions in various parts of the body, sometimes momentary, other times sustained bracing reactions. There are abortive acts to do one thing, rapidly changing to another. The acts are disharmonious, lacking coordination. The subtle tensions, added to the more obvious ones of shifting, restlessness, grimaces and tics, form a basis for inferences about the cognitive processes of the neurotic. By expressing feelings of nervousness and anxiety and relating to the therapist details of the problems and stresses that are faced, the patient can be helped in learning to relax excessive tensions and associated unwanted cognitive processes away.

LEARNING HOW TO RELAX

The method of Progressive Relaxation was very carefully developed, empirically guided through electromyographic records so as to progressively relax the entire body in the most efficient manner that has yet been discovered. The method begins with the person lying prone, legs not crossed, arms slightly to the side of the body and not touching. The eyes are gradually allowed to close. The first region of the body to be controlled in the method of Progressive Relaxation is the arms. For instance, one learns to identify a localized tension in the ventral surface of one arm and then relaxes it away. Bending the hand back at the wrist, the person holds the position for a moment or two (Figure 4). The learner, at this point, studies the tension, the first time in life that the person has ever specifically recognized what tension feels like. Once there is a good clear image of tension, the hand is allowed to relax. This is not an easy step to get across. One of the best ways of teaching it is to watch as you tell

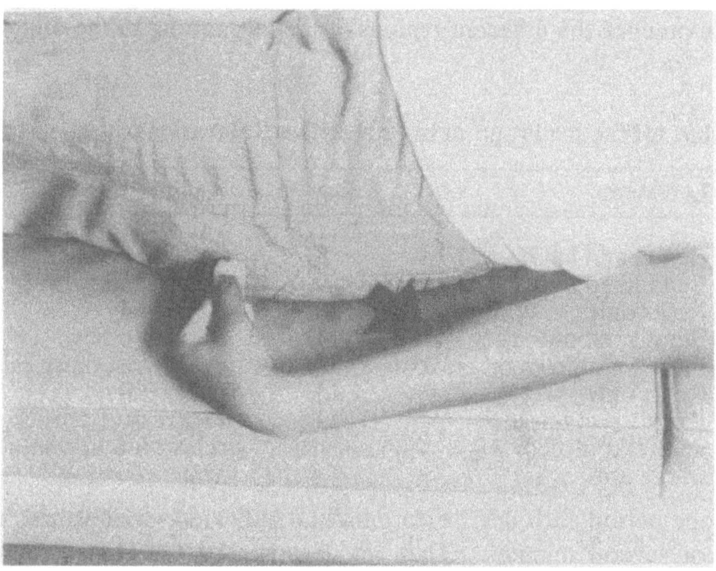

Figure 4. When the learner bends a hand forward the tension signal can be recognized in the front (ventral) part of the forearm.

the learner "now relax the hand," and she/he will *work* the hand down. Work is exactly the opposite of relaxation. You say: "You are making an *effort* to relax. Trying is work! Trying is contracting muscles, so you cannot *try* to relax. You simply allow the skeletal muscle fibers to elongate. And to allow them to elongate, to relax, you simply "let go." An appropriate analogy is that of a limp dishrag--the hand simply collapses when support is removed.

Once the learner has that basic notion, it is simply a matter of repetition. The principles are: l) identify the local sign of tension; and 2) allow it to relax away. You study the contrast between the previous state of tension and the ensuing state of relaxation. The emphasis is on the learner. "*You* identified the tension, and *you* relaxed it away. I didn't do it as a teacher, it's up to you." From this point on, aside from guidance, the teacher cannot do it, it's up to the learner. The key word is redundancy: practice, practice, practice! By systematically repeating the process of identifying a localized tension, the control signal, and repeatedly relaxing it away, one comes to effectively control tension in that region. With practice, the control signal can be relaxed or tensed to an appropriate degree at will.

The method calls for thoroughness. For example, there are a number of control signals in each arm that need to be studied, as illustrated in Table 1. In addition to localized tension (that confined to a specific muscle group) the body also generates a more widespread kind of tension which is carried chronically throughout the striated musculature. This generalized tension is a residual tension in which there is low level continuous contraction of the muscle fibers, along with slight localized movements. Localized relaxation allows one to relax a particular, limited group of muscles, but a different technique is required for generalized tension. An effective procedure for controlling this widespread phenomenon is to very gradually and uniformly stiffen (tense) an entire arm for perhaps one minute and then gradually relax it over an extended period of time (perhaps 20 minutes). This procedure, with sufficient practice, can allow one to relax generalized residual tensions down to a zero level.

After the learner has practiced sufficiently with one arm we proceed on in the same manner with the other arm. Next we proceed with the legs in the same thorough manner. We practice the different regions of the leg, getting to the thigh, up through

Table 1. Practice Program in Progressive Relaxation for the Arms

Day No.	Left Arm	Day No.	Right Arm
1.	Bend hand back.	8.	Bend hand back
2.	Bend hand forward.	9.	Bend hand forward.
3.	Relax only.	10.	Relax only.
4.	Bend at elbow.	11.	Bend at elbow.
5.	Press wrist down on books.	12.	Press wrist down on books
6.	Relax only.	13.	Relax only.
7.	Progressive tension and relaxation of whole arm.	14.	Progressive tension and relaxation of whole arm.

Practice one period each day, performing the indicated tension three times at intervals of several minutes. Then go negative for the remainder of each period. Thus, on day one, bend the left hand back. On day two, bend the left hand forward, and on day three do nothing at all. After fourteen days, you are ready to go on to the leg.

the buttocks, and so on. Without this step-by-step, systematic learning, a person simply is unable to adequately relax the entire body.

After the legs, we move on to the trunk. In the abdominal region we are directly concentrating on gastrointestinal problems such as colitis and ulcers. It is estimated that 90% of the diarrhea and constipation in the country is due to over-tension concentrated in the abdominal region.

Next, we proceed up through the chest, back, shoulders, and then the neck. In the neck we start getting control of the regions directly responsible for headaches.

Moving into the eye region, the individual learns to wrinkle the forehead and to frown. I usually advise one to look into a mirror to distinguish between wrinkling the forehead and frowning. It's a little like learning to wiggle your ears, but with practice one can do it. In this area one can study carefully the extremely small tension signals in the eye region, the ones that are responsible, principally, for cognitive activities involved in visualization. I would say that about 90% of cognitive activities have visual and conjoint linguistic components. To get direct control over those, such as to relax a fear away, one needs to learn to relax these very slight tensions in the eye muscles and speech muscles. Much attention has been placed recently on visual imagery, e.g., "guided imagery." Such practice could have been taken from Progressive Relaxation as it was developed in the 1920s. How often we seem to reinvent the wheel.

Progressive Relaxation of the ocular muscles involves several different eye positions which include looking straight ahead, down, up and right. In looking to the left, very slight tensions can be detected, for instance, in the left side of the eye that are perhaps 1000 times less intense than those which the learner observes in the arm muscles at the outset of training. The perception of progressively smaller levels of tension in tiny muscle groups is the goal in Jacobson's Progressive Relaxation. Critical in achieving the skill of detecting extremely slight tensions is the Method of Diminishing Tension wherein increasingly slight tension signals are observed.

When we proceed on to the speech region, one learns to recognize tension controls in muscles that open the jaws. Next the learner closes the jaws. The learner picks up the jaw tensions rather rapidly, but there are secondary control regions in the temples which usually the learner does not recognize at first. The muscles of the jaw are particularly vulnerable to tension-control problems of bruxism. In my clinical experience, bruxism along with hemorrhoids are among the first symptoms to be relieved among patients who are learning to relax. Control of these tensions needs to be carried over into sleep.

The next step is to study tension controls in the cheeks and in the lips. The most important of the speech muscles is the tongue, a very strong muscle that is active in essentially all of our cognitive activities. The practice position is to pull the tongue back and study those tensions. Then in the next period the tongue is pushed against the teeth, learning to control those tensions. Control of the tongue is effective for helping individuals to relax and to help them go to sleep. The strategy for insomnia is to carry relaxation into bedtime.

Upon completion of the first phase of training,the learner has studied all of the 1030 odd muscles of the body in groups while learning to relax lying down. But we do not want to only relax while prone. We need to generalize relaxation into ordinary life. What the learner needs to do is, through successive approximation, to relax in the various positions that occur in everyday living. The essential concept here is known as *Differential Relaxation*. Differential Relaxation is learning to *optimally* contract (tense) only those muscles that are necessary for performing the act at hand, as in Figure 2. Hence one now learns to relax sitting up, with eyes closed and the head down on the chest, as one proceeds through the program once again.

Then the program is repeated in its entirety as the learner sits with the head up, balanced on the spinal cord. After that is accomplished, the learner proceeds sitting with head up and relaxing with the eyes open. When you totally relax the eyes while leaving them open, with the eye muscles not contracting, there is no visual perception. The eyes must move before you are able to perceive anything so that in this totally relaxed condition there are no visual images whatsoever. Other research in which the visual image is stabilized on the retina has also confirmed that without the eyes moving, there is no visual perception.

In the next stage, one learns to differentially relax in other activities such as reading and writing. For example, in reading, one sits comfortably relaxed with the feet on the floor, optimally contracting the muscles of the arms to hold the book, to move the eyes and to contract the speech musculature in "sub-vocalization." Research has shown that covert speech behavior facilitates the understanding of what is being read (e.g., McGuigan, 1978,1981, 1984). This conclusion has also been confirmed clinically so that if the individual relaxes the speech muscles during reading, the report is that there is no meaning to the text that falls on the eyes.

The final stage of learning to relax is to incorporate Differential Relaxation into everyday life, twenty-four hours a day, including sleeping at night. At this point, it is not really necessary to have an explicit practice period as one is differentially relaxing in all activities. This stage is known as achieving "automaticity" in which any unwanted tensions are automatically and unconsciously released.

The principles of learning to relax are simple enough. The difficulty comes in actually practicing to relax, in the learning process of effectively controlling the 1030 or so striated muscles throughout the body. The task can be enormous in a person who has for decades learned to habitually brace the sizable quantity of striated muscles which comprise almost half the body weight. To effectively reverse maladaptive muscular conditions that are extensively represented throughout the body requires really diligent dedication. After a period of being discouraged when working with patients, I asked Dr. Jacobson, "What are the characteristics of those who will sufficiently dedicate themselves to practice?" His response, off the top of his head was: "Engineers and Catholics!" Perhaps he should have added concert musicians. An analogy for achieving a suitable state of relaxation is to learn to play Bach at a high level of competence on a musical instrument. The principles of manipulating the components of the musical instrument are simple and straightforward enough. The problem comes in sufficient dedicated practice under effective learning conditions.

CLINICAL PROGRESSIVE RELAXATION

The application of Progressive Relaxation for clinical purposes starts with taking a case history of the pattern of complaints that the patient presents. The initial complaint might be of headaches, but with a careful case history there will typically emerge five or six complaints usually concluding with chronic fatigue (continuous bracing is work that tires one). Ideally, the therapist electromyographically (EMG) measures stress-tension profiles. As the patient learns to relax, the tension profile consisting of samples from throughout the body, gradually decreases. In successful cases (usually those who regularly practice relaxation), the complaints are alleviated or eliminated completely. The reduction in EMG stress-tension profiles provides an independent confirmation of progress of the therapy.

There have been sufficient reports of clinical applications of Progressive Relaxation elsewhere, so I will not dwell on them here except to mention one exciting possibility that has been developing in recent research. There is some evidence to indicate that relaxation may have an impact on the resilience of the immune system. If true, there are far reaching consequences. For example, though we may never be able to *prevent* the development of cancer through relaxation, it does seem that we are able to modify the development of a cancer through relaxation once it has occurred. The mechanism probably is that by relaxing the muscles we beneficially affect the immune system in some unknown way. Certainly a high priority research project is to conduct a true conditioning experiment, applying Progressive Relaxation to cancer patients.

In conclusion, let me end on an optimistic thought about prevention. We know that we can prevent many stress-tension maladies by adequately relaxing before they occur. For example, a major development in the last decade or so has been the emergence of the specialized pain clinic in which relaxation is a major weapon against pain. It has been quite clearly established that pain can be prevented or at least considerably attenuated by relaxing--the applications range from preventing pain in the dentist's chair by relaxing, even obviating the use of novocaine during a root canal, through major surgery. More generally, if we could teach our children to learn to relax, the benefits for the rest of their lives would be enormous. They could not only prevent the varieties of psychosomatic and psychiatric disorders that we have discussed, but children could be more productive and joyous throughout their lives. Of even greater importance would be the tremendous benefits for society at large. Financial benefits for industry, and for society generally, are inestimable.

REFERENCES

Jacobson, E. (1929).*Progressive Relaxation*. Chicago: University of Chicago Press.

McGuigan, F. J. (1978). *Cognitive psychophysiology: Principles of covert behavior.* Hillsdale, N.J.: Erlbaum.

McGuigan, F.J. (1981). *Calm down: A guide for stress and tension control.* New York: Guilford (also, San Diego, CA : ISM-USIU, 10455 Pomerado Rd., 92131).

McGuigan, F. J. (1984). How is linguistic memory accessed?--A psychophysiological approach. *Pavlovian Journal of Biological Science, 19*, 119-136.

McGuigan, F. J., & Dollins, A. (1989). Patterns of covert speech behavior and phonetic coding. *Pavlovian Journal of Biological Science, 24*, 19-26.

THE USE AND MISUSE OF SCIENTIFIC RELAXATION IN SPEECH PATHOLOGY

Robert L. Casteel

Speech Pathology
Portland State University
Portland, Oregon

It has been seventy-eight years since Edmund Jacobson wrote his dissertation on *Inhibition*, nearly sixty years since he wrote his landmark text *Progressive Relaxation* and about fifty-five years since he published *You Must Relax*, a text for lay persons. Subsequently, many authors have modified, distorted, misinterpreted or basically changed his program. Changes by others in print have caused fourth and fifth order permutations of the Jacobson program to the point that well-meaning people attribute all types of relaxation schemes to Jacobson. Many of these schemes have scant resemblance to his original work.

The seed for self-discovery of the above was planted at the second international conference of the International Stress and Tension- Control Society at the University of Sussex in 1983. Although I was trained in the early 1960s by Lois Barclay, P.A. and the late Herman Dickel, M.D. who had been directly trained by Edmund Jacobson, I tended to be a non-critical reader of my colleagues in speech-language pathology. It was as though I was delighted that others in my field saw the benefits of "relaxation" for speech and voice. The seed was planted by a simple question from Dr. Wes Sime, physiologist at the University of Nebraska. Upon the completion of my address dealing with the benefits of scientific relaxation as incorporated in my program for the control of stuttering and the modification of voice disorders, Sime asked why my program wasn't used by more professionals in the United States. Caught off guard I replied with some inane comment such as "I guess they think it won't work." Thereupon, a more critical reading of authors who espoused "relaxation" followed.

The purpose of this paper is to overview how speech pathologists have interpreted relaxation training, to high-light Jacobson's principles that are frequently ignored or forgotten, and to share how these principles influence my use of scientific relaxation in speech pathology.

COMMON MISINFORMATION

The speech pathology literature is replete with information on relaxation but not with Jacobson's scientific relaxation (learning to identify the neuromuscular sensations of muscle groups contracting and how to modify the contractions).

Unfortunately, most of it deals with external locus of control (the clinician) rather than having the individual take responsibility for identifying muscle tension and learning to relax. The spectrum includes, but is not limited to, massage, drugs, suggestion and imagery, music therapy, hypnosis or induced relaxation, physical therapy, distraction, yoga, exhortation, relaxation, calm environment and incantations (Van Riper, 1972). Much of the above has been linked to or combined with Jacobson's Progressive Relaxation or even worse, taught as if that were the way to teach Progressive Relaxation, i.e., exercise, imagery, suggestion. As a result, some conclude that Progressive Relaxation does not transfer well to real-life situations.

In scanning the literature, both classic texts and current publications, one finds misinformation, under-instruction and over-generalization. In Greene (1964), a well-known British author, there are 22 pages on relaxation, and one phrase on Jacobson, viz., "abrupt cessation of tension for contrast." In the very next line she recommends stretching exercises, such as extending the arms along the side in order to identify "strain" in the shoulders. According to her, this is to be contrasted with the enjoyment of the resting period. Van Riper (1972) asserts the efficacy of Progressive Relaxation for inducing sleep; however, he concludes that we cannot go through life as a "limp noodle."

Wilson (1979) combines at least four philosophies in his relaxation procedures: 1) Jacobson's Progressive Relaxation, 2) imagery, 3) relax very slowly from a forced tension state, and 4) massage. In Boone and McFarlane (1988), Progressive Relaxation is discussed under "differential relaxation," but does not deal with differential relaxation and, further, the procedure is described as "deliberately relaxing and tensing certain muscles." This is not different from Van Riper and Irwin (1958) who mislabled Progressive Relaxation as "differential relaxation." They instruct that one should tense and relax starting with the toes and working one's way to the throat; and if one should find tension in the throat upon voicing, relaxation should be started over again from the toes. Prater and Swift (1984) had a variation on this theme. They discussed Progressive Relaxation as tensing and relaxing the limbs first and then more proximal body parts with the idea of identifying what tension and relaxation "feel like." I would say, according to Jacobson, they failed to recognize, among other things, that relaxation does not have a feeling. The original goal is to identify the tension signal and the final goal is to learn to "let go" tension (not tense).

In what Leith and Johnston (1986) call tension/relaxation contrast, they submit that "the client may learn the essence of relaxation in one session or less." They start with a clenched fist which they slowly let go. With this amount and type of instruction, I doubt if the client develops any awareness of the fact that the muscles of the forearm are responsible for making the fist. Along this same theme, Stemple (1984) wrote in a short paragraph entitled "Progressive relaxation," "the most popular exercise involves alternately tensing and relaxing all the muscles from the scalp to the toes."

All authors are not as far away from the basic tenets of Jacobson, for Moore (1971) stated "the basis of the technique is the recognition and localization by the patient of muscles in contraction and the voluntary relaxation of the contractions." Unfortunately, however, he talks about exercise and gives no instructions.

In view of all that's been stated here, with the inherent limitations and the obvious deviations from the tenets of Jacobson, perhaps the best professional recommendation comes from Bless (1983). When writing on voice disorder management she stated "...changes almost invariably coexist with excessive tension...in extreme tension...refer them to a relaxation therapist."

In a paper of this length, it is not possible to quote or paraphrase even most of those who have written about relaxation, its limitations and possible benefits to the practice of speech pathology. After fifty years of Jacobson being modified by scientists, clinicians and popular writers, the above may sound normal and differences may not seem to be important. It is my intent, therefore, in the next section, to focus on aspects of Jacobson's program which seem to have been ignored, forgotten or not learned by practitioners in speech pathology. When the basic tenets of Jacobson are ignored, the outcome should not be expected to be the same.

IGNORED JACOBSON PRINCIPLES

A. Distinguish the separate sensations of tension and strain.

Many casual proponents of relaxation do not train subjects to detect the vague sensation of muscles contracting which has been described as: misty, delicate, unobtrusive. The sensation of tension, for most, is difficult to detect. By contrast, the strain at a joint is sharp and easy to detect. The sensation of strain masks the identification of tension or is mistaken for tension. To detect degrees of muscle tension is a learned skill.

B. Do not tense and relax repeatedly for it becomes exercise rather than relaxation.

People who work at relaxation are not learning relaxation. Work is the product of muscles contracting, whereas relaxation is the absence of doing. Students have come to confuse the contraction used to identify tension sites with the relaxation process. Once the muscle sense identification is learned, one does not tense to relax; rather, one simply lets go.

C. Use "relaxation practice" not "relaxation exercises."

It is more than a case of semantics. We tend to work for those things we wish to accomplish--we exercise ourselves. Rather, we need to practice learning the skill of not doing. Exercise is doing and relaxation practice is the absence of doing.

D. Do not use suggestion, for it distracts from attending to the tension signal.

Although Jacobson does not use the word "distraction," he does contend that "suggestion" interferes with the task of skill learning. It becomes little more than a lesson in positive thinking rather than learning to scientifically control muscle contraction.

E. Every third session does not involve tensing.

I cannot find anywhere in the speech pathology literature that every third session is exclusively relaxation. These sessions are conducted without purposeful muscle contraction. To me, this is a critical part of the training which prepares the subject for differential relaxation in life situations.

F. Following tensing a new group for identification of the tension signal, relax all previously learned parts when you relax a given part, but never tense all parts.

Once again, in addition to the new learning, emphasis is being placed upon simply going negative which is the ultimate goal of scientific relaxation, i.e., when one discovers an undue amount of tension, one reduces it.

G. Study one group per session.

Too often in the literature and in clinical practice the subject is instructed to tense and relax from head to toe or to tense and relax all muscle groups at one time. This does not permit focused learning and becomes little more than exercise.

H. "Never contract a part in order to relax it. Avoid movement as an aid during attempted relaxation." (1957).

This is a direct quotation from Jacobson which clearly warns against relaxation exercise. Raising the level of excitability does not lead to calming down. The only reason given for contracting muscles to any degree is to identify the subtle signal of muscles being contracted. Its purpose is identification, not relaxation.

I. Goals for primary muscle group activity and secondary group muscle activity are not the same in differential relaxation.

With primary muscles used to carry out a task, the goal is to achieve the appropriate amount of tonus that the task calls for (minimum tension or optimum tension); with secondary muscle activity (non-participating muscle groups) the goal is to eliminate tension by total relaxation of the muscles not requisite to the task.

Before moving to the next section, it should be emphasized that the reader, whether a speech pathologist or not, should not simply view Jacobson through this writer's filters. We need to re-read Jacobson as if for the first time. Anything sort of that and I would be guilty of promoting error as my well-meaning colleagues have done. Also, these comments are made out of context; so, look for these points in the context of Jacobson's writings.

USE OF PROGRESSIVE RELAXATION IN SPEECH PATHOLOGY

There is increased evidence that stuttering is not associated with *trait* anxiety as much as it is with *state* anxiety. In other words, the person who stutters is no more anxious in general than non-stutterers (Zenner and Shepherd, 1980); but in specific self-esteem threatening situations, i.e., speaking, the individual over tenses and uses too much effort which valves off air flow rather than permitting air to flow. They try too hard and do the wrong things. The more effort they bring to the task, the more severe is their disorder, according to lay people and professionals alike. Obviously, no matter the cause, they need to bring less tension to the task. The problem is they do not know how to relax nor what to relax. They need to learn to "calm down" (McGuigan, 1981) in general and differentially relax speech musculature in specific speaking situations (state anxiety). Damste (1970) states relaxation has "little value...unless {it} leads to tension-control during an increasing number of everyday life situations."

For these reasons, Progressive Relaxation is only part of most treatment programs including mine. It is used in conjunction with other procedures i.e., specific speech modifications are taught to alter old ways of voicing and articulating under stress. Also, frequently incorporated in the procedures is Wolpe's (1958) Systematic Desensitization using a hierarchy of fear-evoking stimuli varying progressively in strength.

It is my belief that when the individual learns to recognize the abnormal tension brought to the task, learns how to reduce or eliminate unwanted tensions (differential relaxation) and is appropriately instructed in what one needs to do to talk, the person can take responsibility for voicing and speaking. This is not an immediately learned thing nor a once-learned thing. The individual has to experience learning, plateauing and even relapsing in order to discover that it is not an immediately learned thing nor a once-learned thing. One must experience learning, plateauing and even relapsing in order to discover that what happens is not magic, but the product of new skills and specific choices being made by the individual.

These subtle muscular adjustments cannot be learned through exercise, suggestion nor admonition. Success, whether in voice disorders or stuttering, is the product of the individual learning how, through self-discovery and self-responsibility, to manage their muscles. Change is the tedious task of learning to respond to life's speaking situations in a new manner. In the beginning, this responding takes place not free of self-doubt, not free of anxiety, nor free of failure, but change is the product of an on-going task of becoming better and better acquainted with what one needs to do with muscles to talk efficiently. Over time the individual is learning to change from tension habits to relaxation habits. In effect, the person is changing how he reacts to perceived stress. Relaxation is *practiced* in a quiet environment in the beginning, but relaxation is *learned* in real life situations doing the things one needs to do to talk.

REFERENCES

Bless, D. (1983). Treatment of functional voice disorders. *In Voice Disorders*, W.Perkins (Ed.),pp.21-30. New York: Thieme-Stratton, Inc.

Boone, Daniel R. and McFarlane, Stephen C. (1988). ,*The Voice and Voice Therapy*, 4th ed. Englewood Cliffs, N.J.: Prentice-Hall, Inc.

Damste, P. Helbert (1970). A behavioral analysis of a stuttering theory. *In Conditionin in Stuttering Therapy*, pp. 77-95. Memphis, Tenn.: Speech Foundation of America.

Greene, Margaret C.L. (1964). *The Voice and its Disorders*, 2nd ed. Great Britain: Pitman Medical Publishing Co., Ltd.

Jacobson, Edmund (1957). *You Must Relax* , 4th ed. New York: McGraw-Hill Book Co., I

Leith, William & Johnston, Robert (1986). *Handbook of Voice Therapy for the School Clinician*. San Diego, California: College-Hill Press, Inc.

McGuigan, F.J. (1981). *Calm Down--A Guide for Stress and Tension Control*. New York: Guilford.

Moore, G. Paul (1971). *Organic Voice Disorders*. Englewood Cliffs,N.J.:Prentice-Hall,Inc

Prater, Rex J. & Swift, Roger W. (1984). *Manual of Voice Therapy* . Boston, Mass.: Little, Brown and Co.

Stemple, Joseph C. (1984). *Clinical Voice Pathology*. Columbus, Ohio: Charles E. Merrill Publishing Co.

Van Riper, Charles (1973). *The Treatment of Stuttering*. Englewood Cliffs, N.J.: Prentice-Hall, Inc.

Van Riper, Charles & Irwin, John V. (1958). *Voice and Articulation*. Englewood Cliffs, N.J.: Prentice-Hall, Inc.

Wilson, D. Kenneth (1979). *Voice Problems of Children*, 2nd ed. Baltimore, Md.: The Williams and Wilkins Co.

Wolpe, J. (1958). *Psychotherapy by Reciprocal Inhibition*. Stanford, California: Stanford University Press.

Zenner, Anthony A. & Shepherd, William Pete (1980, November). Trait anxiety of stutterers and nonstutterers. Research presented at the Annual Convention of the American Speech-Language-Hearing Association, Detroit, Michigan.

BREATHING AWARENESS AS A RELAXATION METHOD IN CARDIAC REHABILITATION

Jan van Dixhoorn[1] and Hugo J. Duivenvoorden[2]

[1]St. Joannes de Deo Hospital
Haarlem, The Netherlands

[2]Erasmus University Rotterdam
Rotterdam, The Netherlands

INTRODUCTION

Opinions differ as to the feasibility and utility of relaxation therapy for cardiac patients. Although it seems obvious that relaxation is helpful for reducing stress in the recovery period after acute myocardial infarction (1-5), as well as for changing risk behavior (6, 7), its usage in cardiac rehabilitation is limited and variable. Only in West-Germany, it seems, is relaxation offered in all rehabilitation centers, mainly as autogenic training classes (5). In the Netherlands, application for admission is rapidly increasing, up to about 50% for all centers (8). Cardiac patients pose a particular challenge with respect to relaxation. They tend to be skeptical, to prefer strategies that allow them to remain in control, to be impatient and to have little power of self-observation (5, 9). Certainly it is true that relaxation may provoke anxiety and resistance (10). Many professionals involved in cardiac rehabilitation consider it useful for all patients to learn relaxation (5, 11), even though it may have appeal to a minority only. Others assume that only some patients need to learn it (12).

On the other hand, the rehabilitation period is suitable for learning more adequate coping styles. The most popular treatment form, aerobic conditioning, has only a modest psychic effect (1, 13, 14). The aforementioned cardiac patients provide the rationale for behavioral intervention such as relaxation to take place. Certainly, introducing relevant coping styles and motivating patients to utilize them poses a significant challenge to health professionals (9).

An adequate strategy depends as much on the relaxation procedure and technique as on the context of the rehabilitation setting. In St. Joannes de Deo Hospital, Haarlem, The Netherlands, a procedure for individual treatment was developed. It centered around respiration, also using EMG-feedback and general relaxation (15). A randomized controlled trial of this relaxation therapy showed that it improved the overall physical benefit of training, in comparison with only exercise training (16). In particular, the risk of a negative training outcome was diminished by 50% and ST-segment abnormalities, indicating myocardial ischemia, were significantly reduced. A two-year follow-up revealed that patients who learned to relax experienced significantly fewer cardiac events (17). With respect to the psychic benefit of rehabilitation, exercise per se did not result in any psychic change, but the combined treatment of exercise and relaxation increased perceived well-being and reduced anxiety and feelings of invalidity (18).

The nature of the procedure employed was breathing awareness. Most relaxation techniques do not address respiration directly, so as not to disturb its autonomic character by voluntary control. The rationale is, that when one relaxes physically and mentally, respiration becomes optimal. On the other hand, regulating (pacing) respiration modulates the stress response and anxiety (19, 20). Teaching diaphragmatic breathing is effective in reducing stress for various disorders (21-24).

Although reduced arousal certainly affects respiration (25), respiratory *habits* do not necessarily change with general relaxation (26). Simply paying attention to breathing without specific instruction can also disturb it, because of an over-consciousness or by evoking faulty or strenuous habits.

An underlying fact is the dual role of respiration as a voluntary and involuntary function. Breathing may be an indicator of tension but functions as well as a regulator of tension. The problem of breathing technique is how to use the latter potential without disturbing its feedback value as a tension indicator. Therefore, techniques derived from voice and breathing therapy were integrated in general relaxation technique, emphasizing body awareness and passive concentration. This resulted in "breathing awareness" as a relaxation method. Its aim is to elicit a shift in the respiratory pattern towards a more easy and natural pattern while avoiding strain and effortful practice. When successful, this has strong subjective effects and usually lowers respiration rate. This method was applied to cardiac patients, because, as was mentioned earlier, it is for cardiac patients of prime importance to achieve an experience of relaxation within the first sessions of relaxation therapy. A limited number of sessions should be sufficient as a first step to master the basic technique. It is of equal importance to emphasize sensory awareness and to notice bodily signals of tension and relaxation. The majority of the patients are not at all used to being aware of these signals, or on the contrary, to ignoring them. "Feeling well" means "feeling nothing," i.e., there is nothing to complain about. Finally, it is important to present relaxation as a psychologically neutral technique and as part of the normal rehabilitation program.

The questions to be answered are,

1) does relaxation, applied in the procedure outlined above, reduce respiration rate and increase body awareness,

2) do respiration rate and body awareness in turn induce beneficial effects with respect to the total rehabilitation outcome,

3) which respiratory parameters are influenced in particular? (fine grain-analysis)

Table 1. Baseline Clinical Data

Variable	Treatment A		Treatment B	
No. of cases	76		80	
Age (years)	55.4	(8.2)	55.7	(8.1)
Males	71	(93)	76	(95)
Working	50	(66)	51	(64)
Married/with Partner	69	(91)	74	(93)
Size of MI:				
unknown	4	(5)	4	(5)
small	20	(26)	27	(34)
medium	27	(36)	22	(27.5)
large	25	(33)	27	(34)
In-hospital signs of heart failure	14	(18)	13	(16)
Medication on discharge:				
beta blockers	20	(26)	25	(31)
diuretics	27	(36)	20	(25)
anti-anginal	13	(17)	18	(23)
Start of physical training (weeks after hospital dscharge)	4.8	(2.8)	5.2	(2.1)
Exercize testing:				
Maximum work load (watt)	136	(24)	132	(21)
ST-segment abnormalities	24	(32)	20	(25)
Angina pectoris	9	(12)	9	(11)

Data are reported as events and percentages of cases or as means (SD), MI, myocardial infarction.

PATIENTS AND METHODS

Patients

After being discharged from several hospitals, cardiac patients are referred to the regional rehabilitation center at St. Joannes de Deo Hospital, Haarlem, The Netherlands. In three intake periods (1981-1983), a total of 156 myocardial infarction patients were found eligible for the study. They were randomly allocated to two treatment protocols. Patients who were considered to need individual (psychosocial) help in addition to exercise training were excluded. There was no age limit. Table 1 summarizes the clinical data at the time of entry to the trial for the two randomized groups.

Treatment Programs

Rehabilitation consisted of a program of relaxation training in addition to exercise training (Treatment A) or of exercise training only (Treatment B). The exercise training consisted of 5 weeks of interval training, once a day for half an hour, on a bicycle ergometer. Training was done in groups of four patients supervised by two physical therapists. Each patient exercised up to 70% of the maximal heart rate attained at the pre-training exercise test.

Relaxation training was given once a week in six individual sessions of one hour, by five specially trained persons. Three of them were a psychologist, a medical doctor and a physical therapist. Several procedures for active and passive relaxation were employed: EMG feedback of the frontalis muscle was used , 1) as a "mental device" (25) to focus attention for passive relaxation, 2) to give feedback of muscle tension and explain the concept of relaxation, 3) to monitor excess inspiratory effort.

For breathing instruction, attention was directed to respiratory movement (rate, depth, location, ease, regularity). In the supine position, one hand was placed on the lower abdomen, accompanied by the words, "the hand notices what the body does." Next, a technique to influence respiration was applied. Audible lip breathing is an example of this method. It is postulated that this technique stimulates inspiration and diaphragmatic activity, while preventing strain in the throat or chest. Then, attention was again directed towards passively monitoring breathing and the patient was asked to compare the result with the previous condition. The point was made that the primary aim of the technique is to become aware of differences, first in quality of respiratory movement, next in body sensation, and finally in thought, mood and feeling.

The patient learned to observe and elicit a "shift" towards a more easy, free and effortless respiratory pattern, with a smooth rhythm of inhalation and exhalation. The therapist monitored respiration and gave feedback so that inspiration expanded both the lower abdomen and the costal margin. Expiration was moderate and slow. Manual techniques were applied to elicit breathing movements which involved the trunk as a whole and required less effort. This was practiced first in the supine, relaxed position, but later also as the subject was sitting and standing ("active relaxation"). The patient was then asked to practice at home and also when experiencing chest discomfort.

Care was taken to introduce relaxation as a part of the routine rehabilitation procedure and not a means of providing special psychological help. The treatment itself was presented in a neutral fashion. It emphasized the technical and physical aspects of relaxation and its utility in dealing with daily challenges. Also provided was a rationale, in the form of the biofeedback instrumentation, for incorporating the treatment. Finally, breathing "exercises," and the masking of psychological implications also made up the rehabilitation treatment.

Measurements

An appointment was made for the physiological test, at which occasion psychological questionnaires were also completed. All patients performed the graded exercise test at the beginning of the physical training. Both tests were repeated after rehabilitation; the physiological test was also repeated three months later.

Psychological Questionnaires

Before and after rehabilitation the patients completed a set of four psychological questionnaires. They were as follows: first, the Heart Patients Psychological Questionnaire (HPPQ), constructed to measure the well-being of cardiac patients (27), consists of the scales: Well-being (HPPQ-W), Subjective Invalidity (HPPQ-I), Displeasure (HPPQ-D), and Social Inhibition (HPPQ-S). The second type of psychological questionnaire was the STAI, measuring: state and trait anxiety (28). Sleep Quality, measured with a 10-item questionnaire was the third (29). Functional Complaints, a 25-item questionnaire constructed to measure complaints often mentioned by cardiac patients but not typical of angina pectoris was the final form.

Exercise Testing

All patients performed on a bicycle ergometer (Monark) before and after the physical training. The test started with a one-minute period of cycling at 60 cycles a minute without load, then for two minutes at 60 Watts. The test was continued by increasing the workload with 30 Watts every two minutes until symptoms limited the patient to continue or until the physician terminated the test. Exercise-induced signs of cardiac dysfunction (ST-abnormalities, angina pectoris, serious dysrhythmias) were noted and heart rate and systolic blood pressure were measured.

Physiological Test

The test was introduced to the patient as a physiological measurement of the resting condition, in addition to the exercise test which measured the condition during effort. The research assistant was blind to the treatment form of the patient. He did not refer to the relaxation therapy and took care not to make any suggestions with regard to "proper" breathing.

Protocol: after attaching the equipment, the patient remained standing for two minutes. Measurements during the second minute ("standing") were used, after which time the patient was to lie down on the back. Measurements in the second minute of lying down were used ("supine"). Next, the use of mouthpiece and nose-clip was explained and they were attached. After this, the patient was to lie quietly without making physical movements or talking. This lasted six minutes. Measurements in the first ("mouthpiece") and last minute ("quiet") were used.

Body awareness: at the end of the test the patient's self assessment, specifically perceptions concerning the body's state, were recorded. Answers were rated as 1 = pleasant, 2 = no particular feeling, 3 = unpleasant.

Respiration: respiratory movements and heart rate were continuously recorded polygraphically with a Psychophysiograph (ZAK). One band was strapped around the chest at the level of the fifth intercostal space, and one around the abdomen at the umbilical level, both bands containing a transducer which provided stretch dependent voltage changes. This was converted into a recording of chest and abdominal expansion and retraction. Respiration rate per minute was calculated.

Respiratory sinus arrhythmia: a finger plethysmograph was used to measure the pulse, converted by a cardiotachometer in a beat-to-beat recording of heart rate, simultaneous with respiration. Respiratory sinus arrhythnmia was calculated as the mean difference between minimum beat interval during inspiration and maximum interval during expiration for five consecutive respiratory cycles.

Ventilation: using a mouthpiece and nose-clip, air was sampled from the mouthpiece and carbon-dioxide concentration (% volume) was measured with a capnograph (Jaeger). End-tidal carbon-dioxide concentration in the exhaled air was used. Ventilation was measured with a wet spirometer (Lode). Tidal volume registrations corresponded with the amplitude of the simultaneous polygraphic recording of rib-cage and abdominal motion. On the basis of this, tidal volume at the beginning (supine) and the end of the text (quiet) was estimated, and minute volume was calculated.

Method of Analysis

For statistical testing: Student's t-test was used for measurements of a metric level and chi square for measurements of a nominal level. It then followed that the measurements, obtained through exercise testing pre and post training, were integrated into a composite criterion for "training benefit" (TB), trichotomized as follows: a. the patients with doubtful or no change (TB=O), b. the patients who improved (TB=+) or c. the patients who deteriorated (TB=-). The procedure is described in detail elsewhere (16). In short, the measurements were ranked into four levels according to their clinical relevance: 1) signs of cardiac dysfunction, 2) maximum work load, 3) maximum heart rate, and 4) systolic blood pressure response. At each level a patient could be selected for TB=+ or TB=- when a significant change in the particular measurement had occurred. Finally, dropouts were included and classified on the basis of the reason for not completing the program.

The next portion of the evaluation involved psychic outcome. In this report psychic outcome is distinguished in 1) well-being, measured by HPPQ-W; 2) psychic function measured by STAI-S, STAI-T and HPPQ-D, representing anxiety and depression; and 3) somatic function measured by HPPQ-I, sleep quality and functional complaints. For psychic and somatic function, the scores on the questionnaires were standardized and summed-up and the resulting scores were dichotomized in favorable and unfavorable changes.

RESULTS

There were no differences between the two treatments in base-line clinical data as shown in Table 1. Infarction size, classified on the basis of the peak serum enzyme levels, was small in 47 patients, medium in 49 patients and large in 52 patients. In-hospital signs of heart failure occurred in 27 patients (17%). On the average, patients visited the rehabilitation centre during the third week after hospital discharge and underwent initial exercise testing two to three weeks later. Most patients (93%) reached a maximum work load of at least 120 Watts, with an average of 133 Watts, or 89% of the exercise tolerance predicted on the basis of age, gender and height. Forty-five patients (29%) were on beta-blocking medication.

Relaxation Effect

Table 2 shows that average respiration rate, prior to rehabilitation, was about 15/minute and did not differ between treatments. At post-test and at follow-up it decreased to 12.5/minute for Treatment A but was unchanged for Treatment B. The differences were significant ($p < 0.0001$). Figures 1 and 2 show that during the test, respiration rate declined from 17/minute (standing) to 16/minute (lying down) to 13/minute after breathing through a mouthpiece and went back to 14/minute (quiet).

Table 2. Effect of Relaxation Training on Respiration Rate

Average respiration rate	Treatment A			Treatment B			p*
	n	$\bar{x}$	(SD)	n	x	(SD)	
pre-test	73	14.7	(3.7)	7	15.2	(3.6)	ns
post-test	66	12.5	(3.7)	70	15.0	(3.2)	< 0.0001
pre-post difference	65	2.1	(2.8)	69	0.2	(1.9)	< 0.0001
three months follow-up	67	12.6	(3.8)	67	15.2	(3.5)	< 0.0001
pre-follow-up difference	66	1.9	(3.0)	66	-0.1	(2.4)	< 0.0001

* Difference between treatments: Student's t-test, two-tailed

This pattern of a steady decline and a slight increase at the end of the test did not change after rehabilitation. For Treatment A, however, after rehabilitation, all values became substantially lower. The difference with Treatment B was highly significant for all measurements at post-test and at three months follow-up. This means that relaxation induced a stable, more quiet respiratory pattern.

Results of the study also involved the following findings. Before rehabilitation the majority of the patients (Treatment A: 63%, Treatment B: 65%) did not notice anything in particular when asked at the end of the test how they felt their body to be (see Table 3). A small number (Treatment A: 10%, Treatment B: 7%) had unpleasant sensations. After rehabilitation most patients in Treatment A (60%) had a pleasant sensation; this change is significant ($p < 0.001$). Patients in Treatment B felt no change. The difference between the treatments in the post-test situation was significant ($p < 0.01$) and also at follow-up ($p < 0.005$). It means that as a result of

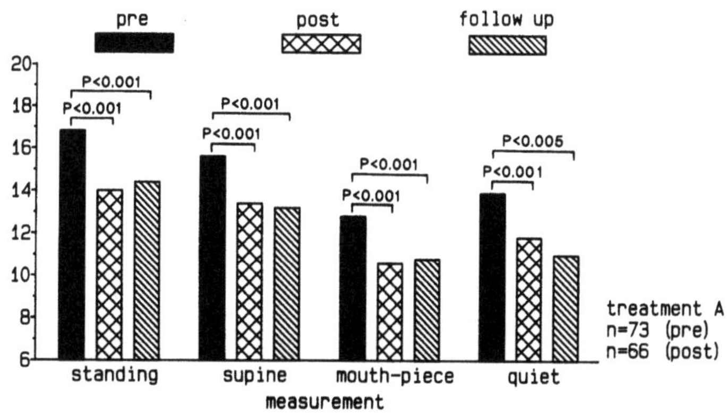

Figure 1. Respiration rate pre-test, post-test and at follow-up for Treatment A.

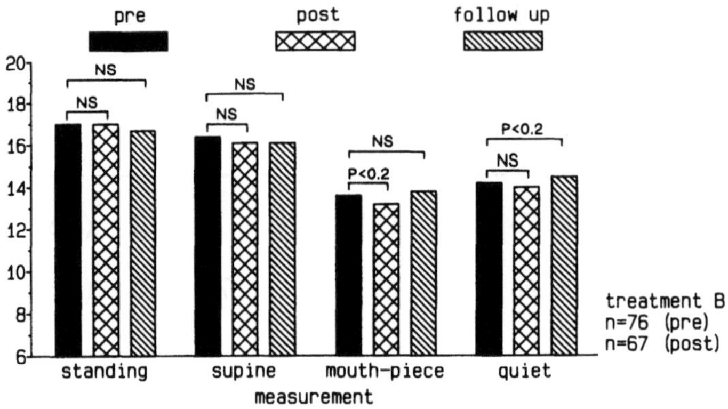

Figure 2. Respiration rate pre-test, post-test and at follow-up for Treatment B.

relaxation training, body awareness increased and physical rest induced more pleasurable body sensations.

Relation of Rehabilitation Outcome To Respiration Rate and *Body Awareness*

The testing procedures produced several outcomes of a significant physical nature. First of all, the composite criterion of training benefit indicated that in Treatment A, 42 patients (55%) improved physically after rehabilitation and 37 patients in Treatment B (46%). Patients were considered not improved when they did not change (Treatment A: 25%,Treatment B: 21%) or deteriorated after training

Table 3 Effect of Relaxation Training on Body Awareness

Body sensation after rest	Treatment A n(%)	Treatment B n (%)	p*
pre-test			
pleasant	16(27)	17(28)	
nothing particular	37(63)	39(65)	
unpleasant	6(10)	4 (7)	ns
post-test			
pleasant	38(60)	23(33)	
nothing particular	20(32)	38(55)	
unpleasant	5 (8)	8(12)	< 0.01
three month follow-up			
pleasant	38(59)	18(28)	
nothing particular	20(31)	39(60)	
unpleasant	6 (9)	8(12)	< 0.005

*Difference between treatment: chi square, df=2, two-tailed

(Treatment A 20%, Treatment B: 33%). Table 4 shows that for both treatments the respiration rate at post-testing was slightly higher with patients who improved physically, in comparison to patients who did not improve. The difference was not significant. Thus, respiratory rate was not related to physical benefit. Positive body awareness had no relation to training benefit either.

The most significant finding related to the psychic nature of the individual was that most patients in Treatment A improved in perceived well-being (HPPQ-W). Those who improved were breathing slower than those who did not improve ($p < 0.05$). Body awareness, however, was only slightly more positive. In Treatment B, well-being only slightly improved after rehabilitation. There was no relationship between improvement and respiration rate or body awareness post-testing.

Importantly, the psychic function (anxiety and depression) showed a positive change in most patients (Treatment A: 69%, Treatment B: 70%). For Treatment A improvement of psychic function had no relation to either respiration rate or body awareness. In Treatment B, patients who improved psychically were breathing faster at post-testing ($p < 0.05$). They did not differ in body awareness from patients who did not improve. Also, the patients' somatic function (sleep quality, feelings of invalidity and functional complaints) showed a positive change (Treatment A: 69%, Treatment B: 60%). Patients in Treatment A who improved somatically tended to breathe slower at post-testing ($p < 0.20$) and had significantly more positive body awareness ($p < 0.02$). This means that somatic improvement was related to the relaxation effect. In Treatment B, patients who improved somatically were breathing slightly faster.

Respiratory Changes: Fine Grain Analysis

Data collected with the physiological test were analyzed for a sub-set of the patients admitted to the study in 1982. Out of 58 patients, post-test measurements were available for 48 (Treatment A: 24, Treatment B: 24).

Estimated tidal volume at the beginning of the test increased for Treatment A from 0.61L to 0.69L (see Figure 3). It decrease in Treatment B from 0.59L to 0.5L ($p < 0.05$). The difference between the treatments was significant ($p < 0.05$). At the end of the test, tidal volume was smaller than at the beginning, particularly for Treatment B, both before and after rehabilitation.

Also, estimated minute volume was 8.0L for Treatment A and 8.5L for Treatment B at the beginning of the test (see Figure 4). It increased slightly for Treatment A and decreased a little for Treatment B after rehabilitation, but not significantly. During the test, minute volume decreased substantially, both before and after rehabilitation, irrespective of the treatment. This means that physical rest clearly reduced ventilation.

Yet another important observation involved estimated effective ventilation. It was calculated as tidal volume minus 0.15L (the average volume of dead air space) times respiration rate. Again, for Treatment A effective ventilation increased (from 5.9L to 6.3L), whereas it decreased for Treatment B (from 6.2L to 5.5L). The difference between treatments was not significant.

Furthermore, end-tidal CO_2 concentration increased significantly in Treatment A from 4.3 (0.5) vol% to 4.5 (0.5) vol% after training ($p < 0.05$). In Treatment B it increased slightly from 4.5 (0.6) vol% to 4.6 (0.6) vol%. The difference between treatments was not significant.

Table 4. Four Outcome Measures, Related to Respiration rate and Body Sensation, for Treatment A and Treatment B.

	Respiration rate at post-test					
	Treatment A			Treatment B		
	n		p*	n		p*
Exercise testing						
improved	38	12.7 (3.6)		35	15.4 (3.1)	
not improved	28	12.1 (3.8)	ns	35	14.6 (3.3)	ns
Well-being						
improved	48	11.8 (3.3)		39	15.1 (2.9)	
not improved	18	14.1 (4.2)	0.03	30	15.1 (3.5)	ns
Psychic function						
improved	43	12.2 (3.6)		46	15.4 (3.1)	
not improved	19	12.4 (3.5)	ns	20	14.0 (2.5)	0.05
Somatic function						
improved	41	11.9 (3.7)		38	15.4 (3.2)	
not improved	20	13.3 (3.2)	0.1	26	14.4 (3.4)	ns

	Body sense at post-test (**)					
	Treatment A			Treatment B		
	n		p*	n		p*
Exercise testing						
improved	36	1.5 (0.7)		35	1.8 (0.6)	
not improved	27	1.5 (0.6)	ns	34	1.8 (0.7)	ns
Well-being						
improved	47	1.4 (0.6)		38	1.8 (0.6)	
not improved	16	1.6 (0.8)	ns	31	1.7 (0.6)	ns
Psychic function						
improved	41	1.4 (0.6)		46	1.8 (0.6)	
not improved	18	1.5 (0.7)	ns	20	1.7 (0.7)	ns
Somatic function						
improved	40	1.4 (0.5)		38	1.8 (0.6)	
not improved	18	1.8 (0.9)	0.02	25	1.8 (0.7)	ns

*Student's t-test, two-tailed;
**1 = pleasant, 2 = nothing particular, 3 = unpleasant

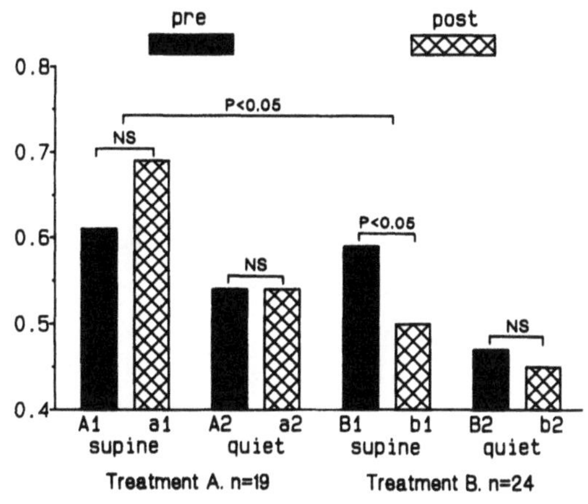

Figure 3. Estimated tidal volume pre-test and post-test for Treatment A and B.

Chest and abdominal motion was also significant. The relative contributions of rib-cage and abdomen to the respiratory movement could be tentatively estimated as being the ratio of the amplitude of the abdominal and rib-cage recording. This ratio was 4.2 for Treatment A and 4.6 for Treatment B at the beginning of the pre-test. During the test it increased for both treatments to 4.5 and 5.0 respectively. This means that abdominal contribution to respiration increased relatively during the test. After training the ratio increased during the test from 5.3 to 5.8 in Treatment A, and in Treatment B from 3.4 to 4.2. Consequently, abdominal breathing had increased in Treatment A but had diminished in Treatment B. The difference between treatments was not significant ($p = 0.14$).

Finally, respiratory sinus arrhythmia was observed (Figure 5). The heart rate variability during slow breathing (6 cycles/minute) both at the beginning and at the end of the test increased for Treatment A after training ($p < 0.005$ respectively $p < 0.02$). For Treatment B respiratory arrhythmia did not change. The difference between treatments was more pronounced at the end of the test ($p < 0.05$) than at the

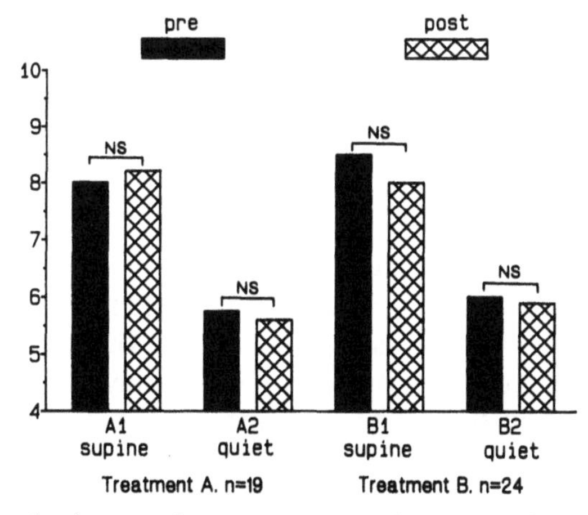

Figure 4. Estimated minute volume pre-test and post-test for Treatment A and B.

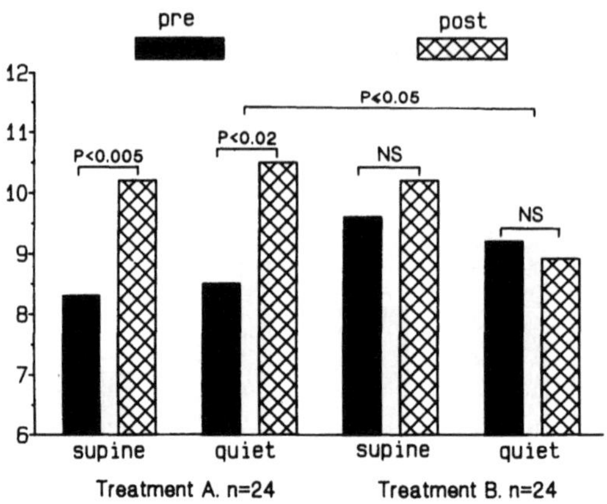

Figure 5. Respiratory sinus arrhythmia pre-test and post-test for Treatment A and B.

beginning (p = 0.10). Average variability differed significantly between treatments (p < 0.04).

DISCUSSION

Effect on respiration: This study showed that breathing awareness as a relaxation method has been successful in calming respiration and inducing positive body awareness for myocardial infarction patients. Regarding the implications of this result, several points need to be considered. First, the exploratory fine grain analysis on a sub-set of patients showed that a slower respiration rate meant that ventilation became more efficient, because tidal volume increased while minute volume remained practically unchanged. Thus, the proportion of inhaled air used for gas exchange increased, as well as the time for oxygen exchange in the lungs. The increased effective ventilation did *not* result in excess ventilation (hyperventilation), which would have been a negative side-effect (30, 31). In fact, the number of patients with CO2 below 4.0 vol% dropped from 3 to 1 in Treatment A, whereas it rose from 4 to 6 in Treatment B.

Second, it was found that physical training did not improve respiration. The fine grain analysis showed that patients in Treatment B even tended to breathe more superficially after training. For both treatments, patients with physical training benefit did not breath slower. Thus, contrary to expectation (32), respiration was not inherent to a physical training effect.

Third, the decrease in respiration rate, although highly significant, was modest. When patients are taught to breathe diaphragmatically and asked to perform their skill, respiration frequencies of 4-8/minute would not have been surprising (20,21). In the approach utilized in this study, however, emphasis was less on voluntary skill and more on a shift in the spontaneous respiration pattern. The idea was that a change in the habitual pattern would be more durable. The stability of the results at the three month follow-up confirmed this. The finding has been confirmed even after two years: in 38 patients a registration of respiration was carried out at the follow-up interview Figure 6 shows that respiration rate was still lower for Treatment A, whereas Treatment B showed an unchanged frequency. The difference was highly significant.

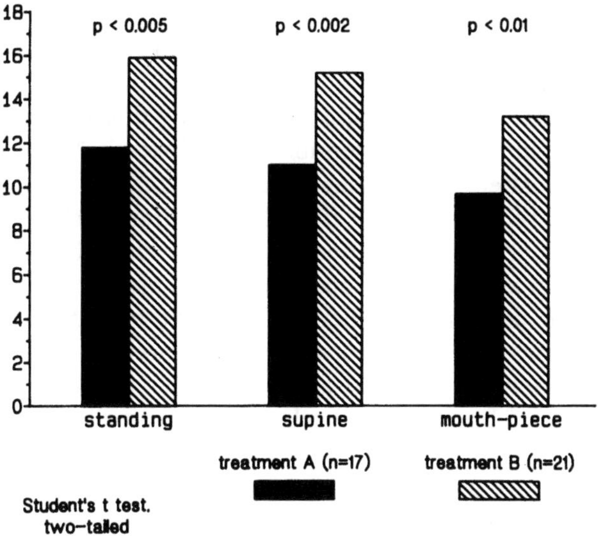

Figure 6. Respiration rate at two year follow-up for Treatment A and B.

Fourth, the study indicated that reducing respiration rate is not an ideal to be achieved. Rather, the express purpose should be to induce a psychophysiological change and to retain the connection of respiration to other physiological and psychological variables (33). The procedure of breathing awareness seemed to have been successful in that respect, because the response of respiration rate to the various phases of the physiological testing (standing, lying down, mouthpiece breathing, quiet) remained unchanged. This means that respiration became more quiet through breathing therapy but was not forcefully controlled and remained a valid tension indicator. Also, respiratory change was not limited to frequency, but included other parameters, e.g., sinus arrhythmia.

However, the interrelation of frequency with other respiratory variables deserves further study, in order to characterize possible changes in respiratory pattern in more detail. For instance, prior to rehabilitation, respiration frequency did not correlate with carbon dioxide. Only after breathing therapy was the expected negative correlation found. This means that breathing awareness strengthened the interrelation of respiratory parameters.

Also, although the relaxing effect of breathing technique is often ascribed to increasing diaphragmatic activity and decreasing upper-thoracic breathing, this seems to be an overly simplistic conclusion. The coordination of the diaphragm with respiratory muscles in the abdomen, the back and in the chest is more important than diaphragmatic strength (34-36). For instance, there was no tendency for upper-thoracic breathing among the cardiac patients (37). Instead, the rib-cage contributed far less to respiratory movement than the abdomen. This tendency was strengthened by the relaxation method, which put emphasis on breathing movement in the lower abdomen. This finding seems paradoxical, considering that efficient breathing involves movement of the whole trunk, including the pelvis, spine and breast-bone (38). It was noted however, that the rib-cage showed small amplitudes, because the chest was rather stiff and usually was wide. In the supine position on the back it became even more fixed. Thus, the absence of gross upper-thoracic breathing did not imply an adequate costo-abdominal rhythm. For that reason, manual techniques were used in various postures to improve the rhythmic expansion and contraction of the whole body under respiration. The technique for home practice started with natural breathing in the lower body, because focusing attention on the chest has a risk of evoking forceful breathing.

Finally, the method employed focused on sensory discrimination of differences in breathing pattern and in bodily tension. The "exercise" was to compare the condition before and after a particular procedure, and to become aware of the difference. Thus, the relatively strong impact of respiratory change was coupled to "passive" awareness and self-observation. It seems that the ability for sensory awareness is the core of all relaxation procedures. The problem was how to introduce this concept to cardiac patients and whether they could tolerate increased sensitivity to inner physical events. When successful, this awareness has the psychological function to reduce anxiety, in particular about the body. Obviously, it is necessary to master the techniques of breathing and relaxation, eventually integrating them into the emotional state.

The outcome of the present study indicated that body awareness had indeed been increased. It should be noted, however, that this concerned a pleasurable experience occurring at the end of the test, i.e., after about 15 minutes. It means that physical rest had become more of a positive experience. Probably a more favorable attitude toward relaxation was induced, rather than the more negative interpretation of the need for physical rest as a sign of weakness. In fact, patients in Treatment A continued taking daytime rests, whereas patients in Treatment B rested less often after rehabilitation. At the two-year follow-up, the treatments still differed in this respect.

The following contentions are therefore justified: that the method of breathing awareness 1) has been effective in changing the habitual respiratory pattern; 2) proved to be a valuable instrument to introduce body awareness and also relaxation.

Two significant factors led to this outcome. First, focusing on breathing "activity," in addition to the feedback signals, made it easier to continue lying down for some time and being passive (25). In case a patient became more restless during passive relaxation (10) the treatment continued with active relaxation, either sitting or standing. Second, the respiratory pattern which resulted from the breathing technique, together with reduced muscle tone (39) induced a "drowsy" state of mind (40,41), which facilitated passive awareness. Practical experience with this procedure showed that it was acceptable to the patients: no one stopped relaxation therapy. After the study, the relaxation procedure was retained as an individual treatment in the rehabilitation. Also, all patients now have one group relaxation session and it is incorporated in the regular physical exercise. In this way, most patients appear to be positive about relaxation.

The rehabilitation outcome can be summarized as follows. Relaxation therapy appeared to improve rehabilitation outcome, as well as respiration and body awareness. The question remains whether the latter effect is instrumental for bringing about an effect on rehabilitation outcome. However, the improvement in patient well-being was clearly related to slower respiration for Treatment A. The effect of relaxation on well-being may therefore be interpreted as partially the result of its influence on respiratory pattern. Improvement in somatic function was related to positive body awareness for patients who learned to relax; they also showed a trend towards slower breathing. Relaxation may have enabled these patients to experience and view their bodies differently, placing different limitations on physical potential. Furthermore, patients in Treatment B improved almost to the same degree, but without concomitant increase in body awareness. Possibly, recovery may have been a different process for them. If that thought is correct, it means that relaxation modifies the influence of rehabilitation on recovery. Another indication for this reality involved the inverse relation between respiration and psychic improvement for Treatment B. A possible interpretation is that, for those patients, heightened activity served as a way to cope with anxiety and depression (42). A kind of masking effect allowed patients to deal with depression.

It is possible that relaxation influences the way in which the patient experiences the rehabilitation, and what he learns from it. There is an enhanced ability to reflect upon lifestyle. The psychological literature on cardiac patients mentions an inability to relax; a preference for activity and resistance to passivity; a need for control and a firm belief in active, effortful coping strategies; a tendency to deny problems and minimize complaints. Cardiac rehabilitation usually addresses these tendencies by focusing on proper aerobic conditioning. The value of breathing and relaxation technique seems to be that it facilitates the ability for the individual to change, and to make rehabilitation more of a learning experience.

Future research is necessary to distinguish patients who were able to learn relaxation from those who could not master the techniques. Inability to relax and to breathe quietly may result from physical handicaps, e.g., intolerance for increased body sensitivity. Also, the motivation of the patient and the relation with the therapist are of importance. An intriguing question involves the degree to which a successful rehabilitation outcome depends upon a potential ability to relax.

SUMMARY

A relaxation method emphasizing sensory awareness and relaxed, diaphragmatic breathing, was introduced into a cardiac rehabilitation program. As compared to a physical exercise program, this method effectively reduced respiration rate and increased pleasant body sensations during physical rest. Simultaneously, ventilatory efficiency increased, hyperventilation was reduced, and heart rate variability increased.

After rehabilitation, slower respiration was associated with a higher level of perceived well-being, whereas positive body awareness signified more adequate psychosomatic function (sleep quality, functional complaints, sense of invalidity). Patients who learned to relax retained the habit of taking a siesta. At the time of a two-year follow-up, respiration rate still persisted to be lower and siesta time was longer than in patients who followed exercise training only.

It is concluded that the method of breathing awareness is suitable to induce relaxation and body awareness for cardiac patients.

REFERENCES

1. Stern, M., Gorman,P. and Kaslow,L. 1983. The group counseling vs exercise therapy study. *Arch. Int. Med.* 143: 1719.

2. Langosch, W., Seer,P., Brodner, G., Kallinke, D., Kulick, B. and Heim,F. 1982. Behavior therapy with coronary heart disease patients: results of a comparative study. *J Psychosom. Res.* 26: 475.

3. Polackova, J., Bockova,E. and Sedivec,V. 1982. Autogenic training: application in secondary prevention of myocardial infarction. *Activ. Nerv. Sup.* 24-3: 178.

4. Krampen, G., and Ohm,D. 1984. Effects of relaxation training during rehabilitation of myocardial infarction patients. *Int. J. Res.* 7-1: 68.

5. Ohm, D. 1987. Entspannungstraining und Hypnose bei Patienten mit koronaren Herzkrankheit in der stationaren Rehabilitation. Roderer Verlag, Ragensburg.

6. Suinn, R. 1974. Behavior therapy for cardiac patients. *Beh. Ther.* 5: 569.

7. Friedman, M., Thoresen,C., Gill, J., Ulmer, D., Thompson, L., Powell, L., Price, V., Elek, S., Rabin, D., Breall, W. Piaget,G., Dixon, T., Bourg, E., Levy, E. and Tasto,D. 1982. Feasibility of altering Type A behavior pattern after myocardial infarction. *Circulation.* 66-1: 83.

8. Dixhoorn, J. van, Bar, F. W. H., Erdman, R.A.M., Keulen, A.M.A. van. 1988. Cijfers en beschouwingen over poliklinische hartrevalidatie: een inventarisatie. *Hart Bull.* 19:11.

9. Sime, W.E. 1980. Emotional stress testing and relaxation in cardiac rehabilitation. *In*: "Stress and tension control," McGuigan, F.J., Sime, W.E., and Wallace, L. Macdonald, eds., Plenlum, New York.

10. Heide, F., and Borkovec,T. 1984. Relaxation-induced anxiety: mechanisms and theoretical implications. *Behav. Res. Ther.* 22-1: 1.

11. Hackett, T.P., and .Cassem,N.H. 1982. Coping with cardiac disease. *In*: "Comprehensive cardiac rehabilitation," Kellerman, J.J., ed., Karger, Basel.

12. Fardy, P. 1986. Cardiac rehabilitation for the outpatient: a hospital-based program. *In*: M.L.Pollock, D.H.Schmidt, D.T., ed. Heart Disease and Rehabilitation. Wiley, New York, 1986. Mason

13. Mayou, M. 1983. A controlled trial of early rehabilitation after myocardial infarction. *J. Cariop. Rehab.* 3: 397.

14. Hughes, J. 1984. Psychological effects of habitual aerobic exercise: a critical review. *Prev. Med.* 13: 66.

15. Van Dixhoorn, J. 1984. Body Awareness: the proper application of relaxation and breathing technique. *Gedrag.* 12: 31.

16. Van Dixhoorn, J., Duivenvoorden, H.J., Staal,H.A. Pool,J. and F. Verhage. 1988. Physical effects of exercise training and relaxation therapy in cardiac rehabilitation, assessed through a composite criterion for training outcome. Submitted.

17. Van Dixhoorn, J., Duivenvoorden, H.J., Staal,H.A., Pool, J. and Verhage,F. 1987. Cardiac events after myocardial infarction: possible effect of relaxation therapy. *Eur. Heart J.* 8: 1210.

18. Van Dixhoorn, J., De Loos,J. and Duivenvoorden, H. J. 1983. Contribution of relaxation technique training to the rehabilitation of myocardial infarction patients. *Psychother. Psychosom.* 40: 137.

19. Cappo,B.R., and Holmes,S.S. 1984. The utility of prolonged respiratory exhalation for reducing physiological and psychological arousal in non-threatening and threatening situations. *J Psychosom. Res.* 28-4: 265.

20. McCaul, K.D., Soloman,S. and Holmes,D.S. 1979. Effects of paced respiration and expectations on physiological and psychological responses to threat. *J Pers. Soc. Psych.* 37-4: 564.

21. Peper, E., Smith,K. and Waddell,D. 1987. Voluntary wheezing versus diaphragmatic breathing with inhalation (Voldyne) feedback: a clinical intervention in the treatment of asthma. *Clin. Biofeedback and Health.* 10-2: 83.

22. Grewal, J., Tan,W. and Sim,M. 1987. Evaluation of a diaphragmatic breathing exercise program for COPD patients. *Clin. Biofeedback and Health.* 10-2: 98.

23. Nagarathna, R., and Nagendra,H. 1985. Yoga for bronchial asthma: a controlled study. *Brit. Med. J.* 291: 1077.

24. Reybrouck, T., Wertelaers, A., Bertrand, P. and Demedts,M. 1987. Myofeedback training of the respiratory muscles in patients with chronic obstructive pulmonary disease. *J. Cardiop. rehab.* 7: 18.

25. Benson, H., Beary,J.F. and Carol,M. 1974. The relaxation response. *Psychiatry.* 37: 37.

26. Lum, L. C. 1976. The syndrome of chronic habitual hyperventilation. *In*: "Modern trends in psychosomatic medicine," Hill, O., ed., Butterworths, London.

27. Erdman, R. A. M. 1981. Welbevinden bij hartpatientedn. Swets & Zeitlinger, Lisse.

28. Van Der Ploeg, H., Defares,P. and Spielberger, C. 1980. Manual for the State-Trait Anxiety Inventory-DY. Swets & Zeitlinger, Lisse.

29. Visser, P., Hofman,W.F. and Kumar, .A. 1979. Sleep and mood: measuring the sleep quality. *In*: "Sleep research," Priest, R. G., Pletscher, A., and Ward, J., eds., MTP Press, Lancaster.

30. Neill, W.A., and Hattenhauer, .M. 1975. Impairment of myocardial 02 supply due to hyperventilation. *Circulation.* 52: 854.

31. Nixon, P.G.F., Al-Abbasi,A.H., King,J. and Freeman, L.J. 1986. Hyperventilation in cardiac rehabilitation. *Hol. Med.* 1: 5.

32. Astrand, P., and Rodahl, K. 1987. Textbook of work physiology. McGraw Hill, New York.

33. Grossman, P. 1983. Respiration, stress and cardiovascular function. *Psychophys.* 20-3: 284.

34. Kapandji, I. A. 1974. The physiology of the joints, III. Churchill Livingstone, London.

35. Parow, J. 1972. Funktionelle Atmungstherapie. Georg Thiem, Stuttgart.

36. Decramer, M., and Macklem, P. 1985. Action of inspiratory muscles and its modification with hyperinflation. *Airways.* 4: 19.

37. Hymes, A., and Nuernberger, P. 1980. Breathing patterns found in heart attack patients. *Res. Bull. Himal. Inst.* 2-2: 10.

38. Balfoort, B., and Van Dixhoorn, J. 1979. Ademen wij vanzelf? Bosch en Keuning, Baarn.

39. Gellhorn, E. 1958. The physiological basis of neuromuscular relaxation. *Arch. Int. Med.* 102: 392.

40. Timmons, B., Salamy, J., Kamiya, J. and Girton, D. 1972. Abdominal-thoracic respiratory movements and levels of arousal. *Psychon. Sci.* 27: 173.

41. Naifeh, K.H., and Kamiya, J. 1981. The nature of respiratory changes associated with sleep onset. *Sleep.* 4-1: 49.

42. Van Doornen, L. 1980. The coronary risk personality: psychological and psychophysiological aspects. *Psychother. Psychosom.* 34: 204.

INFLUENCE OF DANCE AND RELAXATION TRAINING ON THE MORALE AND REHABILITATION OF PATIENTS WITH CRANIAL INJURIES

Suzanne Masson and Walther Luthi

Dept. of Psychomotricité, Hôpital La Salpetrière
University of Paris, France

Severe cranial injuries present a silent epidemic of modern times. As a result of traffic accidents, and in spite of speed limits, the number of cases is increasing, but thanks to progress in Neurosurgery and Rehabilitation, we can also see an increase in survivors with severe brain and cranial injuries. In the whole of the European community, there are nearly half-a-million cases and, in France, about eighty thousand. The majority are male, with a mean age of about 25 years.

The problems of these patients are often specific and invisible, and cannot be compared to the usual categories. The following symptoms are often seen:

a) Sensory defects - seeing, hearing, smell, speech, etc.

b) Partial hemiplegia, incoordination of movement, apraxia

c) Modification of the basic muscle tonus, as spasticity or hypotonia

d) Epilepsy

Problems of intellect and behavior may include

a) Psycho-organical syndrome

b) Problems of memory and learning

c) Psychomotor problems - balance, agonistic, apraxia

d) Affective report - instability

e) Depressions

f) Changes of character and personality

g) Weak self-awareness, mainly regarding the former, normal life

There are also many social problems, so that rehabilitation into social life may take many years. For patients with cranial injuries, this re-integration may present a painful and difficult adaptation. Society often undervalues the potential of these patients, so that they may have great difficulty in returning to daily work. Only about one-third of them are able to find an adequate occupation. Finally, one must not forget the trauma within the family when the patient returns home after long clinical treatment. Often it is left to the family to carry the responsibilities and the burden of daily care of the patient.

It is under these circumstances, and at the request of the "Association des Familles de Traumatisès Cranien Francais" (French Association of Families of Brain-injured Patients) that the center for rehabilitation was set up in the department of Psychomotricité, Hôpital La Salpetrière.

We work with groups of eight to ten patients, all with severe neurological damage, and having experienced long periods of coma. Most of them are young people, between 15 and 30 years old, and all of them are victims of traffic accidents. The specific medical treatment is followed by different rehabilitation programs such as physiotherapy, occupational therapy and so on.

In our own department, the aim is to complement these interventions with special psychomotor activities, by means of music and rhythm under regular instruction and motivation by the therapist. It is our experience that rhythm can help amazingly in the progress of movement performance. This positive influence is particularly apparent in patients with cerebellar damage. It would also appear that the music produces a very positive emotional influence, and a diminution of ever-present stress.

Relaxation is obtained by rhythmic exercises for release of tension, and by dynamic activities such as Ti-Chi-Kan, in which the alternation of movements from one side to the other, executed under very slow rhythm, brings about an improved muscle tone. Exercises for balance and coordination consist of general and purposeful movements.

A very important factor is that, during the performance, the family members, or friends of the patient, join in the exercises at the same time. The gradual progress made, and the improvement of the ability to participate like everybody else in these creative bodily activities and games, changes these patients for the better. Often, by these means, they find new hope for their future, especially for their determination to manage their own future rehabilitation.

From the first year of this work, we have found a great interest amongst the patients, and amongst their families. The therapy group meets weekly for two hours, of which one hour is given to movement and exercise.

Although the numbers are small, the outcome of this work, still in the experimental stage, is very positive, helping to improve the life of patients whose handicap might prove even more severe without this help. It will take some years to gather substantial and reliable data.

VARIED APPROACHES IN BEHAVIORAL MEDICINE

VAGINAL TEMPERATURE BIOFEEDBACK TRAINING FOR PREMENSTRUAL SYNDROME

David B. Van Zak*

Private Practice
West Los Angeles, CA

INTRODUCTION

Premenstrual syndrome (PMS) includes physical symptoms of bloating, and aching pain, and psychological symptoms of depression, lethargy and irritability. The key to the diagnosis of PMS seems to be establishing the timing of the symptoms in relation to the menstrual cycle, but this has not been uniformly defined. Several tests have been designed to assess PMS symptoms, but there is still controversy over how to define and assess the symptoms.

Treatment approaches to PMS have proliferated in the last two decades; the most widely researched have been hormonal, behavioral, vitamin supplementation, diuretic, and biofeedback. Behavioral and biofeedback treatments have recently attracted attention because they offer the possibility of voluntary self-control over the symptoms, without the use of medication.

Recent psychophysiological theories have suggested that the autonomic nervous system may be "plastic," in the sense that its responses may be shaped through reinforcement. Thus, it may be possible to "entrain" the viscera and autonomic nervous system to respond with a new pattern of responses which are not painful, or are at least less reactive to congestive pain, because these "incompatible responses with anxiety" are more relaxed.

Previous research has suggested that vaginal temperature feedback with autogenic training, and vaginal temperature feedback with EMG feedback are effective treatments for PMS. Hand temperature feedback with EMG feedback has been shown as an effective treatment, while pain management training and imagery have also been shown as effective treatments.

---

*The author wishes to thank Ken Njeru, MS, Dept. of Biostatistics, PRUCLA Medical Center (currently at the University of Nairobi, Kenya) for his statistical analysis of the data; and Nancy Newman, Valerie Morgan, Lisa Jaffee and Ernest Carter who were research assistants on the project, responsible for treatment of the subjects and collating the data.

Reviews of the literature have shown that hand temperature training alone is not as effective as EMG feedback with relaxation training. However, no previous study has carried out treatment for more than two months; since PMS symptoms may vary from month to month, the results obtained in several studies may have reflected this variation rather than the effects of treatment. This would affect the external validity of these studies, the ability to generalize results to other populations or settings.

The present study addressed the problem of whether voluntary behavioral control techniques of vaginal temperature biofeedback are effective treatments for PMS.

METHOD

Subjects

A sample of 30 PMS women was recruited as volunteers for an experimental treatment of PMS, by flyers displayed on campuses in the Los Angeles area, and through local gynecologists' offices. All of the subjects had primary dysmenorrhea (absence of organic pathology), as confirmed by their gynecologists within the previous six months; none used IUD's or contraceptive pills, and none were pregnant. This sample was randomly assigned to one of three treatment conditions: (1) true vaginal temperature biofeedback treatment alone, with pretest-posttest testing; (2) false vaginal temperature biofeedback alone, from a prerecorded cassette tape of another subject, pretest-posttest; and (3) a control group which received no treatment, pretest-posttest.

Apparatus and Materials

1. Advanced Electro-Labs Trimode Biofeedback instrument, with two-channels of EMG, one-channel GSR, and one-channel Thermal feedback, modified by the manufacturer to feedback one-hundredth of a Fahrenheit (F) degree through audio tone

2. One all-purpose thermal probe with 4-foot long cables

3. Disposable thermometer covers (thermometer "condoms") to cover the thermal vaginal-feedback probes

4. Daily menstrual symptoms inventory sheets, and stamped post cards, pre-addressed to the principal investigator

The Moos Menstrual Distress Questionnaire, the Millon Behavioral Health Inventory, the McNair and Lorr Profile of Mood States, and the Chesney and Tasto Menstrual Symptom Questionnaire were administered as pre- and posttest measures along with baseline biofeedback data and a subjective daily journal. Monitored variables measured as co-variates included respiration, heart rate, and galvanic skin response (GSR).

PROCEDURES

Subjects were determined to be at minimal risk, according to guidelines published by the American Psychological Association (Association for Advanced Training in the Behavioral Sciences, 1987), and after informed consent was obtained, treatment consisted of 12 weekly 30-minute office biofeedback relaxation sessions augmented by twice daily 10-minute relaxation practice sessions at home.

For four consecutive cycles all subjects recorded the daily subjective severity and duration of their menstrual symptoms: negative emotional and mental states; positive emotional and mental states; bloating; aching pain; depression; lethargy; irritability; headaches; intestinal disturbances; dysmenorrhea; water retention; bleeding; and any other symptoms they related to cyclical changes in their physiology or psychological state. The severity or absence of the symptoms was indicated on a 0-100 scale. The daily symptom indexes were summed for each period for each symptom, then the symptom groups were combined by regression analysis. Before the treatment started, each subject recorded her baseline symptoms through one complete cycle, and the averaged indexes were used to establish the baseline for each subject.

The 30 experimental subjects were matched by initial severity of dysmenorrhea, ethnicity, and socioeconomic status into two treatment groups (true and false feedback), and one control group (no feedback). All experimental subjects had an intake interview with the experimenter and a female research assistant, during which details of the respective procedures were explained and advised consent was obtained. All subjects were required to have had an interview and physical exam within the last year with their gynecologists, in order to get accurate information and to relieve misconceptions about menstruation. All subjects continued symptom recording during the three-month training period. The last month of menstrual records established the after-treatment indexes.

It was predicted that the true biofeedback group would prove superior to the false feedback and control groups in rate of symptom reduction, as measured by group mean data. The experiment was double blind; neither the research assistants who did the training, nor the subjects, knew which group was the experimental group receiving treatment, and which group was control. This design controls for experimenter bias and reactivity.

RESULTS

In analyzing physiological data it is important to test whether the data meet the assumptions of normality; biofeedback data may not be normally distributed, either within subjects or across subjects. Therefore, the biofeedback data were tested for goodness of fit to a linear regression line (Figure 1). Since the data did fit a linear regression line, the data were analyzed using the parametric statistic Analysis of Variance.

To investigate whether the subjects had effectively managed to increase control over the symptoms as they continued to receive more biofeedback treatment, linear regression analysis was used to assess the changes in temperature over the 12-week period. But, on examination of individual changes in temperature over time, it was apparent that there was understandable cyclity in the data. That is, the temperature would increase for some time, then drop, then increase again and drop in cycles of about four weeks (see Figures 1a to 1d).

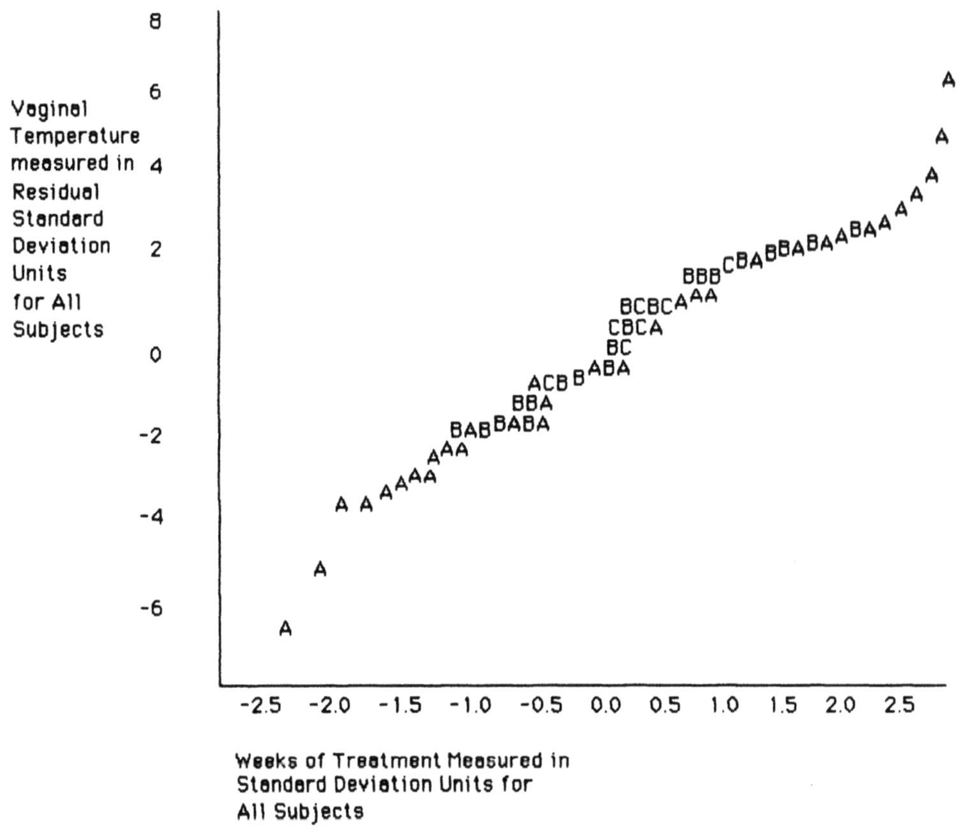

Figure 1. Normal Probability Plot of Goodness of Fit of Vaginal Temperature Biofeedback Data to Linear Regression Line

Table 1 shows the effects of controlling for 'time-to-menses.' An analysis of covariance was performed, wherein the subjects were classified, at each week, by the number of weeks to next menses. The vaginal temperature for each menstrual week can be seen from this breakdown of the data. As can be seen from Table 1, over the course of the 12 weeks of biofeedback treatment, vaginal temperature nearly reached significance at the $p = .05$ level for the premenstrual week. Vaginal temperature did increase significantly ($p > .05$) over the premenstrual week. That is, group mean data for the biofeedback treatment group suggest that by the beginning of the menstrual week, subjects in the experimental (vaginal temperature biofeedback) group had significantly increased vaginal temperature over the premenstrual week.

Results (Table 2) showed that group mean data for the experimental group differed significantly from the group mean data for the control group on the paper-and-pencil tests. The experimental group showed a reduction in overall symptomatology, as measured by the combined Millon and Wahler scales (PERS=personality factors; STRE1=physiological stress; STRE2=psychological stress; and EMOT=emotional factors), Menstrual Distress Questionnaire (MDQ), and Profile of Mood States (POMS). These were cross-referenced to subjective daily symptom journals which all subjects kept for the three months of treatment, as a check on accuracy of measurement. Results of this cross-referencing suggest that the

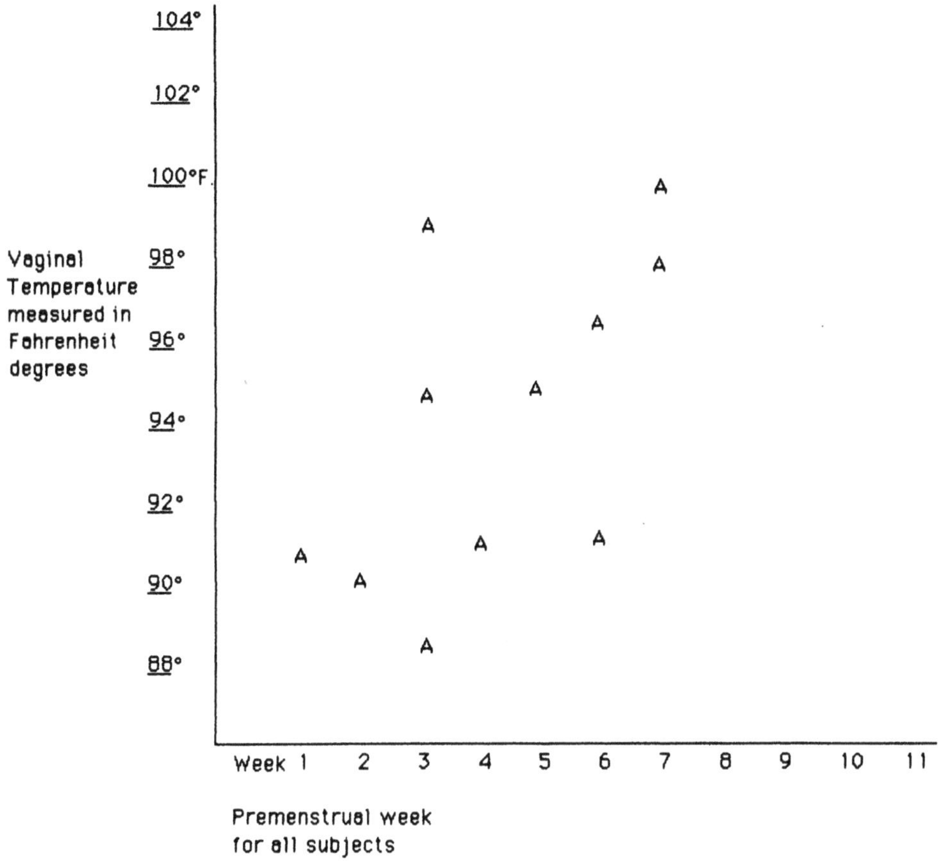

Figure 1a. Individual Obserbvations of Biofeedback Data Showing Cyclicity of Vaginal Temperature, by Week of Menstrual Cycle: Prementrual Week Observations

biofeedback-induced changes in symptomatology were consistent with the changes in paper-and-pencil, self-reported symptoms.

The experimental group biofeedback data (Figure 2) showed overall reduction in symptomatology, an increase in mean vaginal temperature, and high correlation between mean vaginal and hand temperature readings, at least for the premenstrual-to-menstrual week.

Specifically, as can be seen from Figure 2, during the 12 weeks of biofeedback treatment the treatment group increased mean premenstrual week vaginal temperature (T=0) from an average of approximately 89° (Fahrenheit), to an average of approximately 99° (Fahrenheit). During the week following menstruation (T-1) mean vaginal temperature increased from approximately 93° to approximately 97°, over the 12 weeks of treatment. Similarly, for the next week of menstruation (T-2), mean vaginal temperature increased from approximately 93° to approximately 98°. For the last week of the menstrual cycle, mean vaginal temperature increased from 94° to approximately 98.5°.

Hand temperature was measured as a co-variate of vaginal temperature, but was not trained with biofeedback. Evaluation of these results is not as clear as with

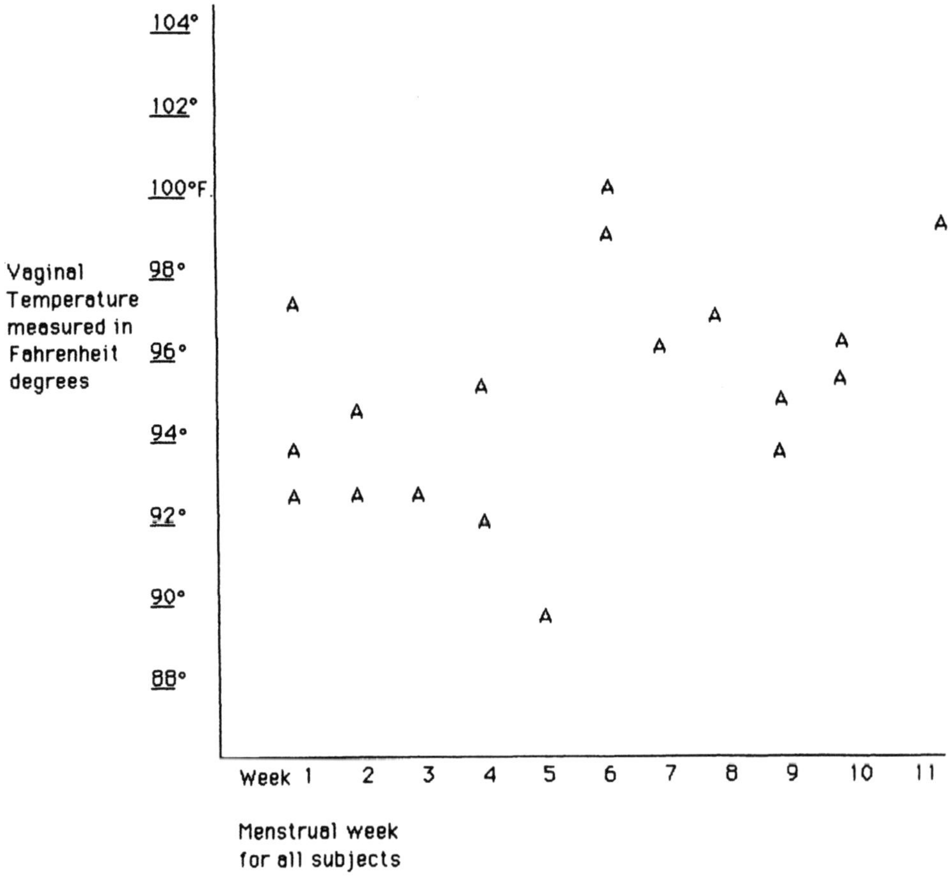

Figure 1b. Individual Observations of Biofeedback Data Showing Cyclicity of Vaginal Temperature, by Week of Menstrual Cycle: Menstrual Week

vaginal temperature. For example, as can be seen from Figure 2, during the premenstrual-to-menstrual week (T-0) the mean hand temperature readings increased from approximately 83° F. to approximately 91° F. over the 12 weeks of treatment. This is roughly parallel to the changes in vaginal temperature. However, for the following weeks of the menstrual cycle, the changes were not consistent. The week following menstruation changed very little (from approximately 83.0° to 83.5°). For the weeks following, the results are more nearly in the direction expected, with temperature increasing over the 12 weeks of treatment. The reasons for this inconsistency are not clear, but may have to do with measurement errors, artifacts, or inconsistent hormonally-induced changes in temperature. It appears that hand temperature may be a reliable indicator of premenstrual syndrome symptoms for most weeks.

As can be seen from Table 3, galvanic skin response (GSR) was also measured as a covariate, but statistical analysis suggested that GSR is unrelated to PMS symptoms and is unrelated to any treatment effects.

Results for the control group can be seen in Figure 3. Neither vaginal nor hand temperature changed significantly from group mean baseline levels, which would be expected from lack of treatment and from the self-control hypothesis. Group mean

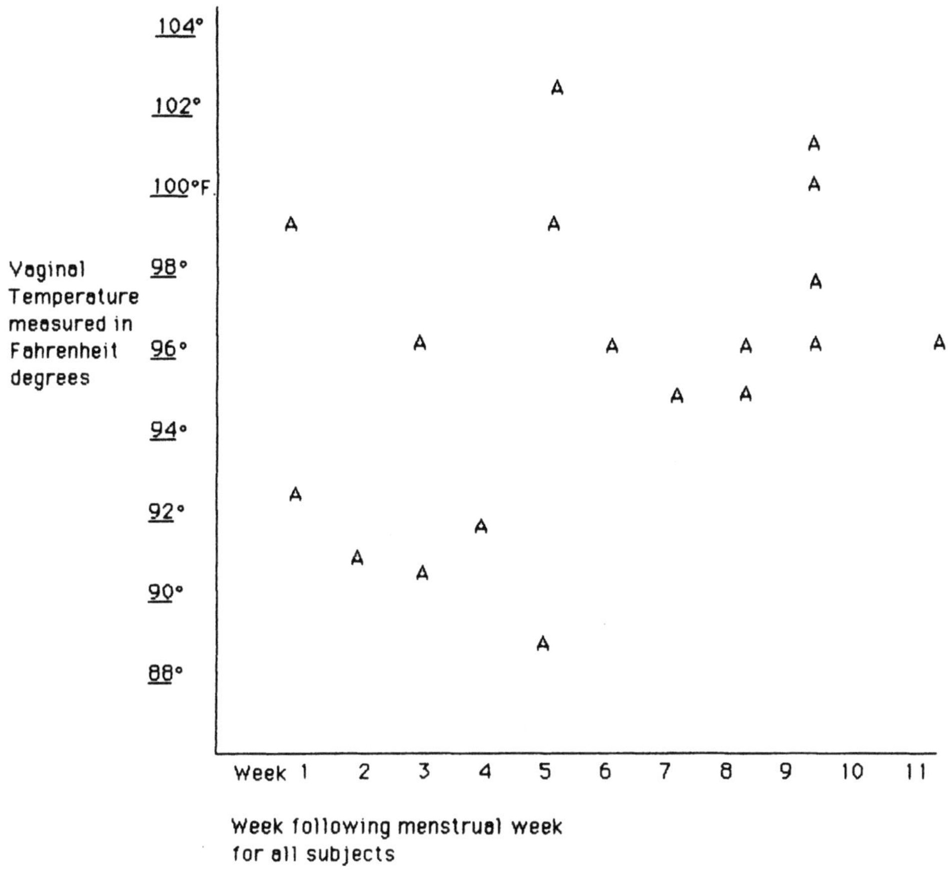

Figure 1c. Individual Observations of Biofeedback Data Showing Cyclicity of Vaginal Temperature, by Week of Menstrual Cycle: Week Following Menstrual Week

vaginal temperature varied from approximately 96.4° F. to 96.6° F. over the course of 12 weeks of measurement, a non-significant difference. Hand temperature group mean data varied from approximately 83.2° F. to 83.7° F. over the 12 weeks of measurement, which was not significant.

Results of Tables 1, 2 and 3 suggest that both physiological and psychological symptoms showed a decrease in severity and an increase in voluntary control. Furthermore, as suggested by Figure 2, voluntary control appeared to increase with treatment, as predicted by the self-control hypothesis. Subjects also reported increasing subjective control over the symptoms. As described, an unexpected result suggested that menstrual phase could be fairly accurately predicted from daily hand temperature and weekly hand temperature measurements. These results have not been reported or explored by any other researchers.

DISCUSSION

Premenstrual Syndrome (PMS) symptoms (Periluteal Phase Dysphoric disorder, DSM-III-R, APA, 1987) may be related to fluid retention, hormonal build-up, involuntary muscle tension build-up, feelings of helplessness or lack of control over

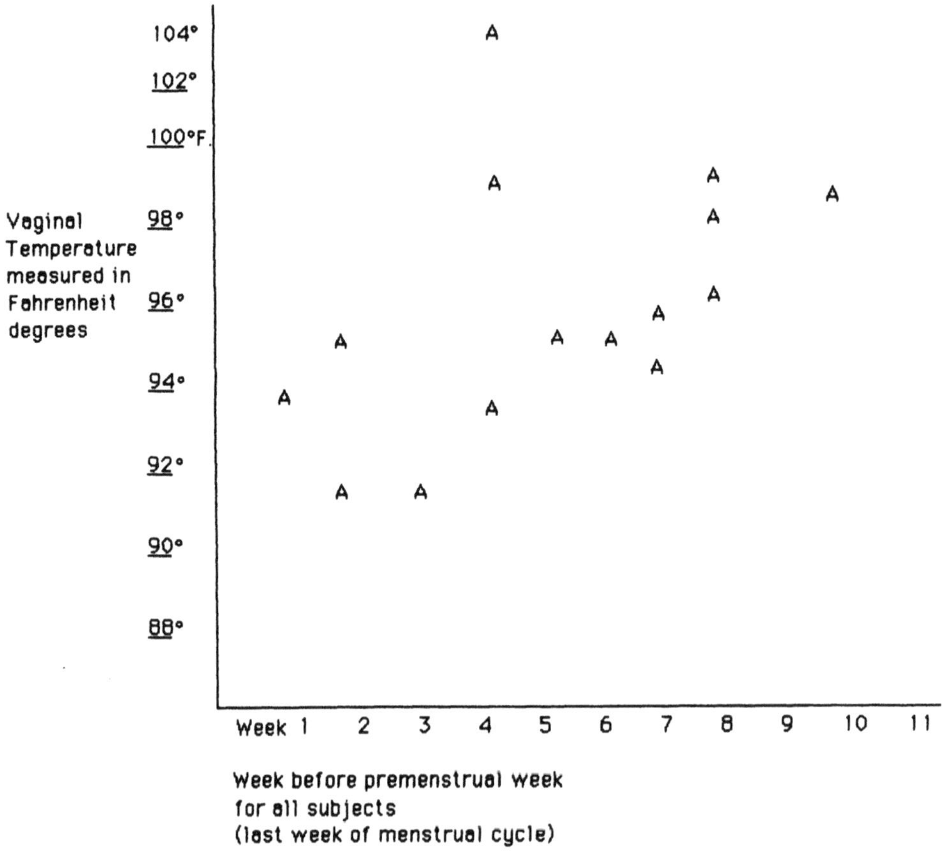

Figure 1d. Individual Observations of Biofeedback Data Showing Cyclicity of Vaginal Temperature, by Week of Menstrual Cycle: Week Preceeding Premenstrual Week (Last Week of Menstrual Cycle)

the symptoms, cognitive loss of control or deficiency, misperception of sensations or other factors.

Vaginal temperature feedback appears to be an effective treatment for PMS symptomatology, and to some extent for reduction of other discomforts associated with the menstrual period. This substantiated the main hypothesis, but the reasons for this effectiveness are not clear. It may be that biofeedback produces a feeling of control over the symptoms; or, biofeedback may produce a feeling of relaxation, which generalizes to the muscles or circulatory system. It has the added advantage, as a voluntary self-control procedure, of being an internal coping skill which appears to be entrainable, with 12 weeks of training. Vaginal temperature feedback appears to contribute to a decrease in physiological stress and psychological symptoms. Subjects reported less mood swings and depression, irritability, bloating, and aching pain. The mechanism for symptom relief appears to be voluntary control and perhaps awareness of, or confidence in, ability to control the underlying physiological processes.

Stage of menstrual cycle also appears to be predictable from hand temperature data. Hand temperature feedback is a familiar form of feedback, and is well-researched in the literature. An initial group mean of approximately 86° to 88° would be expected in a non-patient population. A group mean initial hand

Table 1. Analysis of Covariance of Vaginal Temperature, by Number of Weeks to Next Menses, Showing Effects of Controlling for "Time-to-Next-Menses"

Measure	T=Time to next menses	Sample Size	Slope Estimate	Standard Error	Significance (p-value)
Vaginal	0	11	0.993	0.475	0.066*
Temper-	1	20	0.401	0.158	0.020**
ature	2	18	0.403	0.296	0.193
	3	15	0.397	0.305	0.215
Hand	0	11	1.217	0.664	0.100
Temper-	1	20	0.027	0.207	0.896
ature	2	18	0.378	0.249	0.149
	3	15	0.325	0.336	0.351

*Nearly reached significance at $p > .05$
**Significant at $p > .05$

temperature reading of 83° suggests an abnormally low temperature, typical of a state of stress. This could be due to the presence of pathology, anxiety or stress-related disorders. A group mean final temperature reading of 91° suggests above average temperature, and a relaxed state. That is, this suggests that vaginal temperature produces a relaxed state in patients who are under stress, either from the direct PMS symptoms, or from the attendant cyclical anxiety which may be directly or indirectly related to the PMS symptoms. If these data are replicated by other studies, this suggests that hand temperature biofeedback monitoring could be used to reflect when Premenstrual Syndrome symptoms would be likely to occur. Vaginal temperature feedback, and the resulting psychophysiological voluntary control techniques could perhaps then be used to reduce premenstrual symptomatology. These techniques could perhaps be generalized to other conditions.

INTERPRETATION

Biofeedback appears to assist in the development of voluntary self-control over psychophysiological symptoms of Premenstrual Syndrome. The mechanism of symptom reduction may involve "entrainment" of the autonomic nervous system to a lower state of arousal, generalization of relaxation, changes in hormones or circulation, increased confidence in the ability to control physiological systems, or cognitive control over the symptoms. The familiar signs of increased hand temperature suggests that the subjects learned voluntary control over physiological stress reactions, and learned to relax, or entrain to relaxation, their physiological symptoms.

Biofeedback self-control techniques don't require dependence on medication, external controls, or additional treatments. If these results are replicated, it would suggest that biofeedback techniques are effective voluntary control entrainment treatments for Premenstrual Syndrome symptoms.

An unexpected result of this study suggested that hand temperature could fairly accurately predict stage, or phase, of the premenstrual cycle. This result, if replicated, could hold important implications for prediction of stage of cycle, control of

Table 2. Experimental group paper-and-pencil test scores, p-values and significance levels.

	#Item	Mean Difference (Baseline-end of Study)	Standard Error of the Mean	N	t-Score	P-Value
Personality Factors	PERS	19.75	11.234	8	1.758	0.122
Physiological Stress	STRE1	58.625	18.595	8	3.153	0.016**
Psychological Stress	STRE2	35.625	11.055	8	3.223	0.015**
Emotional Factors	EMOT	14.125	5.626	8	2.514	0.040*
Profile of Mood States	POMS	13.000	5.444	8	2.388	0.048*
Menstrual Distress Questionnaire	MDQ	7.875	2.973	8	2.649	0.033*

*Significant at $p > .05$
**Significant at $p > .02$

Table 3. Analysis of Covariance of Vaginal Temperature Biofeedback Data with Hand Temperature Biofeedback and Galvanic Skin Response (GSR) Biofeedback as Covariates.

Measure-ment	Slope Estimate	Sample Size	Standard Error	Signific-ance (p-value)	95% Confidence Interval Lower Limit	Upper Limit
Vaginal Temperature	0.566	64	0.126	0.0001*	0.314	0.818
Hand Temperature	0.283	64	0.158	0.079**	-0.033	0.599
Galvanic Skin Response (GSR)	-0.667	64	0.832	0.426	-2.331	0.997

*Significant at $p > .0001$
**Nearly reached significance at $p > .05$ ($p > .08$)

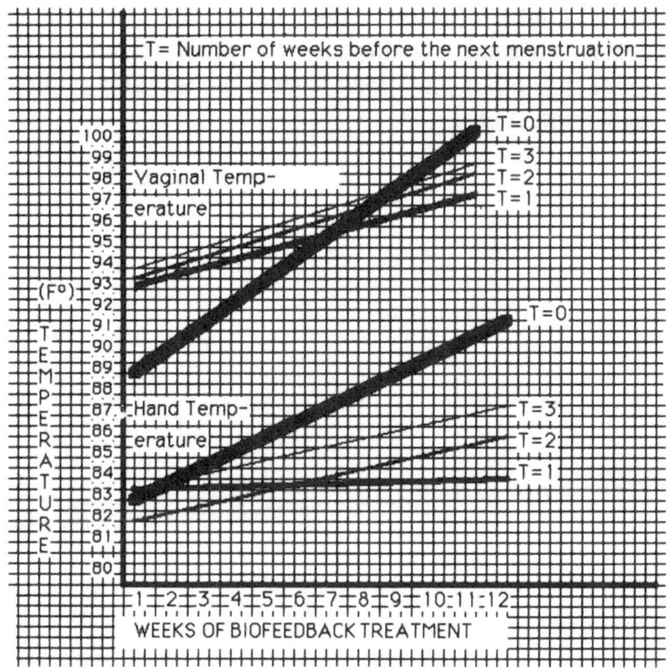

Figure 2. Separate Regressions for Various Times-to-Menses

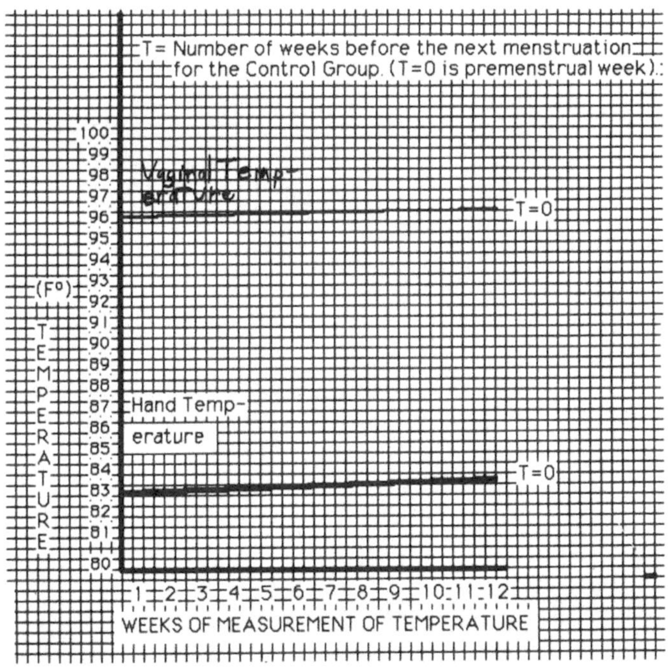

Figure 3. Separate Regressions for Various Times-to-Menses (Control Group)

premenstrual symptoms through biofeedback, and control of birth pain, and other menstrual symptoms.

Further research should focus on understanding the mechanisms underlying voluntary physiological self-control techniques for premenstrual distress, and on applying these techniques to other conditions, such as menstrual cramping, hot flashes (menopause), or vaginal infections.

COPING WITH SOCIAL STRESS THROUGH BEHAVIOR THERAPY

Mélinée Agathon

C.N.R.S. Centre Hospitalier Sainte Anne
Université Paris V
Clinique des Maladies et de l'Encéphale
Paris, France

The concept of stress refers, since Selye and Cannon, etc., to the psychophysiological reaction of an individual who is trying to defend himself against some kind of noxious stimulus and to find means for modifying this stimulus or for adapting his response to it. For many people, some social situations are perceived as being noxious, for instance in meeting strangers or being criticized. It is in this sense that we can conceive the more limited concept of social stress. The term refers to a whole set of psychophysiological, physical and cognitive reactions to situations requiring interpersonal interactions.

Sociological studies on stress have focused on reactions to life events which are universally recognized as aversive health problems. These include bereavement, accidents, catastrophes, war, family or marital discords and unwanted changes in social or occupational status. All these events are unusual and the emotional state they create is considered as being normal as long as it is only temporary.

Unlike these psychosocial stressors which occur in life events and to which an exaggerated vulnerability might, according to DSM III R,[1] reflect some kind of mental illness, there are casual social situations which generate very strong anxiety and are considered by the individual as social stressors.

It has been shown (Agathon, 1987) that in our changing world, social stressors (habit changes, problems of unemployment, for instance) might cause psychological distress. We are not referring here to severe disorders encountered in social phobias which invalidate the social and professional lives of some individuals, such as dysmorphobia, blushing or obsessional fear of blushing. We are referring to a form of social anxiety in which this individual is lacking skills which could help him to cope with interpersonal situations. Anxiety makes him, then, underestimate his abilities to express, in a socially acceptable way, what he feels and inhibits his verbal behavior, his gestures and even his mimic expressions.

---

[1]DSM III R : Diagnostic and Statistical Manual of Mental Disorders (Third Revision Revised), 1987, American Psychiatric Association, Washington, D.C.

In our experience with psychiatric patients who suffer from non-specific anxiety resistant to all previous treatments, behavior analysis often reveals inadequate responses in social situations but does not reach DSM III criteria for social phobia. "Social stress" is evidenced by fear of expressing an opinion in a group context, leading to inhibition or to inadequate verbal and non-verbal responses in a given situation.

It is not, by definition, the aim of behavior therapy to seek why and how this non-assertive behavior has been acquired. But it is necessary to examine under which circumstances it occurred first, sometime during childhood, and when it is still appearing. Gray's (1986) neuropsychological theory on conditioning in the central nervous system tends to demonstrate that anxiety occurs with problems of brain adaptation to its neural environment.

During these last years, our work at Hospital Sainte Anne has focused on anxiety disorders, mostly on phobic disorders (Agathon & Samuel-LaJeunesse, 1981). More recently, we studied phobias and various forms of fears through Wolpe's Fear Survey Schedule (Wolpe & Lang, 1964). Amidst them we found a surprisingly large number of situations generated by social situations, e.g., fear of being observed or criticized during work, of speaking to a large audience and of being ignored by other people. Not only do patients reporting these fears feel uncomfortable when they have to face these situations, but often they try, if possible, to avoid them, anticipating anxiety; e.g., they refuse invitations, keep silent in social or professional groups, avoid expressing their opinion or their disagreement and do not protest against unjustified reproaches.

Behavior therapy is a direct approach to these non-satisfactory behaviors emitted in response to stressors such as socio-environmental demands. It is not oriented on the study of the conflicts which might underlie responses to social stress or of the different models of psychosocial stress which were developed by Kaplan (1983). Nevertheless, behavioral approaches, in many cases, do bring the individual to a better understanding of these conflicts and might, therefore, reduce his difficulties of adaptation and the accompanying physiological, humoral and neuroendocrinal manifestations of stress which are, nowadays, evidenced in psychophysiological diseases (Loo & Loo, 1986).

Cognitive therapy has been used to reduce anxiety, in particular by Ellis (1977) in his Rational Emotive Therapy, and by Meichenbaum through "stress inoculation" (Meichenbaum & Novaco, 1978). But they too rapidly, in our sense, made the hypothesis that, in most people, adaptational difficulties are imaginary. Cognitive therapists aim to persuade their clients that their emotional problems have no foundation. In trying to teach them how to cope with these problems, Lazarus and Folkman (1984), for instance, distinguish, in what they call the regulation of distress, two different coping functions: "emotion-focused coping strategies" and "problem-focused coping" centered on the management of the problem which is causing distress. They underline that teaching someone to behave differently "is not sufficient to reduce stress if the new behavior causes conflicts." So cognitive therapists, as they say, attempt to alter these beliefs that constrain the behavior of their clients, so that behavioral change is accompanied by a change in the underlying values.

It remains doubtful that underlying values which are generally cultural can effectively be changed. This is particularly so when psychosocial stressors arise, making the individual still more vulnerable to his environment. If he wishes, then, to get some control over events, he must first be persuaded that he has control of his own behavior and, notably, of his behavior during social relationships.

As was mentioned above, we found, among patients referred to our behavior therapy unit, a large number of social fears. A more recent study (Agathon, in press) carried on 159 subjects (100 males and 59 females) suffering from anxiety disorders, showed that those patients with the highest scores on a factor of social fears estimated by the Fear Survey Schedule, had the lowest scores on an assertiveness schedule (Rathus, 1973). Lack of assertiveness, no doubt, makes the individual more vulnerable to social stressors and so does excess of assertiveness, leading to habits of anger and of uncontrolled reactions to frustration.

Since Salter's (1949) and Wolpe's (1958) studies on conditional reflex therapy, difficulties in expressing one's feelings in a socially acceptable way have been considered, to some extent, as having a role in the genesis of anxiety. Reversely, the expression of personal feelings, even anger in some cases, is seen as having a sedative effect according to Wolpe's principle of reciprocal inhibition.

Liberman et al (1975) described methods of increasing what was called "personal effectiveness" by teaching new "social skills." Unassertiveness is, in this sense, not only a consequence of anxiety in social situations considered as stressors, but also, and sometimes more so, a consequence of lack of social skills. The individual has, possibly, never been taught what to do, nor what to say on some occasions, whether or not he has met them before. Or possibly--this could be the case of some very handicapped psychiatric patients--he has lost these skills or forgotten them and this accounts for his lack of personal effectiveness.

Liberman and his colleagues have more recently extended methods of acquiring personal effectiveness so as to also bring changes in groups, organizations and institutions. They believe that many of their patients who are the most vulnerable to social stressors can benefit from assertive training to improve their relationship with others, and consequently get more welfare in their everyday lives. Their goal is to instigate change in their consultees so as to help them to function more effectively and efficiently and with greater satisfaction and morale. Training people in personal effectiveness promotes changes in their behavior and also changes in the behavior of others toward them. Therefore it can be of use not only to help an individual in his personal problems of social communication and relationship, but also it can bring more cohesiveness in the management of a group by promoting better leadership or supervision.

Social skills are learned during training in personal effectiveness which focuses on learning new responses to stressful social situations, or re-learning responses or skills which might have been forgotten or inhibited. It is done by analyzing and role-playing, by a procedure of behavioral rehearsal in interpersonal or social situations. Trainees learn to emit these responses in an appropriate and non-aggressive way. They are then positively reinforced by approval, coaching and sometimes by the example of the behavior therapist which they try to imitate. In this social learning procedure, differences are made clear between inhibited, assertive and aggressive behaviors by role-acting these behaviors. When assertive training is being practiced in a group, other members of the group cooperate also, by positive suggestions rather than by criticism, in the change of the inappropriate behavior.

Indications of assertive training, as can be evidenced in the literature, have widened from students anxious to achieve academic success and social approval to most impaired psychiatric patients. In both cases it still has to be established and experimentally demonstrated that social skills acquired during training in a restraint group can be generalized in real life in other stressful situations or events. It still has to be proved that these skills can effectively help the individual to cope with the problems he meets during work, leisure time and family or marital life.

But there is no doubt that learning techniques for coping with social stressors reduces stress and anxiety. For instance, aircraft pilots are trained in acrobatics in order to be able to deal calmly, if ever it occurs, with an unusual position of their engine. It is more important, for the safety of flight, to take into account this training than to speculate on some pilot's personality traits or psychophysiological variables.

Up to now very little can be found in American research on cultural anthropology with reference to the impact of social stress on the behavior of individuals because most of these studies were considered in relation to child rearing and relations with parents and peers. In the cultures examined, for instance by Ruth Benedict and Margaret Mead, the individual was clearly aware of the norms of his social group and helped by others to cope with stressors.

Such is not always the case in our contemporary societies: changes in the environment (technological, cultural) are frequent and might lead to some discomfort in interpersonal relationships, to a fear of not being able to show others the appropriate mimic, to give up-to-date answers to a question, to hurt the feelings of friends, to be unable to reject unreasonable demands.

Assertive training is frequently indicated, in behavior therapy, for individuals who have to cope with social stressors. It has been practiced in our Clinic since 1976. Most trainees are outpatients with normal professional and family lives. They are seeking help because they wish to get better acceptance from the groups to which they belong or which they are aiming to enter. As we have already mentioned, assertive training does not have, as a goal, to normalize the social behavior of an individual so as to make him acceptable for the group. It is rather meant to make him understand that he can also modify the reactions of his environment by acquiring better and more numerous social competences. This might require reappraisal of values, habits and ways of living.

In research carried out in our Clinic (Samuel-LaJeunesse et al, 1985) we studied the therapeutic results obtained by assertive training. Patients (18 males and 13 females aged 21 to 49) had, all except three, professional activities and a good socio-cultural level. They met weekly during a period of six months. Assertive training groups included 3 to 5 patients, the behavior therapist (a psychologist) and an observer who was a student either in psychology or in psychiatry.

At the end of the sessions, the great majority of the patients estimated that they were improved. This improvement was also reported by a psychiatrist, acting as an independent observer, on the symptomatic level. He also found global clinical improvement in 74% of the patients. Socioprofessional and family handicaps appeared statistically diminished.

These results, and many others reported in the literature, enlighten the psycho-sociological aspects of anxiety without reference to psychopathological processes nor to dynamic theories. Many questions remain unanswered on the impact of social stressors on the individual. Do they increase his emotional distress to such an extent that he becomes unable to adapt his behavior to the noxious event? Does learning social skills help him to cope with them? Behavioral approaches for coping with social stress constitute a challenging way of trying to answer these questions.

References

Agathon, M. Behavioral approaches of social anxiety in changing world. International Congress: "Social Change and its Effects on Human Behavior." Athens, November 1987, in press.

Agathon, M., and Samuel, LaJeunesse B. 1981, Bilan de quatee annees de therapie comportementale, *Psychologie Médicale*, 13,1: 107-119

Ellis, A., and Grieger, R. (eds) 1977, Handbook of Rational-Emotive Therapy. Springer, New York

Gray, J.A. 1986, Modélisation de l'anxiété: rôle dy système limbique. *Actualités Médicales Internationales* : Psychiatrie, 22 supp.: 11-13

Kaplan, H.B. (ed) 1983, Psychosocial stress. Trends in Theory and Research. Academic Press, New York

Lazarus, R.S., and Folkman, S. 1984, Stress, appraisal and coping. Springer, New York

Liberman, R. P., King, L.W., De Risi, W.J., and McCann, M. 1975, Personal effectiveness. Guiding people to assert themselves and improve their social skills. Champaign, Illinois

Loo, P., and Loo, H. 1986, Le stress permanent. Masson, Paris

Meichenbaum, D., and Novaco, R. 1978, Stress innoculation: a preventive approach *in* C. D. Spielberger & I. G. Sarasin (eds): Stress and Anxiety 5. Halstead, New York

Rathus, S.A. 1973, A 30-item schedule for assessing assertive behavior*Behavior Therapy* 4: 298-306

Salter A. 1949, Conditioned reflex therapy: the direct approach to the reconstruction of personality. Creative Age Press, New York

Samuel,-LaJeunesse, B., Degleris, N., Brouri, R., and Agathon, M. 1985, Appréciation des effets des techniques assertives en groupe en milieu psychiatrique. *Annales Médico-Psychologiques* 143,5: 458-464

Wolpe, J. 1958, Psychotherapy by reciprocal inhibition. Stanford University Press, Stanford

Wolpe, J. 1983, Tension control for coping and for habit change. Presidential address ISTCS, *in* Stress and tension control-2, McGuigan, Sime and Wallace. 1984. Plenum, New York

Wolpe, J., and Lang, P.J. 1964, A fear survey schedule for use in behavior therapy. *Behaviour Research and Therapy* 2/27-30

PSYCHOSOCIAL FACTORS ASSOCIATED WITH SEVERITY OF MENOPAUSAL SYMPTOMS

Norman Morris[1] and Lucy Morris[2]

[1]Obstetrics and Gynecology, University of London
I.V.F. Unit, Cromwell Hospital
London

[2]Menopause Clinic, West London Hospital
I.V.F. Unit, Cromwell Hospital
London

THE PATIENTS STUDIED

This study was carried out at the Menopause Clinic, West London Hospital, London, W.6. Patients were first interviewed by a gynecologist who assessed their medical condition and determined the treatment that was required. The women were then asked if they would spare time to give further information to a research assistant (counselor). Very few patients refused to cooperate. Patients were encouraged to describe their childhood experiences, and their reactions to their parents, husband and children. Their libido was also discussed. In all, 35 patients were subject to assessment of whom 26 were still married to their first husband. (In view of information that will be described later, this is very surprising.) Five were divorced, of whom 2 had remarried. Two were widows of whom 1 had remarried, and 2 were single. If the counselor thought that counseling would be of value, further sessions were arranged. The additional number of sessions ranged from 2 to 20.

METHODOLOGY

The data were analyzed in relation to a six-point scale, ranging from positive reactions (+3) to negative reactions (-3).

Appearance (Fig. 1)

An attempt was made to assess the woman's overall appearance, namely (1) her expression and demeanour; (2) her state of tiredness, and (3) the care that she took with her hair, her makeup and with her clothes. Fig. 1 indicates the overall pattern that emerged. In all, 20 women presented a positive appearance and 15 had a negative, unkempt appearance. As indicated later, this observation does not match

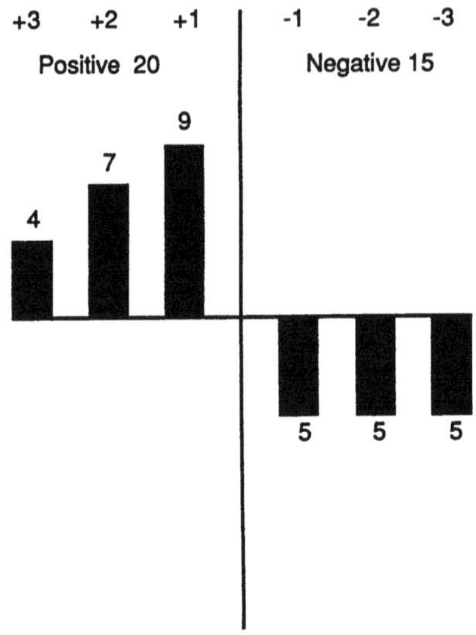

Fig. 1 Appearance

the assessment of their self image (see Fig. 6). Obviously, their reasonable overall appearance often conceals an underlying sense of unhappiness.

Childhood Experiences (Fig. 2)

In this group, 12 patients recalled positive and satisfying experiences of their childhood. The majority (23) described negative reactions and 19 of these had extremely unpleasant recollections.

Relationship with Parents (Fig. 3)

Here again, the majority (19) related that they had negative reactions to their parents. In particular, many claimed that their fathers treated them very badly by

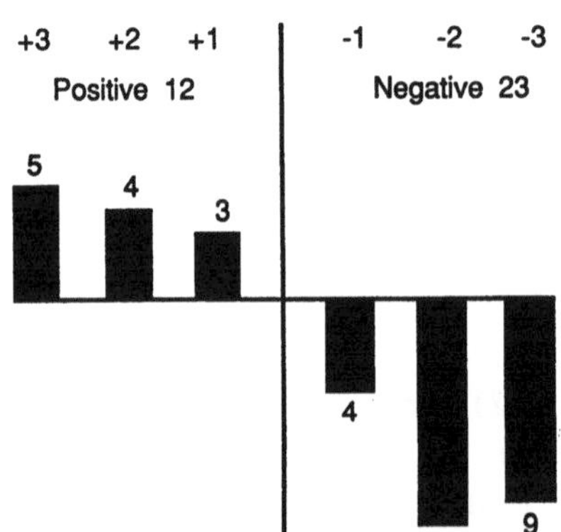

Fig. 2 Childhood Experiences

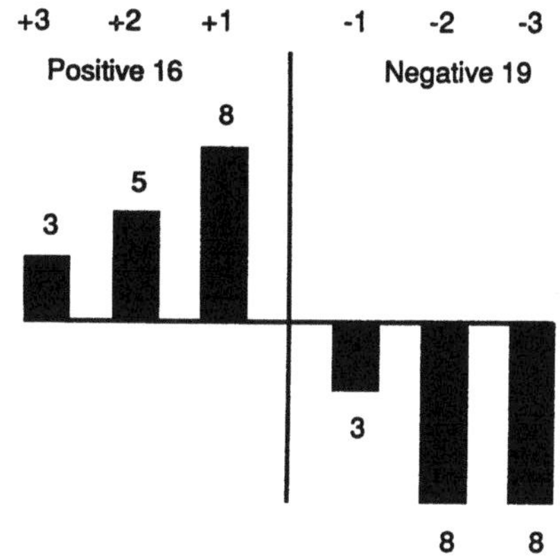

Fig. 3 Relationship with Parents

assaulting them physically, including sexually, as well as humiliating them by their comments.

Relationship with Husband (Fig. 4)

Twenty-one described unhappy relationships with their husbands of whom 15 claimed they were enduring very miserable marriages, where they felt their husbands no longer found them attractive or desirable, or even reasonable companions. In many instances, it was difficult to understand why the marriage had survived except to sustain outward appearances.

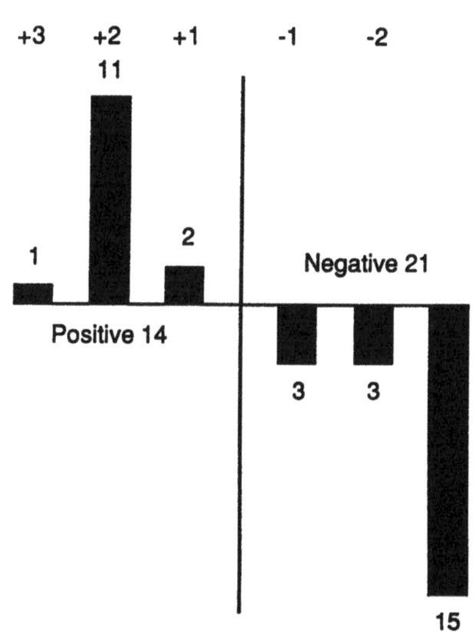

Fig. 4 Relationship with Husband

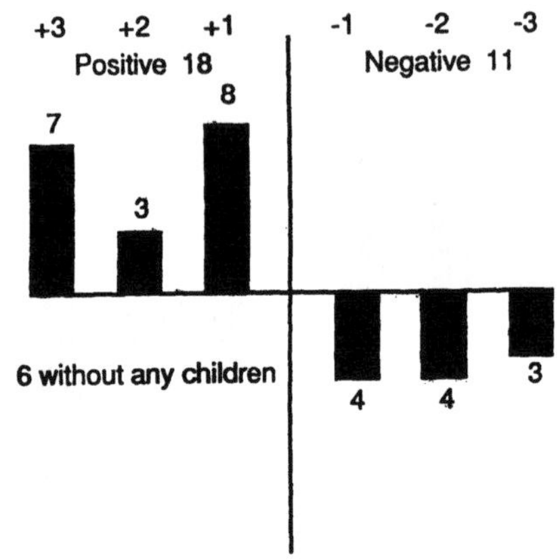

Fig. 5 Relationship with Children

Relationship with Children (Fig. 5)

In this group, the majority (18 out of 29) thought they had good relationships with their children. They appeared to get along with them far better than they did with their husbands. Of the 11 who reported negative relationships, only 3 were in the (-3) category. It would be interesting to interview the children to determine whether they felt that they had equally satisfying relationships with their mothers. Six women in this study did not have children.

Self Image (Fig. 6)

The majority (25) reported a negative self image, and 11 were in the most extreme (-3) category. Many felt that they were no longer of value within the family unit. In addition, they felt that the menopause changes had made them appear and feel unwanted, aged and decrepit.

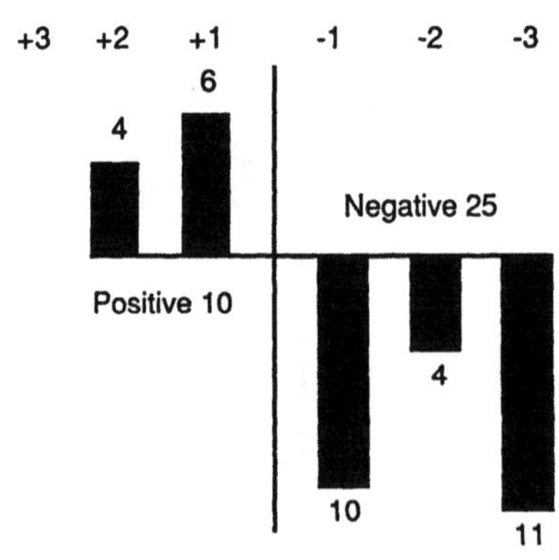

Fig. 6 Self Image

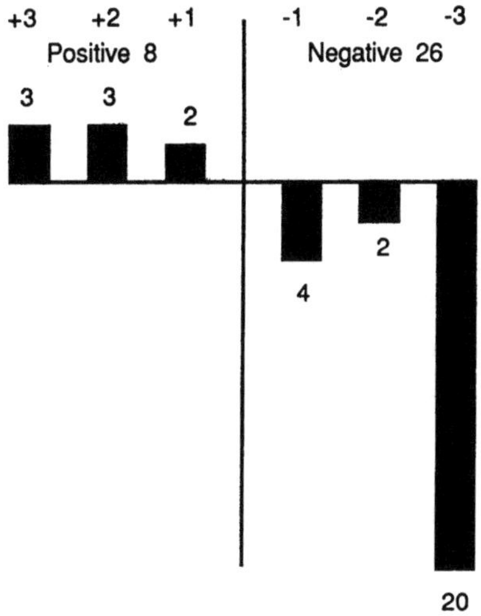

Fig. 7 Libido

Libido (Fig. 7)

In this category, 26 out of the 34 reported loss of sexual desire and response. Twenty claimed that they had no libido whatsoever, and that they seldom had intercourse with their husbands. If they did make love, it was often painful and they derived no satisfaction whatsoever.

SYMPTOMS

These women described the usual range of menopausal symptoms: hot flashes, depression, fatigue, irritability, insomnia, impatience, mood swings, joint and muscle pains, skin rashes, dry vagina and, of course, loss of libido.

TREATMENT

Nearly all these patients received Hormone Replacement Therapy of one kind or another. This treatment gave very effective relief of hot flashes, but the relief of other symptoms varied considerably and was rarely complete. Loss of libido, on the whole, did not respond well to Hormone Replacement Therapy.

Of this group, 25 (71%) required counseling. However, only 14 (40%) received counseling. The reasons given for not accepting counseling varied. The number of counseling sessions varied between 2 and 20. Many women claimed that the counseling was of considerable value to them and it had enabled them to adapt much more effectively to their situation.

Relaxation was also taught during the counseling sessions.

CASE HISTORY

One case history illustrates many of the observations made in this study.

Mrs. B, aged 40, was the youngest of 3 children. She came from an upper middle-class family and is now a barrister. She had a very unhappy childhood--a "weekend" father with a mistress in London. Her mother was obsessive and bad-tempered. She could not retain her servants and as a consequence, used her daughter as a "skivvy." Her mother called her "ugly." She was educated in a strict convent school where sexuality was denied. Eventually she married a barrister from a lower social group who was not an intellectual. She despised his lack of finesse and limited cultural interests.

She stayed up all night cleaning brass rather than go to bed. There was no handle on their bedroom door, so they could not keep out children or make love. She was a Roman Catholic, and could not divorce her husband whom she disliked and feared and for whom she also had no sexual feelings. He beat her from time to time.

Her symptoms were those of tiredness, irritability, anger, depression, and dislike of herself and her early menopause. She felt she was no longer a woman and her husband had convinced her that was really what "menopause" meant.

Her self image was non-existent and she referred to herself as "Clive's mother," and did not feel like a person in her own right. In appearance she was very fat, dirty, slovenly with soiled underwear. Her body was bruised.

CONCLUSION

Women who attend a Menopause Clinic are a special self-selected group. They are certainly not representative of all women going through menopause. They often appear to have had complex and unhappy past emotional histories and poor emotional relationships. These are very much exacerbated by the onset of menopause.

Hormone Replacement Therapy does provide some relief of menopausal symptoms but specially trained counselors should be available to provide additional support and therapy.

PSYCHOSOCIAL LOAD AND SYMPTOMS: WHAT IS THE RELATIONSHIP WITH PERSONALITY FACTORS?

A.J.J.M. Vingerhöets and L.J. Menges

Department of Medical Psychology
Institute for Research in Extramural Medicine
Free University Amsterdam
Amsterdam, The Netherlands

INTRODUCTION

Studying the relationship between "stress" and personality factors may involve the following: 1) the association between personality and (the self-reports of) psychosocial load or stressors; 2) the connection between personality and psychophysiologic/psychosomatic symptoms or strains; and 3) the role of personality attributes as moderating factors in the stress-illness relationship. Therefore, to understand the correlation between the existence of stress and illness, it is necessary to focus on personality factors as determinants of stress-vulnerability or stress-resistance.

Kasl (1983) has suggested that life events cannot simply be perceived as independent of personality characteristics. He mentions, for example, heroin addicts and alcoholics as groups with high frequencies of life experiences. Byrne (1981) and Byrne and Rosenman (1986) have presented evidence that Type A persons have higher scores on life-change questionnaires. Also, Cohen (1982) reported data indicating that sensation seekers also check certain items of life-change questionnaires, such as "trouble with employer" and "sexual difficulties," more frequently than a control group. Finally, Schroeder and Costa(1984) argued that items of life-change scales may be confounded with factors such as neuroticism. According to these authors, the aforementioned principle also applies to items possibly representing symptoms of psychopathology (e.g., change in sleeping or eating habits) and items about events that could be caused by inadequate functioning, such as divorce or being fired from work.

Recently, there has been a renewed concern about stress resulting from minor life events or daily hassles. Some investigators (e.g., Dohrenwend et al, 1984) have suggested that many items of such daily-hassles scales may be interpreted as symptoms indicating disturbed psychological functioning. Consequently, the conclusion has been challenged that daily hassles are better predictors of psychosomatic disturbances than life changes.

There is also some evidence available that emotional strains and personality are related to each other. Neuroticism and hypochondriasis are probably the best examples of such a positive and empirically demonstrated connection (Costa and McCrae, 1985; Luteyn et al, 1985). Provided the often considerable overlap among items of both kinds of scales, these associations can be expected. On the other hand, there is a vast amount of literature on the relationship between personality factors and specific somatic diseases. Probably one of the most frequently reported associations is between Type A characteristics or its presumed components (especially hostility) and cardiovascular disease (see Chesney and Rosenman, 1985); Dembroski and Costa, 1987).

However, seen from the perspective of stress research, the most interesting studies concern the relationship between personality and psychosocial load or symptoms. In these studies, psychosocial factors (e.g., personality factors, coping capabilities or social support) are often treated as moderator variables. The existence of a stress-illness relationship is then examined in particular groups having, and in groups lacking, a specific feature. For example, it has been shown that people who experience social support report experiencing fewer symptoms in stressful conditions than people who lack social support (see, however, Alloway and Bebbington, 1987). The most frequently investigated personality variable seems to be "hardiness" (Kobassa, 1982). Commitment, control, and challenge are the relevant concepts that together constitute this personality style of stress resistance. In several investigations it has been shown that "hardy" people, in spite of a high psychosocial load and job-related pressure, do not frequently report symptoms indicating stress.

Another related concept, Sense of Coherence (SOC), has been proposed by Antonovsky (1979; 1987). The concept was derived from interview data of people who had experienced major trauma, but who were reported to be coping very well. The three core coping elements are: comprehensibility, manageability, and meaningfulness. Although Antonovsky prefers not to speak of a personality variable, his recent description starting with the words "The SOC is a global orientation that..." (Antonovsky, 1987, p. 19) suggests that it is at least very close to a dispositional feature.

The cited investigations have compared personality attributes of two groups: one reporting a high load and many symptoms (referred to as stress vulnerable);the second reporting a high load and few symptoms (the stress resistant people). However, such a comparison does not exclude the possibility of a relationship, as mentioned above, between personality factors and symptom reporting. The point here is that it is not warranted to conclude that differences in personality factors between those two groups really have to do with stress vulnerability and stress resistance. To allow for these inferences, it is necessary to have two additional control groups. This grouping will consist of people reporting low load and many complaints. The second group will consist of individuals having a low psychosocial load and low levels of complaints.

In the present study, on the basis of the psychosocial load and symptom scores, four groups were composed using median splits. It then followed that *personality* is conceived of as the *dependent* variable. This procedure yielded the following groups: 1) low-load, few symptoms;2) low-load, many symptoms; 3) high-load, few symptoms; 4) high-load, many symptoms; and finally, 5) people who could not be classified because they had reported relatively few life events and many everyday problems or vice versa.

The present design allows for the following inferences. In case of a main effect for the factor "psychosocial load," people reporting a high load differ from people reporting a low load, whether or not they also report symptoms. It may be inferred that people reporting many symptoms differ from people reporting few symptoms, regardless of their load levels. However, of major interest are the potential interactions. At this point it may be concluded that a particular personality attribute is connected to stress resistance or stress vulnerability. The focus of the study involves group 3 (the stress-resistant group) and group 4 (the stress-vulnerable group). However, the other groups are important if a correct and thorough interpretation of the results is to be achieved.

The scales of the Dutch Personality Inventory (Luteyn, 1974; Luteyn et al, 1985), will be examined. This includes an assessment of personality factors such as neuroticism, social inadequacy, rigidity, hostility, self-sufficiency, dominance and self-esteem. Unfortunately, little can be written about the relationship between these personality features and the concepts of hardiness and SOC. Nevertheless, based on the literature, the following hypotheses can be put forward:

Neuroticism has been reported to be associated with scores on devices measuring psychosocial load and also on scales measuring symptoms. In addition, neuroticism is mentioned as a factor that renders persons vulnerable to stress. This implies that there are main effects for both psychosocial load and symptoms, as well as an interaction between the factors (Schroeder and Costa, 1984; Wickramasekera, 1986).

Social inadequacy may be assumed to be negatively associated with social support. Therefore, it may be hypothesized that stress-resistant people are more socially adequate than the members of other groups. One may also argue that insufficient social skills may easily lead to a high psychosocial load.

Rigidity, according to Luteyn et al (1985), is associated with maladjustment. Therefore, it follows that stress-resistant people will have lower scores on this factor, whereas the stress-vulnerable group has higher scores.

Hostility has recently been identified as the prime factor in the Type A personality (Dembroski and Costa, 1987). This leads to the hypothesis that the stress-vulnerable group has the highest scores on this personality factor.

Self-sufficiency has never been investigated as a factor in stress research. We speculate that this factor is linked to psychosocial load, the assumption being that interest in other people and their problems might attract persons in need of help. Furthermore, in an analysis of the personality factors that distinguished people who were rarely ill, from those with frequent illnesses, Hinkle (1974) found that those who remain healthy show a lack of concern for other people and life goals. These people rarely involve themselves in life affairs. Such findings lead to the expectation that people with high levels of complaints, generally, are less self-sufficient.

Dominance is hypothesized to be associated with psychosocial load. Dominant persons might be expected to strive for control over their environment. This may result in conflict encounters.

Self-esteem has been reported to be affected by stressors that cannot be adequately dealt with (see Pearlin, 1983). Therefore, we hypothesize that there is a negative association with symptoms. Essentially, people reporting many symptoms will have lower scores on self-esteem than persons who are free of symptoms. Also, evidence has been presented, indicating that solving difficult problems adequately may enhance self-esteem. Therefore, an interaction effect probably exists. This phenomenon is due to high scores for the stress-resistant group.

In Table 1 the hypotheses under investigation are summarized and translated to expected ANOVA-results.

METHODS

Subjects

In two villages in the Mid-Brabant area in the Netherlands, 2500 people (age range 25-50 years) were randomly selected from official documents kept by the Registrar's Offices. Males and females were equally represented. People were informed about the aim of the present study via local papers, during meetings which were organized, and via local broadcasting stations.

Each potential participant received a booklet containing the following six questionnaires: 1) The Everyday Problem Inventory (EPI) (Alledaagse Problemen Lijst, APL {Vingerhoets and Menges, 1988}); 2) The Recently Experienced Events Questionnaire (REEQ) (Vragenlijst Recent Meegemaakte Gebeurtenissen, VRMG {Van der Willigen et al, 1984}); 3) The Dutch Hopkins Sympton Checklist (HSCL) (Derogatis et al, 1974; Dutch version by Luteyn et al, 1984); 4) A lifestyle Questionnaire with items on health habits and social support; 5) The Ways of Coping

Table 1. Summary of the hypotheses formulated in the introduction. A"+" sign indicates that we expected significant effects; a "?" mark means that it was not possible to formulate expectations.

	Psychosocial Load	Symptoms	Interaction
Neuroticism	+	+	+
Social inadequacy	+	?	+
Rigidity	?	?	+
Hostility	?	+	+
Self-sufficiency	+	?	?
Dominance	+	?	?
Self-esteem	?	+	+

Checklist (WCC, Lazarus and Folkman, 1980; Dutch version by Van Heck and Vingerhoets, 1988); and 6) The Dutch Personality Inventory (DPI) (Nederlandse Persoonlijkheids Vragenlijst, NVP {Luteyn, 1974; Luteyn et al, 1985}).

This study deals only with the EPI, QREE and HSCL to compose groups. The DPI will be used to measure the dependent variables (Personality Characteristics).

A completed set of questionnaires was returned by 1197 subjects (47.9%). Mostly because of missing pages, the ultimate sample of subjects with complete data sets was reduced to 998 persons: 465 males (mean age 36.4, s.d.=6.34) and 532 females (mean age 34.9, s.d.=6.33). (For one subject, data on age and sex were missing).

PROCEDURE

Four to six weeks after the questionnaires were sent out, collection of the booklets was begun. When no contact had taken place after two approaches, the subject received a letter with the request to hand in the forms (whether completed or not) at a specified location.

Data Analysis

Data were analyzed separately for both sexes. The aim of the present study was to compose four groups on the basis of psychosocial load and symptoms. As an index for psychosocial load, scores from the EPI and REEQ were used. Median split procedures provided the methodology for selecting subjects who scored either high or low on both questionnaires. Because it appeared that there were considerable differences between occupational levels, both on the independent and the dependent variables, it was decided to compute the medians for each occupational level group separately. The scores were subjective scores, i.e., it was not a mere frequency count of the items checked, but the seriousness and unpleasantness of rating for the EPI and REEQ, respectively, were taken into account. This procedure led to discarding a number of subjects (previously indicated as the fifth group). This group consisted of 81 males and 103 females. In addition, a median split was applied to the HSCL, resulting in groups with either numerous or few symptoms. The following four groups were composed: 1) low-load, few symptoms; 2) low-load, many symptoms; 3) high-load, few symptoms; and 4) high-load, many symptoms. This design allowed the use of a 2X2 ANOVA design with "Psychosocial Load" and "Symptoms" as main factors.The dependent variables were the scores on the seven scales of the DPI: Neuroticism, Social Inadequacy, Rigidity, Hostility, Self-sufficiency, Dominance and Self-esteem.

RESULTS

Generally, the results of the male and female groups showed a close correspondence. This is true of the number of subjects assigned to each category: low-load, few symptoms (men: N=143; women: N=165); low-load, many symptoms (men: N=54; women: N=62); high-load, few symptoms (men: N=52; women: N=51); high-load, many symptoms (men: N=135; women: N=151).

Figures 1a-g show graphic representations of the results, whereas the results of the ANOVAs are summarized in Table 2. In some cases "Psychosocial Load" was the only factor that yielded significant results. In other cases the main factor "Symptoms" was significantly associated with the dependent variables. For some personality variables significant effects were found for both main factors.

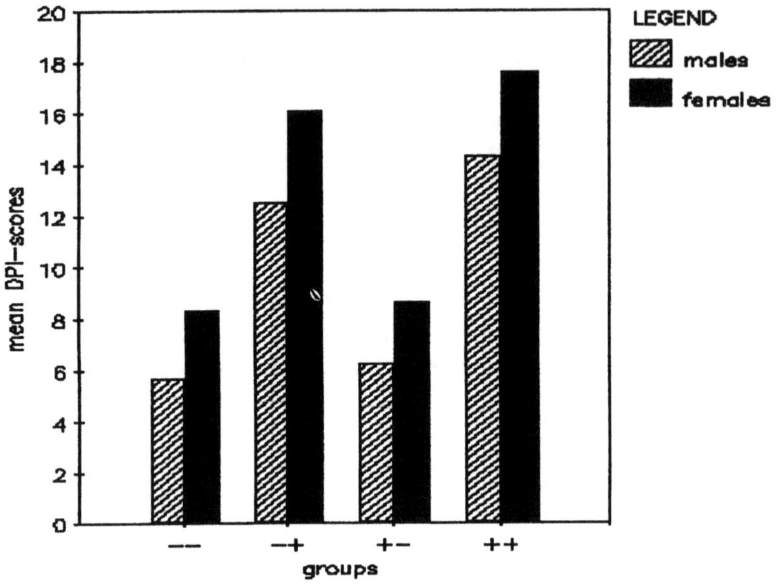

Figure 1a. Neuroticism mean DPI scores (--: low-load, few symptoms; -+: low-load, many symptoms; +-: high-load, few symptoms; ++: high-load, many symptoms).

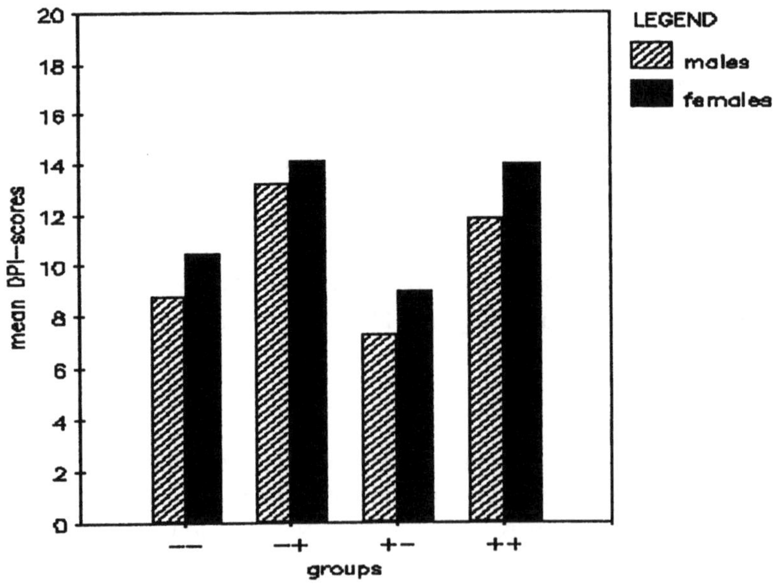

Figure 1b. Social inadequacy mean DPI scores (--: low-load, few symptoms'; -+: low-load, many symptoms; +-: high-load, few symptoms; ++: high-load, many symptoms).

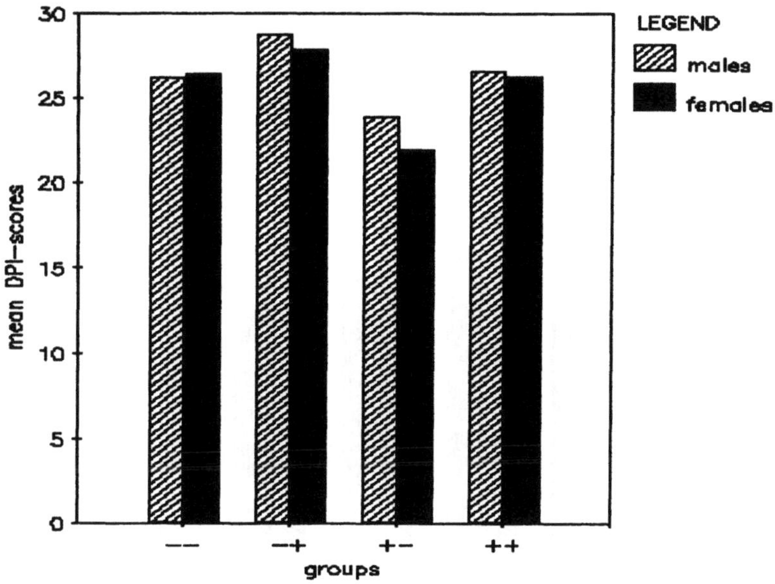

Figure 1c. Rigidity mean DPI scores (--: low-load, few symptoms; -+: low-load, many symptoms; +-: high-load, few symptoms; + +: high-load, many symptoms).

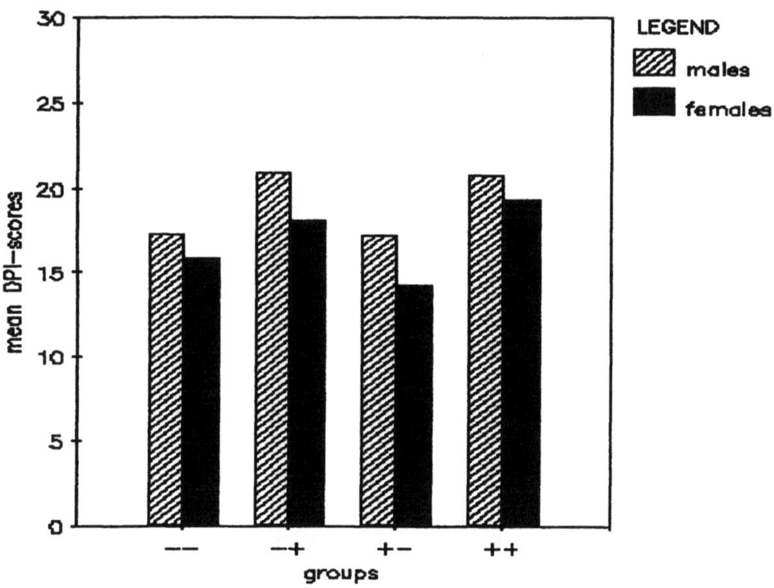

Figure 1d. Hostility mean DPI scores (--: low-load, few symptoms; -+: low-load, many symptoms; +-: high-load, few symptoms; + +: high-load, many symptoms).

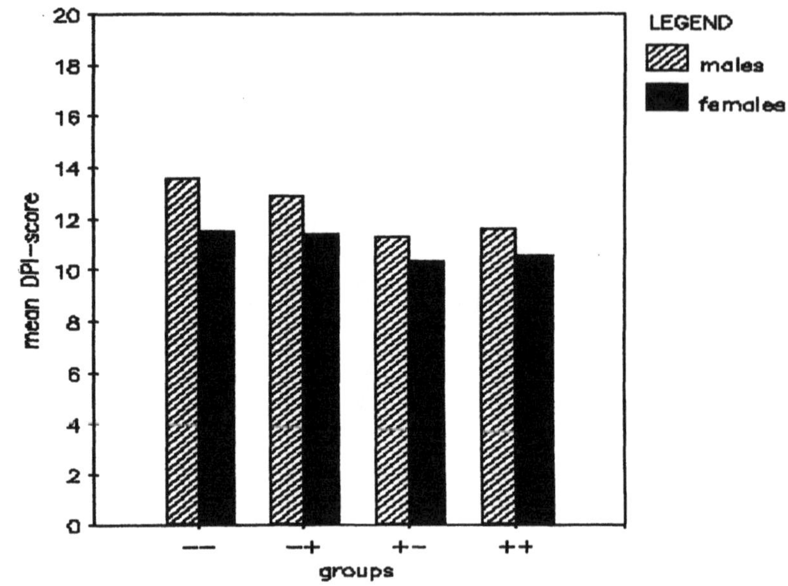

Figure 1e. Self-sufficiency mean DPI scores (--: low-load, few symptoms; -+: low-load, many symptoms; +-: high-load, few symptoms; ++: high-load, many symptoms).

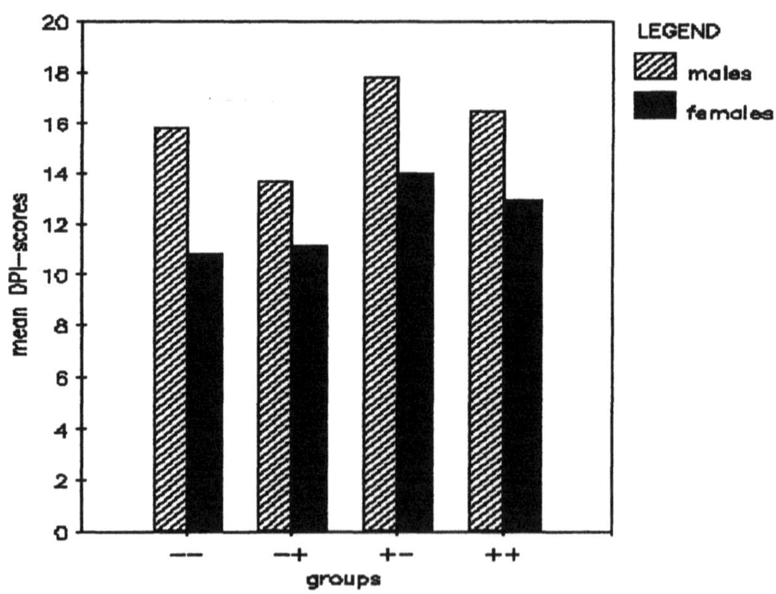

Figure 1f. Dominance mean DPI scores (--: low-load, few symptoms; -+: low-load, many symptoms; +-: high-load, few symptoms; ++: high-load, many symptoms).

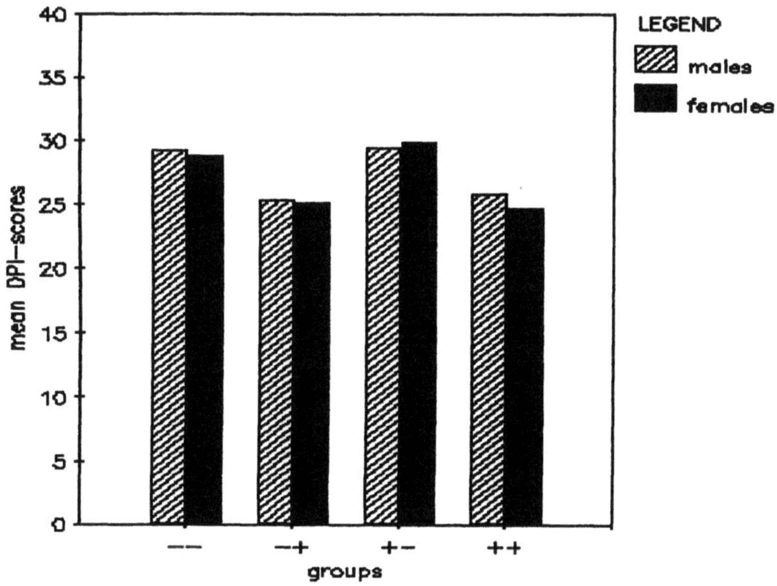

Figure 1g. Self-esteem mean DPI scores (--: low-load, few symptoms; -+: low-load, many symptoms; +-: high-load, few symptoms; ++: high-load, many symptoms).

Self-sufficiency and dominance (only for women) were variables where only significant effects for the main factor, "Psychosocial Load," were found. Individuals reporting a high-load rate were more dominant and less self-sufficient in comparison to people reporting low load. In contrast, neuroticism, social inadequacy, hostility, and self-esteem only yielded significant effects for the main factor "Symptoms." People reporting many symptoms were qualified as more neurotic, less socially adequate, more hostile, and low in self-esteem. Both main factors yielded significant effects for rigidity and for dominance (only for males). Persons scoring high on load were less rigid. In addition, people with many symptoms can be characterized as more rigid and (this holds only for males) less dominant.

Finally, no significant interactions were found, although for rigidity and hostility (only for females) trends could be identified suggesting that the stress-resistant group (high-load, few symptoms) had the lowest scores on both scales.

DISCUSSION

The main purpose of this study was to identify personality characteristics that are associated with psychosocial load, symptoms, and stress-resistance, all indicative of stress vulnerability. Therefore, it was important to find significant interactions in the ANOVAs, in addition to identifying main effects. However, contrary to expectations,we did not find significant interactions for neuroticism, social inadequacy, rigidity, hostility, and self-esteem (although there were trends for rigidity and hostility in the hypothesized direction for females only).

Therefore, the general conclusion that can be drawn on the basis of the present findings is that none of the personality variables tested are related to stress-resistance or stress-vulnerability as defined in the present study, i.e., by combining scores on

Table 2. Results of the ANOVAs with "Psychosocial Load" and "Symptoms" as main factors. The upper panel represents the results of the male subjects, whereas the lower panel summarizes the results of the female groups.

MALES	Psychosocial Load		Symptoms		Interaction	
	F	p	F	p	F	p
1) Neuroticism	2.30	ns	92.98	<.001	.58	ns
2) Social Inadequacy	3.35	=.07	32.28	<.001	.00	ns
3) Rigidity	7.71	<.01	11.15	<.001	.00	ns
4) Hostility	.03	ns	26.00	<.001	.00	ns
5) Self-sufficiency	8.13	<.01	.07	ns	.63	ns
6) Dominance	11.70	<.001	5.97	<.05	.31	ns
7) Self-esteem	.28	ns	34.76	<.001	.05	ns

Note: Degrees of freedom for both main effects and interaction: 1,380.

FEMALES	Psychosocial Load		Symptoms		Interaction	
	F	p	F	p	F	p
1) Neuroticism	1.44	ns	105.39	<.001	.60	ns
2) Social Inadequacy	1.03	ns	32.92	<.001	.81	ns
3) Rigidity	12.93	<.001	11.51	<.001	3.16	=.08
4) Hostility	.02	ns	23.80	<.001	3.53	=.06
5) Self-sufficiency	3.80	=.05	.00	ns	.10	ns
6) Dominance	17.32	<.001	.29	ns	1.26	ns
7) Self-esteem	.26	ns	52.77	<.001	1.48	ns

Note: Degrees of freedom for both main effects and interaction: 1,425

stressor questionnaires and symptom checklists. Consequently, the present data do not warrant statements on personality attributes such as neuroticism, social inadequacy, rigidity, hostility, or self-esteem as predictors of stress-vulnerability or stress-resistance.

On the other hand, analysis revealed some links between the main factors ("Psychosocial Load" and "Symptoms") and the personality variables. People reporting a high psychosocial load can be characterized as less rigid, less self-sufficient, and more dominant in comparison to those reporting low levels of load.The main factor "Symptoms" yielded the following scenario: individuals having high scores on the HSCL appear to be more neurotic, less socially adequate, more rigid, more hostile and low in self-esteem in comparison to their counterparts reporting few symptoms. Consequently, these results confirm the hypotheses concerned with neuroticism, hostility, and self-esteem.

Generally, the results for the main effects corresponded to the expectations formulated in the introduction. Probably the most remarkable and important deviant finding is the lack of a relationship between psychosocial load and neuroticism. This result is at variance with the theoretical position of Schroeder and Costa (1984), as described in the introduction, and it also undermines their plea to remove items in stressor inventories because of the possible contamination by neuroticism.

Having established these relationships, the question remaining concerns the exact nature of certain associations. Because of the cross-sectional design, no conclusions can be reached regarding cause and effect. It is even possible that the directions of the associations are not the same for the different variables.That means, for example, that low self-esteem is the result of having many complaints, whereas, say, high self-sufficiency is the cause of reporting low-load levels.

Because each individual, to some extent, seeks and creates a personal environment, it may be speculated that personality factors are co-determinants of psychosocial load. However, for symptoms there is a somewhat more complex relationship. The classic psychosomatic approach favors the contention that personality factors may be involved causally in symptomatology. On the other hand, the reverse can not be excluded. Symptoms (especially those of a chronic nature) may affect personality.

In conclusion, the present study highlights the importance of an adequate design to investigate the connection between personality and stress-resistance, or stress-vulnerability. The conclusion that those personality factors that were connected with symptoms were characteristics rendering the subject more resistant or, alternatively, more vulnerable to psychosocial stressors is incorrect as indicated by the results of the "low-load, low symptoms" and "low-load, high symptoms" groups. Another interpretation is the so called personality dimension hypothesis (Cohen, 1979). This hypothesis states that some personality dimension may be related both to a response tendency to complain about physical symptoms and life difficulties. Or, alternatively, hypersensitivity to physical symptoms and to negative aspects of one's life situation may affect how symptoms are perceived and reported.

Finally, designing prospective studies in which these variables are measured in order to predict future health status, and the use of adequate control groups are vitally important in formulating an accurate research design.

SUMMARY

In this study, questionnaire data were obtained on everyday problems, life events, psychosomatic symptoms and personality. The sample consisted of 989 subjects.

Using median splits, separately for both sexes and for three occupational levels, participants were classified as either high-load or low-load (combining the subjective scores on the Everyday Problem Scale and on the Recently Experienced Events Questionnaire), and as either reporting many symptoms or few symptoms. This categorization yielded five groups: 1) high-load, many symptoms; 2) high-load, few symptoms; 3) low-load, many symptoms; 4) low-load, few symptoms; and 5) people who could not be classified because they had reported relatively few everyday problems and many life events or vice versa.

Using an ANOVA design (with "Psychosocial Load" and "Symptoms" as independent variables) the personality characteristics of the first four groups were studied. The results indicated few differences between males and females. The factor "Psychosocial Load" yielded significant results for rigidity, self-sufficiency and dominance. In addition, the factor "Symptoms" showed significant effects for neuroticism, social inadequacy, rigidity, hostility, dominance (for males only) and self-esteem. No significant interactions were found. The results are discussed in the light of current knowledge on personality traits as moderators of the stress-illness relationship and on the relationship between personality and psychosocial load and symptoms, respectively. It is emphasized that the designs of previous studies were not adequate to warrant inferences about personality variables as factors rendering subjects more or less vulnerable to "stress."

REFERENCES

Alloway, R., and Bebbington, P. 1987, The buffer theory of social support - a review of the literature, *Psychol. Med.*, 17: 91.

Antonovsky, A. 1979,"Health, stress, and coping: New perspectives on mental and physical well-being," Jossey-Bass, San Francisco.

Antonovsky, A. 1987, "Unraveling the mystery of health," Jossey-Bass, San Francisco.

Byrne, D. G. 1981, Type A behaviour, life-events and myocardial infarction: Independent or related risk factors? *Brit. J. Med. Ps.*, 54: 371.

Byrne, D. G., and Rosenman, R. H. 1986, The Type A behaviour pattern as a precursor to stressful life events: A confluence of coronary risks, *Brit. J. Med. Ps.*, 59: 75.

Chesney, M. A., and Rosenman, R. H. (Eds.) 1985, "Anger and hostility in cardiovascular and behavioral disorders," Hemisphere Publishing Corporation, Washington.

Costa, P. T. Jr., and McCrae, R. R. 1985, Hypochondriasis, neuroticism, and aging: When are somatic complaints unfounded? *Am. Psychol.*, 40: 19.

Cohen, F. 1979, Personality, stress, and the development of physical illness, *in*: "Health psychology - A handbook," G. C. Stone, F. Cohen, and N. E. Adler (Eds.) Jossey-Bass, Washington.

Cohen, L. H. 1982, Life change and the sensation seeking motive, *Person. Individ. Diff.*, 3: 221.

Dembroski, T. M., and Costa, P. T. Jr. 1987, Coronary prone behavior: Components of the Type A pattern and hostility, *J. Pers.*, 55: 211.

Derogatis, L. R., Lipman, R. S., Rickets, K., Uhlenhuth, E. H., and Covi, L. 1974, The Hopkins Symptom Checklist (HSCL): A self-report symptom inventory, *Behavioral Sci.*, 19: 1.

Hinkle, L. E. 1974, The effect of exposure to culture change, social change, and changes in interpersonal relationships on health, *in*: "Stressful life events: Their nature and effects," B. Dohrenwend and B. Dohrenwend (Eds.), Wiley, New York.

Kasl, S. V. 1983, Pursuing the link between stressful life experiences and disease: A time for reappraisal, *in*: "Stress research: Issues for the eighties," C. L. Cooper (Ed.), Wiley, Chichester.

Kobassa, S. C. 1983, The hardy personality: Toward a social psychology of stress and health, *in*: "Social psychology of health and illness," G. S. Sanders, and J. Suls (Eds.), Erlbaum, Hillsdale.

Folkman, S. and Lazarus R. S. 1980, An analysis of coping in a middle-aged community sample, *J. Health & Soc. Behav.*, 21: 219.

Luteyn, F. 1974, "De constructie van een persoonlijkheidsvragen-lijst," (The construction of a personality inventory) Unpublished thesis, University of Groningen.

Luteyn, F., Starren, J., and Van Dijk, H. 1985, "Handleiding bij de NPV (Herziene uitgave)," (NVP Manual {revised edition}) Swets and Zeitlinger, Lisse.

Luteyn, F., Kok, A. R., and Poiesz, A. 1984, "HSCL Hopkins Symptom Checklist (Manual)," Swets and Zeitlinger, Lisse.

Schroeder, D. H., and Costa, P.T. Jr. 1984, Influence of life event stress on physical illness: Substantive effects or methodological flaws? *J. Pers. Soc. Psychol.*, 46: 853.

Van de Willige, G., Schreurs, P., Tellegen, B., and Zwart, F. 1985, "Het meten van "life events": de Vragenlijst Recent Meegemaakte Gebeurtenissen (VRMG)," (The measurement of "life events": the Questionnaire Recently Experienced Events {QREE}) *N. Ts. Psych.*, 40: 1.

Van Heck, G. L., and Vingerhoets, A. J. J. M. 1988, Copingstijlen en persoonlijkheidskenmerken, (Coping styles and personality characteristics) *N. Ts. Psych.*, (in press).

Vingerhoets, A. J. J. M., and Menges, L. J. 1988, Het meten van alledaagse en chronische stressoren: Een literatuuroverzicht. I. (The measurement of daily and chronic stressors: A review of the literature) *Gedrag Gez.*, (in press).

Wickramasekera, I. 1986, A model of people at high risk to develop chronic stress-related somatic symptoms: Some predictions, *Prof. Psycholff.*, 17: 437.

MITRAL VALVE PROLAPSE (MVP) AND VARIOUS PSYCHO-NEUROPHYSIOLOGIC DISORDERS: THE MISSING LINK?

Ph. Jean-Louis

Centre de Cardiologie
Charbonnieres-Les-Bains, France

The histodysplasias are congenital genetic diseases affecting various tissues in the body (nervous tissue, the epidermis, connective tissue, etc.). They are caused by a genetic deterioration of the phase of differentiation of the layers between the fourth and eighth weeks of embryonic development (Robert,41)! Brown (7) in Marfan's Syndrome, Antani (2) and Brandt (6) in Ehlers-Danlos Syndrome, and Etches (14) in neurofibromatosis all found mitral valve prolapse in each of the principle dysplasias. Other researchers have discovered the same condition: Roberts (42) in pseudoxanthoma elasticum, Jean-Louis (23) in hereditary hemorrhagic telangiectasia, and Melaned (36) in Lobstein's Syndrome. Mitral valve prolapse has also been found in chromosomal diseases such as Turner's (Hancock,22) and Down's (Goldhaber, 21) syndromes or in extra-chromosomal formations such as Noonan's disease (Towne, 49), resulting in the formation of histodysplasias.

This communication proposes the hypothesis that mitral valve prolapse is a cardiac manifestation of a neuro-ecto-mesordermal dysplasia (forme frustre).

METHODS - RESULTS

This work is based on the study of 141 patients in whom MVP was established by echocardiography (20), 130 of whom presented no other echocardiographic anomaly. Therefore, research was aimed at pertubations of the central nervous system in patients suffering from mitral prolapse. The first stage of the present work compared the psychopathological data observed in 60 mitral valve prolapse patients and 30 acquired valvular cardiopathy patients. The Rickel's scale (38), with 22 items graded from 1 to 6, was used. Results from the items of depression resulted in significantly higher scores for patients with MVP ($P < 0.001$). Experimental results also indicated disorders in the categories of sleep, appetite, sex, and anxiety ($P < 0.01$).

Mitral valve prolapse was also examined in patients presenting psycho-neuro-physiological disorders. In a control study of 100 female subjects, mitral valve prolapse was found in 4% of the subjects. But in a study of 100 women between eighteen and sixty-five, echo and phonocardiography proved that 23% with psychosomatic digestive disorders presented mitral valve prolapse.

In addition to the nervous system itself, the primitive neuro ectoderm affected the skin. Out of 90 patients with mitral valve prolapse, 77 had epidermal abnormalities. Thirty subjects were found to have at least one of the following conditions: ichthyosis (often very slight and xerodermal in type), lipomata 5, lentigines 37, or polythelia 4. Furthermore, 13 patients presenting at least two of the aforementioned abnormalities were involved in an examination for mitral valve prolapse. Echocardiography showed that 8 had MVP.

An additional echocardiography was conducted on 82 patients presenting a click and/or murmur on auscultation. Fifty subjects had mitral valve prolapse. Eight percent of those cases had an associated cardiac abnormality, which included ASD (4%), ventricular septal defect (2%), and aortic ring dilation (2%). Importantly, in 14% of the cases, asymmetric septal hypertrophy coexisted. Certainly it is possible that in these cases MVP was secondary to the asymmetric septal hypertrophy. However, asymmetric septal hypertrophy is an autosomal dominant trait, as is MVP. Furthermore, authors such as Teare and Elliott believe the anatomical structure of asymmetric septal hypertrophy is close to that of a hamartoma (8).

There is little to say about the vertebrothoracic and skeletal abnormalities that were found in 100% of the cases: straight back and/or antero-posterior narrowing of the thorax, and/or scoliosis, and/or pectus excavatum, and/or pigeon-chest, and/or camptodactilia, etc.

Finally, we studied 130 patients with mitral valve prolapse but without any other echocardiographic anomaly. Thirty-two percent of the cases studied had major neuro-psychiatric abnormalities (psychosis or neurosis). Meanwhile, in 68% of the other cases there were minor psychological disorders corresponding semiologically to "masked depression," presenting the minor clinical forms of periodical psychoses as characterized by a number of psychophysiological disorders associated with asthenia and disorders of sleep, appetite, and sexual disorders. Therefore, psychopathology existed in all MVP cases studied. In addition, epidermal abnormalities were found in 80% of the cases studied. All cases showed skeletal abnormalities. Furthermore, in four instances MVP was associated with Marfan's syndrome. MVP was associated with Ehlers-Danlos syndrome in one case; in one other case it was associated with hereditary hemorrhagic telangiestasia. Finally, one case showed an association between MVP and Noonan's disease.

DISCUSSION

True psychiatric and psychoneurotic manifestations have been reported by authors such as Lian (33), Thompson (48), Johnston (31), Hancock (22), Fontana (15), Jeresaty (30), Giannini (19), Vibert (52), Barlow (3), Wooley (53), Crowe (13), and Jean-Louis (23, 25, 27, 29). Johnston (31) and Fontana (15) found 33% of the tested patients to possess such traits. Hancock (22) found that 38% of the subjects evaluated were psychiatrically abnormal. Interestingly, Jeresaty (30) concluded that 15% of the MVP patients dealt with had psychiatric abnormalities.

Importantly, researchers have shown that central nervous system involvement may find expression in a number of ways. For instance, Stringer and Obeid (47) found central nervous system involvement in various addictions. Gayet, Fischer and Silie (17) concluded that the CNS was involved in neurinomas. Also, CNS involvement found expression in Stickler's syndrome, as shown by Liberfarb, Arstauler and Gooblatt (34). Additionally, Channick, Adlin and Marks (9) found hyperthyroidism to reflect a CNS involvement. Finally, Clarck (10) found mitral valve prolapse in 62% of the patients with hypersomnia.

In cases of mitral valve prolapse, direct linkage to pertubations of the autonomic nervous system have been established by Gaffney (16) and Coghlan (12). Such a relationship has been suggested by Abinader (1), Saintos (44) and Gardin (18). Of course, it is possible that the hyperadrenergic states observed in certain cases of MVP by Boudoulas (5) and Pasternack (38) are related to a deterioration of the autonomic nervous system. In a group of patients suffering from MVP, 23% of the women had psychophysiologic disorders. Venkatech (51) found that 30% of the women with MVP had psychophysiologic disorders. In a group of apparently healthy women, Markiewicz (35) found that 21% of the subjects suffered from MVP.

Jeresaty (30) reported an association of mitral valve prolapse with ASD. Sahn (43) found that dilation of the aortic ring, with or without the appearance of Marfan's syndrome, was related to mitral valve prolapse. Roberts (42) found that Ebstein's anomaly had such a relationship, while Chandraratna (8), in cases of ASH, saw a relationship to mitral valve prolapse. Finally, Rippe (40) found that 34% of the adults with different types of congenital presented mitral valve prolapse.

Similarly, the association between MVP and vertebrothoracic abnormalities has been well known since the work of Bon Tempo (4), Salomon (45), Scampardonis (46) and Udoshi (50).

The original hypothesis was that mitral valve prolapse is a possible cardiac manifestation of a neuro-ecto-mesodermal histodysplasia. As a means of explaining this contention, consider Figure 1. The following helps explain the Figure. Under the influence of genetic factors, the deterioration of the embryonic layers leads to various diseases. The disease type, such as Marfan's syndrome or Ehlers-Danlos syndrome, is determined by the degree to which each layer or group of layers is effected. Similar

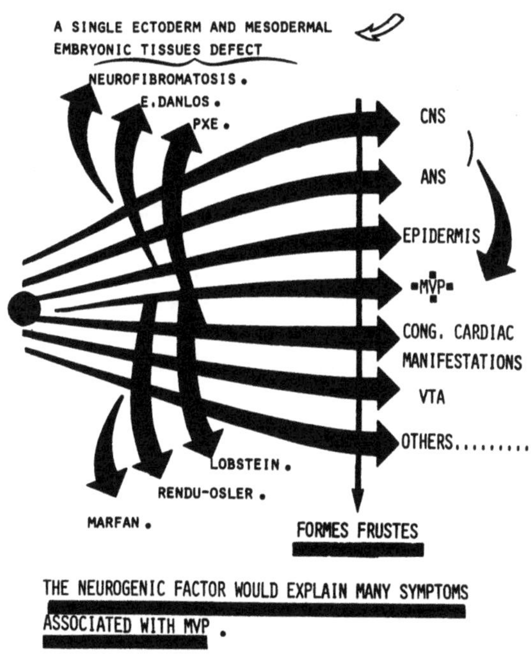

Figure 1. MVP: Cardiac Manifestation of Congenital Neuroecto-mesodermal Dysplasia?

genetic factors, because they are less intense, lead to the creation of the "forme frustre" of these various diseases. Mitral valve prolapse thus appears to be the cardiac manifestation of the "forme frustre" of neuro-ecto-mesordermal histodysplasia. The neurogenic factor explains many symptoms associated with mitral valve prolapse and why chest pain responds better to tricyclic agents rather than to cardioselective beta-blocking agents (26).

REFERENCES

1. Abinader, E.F. : Adrenergic beta blockade and ECG changes in the systolic click murmur syndrome. *Amer. Heart J.* (1976) 91 : 297-302.

2. Antani J., & Srivinas ,H. : Cardiovascular abnormalities in Ehlers-Danlos Syndrome. *Chest* (1974) 65 : 5.10.

3. Barlow, J.B. & Pocock, W.A. : The problem of non ejection systolic clicks and associated mitral systolic murmur. Emphasis on the billowing mitral leaflet syndrome. *Amer. Heart. J.* (1975)_ 90 : 636-655.

4. Bon Tempo, C.P, Ronan, J.A, De Leon, A.C., & Twigg, H.L. : Radiographic appearance of the thorax in systolic click. *Amer J. Cardiol* (1975) 36 : 27-31.

5. Boudoulas, H., Woodey, C.F, & Reynolds, J. : Mitral valve prolapse syndrome : evidence for a hyperadrenergic state. *Amer J. Cardiol* (1979) 43 : 368-372.

6. Brandt, K.D, Sumner, R.D., Ryan, T.J., & Cohen, A.S., : Herniation of "mitral leaflets" in the Ehlers-Danlos syndrome. *Amer J. Cardiol* (1975) 36 : 524-528.

7. Brown, D.R., Demots, H., Kloster, F.E., Roberts A., Menashe, V.D., & Beals, R. : Aortic root dilatation and mitral valve prolapse in Marfan's Syndrome. An echocardiographic study. *Circulation* (1975) 52 : 651-657.

8. Chandraratna, P., Tolentino, A., & Mutucumarana, W. : Echocardiographic observations on the association between mitral valve prolapse and asymmetric septal hypertrophy. *Circulation* (1977) 55 : 622-626.

9. Channick, B.J, Adlin, V.E, & Marks, D.A : hyperthyroidism and mitral valve prolapse. *New Engl Journal Med.* (1981) 305 : 497-503.

10. Clarck, R.W., Boudoulas, H. & Schaal, S. : Adrenergic hyperactivity and cardiac abnormality in primary disorders of sleep. *Neurology* (1980) 30 : 113-119.

11. Claudy, A.L., Seiller, P., & Ortonne, J.P. : Syndrome des Lentigines multiples et dystrophie elastique. *Lyon Médical* (1984) 252 : 114-115.

12. Coghlan, H.C., Phares, P., & Cowley, M. : Dysautonomia in mitral valve prolapse. *Amer J. Med.* (1979) 67 : 236-244.

13. Crowe, R.R., Pauls, D.L., & Slymen, D. : A family study of anxiety neurosis. *Arch Gen Psych* (1980) 37 : 77-79

14. Etches, P.C., Pickering, D. : Apical systolic click and murmur associated with neurobibromatosis. *J. Med Gen* (1978) 15 : 401-403.

15. Fontana, M.E., Rence, H.L., Leighton, R.F., & Wooley, C.F. : the varying clinical spectrum of the systolic click-late systolic murmur syndrome. A postural auscultatory phenomenon. *Circulation* (1970) 41 : 807-816.

16. Gaffney, F.A., Campbell, W.G., Karlsson, B.S., & Willerson, J.T., : abnormal autonomic function in patients with mitral valve prolapse. *Amer J. Cardiol* (1978) 41 : 433-441.

17. Gayet, J.L., Fischer, G., and Silie, M. : neurinome de la fosse cérébrale postérieure et prolapsus valvaire mitral. Association possible et recherche d'éventuelles conséquences rythmiques péri-opératoires. *Ann Cardiol - Angiol* (1985) 34 : 531-534.

18. Gardin, J.M., Isner, J.M., & Ronan, T.A. : Pseudo ischemic valse positive ST segment changes induced by hyperventilation in patients with mitral prolapse. *Am J. Cardiol* (1980) 45 : 952-958.

19. Giannini, A.J., Price, W.A., & Loiselle, R.A., : prevalence of mitral valve prolapse in bipolar affective disorder. *Am J. Psychiatry* (1984) 141 : 991-992.

20. Gilbert, B.W., Schatz, R.A., & Vonrann, O.T. : Mitral valve prolapse : Two dimensionnal echocardiographic and angiographic correlation. *Circulation* (1976) 54 : 716-729.

21. Goldhaber, S.Z., Rubin, I.L., & Brown, W. : Valvular heart disease (aortic regurgitation and mitral valve prolapse) among instutionalized adults with Down's syndrome. *Am J. Cardiology* (1986) 57 : 278-281.

22. Hancock, E.W., Cohn, K. : The syndrome associated with mid systolic click and late systolic murmur. *Amer J. Med* (1966) 41 : 183-196.

23. Jean-Louis, Ph., : Hypothése : Le syndrome du click et souffle méso-télésystolique est un marqueur génétique de la psychose maniaco-dépressive. *Lyon Med* (1976) 236 : 175-176.

24. Jean-Louis, Ph., : Prolapsus valvaire mitral; anomalie ectodermique (lentigines); anomalie mésodermique (hyperelasticité cutanée); une approche progressive vers la vérifécation du concept "Robertien" d'hytodysplasie. *Lyon Med* (1984) 252 : 398.

25. Jean-Louis, Ph. : Syndrome du click et souffle mésotélésystolique (prolapsus Mitral idiopathique) et depression endogène (unipolaire ?); Association génétique probably. *Lyon Med* (1977) 238 : 543-544-.

26. Jean-Louis, Ph. : Imipramine vs acebutolol in treatment of chest pain associated with mitral valve prolapse - Paper presented at the 12th biennal congress of the Southern Africa Cardiac Soceity. (Johannesburg, August 4th - 6th 1980) Abstract vol page 86.

27. Jean-Louis, Ph. : Mitral valve prolapse : possible manifestation of a congenital neuro-ecto-mesodermal histodysplasia. *Amer J. Cardio* (1980) 45 : 443.

28. Jean-Louis, Ph. :Prolapsus valvaire mitral : un exemple d'histodysplasie neuro-ecto-mesodermique (lettre). Arch Mal Coeur (1979) 72 : 1047-1048.

29. Jean-Louis, Ph., Vibert, F., Perinetti, M., & Couturier, H. Données psychopathologiques associées au prolapsus valvaire mitral. Conception histodysplasique de la maladie. Communication La Sociétée Francaise de Cardiologie. Paris 19 Janvier 1980.

30. Jeresaty, R. : Mitral valve prolapse - Raven Press, New York (1979).

31. Johnston, F.D. : Extrasounds occurring in cardiac systole. *Amer Heart J.* (1938) 15 : 221.

32. Kantor, J.S., Zitrin, C.M., & Zeldis, S.M. : Mitral valve prolapse in agoraphobic patients. *Am J, Psychiatry* (1980) 137 : 467-470.

33. Lian,C., Deparis, M. : Le claquement méso-systolique pleuro-péricardique. *Bul Mem Soc Med Hop*, Paris (1933) 57 : 496.

34. Liberfarb, R.M., Arstauler, E. E., & Gooblatt, A. : Prevalence of mitral valve prolapse among patients with Stickler's Syndrom. *N. Engl J. Med* (1984) - 310 : 1054.

35. Markiewicz, W., Stoner, J., London, E., Hunt, S.A., & Popp, R. : Mitral valve prolapse in one hundred presumably healthy young females. *Circulation* (1976) 53 : 464-473.

36. Melaned, R., Aygen, M.F., & Lowstein, A. : Osteogenesis imperfecta with mitral insuffisency due to baloony of the mitral valve. *Israel J. Med Sci* (1976) 12 : 1325-1332.

37. Panger, S.F., Pank, E.R., & Jones, B.A. : Mitral valve prolapse syndrome and anxiety neurosis, panic disorder. *Am J. Psychiatry* (1979) 136 : 106-108.

38. Pasternack, A., Tubau, J.F., & Cousineau, D. : Increase plasma catecholamins in Symptomatic Mitral Valve Prolapse. *Circulation* (1979) 59-60 : II : 156.

39. Rickels, K. Howard, K., : The physicin questionnary. *Psycho pharmacologia* - Berl (1970) 17 : 338-344.

40. Rippe, J.M., Sloss, L., & Ancoff, G. : Mitral valve prolapse in adults with congenital heart disease. *Amer Heart J.* (1979) 97 : 561-573.

41. Robert, J.M. : Histoire naturelle des maladies d'origine génétique. Revue du praticien (1974) 24 : 341-342.

42. Roberts, W.C., Glaney, D.L., Geninger, R.P., Marow, B.D., & Epstein, S.E. : Prolapse of the mitral valve associated with Ebstein's anomaly of the tricuspid valve. *Amer J. Cardiol* (1976) 38 : 377-380.

43. Sahn, D.J., Allen, H.D., Golimberg, J., & Friedmann, W.F. : Mitral valve prolapse in children; a problem defined by realtime cross sectional echocardiography. *Circulation* (1976) 53 : 651-658.

44. Saintos, H.D., Mathew, P.K., & Hilal, A. : Orthostatic hypotension: a commonly unrecognized cause of symptome in mitral valve prolapse. *Am J. Med* (1981) 71 : 746-750.

45. Salmon, J, Shah, P.M., & Heinole, R.A. : Thoracic skeletal abnormalities in idiopathic mitral valve prolapse. *Amer J. Cardiol* (1975) 36 : 32-36.

46. Scampardonis, G., Sing Sang Yang, Marahnad, V., Golberg, H. and Gook, A.S.: Left ventricular abnormalities in prolapsed mitral leaflet syndrome review of eighty-seven cases. *Circulation* (1973) 48 : 287-297.

47. Stringer, J.C., Obeid, A. : Mitral valve prolapse and addictions. *Amer J. Cardiol* (1985) 56 : 808-809.

48. Thompson, W.P., Levine, S.A. : Systolic gallop rhythm: a clinical study. *New Engl J. Med* (1935) 213 : 1021-1031.

49. Towne, W.D., Fabian, J. S., Rosen, K.M., & Rahimtoola, S.H : Systolic prolapse of the mitral valve in Noonan's syndrome. *Amer Heart J.* (1975) 90 : 499-502.

50. Udoshi, M., Shah, A, & Fischer, V. : Incidence of mitral valve prolapse in subject with thoracic skeletal abnormalities. *Amer Heart J.* (1979) 97 : 303-3ll.

51. Vankatech, A., Pauls, D., & Crowe, R. : Mitral valve prolapse in patients with anxiety neurosis. Clin Res (1978) 26 : 656 A.

52. Vibert, F. : Troubles psychiques et psychofonctionnels associés au prolapsus valvaire mitral. Thèse Lyon-Nord (1978) N 480.

53. Wooley, C.F. : Where are the diseases of yesterday? *Circulation* (1976) 53 : 749-752.

NEUROTIC FACTORS IN STRESS

Yves Chesni

International Stress and Tension Control Society
Saint Philbert de Grand Lieu, France

"What disturbs men," taught Epictetus (A.D. 50 - A.D. 130) - "are not things, but their judgments on things." Nineteen centuries later, Hans Selye (1978) echoed the words of the ancient Stoic philosopher: "In other words, here again, we meet the basic principle that what matters is not really what happens to you but the way you take it." And he adds to and clarifies his thought: "It may be said without hesitation that for man the most important stressors are emotional, especially those causing distress....Thus, it is especially true that, in our life events, the stressor effects depend not so much upon what we do or what happens to us but on the way we take it....As a rule a problem arises because we are conditioned or predisposed to react in a certain way when meeting the stressors of daily life..." This is one of the major problems of neuroses, the "daily bread" of psychiatrists and psychotherapists: the neurotic is plunged into despair because he takes the world, life, situations, people and things badly. The radical treatment of pathological stress caused by neurosis calls for the elimination of this latter. I shall briefly discuss neuroses, their mechanisms and some ways of treating them. I will focus on psychoanalysis, relaxation, and desensitization, as taught to me by my mentors and friends Raymond de Saussure, Edmund Jacobson (1929, 1982), Joseph Wolpe (1973), F. J. McGuigan (1978, 1981), and J. Macdonald Wallace (1988), and which I practice every day separately, successively or together with other therapies.

Neurosis is the disease of fixation and repetition. Under the influence of a certain constitutional or precociously acquired typology, an inadequate environment during childhood or of an erroneous perception of it by the child, infantile attitudes become established and repeat themselves indefinitely. These neurotic automatisms are unconscious, involuntary, and compulsive. As age and circumstances change, this behavior, perhaps not without sense in childhood, becomes less and less adaptive. Problems in human relationships follow, as do fear, anxiety, obsessions, feelings of incapacity, of failure, aggressiveness or inhibition, and feelings of persecution.

By the analysis of associations of ideas, of dreams, and above all of transference, i. e., of the repetition of the neurotic automatism in the therapeutic situation, psychoanalysis, aims to increase the awareness, the "insight." The awareness focuses on the neurotic repetition and its meaning, in other words, its analogy with childish behavior, and the cause of this latter. Once the awareness has become deep and durable, the neurotic automatism, unconscious in nature, disappears. The interpersonal relationship with the therapist improves and subsequently, by analogy, so do the other relationships. An important factor of pathological stress is removed.

With regard to emotional stress in general and neurosis in particular, Progressive Relaxation (PR) according to Jacobson (1929) and McGuigan (1981) has a twofold objective. 1) To eliminate directly obsessive thoughts and abnormal emotions by relaxing their neuromotor component, i.e., by relaxing ocular and inner speech muscles, and other muscles implicated in emotion. 2) To tranquilize the whole of the nervous system by relaxing the sensory, retroactive influx from abnormally tense muscles, a pathological excitement which tends to diffuse.

The relaxation is controlled either clinically or by electromyographic biofeedback. As does psychoanalysis, it calls for introspection but PR introspection is only of the muscular sensations. As behavioral therapy, but unlike psychoanalysis, it treats the symptom "here and now," without bothering with its cause: it is enough that the effects of the latter disappear. Still we must wonder if, in neurosis, the distinction between the cause and the effect is not an artificial one, if the neurotic automatism does not form a whole, and if the elimination of a part of it does not mean the elimination of the whole; let us not forget that, for the neurotic, time is suspended and, with it, development, the order of succession and the relation of cause and effect.

According to Wolpe (1973), systematic desensitization, i.e., the elimination of abnormal anxiety in certain situations, is achieved by imagining these situations under deep relaxation, especially of the muscles involved in emotion. When the abnormal anxiety is transferred to the therapist, it is through the presence of the latter, through conversation with him, through the reciprocal look in the face, that the desensitization is achieved, under electromyographic and above all electrodermographic control. Experience shows that anxiety decreases by the repetition of the process and that, when it has been completely eliminated in the situation imagined or in the relationship with the therapist, the result is transferred into everyday life. Wolpe uses introspection in a threefold way: self-control by the patient of his neuromuscular tensions; communication of the intensity of his emotions; definition, classification, hierarchization of the situations giving anxiety. We have come a long way from Watson's reductionism in which, according to Freud, he "thought he could establish a psychology which does not take account of that fundamental fact: consciousness." All the behaviorism has to do is to take account of the Freudian unconscious...[1]

How can systematic desensitization be really curative, i.e., exclude the later occurrence of substituted neurotic symptoms? Wolpe thinks that there is a deconditioning in the Pavlovian meaning of the word, an opinion which is not shared by everyone. I have suggested the following additional explanation: indeed, desensitization aims only at the patient's present, conscious circumstances causing abnormal anxiety; but what would be eliminated is a pathological *structure* common to current, conscious situations, to past, even unconscious situations, and to future, i.e., possible situations (Chesni, 1980, 1983). Added to this are the good effects of simple relaxation.

---

[1]Editor's note: It is frequently and erroneously said that Watson ignored consciousness and unconsciousness. Actually, Watson and the other early behaviorists took these and other mentalistic terms quite seriously, developing theories about them and defining them behavioristically.

As for chemotherapy, it is used in the treatment of psychoses, which does not exclude a complementary psychotherapy, behavioral or other rather than analytical. Under certain conditions and according to certain modalities, it can sometimes help the psychotherapeutic treatment of a neurotic. At our meeting in London, I showed you the happy conclusion of a never-ending psychoanalysis by relaxation and desensitization (Chesni, 1980). More often, it is a further analytic investigation which can be necessary to complete behavioral psychotherapy. So to speak, the symptom is treated, successively or alternatively, from the "outside" and the "inside."

SUMMARY

"In other words," claimed Hans Selye as the ancient Stoic philosophers did - "here again we meet the basic principle that what matters is not really what happens to you but the way you take it." The neurotic way of taking the world, life, things, persons, situations badly is a great factor of "distress." Here we dealt with neuroses as an internal factor in stress, their mechanisms and treatments.

REFERENCES

Chesni, Y., 1980, A happy conclusion of a pscyhoanalytical psychotherapy by progressive relaxation and systematic desensitization, *in* "Stress and Tension Control," Plenum Press, New York.

Chesni, Y., 1984, Buts, moyens, limites de la psychotherapie, *in* "Recherches sur le Développement de la Conscience," La Baconnière, Neuchâtel, Champion-Slatkine, Paris.

Epictetus, A. D. 50 - A.D.130, "Discourses" and "Manual" by Flavius Arrien.

Jacobson, E., 1929, "Progressive Relaxation," University of Chicago Press, Chicago.

Jacobson, E., 1982, "The Human Mind. A Physiological Clarification," Charles C. Thomas, Springfield, Illinois.

McGuigan, F. J., 1978, "Cognitive Psychophysiology. Principles of Covert Behavior," Erlbaum, Hillsdale, New Jersey..

McGuigan, F. J., 1981, "Calm Down: A Guide for Stress and Tension Control," Guilford, New York.

Macdonald Wallace, J., 1988, "Stress. A Practical Guide to Coping," The Crowood Press, Ramsbury, Marlborough, Wiltshire.

Selye, H., 1978, "The Stress of Life," revised edition, McGraw-Hill, New York.

Wolpe, J., 1973, "The Practice of Behavior Therapy," revised edition, Pergamon Press, New York.

STRESS AND COPING STRATEGIES AMONG PROFESSIONALS IN HEALTH CARE AND HUMAN SERVICES

STRESS AND PROFESSIONAL BURNOUT

Desmond Kelly[1]

The Priory Hospital
London, England

INTRODUCTION

Stress can be good for you, which is just as well, because it can't be avoided. Too little stimulus results in boredom and apathy, i.e., living in the "Drone Zone." Too much stress can result in panic and damage your health. The art is to learn to live a full life with a minimum amount of wear and tear. To live more intelligently, in the "C Zone." When people get stressed they use alcohol to calm their nerves and coffee to keep going. They smoke more and this can lead to cancer and heart disease. The UK has the highest rate of heart disease in the world. Type A behavior, which can increase heart disease and lead to burnout, is discussed. The victim is exhausted on all levels, physical, emotional and attitudinal.

Burnout can be prevented, anger used constructively and much psychosomatic disease avoided. Ten tips for coping with stress are suggested that can result in improved health, lower blood pressure and reduced cholesterol in the blood. There is a spontaneous reduction in the use of alcohol, cigarettes and tranquilizers. People sleep better and use fewer hypnotics. Type A behavior is modified, there is less liability to burnout, and people spend more of their lives in the C Zone. The effects on hospitalization are dramatic; an 87% reduction for diseases of the heart and nervous system; and a 55% reduction for benign and malignant tumors. One of the challenges in life is to live near the top of the Human Function Curve and fulfil our potential. By behaving intelligently we can achieve what money cannot buy - serenity.

STRESS CAN BE GOOD FOR YOU

It is part of the driving force by which we achieve our goals. Human endeavor thrives on challenge and realistic ambition; without it boredom and apathy set in. The level of stress experienced depends not on the stressors themselves but on the way you react to them. Joe Macdonald Wallace (1988) has also stated that "Too much stress can diminish the quality of your life at work and at home and eventually lead to many forms of illness." To illustrate this concept he conceives the individual as beset by common stressors which can be real or imagined. This is important because an imagined stressor can cause just as much emotional upheaval as a real one. In the main, stressors come from (i) the place of work, or from (ii) people's personal lives.

---

[1]UK President of The International Stress & Tension-Control Society

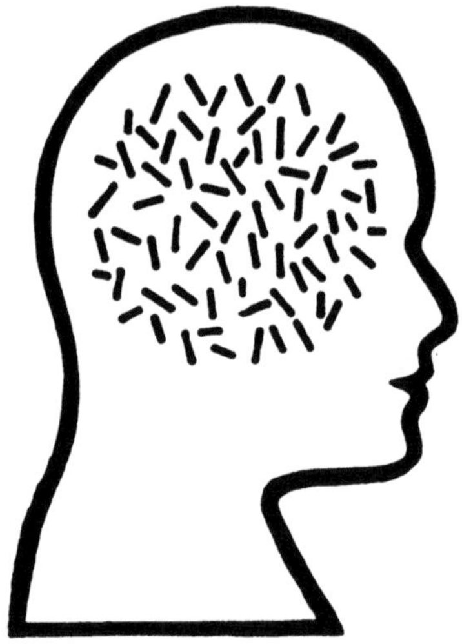

Figure 1. Stress results in disorderly thinking.

At work common stressors are the boss, colleagues, subordinates, isolation, ambiguous tasks, frustrations, the unions, the environment, commuting, promotion and unemployment. Common *personal stressors* include spouse, family, self-concept; temperament, health, economics or other interests, life changes and memories.

Working mothers are especially prone to be torn in two directions by conflicting pressures; work on one side and their personal life at home and children on the other. It is now estimated that 65% of women in Britain have a job. There is a lot of pressure on dual career couples: whose career takes priority if promotion of one requires relocation and causes a potentially adverse effect on the other? Who copes with the children when they are ill?

STRESS CANNOT BE AVOIDED

The art is to learn to live a full life with a minimum amount of wear and tear. The secret is...to live more intelligently. Hans Selye, the founding father of stress research, also observed that there is an optimum level of stress compatible with our health, both mental and physical. Stress can result in disorderly thinking (Figure 1) and in extreme form leads to panic (Kelly, 1980). *The panic zone* is characterized by too much challenge: not enough mastery, being over-committed, under-confident, out of control, scattered, nervous and hyper.

Under-stimulation may also lead to "distress."

The Drone Zone is characterized by not enough challenge, too much mastery, being uncommitted, over-confident, lethargic, sluggish and bored. The aim of good coping behavior is to spend more time living in the *C Zone* which is characterized by being committed, confident, calm and in control; energized, feeling that one can do things, having better mastery and less Type A behavior.

The C Experience is transcendent, effortless, positive, spontaneous, focused and vital. The kind of thing that is described by a member of the winning Cambridge Boat Race crew when leading and approaching the finish. He described that rowing was

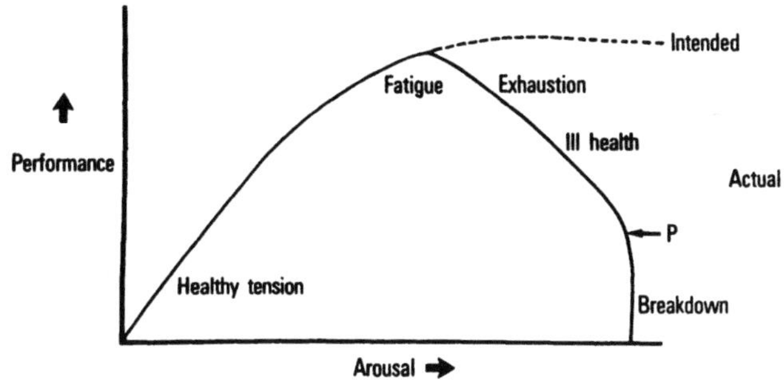

Figure 2. With an increase of healthy tension, performance increases, but at the top of the curve fatigue, if ignored, leads to exhaustion and a fall-off in performance. At point P a small amount of extra work pressure can cause panic followed by breakdown and burnout. (Personal communication from Dr. Peter Nixon.)

almost effortless, that he could go on forever and the boat was moving with an extraordinary rhythm and, as a consequence, it felt as though it was flying through the water. A truly C experience. On the treadmill of life, C experiences can be elusive.

The Human Function Curve

This is a way of looking at "coping behavior" and the relationship between arousal and performance. At the bottom of the curve (Figure 2) is the Drone Zone where there is little arousal (work pressure) and poor performance. As healthy tension increases, so does performance. Near the top of the curve there is high performance, but with extra work pressure fatigue sets in; people go over the top and performance begins to deteriorate. With continual pressure, exhaustion develops. At point P on the curve, it only needs a small amount of extra pressure for panic to set in and drive people over the edge of the cliff into physical breakdown or the burnout syndrome.

THE PROBLEM

A great deal of illness is self-inflicted. When people get stressed the commonest thing they turn to is alcohol, and yet 25,000 people die each year as a direct result of alcohol abuse. Alcohol is a hidden epidemic in British industry and its effects cost the country 1.7 billion pounds a year. Ten to fifteen million days a year are lost at work because of heavy drinking. Alcohol causes road accidents, violence, crime and family disruption, and it is estimated that there are over 2 million husbands, wives and children who are suffering from its effects. Alcohol consumption in Britain has doubled over the past 20 years. Of every leisure pound, 38p is spent on alcohol. Alcohol consumption could be reduced to the level it was 20 years ago, with a tremendous saving to the National Health Service and the family.

What Is a Safe Amount to Drink?

A unit of alcohol is half a pint of beer, a glass of wine, a glass of sherry or a pub measure of spirits. Estimates vary, but since women are more susceptible to alcoholic cirrhosis than men the total number of units for women, that are thought to be safe, vary between 20 and 14 units *per week*, for men between 30 and 21 units. There should be *two alcohol-free days every week* to stop the brain getting used to a regular daily dose of alcohol. The maximum for women would be four units *in any one day*, for men six. The legal driving limit is likely to be exceeded by four units of alcohol. People are most likely to resort to alcohol for "medicinal purposes" when they are anxious, angry, lonely, tired or hungry. Many who pride themselves on never taking pills are drinking like fishes. The definition of an alcoholic as anybody who drinks more than his doctor, is a dangerous one.

THE THREE MAJOR CAUSES OF PREMATURE DEATH

The three major causes of premature death in middle-aged men in Sweden, aged between 46 and 48 years, are: 1) Cancer, 28%, 2) Alcoholism, 25%, 3) Heart Disease, 23% (Petersson et al, 1984). In Britain in 1978, 40% of all deaths in men aged between 35 and 64 were caused by cardiovascular disease (Marmot, Booth, and Beral, 1981). Heart disease is the leading cause of premature death in the UK, accounting for nearly 180,000 deaths each year.

Cancer and Smoking

Forty percent of cancer deaths in Britain are preventable. Nearly 59,000 people in the UK die unnecessarily of cancer every year. Two-thirds of those deaths could be prevented if people stopped smoking cigarettes. Lung cancer is the UK's commonest lethal cancer and, in 1981, killed nearly 40,000 people. It is estimated that smoking accounts for 100,000 deaths annually. One in every four smokers will be killed before their time by smoking, and in Britain tobacco now kills four times as many people as the total killed by drink, drugs, murder, suicide, road, rail or air accidents; poisoning, drowning, fires, falls and every other known cause of accidental death. In America, the percentage of Americans who smoke dropped from 37% in 1976 to 30% in 1986, compared with 34% in the UK. The clamp-down against smoking in public places is much more comprehensive in the USA than in Britain, as a result of the health danger from "passive" smoking. It is predictable that the publicity given to passive smoking will increase in Britain.

Heart Disease

The UK has the highest death rate from coronary heart disease in the world for both men and women. The death rate for men between the ages of 35 and 44 doubled between 1950 and 1965. Type A behavior results in twice the incidence of heart disease as Type B behavior. Type A is characterized by a chronic sense of time urgency, free-floating hostility, easily aroused anger, irritation and impatience over minor provocations. Type B is a more relaxed approach to life (Friedman and Ulmer, 1985).

Each year, 255 million pounds is spent by the National Health Service in treating patients suffering from coronary heart disease. Coronary bypass surgery for blocked arteries is expensive: an incredible $4 billion industry in the USA. A more cost-effective approach would be to educate the public so that Type A characteristics were modified. Since 1968 the death rate due to heart disease in the USA has fallen by 30%. In fact, between 1968 and 1978 alone, the rate fell by 25% while in England and Wales it rose by 14% and by 5% in Scotland. Major reductions have also occurred in Finland (the former world leader in this macabre league table), Canada, Australia and New Zealand. Why this difference?

If we look at the USA, the reduction in the number of heart attacks has taken place during a period when an active health policy has been in operation. In fact, advice about prevention was first publicized by The American Heart Association in 1961. Similar action has been taken in the other countries mentioned, whereas the United Kingdom has lagged behind.

Most people enjoy their Type A behavior and their work gives them a lot of satisfaction but if carried to excess, the damage to their health can turn them into losers overnight. Type A personalities are much more likely to push themselves over the top of the Human Function Curve. Their drive and competitiveness often gives them a faulty perception of priorities and, as they attempt to do more and more in less and less time and push higher up the curve, they become more and more aloof, cynical, quarrelsome, hostile and vulnerable to burnout. As frustration, anger and anxiety increase, so do the stress hormones, adrenaline and noradrenaline and the distress hormone cortisol. Type A's produce a higher level of adrenaline than Type B's during working hours and their blood clots faster. This is accentuated by smoking and can lead to an elevation of blood pressure and the release of fat into the blood stream, which is made worse if the person is unfit or overweight. Fatty acids are then converted into cholesterol which can clog the arteries to the heart and lead to angina or heart attacks.

The level of blood pressure has a very dramatic effect on people's life expectancy. A man at the age of 45 with a blood pressure of 120/80 can be expected to live 32 years. If his blood pressure is 150/100 he will only live 20-1/2 years, i.e., 11-1/2 years will be taken off his life on average. For women of the same age the figures are 37 and 28-1/2 years respectively, i.e., a reduction of 8-1/2 years. It is known that the emotions of hurry, worry and anger increase the blood pressure.

Sir William Osler in 1892 described a type of individual who appeared to be over-represented among his patients with coronary artery disease. "A robust...keen...ambitious man, the indicator of whose engines is always at 'full speed ahead.'" A good description of Type A behavior, which has also been called "hurry sickness."

Pets

During the first year after a heart attack, patients not owning pets died at five times the rate of pet-owning patients. Friedman & Ulmer (1985) consider that the affection and love shown to pets can help prevent even a first heart attack. Feeding cholesterol to a rabbit will produce coronary heart disease in a few months. If, however, the rabbit is gently fondled several times a day, its coronary artery disease can be strikingly inhibited.

Caffeinism

One of the major causes of anxiety, irritability and insomnia is the consumption of too much caffeine. Over 150 mg of caffeine per day, usually two cups of coffee, reduces sleep time, and increases the time it takes to get off to sleep. Caffeine has a half-life of 6 hours. This means that 6 hours after drinking a cup of coffee only half of it has disappeared from the bloodstream. Because it is only metabolized slowly, it can accumulate in the blood and brain during the day. It can also cause restlessness, nervousness, dizziness; irritability, tremulousness, agitation; depression, anxiety, palpitations; headaches and stomach upsets. It is estimated that in the USA 10% of people suffer symptoms of caffeinism. Physicians seldom ask their patients how many cups of coffee they have a day. Many people approaching burnout have over-indulged in caffeine to a very great extent. I know of executives who either drink 8-12 cups of coffee a day or use cocaine to stimulate them to keep going in a high pressure business environment.

THE MEDICAL PROFESSION

Physicians

They have been studied in some detail and statistics from the Registrar General indicate that deaths from cirrhosis of the liver due to too much alcohol are almost three times as common in the medical profession as in the rest of the population. First admissions to psychiatric hospitals are 2.5 times average and especially common are admissions for depression, alcoholism and drug addiction. Physicians have 3.3 times the suicide rate of the rest of the population.

Junior physicians have many stressors. One of the main ones is the long hours of work they are expected to put in at a time when they are relatively inexperienced. Many work on average 91 hours a week and find overwork the most stressful aspect, but emotional disturbance is complained of by 50%, depression 28%, heavy drinking 20% and 25% are using drugs for treating their own physical illnesses. Recent research has shown that the most empathic physicians are the most vulnerable (Firth-Cozens, 1987).

Later in life, disenchantment and the drone zone can set in. In one study of 156 physicians, 47% complained of enduring boredom. "Medicine, as they were then practising it, seemed unlikely ever again to offer them the challenge and excitement that it had in the early days of their careers." (O'Donnell, 1983). When this figure was broken down, 50% of general practitioners complained of being bored, compared with only 27% of psychiatrists. For the whole group it was not surprising to find that 83% complained of periods of exhaustion and 68% found their work stressful. Eight percent complained of being depressed (Morrice, 1984).

Physicians have twice as many road accidents as the general population, and a drug addiction rate at least 30 times higher. They also have a high incidence of unresolved marital conflict and emotional problems. Surgeons and anesthetists have abnormally high blood cortisol concentrations.

There is also the threat of negligence which has been fueled by more patients suing physicians and, as a consequence, there has been a very sharp increase in the fees of the various medical protection societies, including the Medical Defence Union. It only takes a momentary lapse of concentration for a mistake to be made, which can have fatal consequences, and this is more likely to occur if the physician is sleep-deprived.

Nurses

Stress in nurse managers was discussed by the Kings Fund and it was found that suicide is "almost at the top of the league" with 5 or 6 times that of teachers and social workers. Nurse managers have a shorter life expectancy and nurses top the list of psychiatric out-patient referrals. They smoke heavily, in contrast to doctors who have largely given up smoking. Sickness and absenteeism has been estimated at running between 5 and 12%. One in six are considering leaving nursing. Eighty-five percent of senior nurses feel they are overloaded at work and 30% of nursing managers say they face considerable or extreme pressure. Social workers are also under a lot of pressure; this is especially so when dealing with cases of child abuse. Poor management is one of the commonest sources of stress in health professionals. Good management helps people cope with stress.

The medical profession seems to attract people with Type A behavior. The competition to study medicine in the first place is intense, and those without drive and stamina are unlikely to succeed. Type A behavior, like other personality traits, can be taken to excess, however, and is then neurotic. When this happens it is maladaptive and tends to be compulsive, inflexible, irrational and ultimately non-satisfying. "You don't quench ambition by feeding it any more than you quench a fire in the same way. To the ambitious man, what he already has is nothing. It's what he doesn't have that counts." (Condon, 1987).

Stress in the medical profession is common. It is not SEP - somebody else's problem - but very much the concern of the medical profession itself. Who is going to heal the caretakers and prevent them, especially the most empathic and the medical superstars, from burning out?

BURNOUT

Burnout is a condition that develops when a person works too hard for too long in a high pressure environment. It is particularly likely to occur in Type A personalities who ignore the symptoms of fatigue, try and overcome exhaustion by drinking more coffee, and although they intend to continue at the top of the Human Function Curve (see dotted line in Figure 2), they go over the top. The burnout victim is exhausted on all levels, physical, emotional and attitudinal. There is no age limit. It can effect students, physicians, secretaries and captains of industry. Burnout is usually thought to be an emotional state but physical breakdown can also be a consequence. Dissatisfaction at work causes hostility, resentment and frustration; increased smoking and drinking; over-eating, insomnia, psychosomatic illnesses and premature ageing.

At the Priory Hospital in London, where I work, many victims of burnout are seen. These people are irritable, they have a sleep disturbance, massive fatigue and become cynical, with the "I don't care" attitude. They are defensive and have increased susceptibility to abuse coffee to keep going, alcohol to relieve tension or tranquilizers to overcome stress and insomnia. Ulcers are not caused by what you eat, but by what is eating you.

Burnout can be sub-divided into:

a) *Emotional exhaustion* with tiredness, somatic symptoms, irritability, accident proneness, depression and excessive alcohol consumption.

b) *Depersonalization*. Treating people as if they are objects.

c) *Low Productivity* accompanied by feelings of low achievement, high absenteeism and a high sickness rate.

One burnout victim described how it affected him: "The 'old me' exhibited supreme confidence and knowledgeable experience and used to thrive under pressure and did the work of two men, working efficiently and conscientiously every minute of the day, taking short lunch hours and working a lot of overtime. Now I feel a sort of general nervousness, with a feeling that if anybody said or did something to upset me I would be likely to erupt like a seething volcano. I have a couldn't-care-less attitude towards what other people might think of me and a deep desire to be left alone and at peace. My self-confidence has been shattered and I no longer feel capable of handling anything that is thrown at me. I have lost interest, enthusiasm, feel disillusioned, resentment and despair. A great lethargy and pall of depression like a dark cloud hangs over my head. I feel squeezed dry."

Those most likely to develop burnout are very productive but feel indispensable, have high levels of energy, like doing three things at once but don't know when to stop, have high ideals but are too conscientious, have high expectations of themselves and others and are poor delegators. The most vulnerable are the highly competitive who are perfectionists and addicted to setting themselves unrealistic daily targets at work and at play. An example is making more than 40 telephone calls between London and Edinburgh on a car phone, and even trying to fill the car up with petrol, with the nozzle in one hand, while talking long distance on the phone with the other.

Dr. Herbert Freudenberger (1974) described burnout as physical and emotional exhaustion. There are four stages in its development:

Stage 1 is especially common in the newly qualified or when starting work or after a promotion. There is a feeling of uncertainty about coping with the demands of new pressures. There is a tendency to be over-conscientious or to overwork, and in some there is a great deal of enthusiasm and energy.

Stage 2. Short-lived bouts of irritation, tiredness, anxiety and frustration. There may be feelings of stagnation or "banging your head against a brick wall;" and a tendency to "awfulize" - everything is awful!

Stage 3. Increasing anger and resentment, lasting for longer periods. There will be feelings of failure and general discontent at work accompanied by guilt, a lowering of self-esteem, feelings of inadequacy. Apathy and cynicism will increase - "Why bother?"

Stage 4. Extreme personal distress. There may be physical complaints such as ulcers, headache, and backache; angina, severe insomnia, and other symptoms, with the abuse of coffee and alcohol. Extreme anxiety or panic leading to reluctance to go to work, depression or even suicidal feelings.

Burnout does not necessarily follow this progression nor is it always seen in pure culture, but many people may recognize parts of the syndrome. Early recognition is important, to enable corrective steps to be taken.

Burnout can be prevented by redesigning the job, increasing variety, preventing excessive hours of work. Have enough challenge to keep boredom, complacency and the drone zone at bay. Provide variety and time-out at work. Recreation and holidays are vital for health and efficiency. Short breaks and a healthy lifestyle are better than very long holidays with a lot of pressure building up before going away and a mountain of problems to come back to. The panic zone should be avoided, or seen as the flashing amber warning light. Many of my patients crash on through the red light to disaster.

Use anger constructively. Try and use the energy of anger to get things done, to put things right, rather than suppressing it or dumping it on people who do not deserve it (Lamplugh, 1988).

I use the "One Minute Reprimand." I tell the person precisely what was wrong, as soon as possible after the event, and how I feel about it (angry, annoyed, frustrated, etc.). I am not criticizing them as a person but it is the action which is unacceptable. I ask them if they understand and will they undertake not to do it again and then explain that the matter is at an end. That way anger is expressed and dealt with constructively, rather than rumbling on like thunder to come out at a later stage like lightning.

Reward should include praise as well as pay. Attention should be paid to the environment and holidays. The support of senior staff is indispensable. Flexibility should be encouraged and increased enjoyment at work; a sense of humor will be a great asset in most work places.

Hormone and the Immune System

Stress therefore results in increased smoking, drinking, elevation of blood pressure and heart disease. It also results in the release of the stress hormone, cortisol, and weakens the immune system of the body. The stress response may also prove to be lethal. When a person is under chronic stress the production of the body's natural killer cells called T lymphocytes is inhibited. These can protect the body against opportunistic infection and even cancer. These are the cells which are attacked and destroyed by the AIDS (Acquired Immune Deficiency Syndrome) virus, HIV (Human Immunodeficiency Virus) and as the virus attacks more and more T lymphocytes so the body becomes more and more vulnerable, until an intercurrent infection or cancer leads to death. One of the tasks before us is to keep our T lymphocytes in good shape.

PSYCHOSOMATIC DISORDERS

The cost of inconvenience, pain and suffering of psychosomatic disorders is considerable, for example duodenal or stomach ulcers, asthma, migraine and tension headaches; the irritable bowel syndrome, eating disorders, angina; skin conditions, insomnia and psychiatric problems.

Exercise

Exercise can be an important contributory factor in keeping the body healthy. There are those who produce endorphins when they exercise: "good mood" hormones in their brains, and including regular exercise into one's lifestyle is highly beneficial for most people. It burns up the adrenaline released by anxiety or anger and produces a natural feeling of tiredness which promotes good sleep. The effect of physical tiredness is quite different from mental tiredness. The brain has a design fault; the more tired it gets the more elusive sleep becomes, and in its place the head is full of repetitive, often distressing thoughts.

TEN TIPS FOR COPING WITH STRESS.

1. Avoid self-medication with nicotine, too much alcohol, coffee or tranquilizers.

2. Work off stress. Physical activity is a terrific outlet.

3. Don't put off relaxing. Use a stress reduction technique daily. Anxiety can lead to insomnia and as one gets more tired, sleep becomes elusive until a clinical depression can be precipitated.

4. Get enough sleep and rest to recharge your batteries. Sleeping pills will rarely be necessary if you set about changing your lifestyle.

5. Eat sensibly. High fibre, fruit and vegetables: low in salt and animal fat and dairy products which contain a lot of cholesterol.

6. Agree with somebody. Life should not be a constant battleground. Avoid entrenched interpersonal conflicts. Think of your coronary arteries instead. Pets can play a useful role in reducing stress. Dogs are constant and loyal, irrespective of the triumphs or disasters of the day. Kindness to animals is therapeutic and stroking them reduces your blood pressure. An animal's affectionate response to kindness is good for you, too, and will make you feel better.

7. Learn to accept what you cannot change. To ignore this only leads to unhappiness, cynicism and bitterness. "I have no time to spare for yesterday: let it rest in peace."

8. Manage your time better. You need a system that works for you, not against you. Take one thing at a time and beware of over-doing Type A behavior.

9. Know when you are tired and do something about it. When we are tired we are attacked by ideas we conquered long ago. It is very difficult to go to sleep when either very anxious or angry.

10. Plan ahead by saying "No" now. You may prevent too much pressure piling up in the future.

RELAXATION

How then to provide regular relaxation? For most of us, when we close our eyes and try to relax we are bombarded by thoughts, many of which carry emotionally charged connotations. Using a relaxation cassette either with or without biofeedback can be valuable. Different methods work for different people but the scientific evidence of the benefits to health and mental well-being are considerable.

CONCLUSION

Stress can result in increased smoking, drinking, elevation of blood pressure, cardiovascular disease, psychosomatic disorders, and psychiatric illness. The International Stress and Tension-Control Society is in existence to promote a better understanding of the adverse effects of excessive stress and tension, and the principles underlying their control. It is an important objective. Not only lay people but professionals and academics, too, are keen to know how they can get more out of life, without breaking down with a physical illness or burning out.

With good health we have freedom. One of the challenges in life is to live near the top of the Human Function Curve so that we can fulfil our potential without too much wear and tear. Life is a constantly changing kaleidoscope and has a different meaning for different people. For some it is a religious belief, while others are obsessed with the accumulation of wealth. But remember, no riches can purchase serenity.

REFERENCES

Chopra, D. (1987). "Creating Health, Beyond Prevention, Towards Perfection," Houghton Mifflin, Boston.

Condon, J. T. (1987). Type A Coronary-prone behaviour pattern and pathological narcissism, Aust. N.Z. *J. Psychiatry*, 21:16

Firth-Cozens, J. (1987). Emotional distress in junior house officers, *BMJ.*, 295:533.

Freudenberger, H.J. (1974). Staff burn-out, *J. of Social Issues*, 30.1:159.

Friedman, M. and Ulmer, D. (1985). "Treating Type 'A' Behaviour and Your Heart," Joseph, London.

Kelly, D. (1980). "Anxiety and Emotions: Physiological Basis and Treatment," Charles C. Thomas, Springfield, Illinois.

Lamplugh, D. (1988). "Beating Aggression. A Practical Guide for Working Women," Weidenfeld and Nicolson, London.

Marmot, M.C., Booth, M. and Beral, V. (1981). Changes in heart disease mortality in England and Wales and other countries, *Health Trends*, 13:33.

Macdonald Wallace, J. (1988). "Stress: A Practical Guide to Coping," The Crosswood Press, Marlborough.

Morrice, J.K.W. (1984). Job stress and burnout, *Brit. J. Psychiat. Bulletin*, March 45.

O'Donnell, M. (1983). One man's burden, *BMJ.*, 286:318.

Osler, W. (1892). "Lectures on Angina Pectoris and Allied States," Appleton, New York.

Petersson B., Trell E., Henningsen N-C, and Hood, B. (1984). Risk factors for premature death in middle-aged men, *BMJ.*, 288:1264.

STRESS IN GENERAL MEDICAL PRACTITIONERS OF THE UNITED KINGDOM

A. M. D. Porter, J. G. R. Howie, and J. F. Forbes

Department of General Practice
University of Edinburgh
Scotland

INTRODUCTION

In 1981, the Review Body on Doctors' and Dentists' Remuneration (DDRB) contained a section in the chapter on general medical practitioners (GMPs) entitled "Workload and Stress." It concluded: "We are not convinced on the evidence so far presented to us, which has been largely of an unquantified nature, that there has been a significant increase in workload; but we shall examine this matter more specifically next year." No further comment was made about stress.

The General Medical Services Committee of the British Medical Association, in collaboration with the Health Departments, responded to the DDRB's concern for better information on workload by carrying out a survey of GMPs' workload which was published in 1987 (DHSS, 1987). At the same time, the Royal College of General Practitioners (RCGP) was involved in discussions about quality (RCGP, 1985; Pendleton et al, 1986), the government was reviewing the provision and financing of primary care (Cmnd 9771, 1986; Cm 249, 1987), and the Social Services Committee of the House of Commons was examining Primary Health Care (House of Commons, 1987). In spite of this activity, there has been relatively little research into the stresses associated with medical work and even less into the implications of GP stress on the care they provide to patients.

Stress in Health Professionals (1987), edited by Payne and Firth-Cozens, was an attempt to begin to fill this gap, and one chapter in that book described a theoretical model for looking at stress in general practitioners and summarizes some findings from a pilot study in Edinburgh. More recently, Rankin et al (1987) have reported on their findings from a questionnaire and self-monitoring diary inquiring about determinants of hassle and mood, which was completed by 51 "motivated" GPs, and Mackin et al (1988) have reported their findings of a pilot questionnaire survey of 100 GPs (they had a response rate of 50.5%) asking about job satisfaction and sources of job stress.

The Edinburgh research program has followed up its theoretical model and pilot study with a one-year study of general practitioners' (GPs') work, their patterns of daily life and feelings of stress, and the relationships between practice organization, the flow of patients through surgeries, and the quality (process and outcome) of patient care.

AIMS

Ideally, we hope to identify the different causes of stress that GPs experience, describe the supports they rely on, examine the coping strategies they have developed, and analyze the effects of these coping strategies on patient care. From this, and our other research interests, we plan to make practical personal, organizational and policy suggestions for general practice and its practitioners.

This paper reports on our progress *half way* through the data collection phase of the program. For this reason, the paper is descriptive and inductive.

THE PARTICIPANTS

In May 1987, all 496 general practitioners in the Lothians were invited to attend one of a series of three meetings at which we explained the aims and methods of our research program. All attenders (and those physicians who sent their apologies) were subsequently invited to participate.

During the summer, every interested GP was visited in his/her practice and the details of the research methods discussed with them and their reception/administrative staff. Each GP participated in a trial recording day in Sept/Oct, and the study proper began on November 9, 1987. Since then, two GPs have withdrawn from the project (one because she was moving to a practice outside the study area, and one because he found the research methods too invasive on his daily work). One single-handed physician joined the project in February, 1988. Overall, 95 physicians are currently participating in the program: 78 full-time, 7 part-time physicians, and 10 trainees. These 85 non-trainee physicians represent about 17% of general medical practitioners in Lothian. Twenty-one of the 85 are female.

On the basis of this method of recruitment, the participating physicians cannot be said to be a representative sample. However, we do have a good mix of participants: from single-handed male and female physicians to those working from group practices with 5 or 6 partners; from physicians working in the more deprived areas of Lothian to those in more affluent areas; from city to town and country physicians; from younger to older. A comparison of the socio-demographic characteristics of participating and non-participating physicians is in preparation.

METHODS

Each physician records information on one day in every 15 days. Half-days, holidays and weekends (whether on-call or not) are included in the "sample" of days. Thus, if a physician's first recording day was a Friday, the second day will have been the Saturday two weeks later.

Data on stress are collected using two self-report instruments. First, the physicians are given a small buzzer which emits two short 'beeps' every half hour (like the hourly beeps which sound on some digital watches). They use this to remind them to record on a daily diary card (Figure 1) how pressured they feel on a scale from 1-7 marked "relaxed - tense." This instrument was tested in the pilot study and validated against the Stress Adjective Check List developed at Nottingham University (Cox and Mackay, 1985; Porter et al, 1987). Second, at the end of each recording day, the physicians complete a questionnaire which asks for details related to: (a) clinical,

Form Q4

Department of General Practice
University of Edinburgh
(031-667 3805)

DIARY CARD

Doctor ______________________

Practice ______________________

Date ______________________

Were you personally on call last night? YES / NO

No. of telephone calls received ____

How many of these were between 11.00 p.m. and 7.00 a.m.? ____

No. of times you were out ____

How many of these were between 11.00 p.m. and 7.00 a.m.? ____

Are you personally on call tonight? YES / NO

Time	ANTICIPATED COMMITMENTS (To nearest 30 minutes)	NEW/CHANGED COMMITMENTS (Reasons for change in pressure)		What are your feelings of pressure just now? (relaxed ------ tense)
8.00			8.00	1--2--3--4--5--6--7
9.00			9.00	1--2--3--4--5--6--7
10.00			10.00	1--2--3--4--5--6--7
11.00			11.00	1--2--3--4--5--6--7
12.00			12.00	1--2--3--4--5--6--7
1.00			1.00	1--2--3--4--5--6--7
2.00			2.00	1--2--3--4--5--6--7
3.00			3.00	1--2--3--4--5--6--7
4.00			4.00	1--2--3--4--5--6--7
5.00			5.00	1--2--3--4--5--6--7
6.00			6.00	1--2--3--4--5--6--7
7.00			7.00	1--2--3--4--5--6--7
8.00			8.00	1--2--3--4--5--6--7

Figure 1. DAILY DIARY CARD

organizational and administrative events which have caused stress, (b) the fitting together of work, personal and domestic responsibilities and commitments, (c) other causes of stress,(d) a summary of the morning and afternoon, and (e) a short scale to measure feelings of well-being.

The physicians also complete the inside pages of the diary card to give us their anticipated commitments for the day, any changes in those commitments, and new commitments that may occur.

For every face-to-face contact with a patient (whether at the surgery or at the patient's home), the physician completes a record card giving details of diagnoses, treatment/management, interruptions, and the physician's feelings of satisfaction. The physicians also use a digital clock, synchronized with one at reception, to record the time each patient spends with him/her, and information is also collected on the time patients arrive at reception and their appointment times (if such exist).

This paper looks at the stresses reported over the first six months by the GPs who have been participating, but excludes the trainees and the GP who joined the project after the New Year. At this stage we cannot say much about aggregated pressure scores because each GP may perceive pressure and tension differently, and may locate "normal" at a different place in the scale. Until we have carried out more detailed analysis on these data, and until we have more information on GPs' attitudes and personalities (which we plan to collect later this year) we do not wish to draw conclusions on the differences among GPs. Rather, we are more interested in looking at each GP individually, and comparing stressed days with relaxed days within each GP's six months of recording experience. Recordings on the pressure scale of 5 or over have been taken as the level at which GPs were experiencing undesirable feelings of pressure or tension.

It was our intention at the start to simply examine the ten most stressful days that different physicians had experienced, and compare them with non-stressful days. However, observations relating to booking times and consultation times led us to separate the experiences of physicians who consulted at an average of more than 8 minutes per patient (the slower physician) from those who consulted at an average of less than 6 minutes per patient (the quicker physician). Shortage of space will restrict descriptions to these two groups and little will be said about the larger number of physicians who consulted at an average of 6-8 minutes per patient.

RESULTS

The average consultation time for all consultations for all the physicians was seven minutes. Figure 2 shows that 17 physicians consulted at an average of nine or more minutes per patient (slower physicians), and that ten consulted at an average of five or less minutes per patient (quicker physicians). Table 1 shows that, for six of the 17 slower physicians, their average number of pressure scores greater than 4 per morning, or afternoon, was 2 or more. On the other hand, not one of the 10 quicker physicians had an average number of pressure scores greater than 4 recorded per am/pm of 2 or more.

The Slower and More Pressured Physicians

For linguistic convenience we have given each physician an identification letter which has no significance other than order of appearance in this paper.

Physician A experienced a Thursday during which he frequently recorded pressure scores >4. Figure 3 shows how he spend the day, and his half-hourly

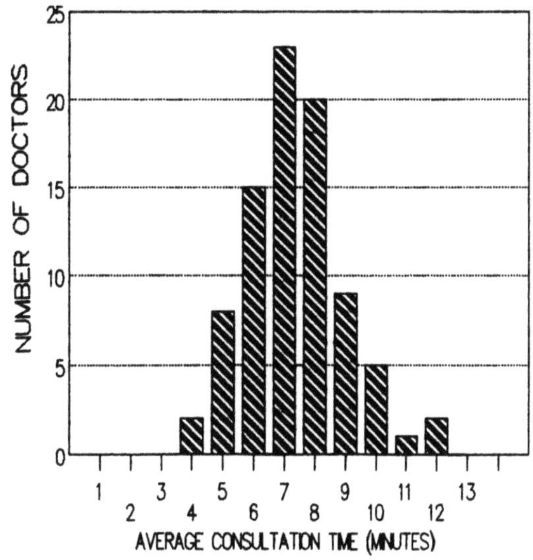

Figure 2. DOCTORS' AVERAGE CONSULTATION TIMES
All doctors except trainees.

pressure scores. He had been on-call the night before and reported that he had not got much sleep. He had received three calls and made three visits between 11:00 pm and 7:00 am.

Table 1. Average number of pressure scores >4 per morning (9:00am - 1:00pm) and afternoon (2:00-6:00pm) for doctors with different consultation times.

Av. No. scores >4	Doctors with average consultation times of: --<6 mins-- am	pm	-- >8 mins-- am		pm
0	3	1	0		1
<1	4	5	8		7
1+	3	4	4		4
2+	-	-	1)		(2
3+	-	-	2)	6 GPs	(-
4+	-	-	1)		(-
5++	-	-	1)		(1
Total	10	10	17		15
			Off duty on afternoons:		2

He started his 8:30 am open (non-appointment) surgery session in a branch surgery early at 8:10 and was due to finish at 9:30 so that he could get on with home visits. However, the surgery didn't finish until 11:20 - after seeing 19 patients and failing to see three who had left because they couldn't wait any longer. No other GPs and no nurse were at the branch surgery to help out. He then tried to get his house calls done before an important case conference (and sandwich lunch) at 1:00 pm at the Health Centre with the local psycho-geriatrician and geriatrician, and he reported feelings of maximum stress at noon when he was trying to finish the calls before the

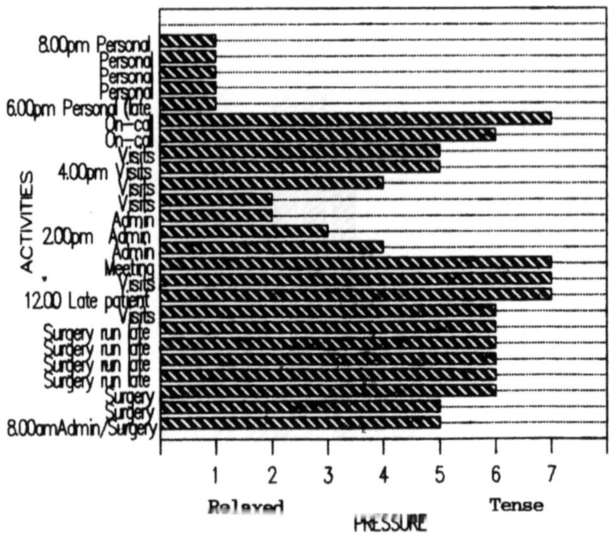

Figure 3. GP ACTIVITIES AND PRESSURE
GP(A) MALE THURSDAY(1)

meeting. After the meeting, he was able to relax a little over some administrative work while his undergraduate student (who was with him throughout the day) was being assessed at the Health Centre by a member of staff from the University Department. He then did two hours of home visits, but still had administrative work to do before going home. This made him late for supper and a function at 6:30 pm. When he got there, he relaxed, but he was to return to practice administration again at 10:30 pm, commenting that routine administration was seldom completed during the working day (8 am - 6pm), and that he had worked on administration until 2:30 am on the previous two nights. Not surprisingly, he had not been feeling "on top of the world" over the previous two weeks, but he was generally feeling pretty positive and reported no negative feelings.

One important factor should be mentioned: one partner was off ill and another was away on holiday, and although a locum had been employed this had not totally compensated for the loss of the two experienced, full-time colleagues. The time of year didn't help either. Apart from his own commitment to a Christmas party in the early evening, he had encountered difficulty contacting the social work department (who were having their own Christmas party) to arrange an emergency admission to Part IV accomodation for a patient who had been inappropriately discharged from hospital.

Fortunately for this physician, not all his days were quite so stressful, though most mornings were pressured to some degree. Figure 4 illustrates a Thursday which was more relaxed. He had not been on-call the night before, nor was he on the coming night. Although his early morning surgery (by appointment at the Health Centre) ran late (largely because patients were booked at six minutes but were seen for ten minutes), he had no visits to do and no lunch appointment. His afternoon surgery also ran late (this time more because of extra patients than because of consulting at a slower rate than the booking rate) but he had no pressing personal commitment early in the evening. As on the previous Thursday, one colleague was

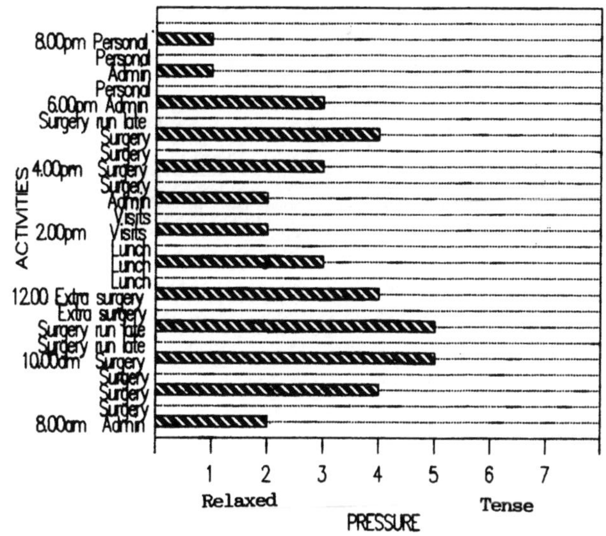

Figure 4. GP ACTIVITIES AND PRESSURE
GP(A) MALE THURSDAY(2)

away on holiday, but demand was low because it was the Easter holidays - the only source of additional stress mentioned by the GP was the heavy holiday traffic.

The outstanding feature of both days was the running late of the surgeries, but it appears this was only associated with raised feelings of pressure when trying to fulfil other commitments, be they practice or personal. It is a regular feature of open surgeries that they run late, but for appointment-system surgeries it is perhaps surprizing that a physician who consistently consults at an average of nine to ten minutes per patient books at a flow rate of ten patients per hour. To reinforce this point:

On a half-day when he had a commitment to get his car to the garage at 1:30 pm, he was, as he put it, only "ahead of the game" by moving the start of his morning surgery from 8:30 to 7:45. Even so, he ran half an hour late and he recorded pressure scores >4 as he worked through the 20 patients. As on the previous days, patients were booked at 8.8 minutes but were seen at an average of 10.8 minutes per patient.

He experienced another stressful morning and early afternoon on a Wednesday. Morning surgery only ran 30 minutes late, but he spent the day rushing to get to meetings: Rotary Club, son's school, evening meal at home and BMA meeting in evening. The surgery was booked at 8.5 minutes per patient but he consulted at an average of 10 minutes per patient.

These examples from one GP's experience raise three factors that seem to be associated with stress on GPs. First, the rate at which physicians book patients and then see them; second, the organization of commitments/meetings at lunch time and of personal commitments in the early evening, and third, the issue of night work which is not pursued in this paper.

Figure 5 illustrates a Thursday for Physician B who also recorded high scores for at least part of most days. She had not been on call the night before, but her 9:00 am surgery ran late by almost an hour, largely because she had 16 patients booked at an average of 8 minutes per patient, whereas she consulted at an average of 10.5 minutes per patient. Then, whilst she was busy catching up on letters, etc., she discovered at

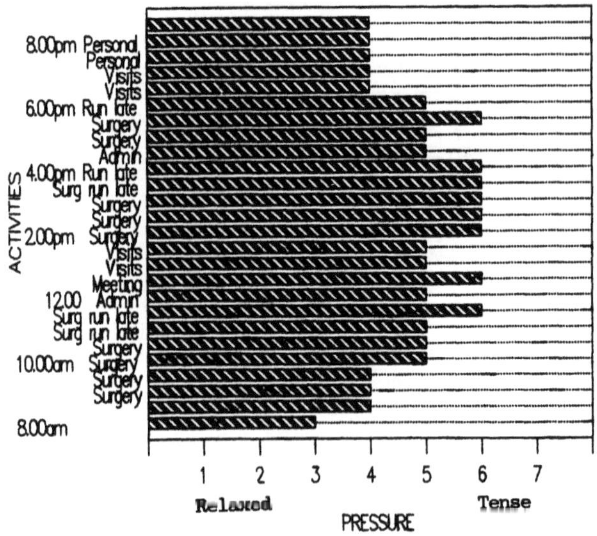

Figure 5. GP ACTIVITIES AND PRESSURE
GP(B) FEMALE THURSDAY(1)

12:30 that she had misunderstood a new system of sharing the on-call rota which meant that she had to go out on visits, and had no time for a lunch break. She started her 2:00 pm surgery ten minutes late and ran half an hour late, again largely because patients were booked for an average of 8.2 minutes but she consulted at an average of ten minutes. There were ten patients booked into her 5:00 pm surgery which was due to finish at 6:00 pm. In the end, she saw seven patients at an average consulation time of ten minutes, and finished at 6:30..."exhausted, but not really tense."

On another Thursday, her morning was more relaxed (Figure 6). Her 9:00 am surgery ran 30 minutes late, again largely because patients were booked for eight

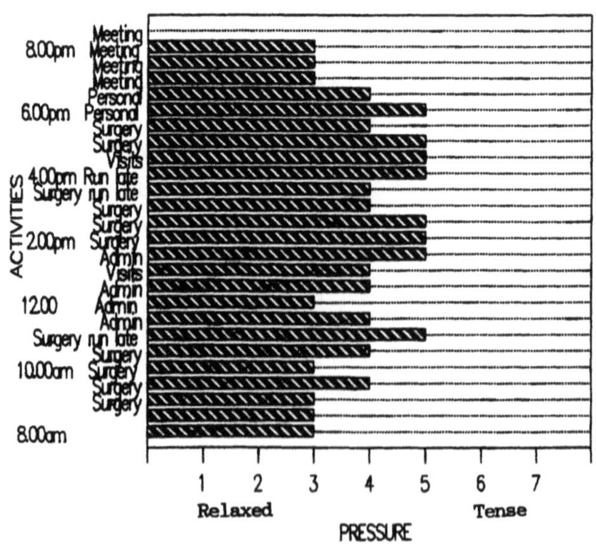

Figure 6. GP ACTIVITIES AND PRESSURE
GP(B) FEMALE THURSDAY(2)

minutes and seen an average of ten minutes. She had time to catch up on administration and had fewer visits to do, leaving her time for a lunch break while she finished more administration. Her 2:00 pm surgery ran an hour late - again because of spending longer with patients than scheduled for. She then went out on a house call, but was able to start her 5:00 pm surgery and finish it on time, helped by two patients who did not attend. Her pressure score of 5 at 6:00 pm is explained by her concern to finish surgery on time in order to get home and have something to eat before going out at 7:00 pm for a clinical meeting.

One of the four other participants (Physician C) experienced considerable strain on two consecutive recording days. On his Thursday half-day, the morning started with a 5 at 8:30, and his 9:00 am surgery began on time but was rated as 6. There was nothing in particular to explain these scores, but it was clear that he was feeling the effects of pain and restricted activity following an injury. By 10:40 the surgery had run past its official finishing time and didn't conclude until after 11:30 (90 minutes late), partly because of a patient in the waiting room with suspect cardiac failure, and partly because of two extra, prolonged consultations at the end of the surgery. This made him late for his house calls, but he finished before 1:00 pm and had time for an hour's lunch at the start of his half-day.

Two weeks later (Friday), the hour before the surgery was more relaxed, but its start at 9:00 am was scored 6, and he stayed tense as it ran 30 minutes late, (one extra patient added to an already fully booked surgery), making him late again for home visits. He relaxed a little over lunch, and early afternoon visits were not stressful. However, his 3:00 pm surgery ran an hour late, largely because there were many more "difficult patients" than expected, and up went his tension. The two factors that appear to be associated with this GP's feelings of pressure are: first, his own physical health and mobility which slowed him down, and second, fitting extra patients into appointment surgeries already fully booked.

Physician D, who works part-time, tended to record pressure scores greater than 4 as she worked through morning surgeries and tried to finish so that she could get home for 1:00 pm..."but I never do!" Her most pressured day was a Tuesday. It began at 8:30 am with a pressure score of 5, probably because she had been up much of the night with her three-year old child. She did visits for 2.5 hours, when she was more relaxed, but she arrived late for her surgery at 11:15 and had to deal with four unexpected phone calls, putting her back almost 30 minutes, and her pressure score rose above 4. The surgery was due to end at 1:00 pm and she was anxious to get home to see her sick son. She worked at the booking rate (8.75 minutes per patient), saw 12 patients and finished at 1:30 pm. She had a similarly stressful experience on a Monday when she had hoped to be home at 1:00 pm but didn't make it until 2:00 pm because she started the surgery 20 minutes late (she had lost her research study digital clock), and the surgery ran an hour late (even though three patients did not attend). On the mornings that she had no surgeries, when she was either catching up on administration or doing school medicals, she recorded no pressure scores greater than 4.

Rather similarly, Physician E also experienced one half-day (also a Thursday) of considerable high pressure. He had been on-call the night before and was called out on a home visit at 7:00 am, worried that he might not get back in time to take his daughter to school. His surgery ran over an hour late, but he managed to squeeze in a coffee break before doing three visits before 2:00 pm, when he had to leave for a personal commitment. He only made it on time because the last patient he was to visit had already gone to hospital. His only other half-day was a public holiday and his emergency morning surgery passed without pressure scores rising above 4.

Physician F experienced feelings of tension on Two Friday afternoons, and her tension appeared to be greatest at this time of week. The first Friday began stressfully at 9:00 am when she was asked to do a surgery for a partner who was off sick, but otherwise the morning was uneventful and relaxed. Her afternoon surgery started slightly late, and some late patients constrained her ability to get visits done before going home to a personal commitment at 7:30 pm. The strain on the second Friday afternoon seemed similar in that she had a fully booked surgery with many interruptions, and then had late house-calls at 5:30 and 6:55 pm, just before she was due to leave for an important personal commitment.

The common theme from these examples appears to be that surgeries which run late *and* which are followed closely by another commitment (be it professional or personal) are commonly, and not surprisingly, associated with raised pressure scores.

The Slower and Less Pressured Physicians

Physician G might have been expected to have experienced some pressure. On his first recording day (a Friday), his 9:00 am surgery ran 90 minutes late. Again, on a Thursday, both his morning and afternoon surgeries ran an hour late. However, on none of these occasions was he in any hurry to do anything, or be anywhere else, and his only flicker of pressure occurred on a Wednesday morning when his 9:00 am surgery started late and finished half an hour late. He was then due to be at a prearranged industrial health session, but he still had time for a coffee break before he went.

Physician H recorded details on ten surgeries. Three ran at least one hour late and two of them were associated with a pressure score of 5. One surgery which ran 90 minutes late was not associated with pressure scores greater than 4, but it was quite apparent from her pressure recordings that she began to feel less relaxed as the surgery ran over time, largely because of 7 extra patients being fitted in at the end. Luckily, the surgery was followed by time to sign repeat prescriptions and then by visits.

Physician I, who works part-time, had an emergency morning surgery which ran an hour late because more patients kept arriving, and she was forced to reschedule a hair appointment for an hour later. However, her recorded pressure scores remained at or below 4. She did experience some tension on a Wednesday morning at 9:30 - 10:00 when she visited a patient with severe rheumatoid arthritis who had developed melaema during the night and who had been visited by a duty physician. She also recorded feeling tense on a Monday morning after a hospital session ran late, and she was then late by five minutes for meeting her children off a train. She had not been on-call the night before on any of these days.

These three examples tend to confirm the suggestion that surgeries which run late are likely to be associated with feelings of pressure only when running late impinges on another commitment, and that pressure can be avoided if a commitment can be re-scheduled. The last example is interesting because it raises the important factor of an acute medical problem causing stress, partly because of the problem itself and partly because solving the problem can take time which then impinges on another commitment. Two other physicians recorded on days when they felt stressed for this kind of reason:

Physician J recorded five surgeries which ran one hour late and four which ran half an hour late. In general, these surgeries were not associated with raised pressure scores, but one Monday morning was particularly stressful. He had been on-call on the Sunday night but no calls came through until 7:30 am, when he was called out on a visit and found a complex social problem which took him until 9:00 to sort out. By then he was 30 minutes late for the start of his surgery. He eventually got some breakfast when he finished the surgery (after seeing two extra patients) at 10:30. He then went off to do more visits and his pressure scores returned to normal. His other experience of pressure scores greater than 4 were associated with a long visit to a terminally ill man and his sick wife, and a visit to the widow of a young man who had suddenly died. He coped with the extra time he spent on these visits by putting off other routine visits until the following day. A practice meeting was another event which was associated with raised pressure scores.

Physician K recorded details of eight surgery sessions. One ran two hours late but was not associated with pressure scores greater than 4, largely because he had nothing else arranged. Two surgeries ran one hour late and one of these was associated with a slight rise in tension. His most stressful time was a Friday morning (he hadn't been on-call the night before) when he heard at 9:00 am of the death of a young patient and he went to visit his widow. This led to him starting his fully-booked surgery slightly late. Generally, his surgeries ran late because of extra patients being added to fully booked surgeries.

Six other slower physicians also experienced surgeries which ran late and which were associated with feelings of tension.

It appears, therefore, that the physicians who consulted at 8 minutes or more per patient experienced surgeries which ran late...some of them very late, and that they were most likely to record feeling under pressure when surgeries ran late *and* they had another (unchangeable) commitment to meet. Physicians most frequently recorded feeling pressured when they were working with schedules that did not allow them sufficient time to catch up before their next commitment. The main reasons for running late were: consultation times running longer than booking times, extra patients being fitted into fully booked surgeries, patients arriving late for their appointment at the end of a surgery session, interruptions during a busy surgery, and starting a surgery late because of having to deal with an unexpected house call of phone calls.

This pattern of factors associated with pressure and stress is also to be found among the physicians who consulted at 4 or 5 minutes per patient. For example:

The Faster Physicians

Physician L has recorded details on 12 surgeries. Eight of them ran an hour late or more. Five of these were associated with pressure scores greater than 4, and he was most likely to feel pressured during the late afternoon surgeries which ran late (and when he was feeling tired) rather than during the morning surgeries which ran late. Thus, for example, one of his Tuesday afternoon surgeries which was fully booked with 21 patients to be seen between 4:50 and 7:00 pm, started on time but ran on until 7:50 after he had seen 23 patients. He commented at 6:00 that he was running late, and at 7:00 an extra patient appeared. He only began to record pressure scores greater than 4 at 7:30, but he stayed tense until 8:30 as he started a night on-call. Another Tuesday afternoon and a Friday afternoon followed a similar pattern and were similarly stressful. This doctor did not record feelings of pressure greater than 4 when engaged in other activities.

Physician M recorded details on 12 surgeries. Seven ran to time, four ran 30 minutes late and one started late and ran 90 minutes late. The last hour of this latter surgery was associated with two pressure scores greater than 4. However, her most stressful time was a Tuesday morning. She had been on-call the previous night and was on again the coming night. She went out to an emergency call at 8:30 am which made her late for her 9:00 surgery which then ran 30 minutes late. She then went out on two more emergency calls. Her pressure scores were greater than 4 from 8:30 am until she finished the emergency calls at noon.

Physician N recorded details on 13 surgeries, eight of which finished on time, one ran an hour late, and four ran half an hour late. He recorded one 5 for the last half hour of the afternoon surgery which ran an hour late and he wanted to be away to a personal commitment. The surgery apparently ran late because of several psychiatric patients who required time.

Physician O recorded details on 14 surgeries. Ten of them finished "on time", three finished half an hour late, and one (non-appointment) afternoon surgery an hour late. His only pressure scores greater than 4 were associated with this afternoon surgery and he commented: "patients getting impatient."

Physician P did not record any pressure scores greater than 4, and even scores of 4 were pretty rare. He recorded details on six surgeries, four of which finished on time and two ran half an hour late.

These latter examples draw attention to a factor which appears to differentiate between the quicker and the slower physicians. Although this paper was not intended to make comparisons among physicians, it is worth observing that the quicker physicians recorded fewer surgeries which ran an hour or more late than the slower physicians (Table 2); and we have already seen that they recorded fewer morning or afternoon pressure scores greater than 4 than slower physicians. It is possible, of course, that these two factors might be associated with a third factor like personality and/or recording differences, but it is interesting that although the quicker physicians were less likely to find themselves rushing to keep time with their other commitments, when they did fall behind their pressure levels rose in the same way as occurred for slower physicians.

Table 2.

	Number (%) of surgeries: Running to time	Running 1/2 hour late	Running 1 hour late +	TOTAL
Slower, more pressured GPs	20 (38%)	15 (29%)	17 (33%)	52
Slower, less pressured GPs	44 (39%)	42 (37%)	27 (24%)	113
Quicker GPs	85 (67%)	30 (24%)	11 (9%)	126

CONCLUSIONS

It is obviously not appropriate to draw firm conclusions from the descriptions presented here. However, a picture emerges that most of the participating physicians experienced days, or parts of days, when they felt stressed, and that a major factor associated with these feelings was the running late of surgery sessions which impinged on other (unchangeable) commitments, be they personal (at the end of the working day) or professional. The main reasons why surgeries ran late appear to be: when the physician consults at a slower rate than the booking rate, extra patients being fitted in at the end of a busy surgery session, patients who arrive late at the end of a surgery, interruptions during a surgery session, and having to make a home visit or deal with a number of phone calls before a surgery is due to start. This latter reason is also, of itself, associated with stress.

For a variety of reasons this paper has not been able to examine the relative importance of these various factors, nor has it drawn attention to other factors which may be important. For example: the availability of a practice nurse and other partners; practice list size; tiredness as a result of being on-call the night before; personality, attitudes, satisfaction and health of the physician.

We hope that, by the end of this research program, we will have some quantified information on these complex issues, and be better informed on the relationships among consulting styles, practice organization, stress and the outcome of care on patients' health and satisfaction. How is it, for example, that physicians who consult at less than 6 minutes per patient manage to keep their surgeries running closer to time than those who consult at greater than 8 minutes per patient? And could it be that attempts to encourage physicians to move from five to ten minute consultations might result in physicians feeling more, rather than less, stressed?

ACKNOWLEDGEMENTS

We wish to thank all of the physicians and their administrative and reception staff for providing the data for this study, even though it has caused them some additional stress. Also, thanks to our research team who have processed all the data in such an efficient and good humored manner.

REFERENCES

Cm 249, 1987, "Promoting Better Health. The Government's Programme for Improving Primary Health Care," HMSO, London.

Cmnd 9771, 1986, "Primary Health Care. An Agenda for Discussion," HMSO, London.

Cox, T., Mackay, C., 1985, The measurement of self-reported stress and arousal. *Br. J. Psychol.*, 76, 183-186.

Department of Health and Social Security, 1987, "General Medical Practitioners' Workload, A Report Prepared for the Doctors' and Dentists' Review Body," Mimeo.

House of Commons, 1987, "First Report from the Social Services Committee, Session 1986-87, Primary Health Care," Vols I & II, HMSO, London.

Mackin, P. J., Rout, U., and Cooper, C. L., 1988, Job satisfaction and occupational stress among general practitioners - a pilot study. *J. Roy. Coll. Gen. Practit.*, 38, 303-306.

Payne, R., Firth-Cozens, J., 1987, "Stress in Health Professionals," Wiley, Chichester.

Pendleton, D., Schofield, T., and Marinker, M., 1986, "In Pursuit of Quality. Approaches to Performance Review in General Practice," RCGP, Exeter.

Porter, A. M. D., Howie, J.G.R., and Levinson, A., 1987, Stress and the General Practitioner, *in*: "Stress in Health Professionals," R. Payne and J. Firth-Cozens, eds., Wiley, Chichester.

Rankin, H. J., Serieys, N. M., and Elliot-Binns, C. P., 1987, Determinants of mood in general practitioners, *Br. Med. J.*, 294, 618-620.

Review Body on Doctors' and Dentists' Remuneration, 1981, "Eleventh Report," Cmnd 8239, HMSO, London.

Royal College of General Practitioners, 1985, "Quality in General Practice. Policy Statement 2," RCGP, London.

STRESS OF DENTISTS CAUSED BY ANXIOUS PATIENTS

Hella Heering-Sick and Sven Tönnies

Psychologisches Institut III der Universitat Hamburg
Von-Melle-Park, Hamburg, West- Germany

INTRODUCTION

The starting point of our research project was the fact that anxiety before and during dental treatment is a significant stress factor not only for the patient but also for the dentist. In former research, though, only little attention was given to this viewpoint because the patient as the holder of anxiety automatically slipped into the center of interest (2,3,8,12,18).

When the dentist was included in the question, the main interest focused on the physiological stress of his profession (14), while the psychological and social stress factors were of less interest. In West- Germany only one study by Micheelis (9) is citable in this context, although the original frame of that study was aimed at the understanding of the work aspects of dentistry.

In the USA, however, more research has recently been done, where more psychosocial questions are asked under the concept of "behavioral dentistry" (4), as when anxious patients are questioned about their satisfaction with their dentists' dealing with them (5,7). Their replies showed that a caring and accepting style of communication by the dentist is an important factor for those patients, even if the anxiety is still not substantially reduced.

In the US, a new trend is visible where patient anxiety as a stress factor for the dentist is not just a discussion any more, but where possibilities for stress-reduction are looked for. Our study also tried to take this interest into consideration by not only documenting the subjective working experience of dentists, but also making a connection between experienced stress and certain personality traits. We assume that the personality of the dentist can help to reduce anxiety and stress in the interaction between anxious patients and dentists.

THE PROBLEM AND A DESCRIPTION OF THE SAMPLE[1]

The main questions of this study were: how do dentists perceive the anxiety of patients, how do they react toward themselves, and which causes do they ascribe to

---

[1]Our thanks go to Dr. Hartmut Jost for his part in the research project, especially his help in the development of the questionnaire.

patient anxiety? Furthermore, it considered how experiencing and dealing with anxious patients is interdependent with certain personality traits of the dentists.

Between May and August, 1986, a specially developed 12-page questionnaire was given to all dentists in Hamburg. Of these, 342 were fully answered and came to evaluation, which is equivalent to a 35% response rate. Of the questioned dentists, 82% were male which corresponds to the total of 81% of all male dentists in Hamburg. The average age was 47 years; 80% were married, 76% had one or more children. The average professional experience was 20 years, and 82% had their own practice while the rest worked in association practices; 85% had one or more assistants. More than half (54%) of the dentists had two treatment chairs, 23% had three, 12% had only one, but 9% worked with four chairs. The majority of practices were located in residential areas (43%) and in the City (30%).

RESEARCH RESULTS[2]

The significance of patient anxiety for the dentists.

More than half of those questioned (52%) stated that patient anxiety is a very important subject, only 4% thought it unimportant. However, dentists seem to see this subject as an individual problem which is shown by the fact that only 29% stated that anxiety of the patients is a serious topic amongst colleagues. Nevertheless, they often experience restrictions and stress during the treatment of anxious patients (Table 1): 71% of the questioned dentists felt more or less restricted/stressed by patient anxiety. This rather high percentage is even more significant when one considers the number of anxious patients. Every third patient (34%) is considered anxious, although dentists seem to have quite different ideas about anxiety patients, which becomes clear when looking at the rather wide dispersion (s=26) of their answers.

Rather interesting in this context is that 29% of the questioned dentists are classified as anxiety patients themselves - a quota which is remarkably similar to the general quotas.

As main reasons for patient anxiety, 81% named general pain anxiety, 75% saw negative experiences with physicians, especially during childhood, and finally 58% suspected lack of information on the patients' side about treatment, instruments, etc.

Which reactions and experiences are provoked as a consequence of treating anxious patients?

About half of the questioned dentists named overcarefulness, weariness, fatigue and nervousness as the most frequent reactions (Table 2). The reasons were scaled according to the frequency of their mention. Multiple mentions were possible. More than 33% mentioned that their pulse increases, around 25% become irritated, feel neck or shoulder pain, and their work becomes less accurate. This last figure can have especially negative consequences for the patient, so that the breaking off of the treatment, which is mentioned by 17% of the dentists, can also be seen as a protection for the anxious patient from possible harm.

---

[2]Details and further results are to be found in: Heering-Sick, Hella: Patientenangst im Erleben von Zahnärzten mit unterschiedlichen Persönlichkeitshaltungen. Diplomarbeit, Universitat Hamburg, Fachbereich Psychologie, Hamburg, 1986.

Table l. Degree of restrictions/stress in treatment of anxious patients.

Degree	Mentions	Percent
very	54	(16%)
little	186	(55%)
scarcely	74	(22%)
not at all	24	(7%)

For what reasons do dentists think it important to reduce patient anxiety?

Two reasons are mentioned almost equally often by 3/4 of the questioned dentists: the improvement of prevention and the improvement of the dentist-patient relationship (Table 3). The reasons were scaled after the frequency of their mentions.'Several answers were possible. Through the latter it becomes clear that anxiety of patients is often affecting the interpersonal relationship between dentist

Table 2. Reactions during treatment of anxious patients

Reactions	"Yes" or "rather yes"	"No" or "Rather no"
I become overcareful	160 (57%)	121 (43%)
I become weary and tired	149 (52%)	135 (48%)
I become nervous	120 (44%)	155 (56%)
My pulse increases	97 (37%)	165 (63%)
I become irritated	77 (29%)	186 (70%)
I get neck and shoulder pain	69 (27%)	191 (73%)
My work becomes less accurate	67 (25%)	197 (75%)
I get throbbing of the heart	59 (23%)	196 (77%)
I break off the treatment	46 (17%)	221 (83%)

Table 3. Important reasons to reduce patient anxiety.

Reasons	Very important	A little important	Scarcely or not important at all
Improvement of prevention	234 (74%)	56 (18%)	26 (8%)
Improvement of dentist-patient-relation	237 (73%)	58 (18%)	29 (9%)
Improvement of dental hygiene	196 (63%)	49 (16%)	67 (21%)
Easier treatment	191 (60%)	88 (28%)	40 (13%)
Less stress for the dentist	167 (52%)	100 (31%)	55 (17%)
Reducing cost	103 (34%)	76 (25%)	122 (41%)

and patient. The two following reasons are also of rather interpersonal character: easier treatment and less stress for the dentist. This order indicates that dentists in the meantime ascribe a great importance to the psychological aspects of dentist anxiety. On the contrary, the permanent public discussion over cost reduction is in this context of least importance to the dentist.

Which are appropriate means to reduce patient anxiety?

The questioned dentists think in their majority (82%) that more information, and counseling talks with the patient, are very effective (Table 4) The means were scaled after the frequency of their mention; several answers were possible. Almost all of them (94%) see the reduction of the anxiety as their own responsibility. Therefore, most of them object to the consultation of a psychotherapist as not appropriate. However, 26% of those questioned attest to the promising influence of their own psychotherapeutic training. Conclusively, it seems that dentists judge psychotherapeutic methods to reduce patient anxiety as very important, but want to apply these methods themselves, and see a delegation of specially trained experts as having little effectiveness. When we stress here the importance of psychological means, we should not forget to mention the application of local anesthetics to reduce anxiety, which was after all placed at second rank in 45% of all mentions of promising means.

Do different ways of experiencing and reacting to stress cohere with personality factors?

According to Rogers (11) and Tausch & Tausch (17), the three personality attitudes - respect-warmth, empathetic understanding, and genuineness - have proven necessary for a positive interpersonal interaction. Persons independent of education

Table 4. Promising means against patient anxiety

Means	Very promising	A little promising	Scarcely or not promising at all
More explaining and counseling talks	276 (82%)	56 (17%)	6 (1%)
Application of more local anesthetics	147 (45%)	86 (26%)	93 (29%)
'Unmedical' furnishing of practice	84 (26%)	121 (38%)	113 (36%)
Own psychothera-peutic training	79 (26%)	108 (35%)	118 (39%)
Optic and acoustic distraction	39 (12%)	105 (34%)	169 (54%)
Consultation of a psychotherapist	17 (6%)	39 (13%)	235 (81%)

and theoretical orientation who own these attitudes have shown themselves as especially successful and beneficial in the interaction with others (16).

We tested the hypothesis that those attitudes are helpful in dealing with anxious patients by comparing two groups of dentists statistically: one group of 80 dentists (23%) who according to self-judgment showed a higher degree of client-centered attitudes, and a second group of 70 dentists (20%) with a lower ranking in those attitudes. According to expectation, client-centered dentists felt significantly less restrictions and stress through anxious patients. They experienced anxiety reactions from their patients less frequently, such as nervousness, aggression, exaggerated denial of anxiety, distractions or treatment-refusal.

Equally, the client-centered dentists showed significantly less stress reactions, such as weariness/fatigue, headache, nervousness, increased pulse rate and heartbeat, irritation. in addition they broke off treatment correspondingly less often. More common anxiety reactions such as sweating, trembling, or cramping, however, were perceived equally often by both groups. Further, it showed that the way of handling stress through patient anxiety was independent of sex and age of the dentists.

DISCUSSION OF RESULTS

The unexpectedly high response rate of the questionnaire shows that the subject of the study is of great importance. Nevertheless, we cannot claim our results to be representative of all dentists in the FRG. On the one hand, we questioned dentists in the Hamburg area who are probably similar to those in other city areas. On the other hand, though, there may be differences in practices in small towns and the countryside. Furthermore, it is likely that the dentists who answered our questionnaire represent a group more open towards this subject which could influence the results accordingly.

Another problem arose from the difficulty in defining the term "anxiety" so clearly in a questionnaire that everybody had the same idea of the matter in question. Our results, therefore, are based on the subjective estimations by the dentist of what he perceives as anxiety and which stress reactions emerge from those perceptions. Accordingly, we are not talking about the very small group of patients with dental phobia (ca. 5%), who rarely appear in the dental office any more, but about the patients whose anxiety the dentists confront daily.

Despite these restrictions, it seems a very important result to keep in mind that every third patient was classified as anxious by the dentists, and that almost three-fourths of all dentists feel restricted and stressed when treating those patients. This finding is also supported by the study of Micheelis (10) where 64% of the dentists mentioned middle-to-strong stress experiences.

Considering the stated reactions and feelings during the treatment of anxious patients, it becomes quite obvious that the dentist often has to perform his work under psychic stress which is as effective a handicap, and is in addition to, the well known physiological stress factors. Additionally, lack of time and administrative work were named by 50% and 59%, respectively, of the dentists as quite unpleasant aspects of their profession.

The psychosocial stress is also mentioned in the study of Arnetz et al (1) who found that in Sweden the suicide rate was higher among dentists than in other academic professions. Even though empirical evidence for a direct influence of such stressors is still not known, it seems very probable that they contribute to the increased suicide risk of dentists. This is also supported by findings in the field of "burn-out" research where dentists rank as highly endangered for this symptom.

From our study it becomes clear that the stress of the dentist is not the primary concern in reducing the anxiety of the patients. The first consideration is usually prevention, which is in accordance with the important concern of dentistry to better the prophylactic situation and give more attention to preventive methods of dental work (described in Schneller & Fleischer-Peters, 13). Nevertheless, dentists should pay more attention to their stress experiences, and increasingly use all possible ways to reduce them.

The dentists considered informational and counseling talks with the patients the most promising way to reduce patient anxiety. This result supports the findings of "behavioral dentistry" (4) in the US, indicating that offering to interact with clients is regarded as more sensible than giving medication. This is very encouraging because it shows the openmindedness of the dentists towards communicative interpersonal concepts. A special training in client-centered communication would meet an obvious need for the dentists. Besides that, the matter of dealing with patient anxiety should have more consideration during medical schooling: 78% of the questioned dentists were never, or very seldom, confronted with this problem in their schooling.

The second most promising means, application of local anesthetics, is rather overestimated in its anxiety reducing effect. As Schulte (15) concluded from his study, the dentist anxiety could not be reduced through the use of more local anesthetics. Yet we have to concede that the possibility of using narcotics for pain lessens that part of the patient's stress caused by anxiety and relieves a stressful dentist-patient interaction.

As mentioned, the statements of the dentists about important aspects of the dental anxiety varied considerably. Not only the number of anxious patients, but also the nature and degree of stress when treating those patients, were judged quite differently. It showed that the different perceptions and experiences were connected with the personality of the questioned. Dentists who described themselves as "respectful," "empathetic," and "genuine" had fewer problems in dealing with anxious patients. They felt more competent and secure in explaining and counseling and applied this successfully in the daily contact with anxiety patients, according to their own judgment.

We assume that dentists with client-centered attitudes create a more pleasant and relaxed climate with anxious patients and reduce tensions so that anxiety reactions occur more seldom and are less intensive. The dentist consequently experiences less stress, which again affects the therapy situation positively. Thus, such behavior of the dentist towards his patients can initiate a process which affects the dentist-patient relationship positively and mutually.

For interested dentists, the GWG[3] offers training programs in "communication style" where the mentioned attitudes are taught. Additionally, we hold practical knowledge and experience in certain methods of relaxation such as Autogenic Training or Muscular Relaxation to be sensible. The dentist could integrate these into his treatment for the patient, and could also use them to reduce the professional stress aspects for himself.

REFERENCES

1. Arnetz, B.B., Hörte, L-G., Hedberg A., & Malker, H.: Suicide Among Swedish Dentists. *ScandJ. Soc. Med.* 15: 243-246, 1987.

2. Bernstein, D.A., Kleinknecht, R.A.,& Alexander, L.D. : Antecedents of Dental Fear. *J. Public Health Dentistry* 39: 113-124, 1979.

3. Boon, E.T.: Adults' Fear of Dentistry: Origins And Characteristics. *Gen. Dent.* Sept./Oct.: 369-373, 1983.

4. Bryant, P.S.: Behavioral dentistry: concepts and challenge. In: Ingersoll, B.D., & McCutcheon, W.R. (Hrsg.): Clinical research in behavioral dentistry. Morgantown, West Virginia, 1979, I-8.

5. Corah, N.L., O'Shea, R.M., & Ayer, W.A.: Dentists' management of patients' fear and anxiety. JADA 110: 734-736, 1985.

6. Corah, N.L., O'Shea, R.M., & Bissel, G.D.: Thke dentist-patient relationship: perceptions by patients of dentist behavior in relation to satisfaction and anxiety. JADA III: 443-446, 1985.

7. Glassman, P., Brody, H., Rappoport, A.: Dental fear and its dental practice implications. CDA J 13: 21-25, 1985.

8. Kleinknecht, R.A., Klepac, R.K., & Alexander, L.D.: Origins and characteristics of fear of dentistry. J. Dent. Res. 51: 964-966, 1972.

---

[3]Gesellschaft für wissenschaftliche Gesprachspsychotherapie. Richard-Wagner-Strasse 12, Postfach 270 165, 5000 Koln 1, W-Germany.

9. Micheelis, W.: Merkmale zahnärztlicher Arbeitsbeanspruchung. Deutsch Arzte Verlag, Koln-Lovenich, 1983.

10. Micheelis, W.: Streß und Arbeitsbeanspruchung im zahnärztlichen Tätigkeitsfeld, Zahn-ärtzl. Mitt 75: 683-686, 1985.

11. Rogers, C.R.: Die nicht-direktive Beratung. Kindler, München, 1982.

12. Scott, D.S., & Hirschman, R.: Psychological aspects of dental anxiety in adults. JADA 104: 27-31, 1982.

13. Schneller, T., & Fleischer-Peters, A.: Anwendung psychologischer Methoden in der Zahnmedizin. Fachbuchhandlung f. Psychologie, Frankfurt, 1985.

14. Schön, F., & Kimmel, K.: Ergonomie in der zahnärztlichen Praxis, Quintessenz, Berlin, 1972.

15. Schulte, W.: Das Ansehen unseres Standes, der Schmerz-, Angst-, und Anasthesiekomplex-vor 10 Jahren und heute. Zahnarztl. Mitt 67: 381-386 u. 661-666, 1977.

16. Schulz, W., & Huttner, H.: Personlichkeit des Therapeuten. In: Grunwald, W., (Hrsg.): Kritische Stichworter zur Gesprachspsychotherapie, Fink, München, 1979, 192-193.

17. Tausch, R. & Tausch, A.: Gesprachspsychotherapie. Hogrefe, Gottingen, 1981.

18. Wetzel, W.E.: Die Angst des Kindes vor dem Zahnarzt. Hanser, München, 1982.

PHARMACOTHERAPY FOR STRESS DISORDERS

David Wheatley

Stress Clinic
Maudsley Hospital, London

Psychopharmacology Research Group
Hinchley Wood, Surrey, U.K.

INTRODUCTION

The Maudsley Stress Clinic was established three years ago for the purpose of diagnosing and quantifying stress factors that might be exerting adverse effects on the patient. General practitioners in the area were asked to refer patients to the Clinic who were suspected of having stress problems of whatever kind, and to include not only local patients, but also those from Essex, Kent, the Midlands and elsewhere. Standardized questionnaires were developed to determine the nature and severity of the stresses that might be causing problems to the patients so that they might then be better enabled to cope with them. Psychopharmacology is the form of treatment most usually employed, but patients for whom it is inappropriate are referred to other departments in the hospital for counseling, psychotherapy, etc.

STRESS FACTORS

At present, nine stress areas are being investigated in a routine manner and quantified in order to construct a Stress Profile for each patient (q.v.).

Social Habits

Many individuals use alcohol and tobacco as a means of coping with stress (Stockwell 1985; King 1986). Excessive consumption of stimulant drinks (tea, coffee, cola) may contribute to the physiological effects of stress and its adverse effects on the cardiovascular system (Kenny and Darragh 1985; Boulenger and Uhde 1982; Onrot et al 1985). The social-habits questionnaire assesses consumption of alcohol or stimulant drinks, smoking habits, and any use of addictive drugs (marijuana, heroin, etc.).

Social Stress

This is concerned with the patient's attitudes and involvement in his or her daily life, and is divided into four sections: work, recreation, marriage (etc.), and relations with others. Stress at work mAy be engendered by the job itself, which may be boring and unrewarding or alternatively may involve long hours and high pressures (McKenna and Scholl 1985). Other problems at work involve interpersonal relationships, opportunities (or lack of them) for advancement, and, of course, the particular stresses that may arise from unemployment and retirement. Recreation may take many different forms, some of which involve mental stress, irrespective of the physical stress or the individual's role as participant or spectator. For example, watching a football match may produce intense excitement and mental stress, although no physical exertion is involved. Stresses that may arise in marriage or established cohabitation are concerned with the many aspects of compatibility between the two persons involved, and stress may or may not be a factor for those who are unmarried, divorced or separated. Finally, stresses may arise in relationships with various family members, with other people generally and with friends. Under the last-named category, the individual's desire for social contacts is considered in relation to his or her ability to achieve them.

Life Events

The Social Readjustment Rating Scale of Holmes and Rahe (1967) lists many life events in relation to their relative stressfulness to individuals. However, life events, good or bad, can produce varying degrees of stress in different individuals and under different circumstances. For example, divorce may constitute a tragedy for one but a welcome release from purgatory for another! Therefore, the impact of the event, whether recent or in the past, is considered in relation to the amount of stress that it is producing at the present time. We have categorized events into five groups, based on work undertaken by the Psychopharmacology Research Group when investigating the influence of life events on treatment of affective disorders (Wheatley 1982a).

Emotional events are concerned with interpersonal relationships, examples of good events being: happy love relationships, engagements, marriage, birth of babies; and of bad: broken romances, separation, unwanted pregnancies, abortion, etc. *Living (earning)* events are associated with work and financial affairs. Thus, examples of good events are: promotion at work, passing examinations, successful ventures, financial gains, and so forth; and bad events: dismissal from work, failing examinations, financial losses, demotion, etc. *Living (enjoying)* includes: domestic events, social occasions, local and world events. Examples of good events are: acquisition of prized objects for the home, (a new car, for instance), parties, outings, happy world events; whilst bad events are: domestic mishaps (burst water pipes or other causes of damage to the home), car accidents not involving injury, failure of domestic apparatus, and the like. *Health* concerns illness, accidents, operations, etc., either happening to the individual or to others, but excluding life-endangering illness. Examples of good events are: passing a medical examination, recovery from an illness, successful operations; whilst bad events are: minor illnesses such as colds, sore throats, bronchitis, and longer partially incapacitating illnesses such as anaemia, arthritis, etc. *Illness/death* embraces life-endangering illness involving the patient or close friends or relatives, or the death of close friends or relatives.

Psychiatric

This records family and previous history of psychiatric disorder and the patient then completes the Raskin-Covi diagnostic scales for depression/anxiety (Raskin et al 1970; Covi et al 1974). If the score on either the depression or anxiety subscales exceeds the normal cut-off point, then either the Hamilton depression or Hamilton anxiety rating scale is completed, as appropriate.

Sexual Stress

The sexual urge constitutes one of the most potent stress factors in human life and may produce numerous sequelae when the response to it is inadequate for whatever reason (Wheatley 1983). This is a particularly important aspect of stress assessment, since many patients are reluctant to mention such problems to their physicians who, in turn, frequently omit questions concerning this potent cause of ill-health.

The sexual-stress questionnaire is divided into four parts concerned with the following aspects of sex: mental, physical, female and psychological. The mental aspects of sex involve the degree of enjoyment experienced in sexual activities and the amount of libido of the individual. Physical problems may arise in relation to frequency of performance, erection difficulties, premature ejaculation, partner's response (which may be too passive or too demanding) and the partner's technique. These problems are, of course, not only confined to males, since poor erection and premature ejaculation, for example, can produce as much or more stress in the female partner as in the male who experiences them. Contraceptive usage may introduce further stresses, such as side-effects from oral contraceptives in the female, distaste for mechanical methods, etc. Two stresses which are considered to be peculiar to the female are dysparunia and fear of pregnancy. Finally, other psychological aspects are considered: concern about illicit sex, degree of guilt or distaste, fear of sexually transmitted diseases, feelings of bodily inadequacy such as small penis or breasts, jealousy concerning partner and stress in relation to masturbation.

Sleep

Lack of sleep is a subtle form of stress that may undermine the sufferer's health (Mendelson et al 1984), influencing not only his or her whole life but also exerting an adverse effect in almost every illness known to man. Yet many physicians fail to question patients concerning their sleep, unless they volunteer complaints about it. The sleep questionnaire is concerned with the following aspects of the sleep pattern: time taken to fall asleep, number of awakenings during the night, early morning wakening, total nightly sleep duration and how refreshed the patients feel on final awakening.

From the point of view of subsequent management, the etiology of insomnia (Wheatley 1981) is then classified as follows: physical (symptoms of organic illnesses causing insomnia); physiological (external factors interfering with sleep, i.e., shift work); psychological (emotional impact of life events); psychiatric (anxiety, depression, psychoses); iatrogenic (medicinal drugs causing insomnia, i.e., adrenergic agonists) and idiopathic (insomnia for no apparent reason).

The Elderly Patient

The elderly are particularly vulnerable to the assaults of stress and, with increasing age, there is hardly any aspect of life that is not so influenced (Wheatley 1982b). These influences may be of a subtle nature and are not always appreciated by those who strive to help the elderly. The geriatric questionnaire is administered to those aged 60 years and over and concerns the patient's degree of contentment with the way they live: any stress occasioned by deafness, defective vision or physical defects such as arthritis; and how much it bothers them if they cannot do the things they used to.

One of the main problems is increasing isolation from others in the community, and this is often aggravated by the failing senses. For example, an elderly person who shuns social contacts may merely be self-conscious of (or may not even be aware of) a hearing deficit. A hearing aid may be all that is required to treat such a major stress factor. When indicated, a modified form of the Crichton geriatric rating scale (Robinson 1964) is used to assess mental and functional abilities by excluding items concerned with sleep and mood that are already covered, and with the addition of items concerned with mental alertness or confusion and memory for recent events.

Menstrual Questionnaire

This is divided into two parts to distinguish between premenstrual syndrome and menopausal symptoms. Details are also recorded of menstrual irregularities and the amount of mental stress that they may cause, i.e., menorrhagia, amenorrhoea, irregular periods, etc.

Stress and the Heart

Since stress, particularly when accompanied by anxiety, may affect a number of cardiovascular parameters (Wheatley 1982c) this questionnaire is included to determine underlying cardiac disorders, such as coronary heart disease and hypertension, that might be influenced by, or be the cause of, stress. Details are recorded of personal and family history of cardiac disorders, hypertension or diabetes, since fear of succumbing to the illness that killed one's forebears is a potent stress factor. Blood pressure and pulse rate are taken and if abnormalities are present, these are assessed as part of the stress factor under this heading. Finally, the degree of worry that the patient feels about his or her heart is assessed.

PATIENT POPULATION

Analyses have been undertaken on the first 100 patients attending the Clinic and it is interesting to note that males and females occurred in virtually equal numbers, 51 and 49 respectively. Furthermore, the majority of patients were in the younger age groups with a mean of 36.5 years in the males and 41.6 years in the females. Although it has been said that the Maudsley Hospital is a "DSM III - free area," it is convenient to use the diagnostic categories from that system and the principal diagnoses in these patients is shown in Table 1.

In some cases there was more than one "principal" diagnosis, i.e., insomnia and anxiety together, but in such cases both diagnoses have been shown because of the treatment implications (q.v.).

Perhaps one of the most striking features of this analysis is that virtually half of the patients were suffering from major depression, which in most cases had not been diagnosed prior to referral to the Clinic. Another feature of interest is the equality of the sexes in relation to this diagnosis, since in clinical practice there is usually a preponderance of females to males of approximately 3:1. Insomnia as a stress factor occurred in one-fifth of these patients and the various facets of anxiety that are traditionally associated with stress were prominent.

THE STRESS PROFILE

Each of the stress items described is quantified and the relative severities can be expressed as percentages of the total possible severity in each case. From these the

Table 1. Diagnoses in the first 100 patients seen at the Stress Clinic

PRINCIPAL STRESS	N.	MALES	FEMALES
GENERAL ANXIETY	24	14	10
SOCIAL PHOBIA	8	4	4
PANIC DISORDER	9	6	3
AGAROPHOBIA	1	-	1
SIMPLE PHOBIA	3	2	1
MAJOR DEPRESSION	49	21	28
INSOMNIA	20	8	12
ORGANIC ILLNESS	9	6	3
EMOTIONAL	1	-	1
SITUATIONAL	1	1	1

patient's Stress Profile can be constructed and then used as a measure of change, providing information on the inter-relations between the different stresses and the extent to which one stress will improve when another one is treated. An individual example is shown in Figure 1.

The patient was a middle-aged London taxi-driver, suffering from anxiety symptoms and cardiophobia. A major stress in his life was concerned with his work, as he was a gregarious person who liked to converse, but his fares seldom wanted to talk to him. The other factor was concerned with his marriage to an overbearing and domineering wife. Since insomnia was the main diagnosis in this case, he was treated with a short-acting hypnotic drug (temazepam) and at the end of three weeks his Stress Profile showed great improvement. At the same time, he had come to two important decisions: to change his job and to divorce his wife!

Antidepressant Drugs

Major depression has been one of the most satisfying stress factors to treat, in view of the excellent response that is usually obtained with antidepressant drugs. Considerable effort and persuasion is needed to explain the rationale of this treatment to depressed patients, because this is an illness in which lack of desire to get better is an intrinsic component. The "lag period" of 10-14 days before the

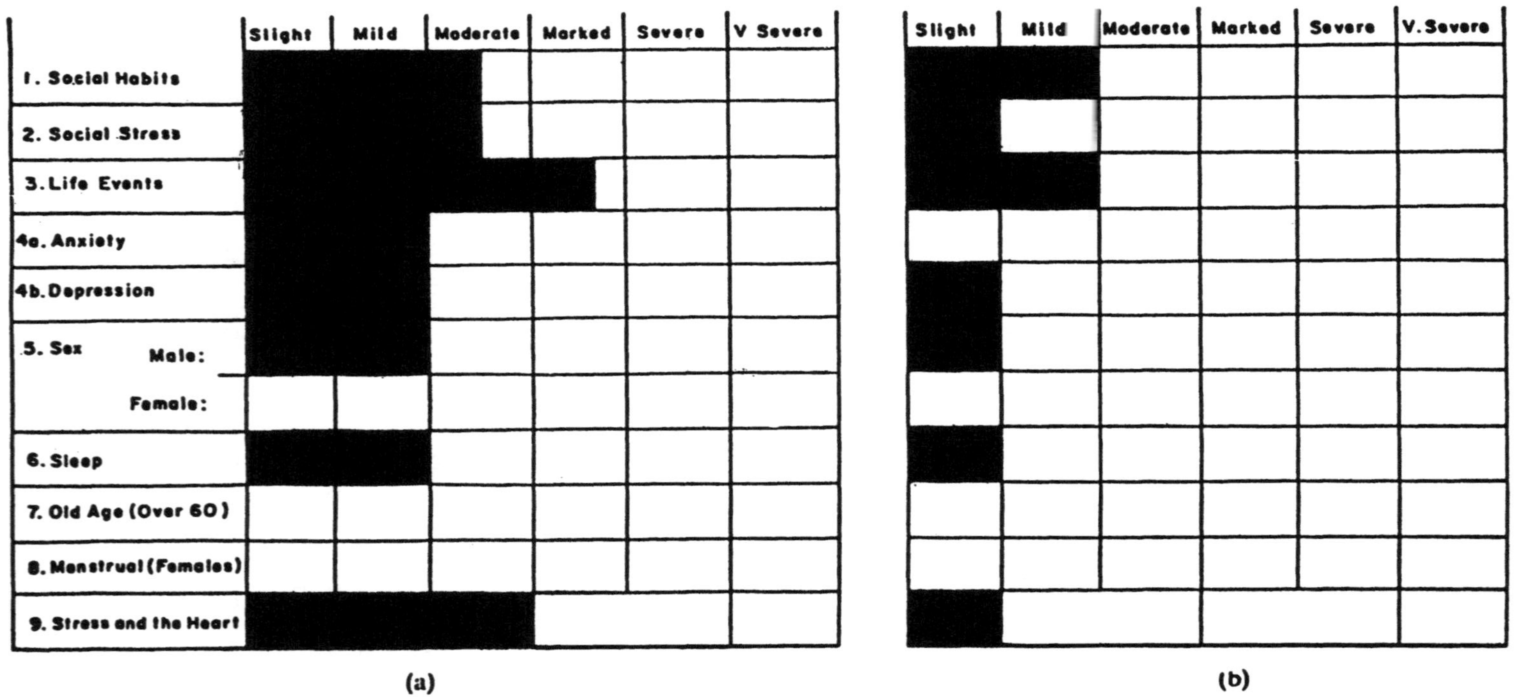

Figure 1. Stress Profile of a patient with anxiety symptoms and cardiophobia: (a) before and (b) after treatment with a centrally acting beta-blocker.

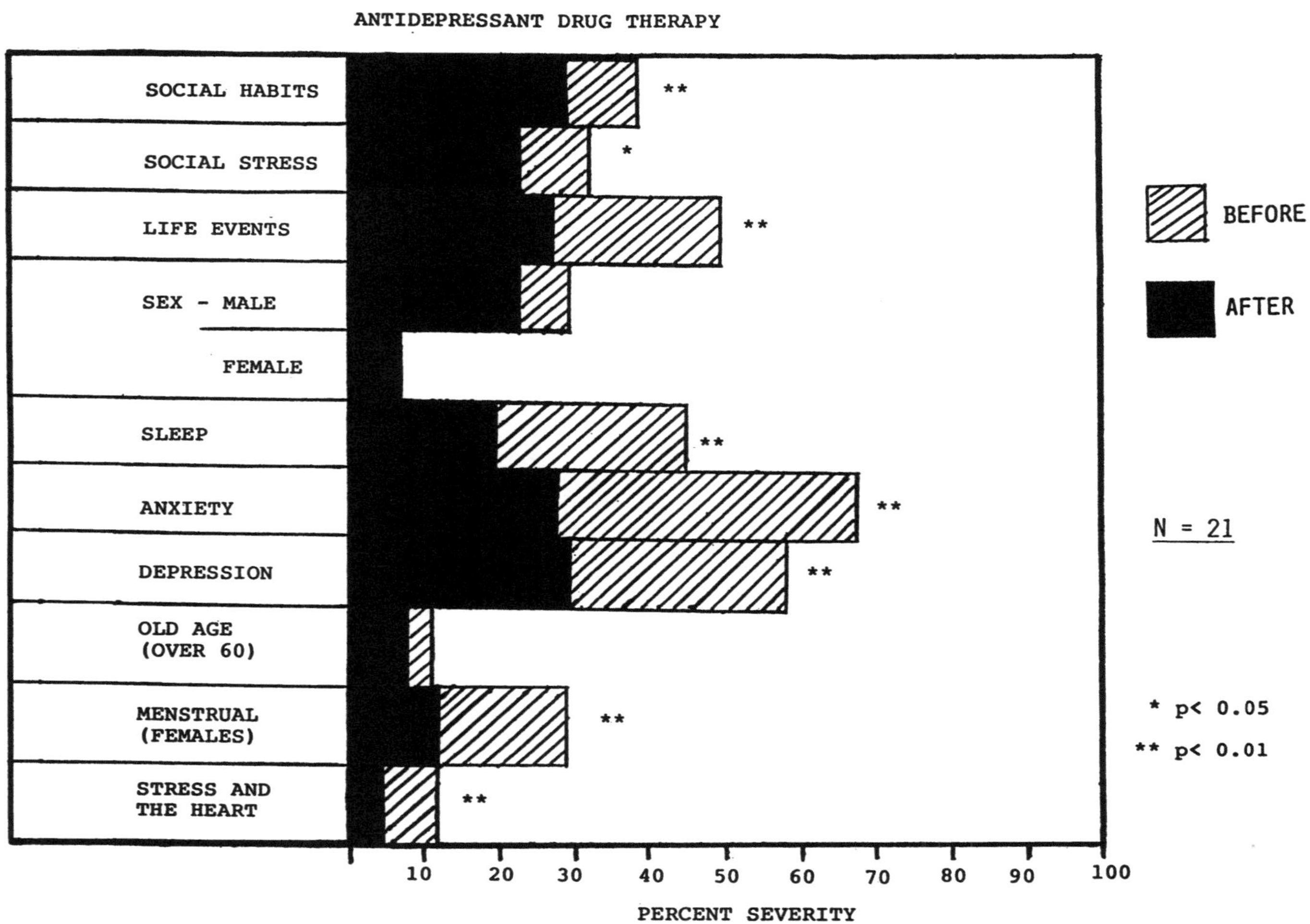

Figure 2. Mean Stress Profiles for 21 patients suffering from major depression before and after treatment with antidepressant drugs.

antidepressant effect becomes established, and the occurrence of side-effects are ready excuses for the patient to abandon treatment before it has had time to work. However, once these problems have been overcome, response is excellent and the mean Stress Profiles of 21 patients before and after treatment are shown in Figure 2.

Once again, successful lifting of the depression resulted in relief of many of the other stress factors.

Beta-Blockers in Anxiety

At the present time there is considerable resistance on the part of patients and their prescribing physicians alike to treat anxiety symptoms and panic attacks with anxiolytic drugs. An alternative approach is to use a beta-blocking drug. Although the main effect of such drugs may be peripheral and on the somatic symptoms of anxiety, nevertheless there may be a central component, in which case a drug with high lipo-solubility would be indicated. Propranolol has the highest lipid solubility of all beta-blocking drugs available in the U.K., and is highly concentrated in the central nervous system. Of the cardioselective beta-blockers, betaxolol is the most highly lipid soluble, although much less so than propranolol. We have used both these beta-blocking drugs in the Clinic and Figure 3 shows the results recorded on the mean Stress Profiles for an initial sample of six patients.

As in the case of the previous analysis, reduction in severity occurred in many of the stress areas but was particularly marked in the relief of anxiety symptoms.

CONCLUSION

Stress is a normal component of life, and indeed a life without stress could be compared to a cocktail without alcohol. In many cases, lack of stress may even constitute a potent stressor per se. It is when individuals fail to cope with stress that adverse effects may ensue which then constitute stress-induced illness. In many parts of the world there has been a rapid growth of facilities aimed at teaching stress-relief,

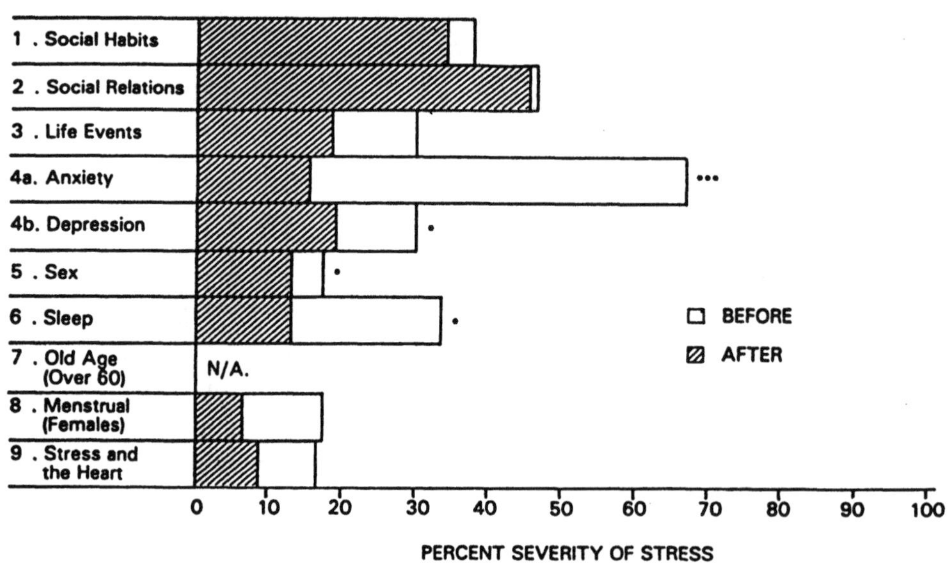

Figure 3. Mean Stress Profiles for six patients suffering from anxiety before and after treatment with beta-blocking drugs. $^{*}p<0.05$, $^{***}p<0.001$.

usually by counseling, relaxation techniques, biofeedback, etc. However, before therapy must come diagnosis, and little attempt has been made in the past to accurately define the factors that are involved in stress-induced illness. The aim of the Maudsley Stress Clinic is to provide an initiative in the systematic evaluation of stress factors by means of the stratified components of the Stress Profile. A better understanding of the effects of stress in human lives may then lead to the development of improved coping with its effects.

REFERENCES

Boulenger, J-P., and Uhde, T.W. 1982, Caffeine consumption and anxiety. Preliminary results of a survey comparing patients with anxiety disorders and normal controls. *Psychopharm. Bulletin*. 18: No.4, 53-57.

Covi, L., Lipman, R.S., Derogatis, L.R., Smith, J.E., and Pattison, J.H. 1974, Drugs and group psychotherapy in neurotic depression. *AmerJ. Psychiat*. 131: 191-198.

Holmes, T.H., and Rahe, R.H. 1967, The social readjustment rating scale. *J. Psychosom. Res*. 11: 213-218.

Kenny, M., and Darragh, A. 1985, An innocuous stimulant? *Psychiatry in Practice*. October, 15-18.

King, M. 1986, At risk drinking among general practice attenders; prevalence, characteristics and alcohol-related problems. *Brit. J. Psychiat*. 148: 533-540.

McKenna, J.F., and Scholl, R.W. 1985, The interactive patterns of occupations and workers in predicting excessive occupational stress. *Stress Medicine*. 1: 93-100.

Mendelson, W.V., Garnett, D., Gilling, J.C., and Weingartner, H. 1984, The experience of insomnia and daytime and night-time functioning. *Psychiatry res*. 12: 235-250.

Onrot, J., Golfberg, M.R., Biaggioni, I., Hollister, A.S., Kincaird, D., and Robertson, D. 1985, Hemodynamic and houmoral effects of caffeine in autonomic failure. *New EnglJ. of Med*. 313: No.9, 549-554.

Raskin, A., Schulterbrandt, J.G., Reatig, N., and KcKeon, J.J. 1970, Differential response to chlorpromazine, imipramine and placebo. *Arch. Gen. Psychiatry*. 23: 164-173.

Robinson, R.A. 1964, *in* "The Diagnosis and Prognosis of Dementia, Current Achievements in Geriatrics," W.F. Anderson, ed., Cassell, London, pp. 190-203.

Stockwell, T. 1985, Stress and alcohol. *Stress Medicine*. 1: 209-215.

Wheatley, D. 1981, Effects of drugs on sleep. *in*: "Psychopharmacology of Sleep," D. Wheatley, ed., Raven Press, New York. pp. 153-176.

Wheatley, D. 1982a, Buspirone: multicenter efficacy study. *J. Clin. Psychiatry*. 43: No. 12, 92-94.

Wheatley, D. ed. 1982b, "Psychopharmacology of Old Age," Oxford University Press, Oxford.

Wheatley, D. 1982c, Treatment of the anxiety factor. *in*: "Stress and the Heart," 2nd edn. D. Wheatley, ed., Raven Press, New York. pp. 39-62.

Wheatley, D. ed. 1983, "Psychopharmacology and Sexual Disorders," Oxford University Press, Oxford.

RELIGIOUS BELIEF AND STRESS: A REVIEW OF COGNITIVE AND BEHAVIOR STRESS-COPING STRATEGIES INHERENT IN RELIGIOUS BELIEF

William Sim Munro

Area Medical and Safety Department
The Post Office
South East Area, England

INTRODUCTION

Numerous types of therapy and techniques have evolved into effective means of managing and preventing stress. As a consequence, a positive living environment is created. To illustrate these ideals, models taking into account the different values and different views of man as endorsed by the professional are constructed. Unfortunately, patients often may have little knowledge of these philosophies.

Achieving optimum performance from an automobile or computer requires that undue stress be avoided. Also, operating these machines according to the makers' manual, or according to the advice of those who have studied that manual, is most sensible.

A significant number of people in this country believe that God made them and that the Bible is God's word. Therefore, it would seem reasonable that these people be offered, as a viable alternative to current treatment strategies, stress counseling based on the information and guidance given in the Bible--our Maker's Manual--about living successfully. Essentially, the Bible promotes the belief that man is a tripartite being - spirit, soul (mind, emotions, will) and body (1 Thessalonians 5:23) together with His absolute values. Consequently, this paper considers three factors - stressors, the individual, and social support - which influence stress outcome or strain, and with each gives the alternative (Christian) view.

STRESSORS

Studies have been conducted assessing the relevant magnitude of stressors and their relationship to "disease" (Selye, 1956; Hinkle and Wolff, 1958; Holmes and Rahe, 1967; Rahe, 1968; Paykel et al, 1969; Paykel et al, 1971; Theorell and Rahe, 1971; Theorell and Rahe, 1972; Dobson, 1982;Kaplan, 1983; Jenkins, 1983; Cooper, 1983; Cooper, 1984; Wells, 1985; Glaser et al, 1985). In preventing and managing stress, chronic stressors need to be evaluated and successfully dealt with. A philosophy must also be developed where the realities of stress are avoided or relieved, possibly even discarded.

The Bible also deals at some length with this (Matthew 10:39; 13:22; Luke 12:15; 12:22-31; Proverbs 14:30).There is particular emphasis on self-inflicted stressors, a phenomenon that occurs when an individual's actions or behavior may lead to an event that produces stressful circumstances. For example, adultery may lead to divorce, an occurrence resulting in a complete range of stressful circumstances involving the household, the children, finance, solicitors, law courts, and so on. Too great an ambition for power or wealth can lead to long working hours with ensuing pressures within the marriage and the family. Dishonest or questionable practices in business can lead to fear of discovery and guilt, two emotions capable of producing extreme anxiety. Finally, irresponsible action can lead to pressures being created in the family and at the workplace. Biblical counsel is given concerning potential resolutions to the aforementioned problems. The resultant distress is also outlined (Proverbs 5:3-23; 6:25-29;6:32-35; 7:24-27; 10:9; 11:29; 12:24-25; 13:7,8; Ecclesiastes 2:17-26; 4:6; 4:8-12; 5:10-17).

The Christian minister must not exclude himself from the need to review his own stressors. If there is a desire to prevent the effects of stress from becoming destructive, the Christian minister must be aware of the existence of stressors. Importantly, the effects of stress are determined not only by the type, severity, number or duration of stressors, but also by mediators or moderators. Examples of mediators and moderators are the individual's reaction to the stressor or potential stressor, and the amount of social support available to and utilized by the affected personality. Similarly, the Bible places particular emphasis on the individual and the importance of the exhibited reaction. There is need to be aware of more than just the stressor. Finally, social support for the individual is also one of the central aspects of theological teachings (Galatians 6:12; 9:10; Ecclesiastes 4:9-12).

The individual's reactions to stressors or potential stressors are greatly influenced by a number of factors.

a) The perception of self or a person's self-image or self-esteem is a central determinant factor in regulation of a person's stress response (Paulhus and Christie, 1981; Gottlieb, 1983; Wills, 1985). Man believes that his worth depends on his achieving (Ivancevich and Matteson, 1988). This becomes incorporated into the human psyche from an early age, especially if parents are attentive and loving only when the child succeeds or achieves. The resultant mentality is often reinforced at school, in games, in the media, and in almost all other cultural aspects. If the individual continues to achieve, a genuine belief in the value of self is formed. If, however, achievement is not attained, especially if this failure is not from lack of diligence or application, then emotions of frustration, worthlessness, and rejection affect the individual. In turn, feelings of anxiety and inappropriate behavior take place, especially when there are attempts to pursue goals even more diligently. Tension and anxiety are also present, as are disillusionment and long term resentment and bitterness. There is a great possibility that psychiatric, psychosomatic or physical illness may then occur.

Efforts are frequently made to change the self-image, but this can be difficult unless cognition is also changed. This is true especially if achievements have been few, and frequent failures have been experienced, particularly if recent failures or fear of failures have been a perceived stressor.

The Christian view is that the individual is most worthwhile (Matthew 6:26; 10:30,31; 12:12; John 3:16). He is made in the image of God (Genesis 1:26,27) and through the born-again experience he can have a new spirit born of the Spirit of God (John 3:5-8). He is then of untold value to his Creator, and becomes a son and heir of God (Galatians 3:26; 4:4-7; Romans 8:15-17), a member of God's royal family (Ephesians 1:4,5; 1 Peter 2:9). Consequently, because of the importance of the aforementioned ideas, it is difficult to conceive of how a poor self-image comes to exist.

Moreover, man is totally forgiven (Romans 5:1,2; 8:1-4), so that any feelings of worthlessness from guilt can be successfully and meaningfully dealt with (1 John 1:7-10).

b) The individual's reactions also depend on individual traits or personality traits (Eysenck, 1967; Rosenman et al, 1975; Roskies, 1978; Haynes et al, 1980; Review Panel, 1981; Cooper et al, 1981; Price, 1982; Roskies, 1983; Eysenck, 1985a; Eysenck, 1985b; Wright et al, 1985; Matthews and Haynes, 1986; Goodkin et al, 1986; Friedman and Booth-Kewlcs, 1987).

Some studies have attempted to show that if personality type or behavior can be changed, it may be possible to prevent the ill effects of stress.

Would cancer be less likely to develop, as it appears may be the case, if expressions of emotion are encouraged (Grossarth-Maticek et al, 1986) and if the helpless, hopeless, depressant personality's reaction to stressors could be changed (Eysenck, 1988)? Modification of the Type A behavior pattern may protect from heart disease (Suinn, 1975; Roskies, 1978; Suinn, 1978; Suinn, 1982; Roskies, 1983; Jacob and Chesney, 1986; Matthews and Haynes, 1986). Preliminary results of studies are promising. However, attempts to change the Type A into a Type B have largely been a failure.

The Christian answer claims that the individual and not just behavior patterns can be miraculously changed (1 John 3: 9,10; Romans 7:6; 2 Corinthians 5:17; Ephesians 4:20-24; Galatians 3:9,10; Ezekiel 36:25-37). Real hope about life now (John 4:13,14; 5:21; 10:9,10) and the hereafter (John 3:16; 3:36; 5:24-30) can banish the helplessness, hopelessness and depression associated with the negative personality, and encourage free expressions of emotion (Romans 15:13; Ezekiel 36:26). If all significance and security is found as it is meant to be in God (Proverbs 10:29,30; 14:26,27; 15:16; 16:7; 16:20; Psalm 94:17-19; 94:22), the Type A personality can be changed together with its aggression and hostility (Luke 12:31).

c) The individual's reactions depend also on the perception of a potential stressor and the degree to which it is seen as a possible threat to the physical or psychological well being (Lazarus, 1966; House, 1981; Cohen et al, 1986). Efforts are made to correct faulty cognition (Jacob and Chesney, 1986). Obviously, much good can result from changing inadequate thinking patterns.

The Christian, born again of the Spirit of God, has hope of an eternal future in the presence of God (Ephesians 1:9-14; 2:4-7; Romans 6:5-10). Consequently, thought processes should put present potential threats in perspective (Romans 8:31-34). Therefore, an individual can be totally secure in the knowledge that God's love is constantly present. In such an environment nothing can be harmful, not even death (Romans 8:35-39). There can be no impairing threat.

Also, man has crucial needs for love, security, and significance (Maslow, 1954). There is a tendency to believe that these needs can be met in a variety of ways (Romans 1:21-32). The individual's needs are met through love and security as provided by other human beings, money, government, and the sense of being in complete control at all times (Glass and Singer, 1972). Furthermore, there is a tendency to believe that significance can be met through professional accomplishment, status, professional authority, knowledge, degrees, possessions, spouse or partner, and affairs (Ivancevich and Matteson, 1988).

As long as the need for love, security, and significance are being met, then emotions and life are stable. However, if there is a loss of an important component or even a possibility of loss, this perceived threat results in creating stress. Negative effects may well follow (Lazarus, 1966; House, 1981; Cohen et al, 1986).

Moreover, it must be noted that there is no sense of possessing ultimate control over anything on which dependence is based. Because events are seemingly beyond control, the individual functions within a constant vulnerable state. The Christian is not immune if there is a reliance on material sources for obtaining love and security. However, the Christian view is that man can obtain his crucial needs from God, who is utterly dependable (Phillipians 4:19; 1 Corinthians 1:9; Hebrews 13:8). This does not mean that God does not provide for these needs, to an extent, through human agencies such as the spouse, work, etc. If these sources no longer meet the individual's needs, they will obviously be missed, but if the belief is that the aforementioned can fulfill all needs, therein lies the problem if they become unavailable. Cognition, therefore, must be changed to respond according to the Maker's plan of how man was created to think (Romans 12:2).

d) The individual's tendency to react in a certain way is also influenced by the state of general physical and mental fitness. This fitness state can be enhanced by exercise, diet, enhanced life-style, and the avoidance of smoking, excessive alcohol and stimulants. Help is given through relaxation and other specific techniques (Jacob and Chesney, 1986).

The Bible deals with all of these factors. Particular emphasis is placed on the benefits of Biblical meditation (Psalms 1:1-3), adequate sleep, and relaxation (Psalm 127:2), and what will benefit the mind and bring peace to the soul (Ecclesiastes 5:19,20; Philippians 4:8).

CHANGE OF COGNITION AND BEHAVIOR

Proper changes in self-image, security sources, and personality type so that they coincide with the thinking and behavior as delineated in the Bible, are seen as being worthwhile. Therefore, the following must be considered.

1. How can the Biblical concepts outlined, which are often so much at odds with man's own manner of thinking, be accepted (2 Corinthians 4:4)?

2. How can thinking and behavior be changed?

Both of these are answered in Christian beliefs about the Holy Spirit. Man's spirit can only be made whole through the born-again experience (clear guidance is given about man's part in this in the Bible). At that time the human spirit is born of the Holy Spirit and the Holy Spirit comes to reside in the human spirit (Acts 2:37-39). Thus, the spirit becomes whole and direct communion with God is re-established. More than this, the Holy Spirit then illumines the soul, especially the mind (2 Corinthians 4:6; Ephesians 1:17-20), so that the truth about cognition and behavior become not only believable and acceptable, but are seen to be The Way (1 Corinthians 1:18).

Ability to change thinking and behavior then is a reality, if the Holy Spirit is allowed to flood the soul, as reflected in "Baptism in the Spirit" (Acts 1:5; 2:4; 4:8;

9:17). This is made possible if the mind, emotions and will come to be operational under the guidance and power of the Holy Spirit (Romans 8:12-14).

SOCIAL SUPPORT

It has been hypothesized that social support serves as a buffer or mediator between life's stressors and poor health and other negative reactions (Medalie et al, 1973; Cassel, 1974; Berkman and Syme, 1979; Vachon et al, 1980; Gottlieb, 1981; Holohan and Moos, 1981; Williams et al, 1981; Blayer, 1982; Dean and Ensel, 1982; House, 1982; Kasl and Cobbs, 1982; Roskin, 1982; Berkman and Breslow, 1983; Broadhead, 1983; Gottlieb, 1983; Reed et al, 1983; Ruberman et al, 1984; Berkman, 1985; Cohen and Wills, 1985a; Cohen and Syme, 1985b; Kasl and Wells, 1985; Caspi et al, 1987; Roos and Cohen, 1987; Ganster and Victor, 1988).

Unfortunately, willingness, ability and funding are not always available to provide adequate support, either through the State or voluntary organizations, to those needing it. Sadly, the family, formerly a source of such support, may not exist in a form to provide it (Kessler and McLeod, 1985). Christians are given a duty to support each other (Galatians 6:2) and are given a local framework, an extended family within which to do it - the Church (Galatians 6:10). Unfortunately, this has too often been only an institution and the source of religious activity. The present move to less traditional, rigid organizations with a more loving and caring concern should bring back the role of the Church family as a buffer to stressors. Indeed, it has been shown that members of some Churches have a low incidence of ischaemic heart disease which, while also possibly associated with lifestyle characteristics, has been attributed to their close-knit communities. Similarly, it has been suggested that social support from wives may protect husbands from some of the ill effects of stress. Some studies have indirectly demonstrated this (Cohen and Syme, 1985; Haynes and Eaker, 1983). Wives, as described in the Biblical tradition, are required to be supportive, and certainly marriages where this is accompanied by reciprocal love and respect from the husband (Ephesians 5:22-31) are more stable and eventually create a less stressful home environment.

It can now be seen that much of what is now postulated about mediators of stressors and the possibility of suitable intervention was defined in the Bible centuries ago. Of course, the Bible goes much further in dealing with this problem. While there is reference in some works to stress prevention and management as if they relate to religion (Bradley and Cox, 1978), references to Christianity often see the problem in terms of a religion, religious practices, and faith and beliefs to be followed, rather than the possibility of a completely life-changing dynamic.

There is much anecdotal evidence that seeking wholeness of body, soul and spirit as illustrated in the Bible leads to successful living and the prevention of the ill effects stress can bring about. Consequently, a study of cases being exposed to and accepting the Bible's guidance as related to the solution of stress should be encouraged.

Meanwhile, there is enough evidence to encourage those who accept the Bible and who are engaged in helping clients avoid or manage stress, to use it as a basis for counseling or to refer clients to others who do. Similarly, there is a need for those who are seeking help and who accept the Bible to be encouraged to ask for or to be referred to such theological based therapy.

Such a reality can only exist if there are sufficient Biblical Counselors available to meet client demand. If training and skill is such as to merit credibility and gain the confidence of those seeking such counselors, this outlined treatment strategy will be successful. There is thus a need for schools to promote training counselors capable of successfully incorporating the Bible in the treatment methodology.

REFERENCES

Berkman, L.F. and Syme, S.L., 1979, Social networks, host resistance, and mortality: A nine year follow-up study of Alameda county residents, *Am. J. Epidemiol.* 109:186.

Berkman, L.F. and Breslow, L., 1983, Health and ways of living: Findings from the Alameda county study, Oxford University Press, New York.

Berkman, L.F., 1985, The relationship of social networks and social support to morbidity and mortality in: Social support and health, S. Cohen and L. Syme eds., Academic Press, New York.

Blayer, D.G., 1982, Social support and mortality in an elderly community population, *Am J. Epidemiol.* 115:684.

Bradley, C. and Cox, T., 1978, Stress and health, in: Stress, T. Cox ed., The Macmillan Press, London.

Broadhead, W.E., Kaplan, B.H., Shermann, S.A., Wagner, E.H., Schoenback, V. G. and Gehlbach, S.H., 1983, The epidemiological evidence between social support and health, *Am. J. Epidemiol.* 117(5):521.

Caspi, A., Bolger, N. and Eckenrode, J., 1987, Linking person and context in the daily stress process, *J. Pers. Soc. Psychol.* 52:184.

Cassel, J., 1974, Psychosocial processes and stress: Theoretical formulations, *Int. J. Health Services.* 4:471.

Cohen, S. and Wills, T.A., 1985, Stress, social support, and the buffering hypothesis, *Psychol. Bull.* 2:310.

Cohen, S. and Syme, S.L., eds., 1985, Social support and health, Academic Press, New York.

Cohen, S., Evans, G.W., Stokols, D. and Krantz, D.S., 1986, Behavior, health and environmental stress, Plenum, New York.

Cooper, C.L., 1983, Stress research, Wiley, New York.

Cooper, C.L., 1984, Psychosocial stress and cancer, Wiley, New York.

Cooper, T., Detre, T. and Weiss, S.M., 1981, Coronary prone behavior and coronary heart disease: A critical review, *Circulation.* 63:1199.

Dean, A. and Ensel, W.M., 1982, Modelling social support, life events, competence and depression in the context of age and sex, *J. Community Psychol.* 10:392.

Dobson, C.B., 1982, Stress: The hidden adversary, Lancaster Medical and Technical Publishers.

Eysenck, H.J., 1967, The biological basis of personality, Thomas, Springfield, IL.

Eysenck, H.J., 1985a, Personality, cancer and cardiovascular disease: A causal analysis, personality and individual differences. 5:535.

Eysenck, H.J. and Eysenck, M.W., 1985b, Personality and individual differences, Plenum Press, New York.

Eysenck, H.J., 1988, Personality, stress and cancer: Prediction and prophylaxis, *Br. J. Med. Psychol.* 61:57.

Friedman, H.S. and Booth-Kewles, S., 1987, The disease prone personality, *Am. Psychol.* 42:534.

Ganster, D.C. and Victor, B., 1988, The impact of social support on mental and physical health, *Br. J. Med. Psychol.* 61:17.

Glaser, R., Kiecolt-Glaser, J.K., Stout, J.C., Tarr, K.L., Speicher, C.E. and Holliday, J.E., 1985, Stress-related impairments in cellular immunity, *Psychiatric Res.* 16:233.

Glass, D.C. and Singer, J.E., 1972, Urban stress: Experiments on noise and social stressors, Academic Press, New York.

Goodkin, K., Antoni, M.H. and Blaney, P.H., 1986, Stress and hopelessness in the promotion of cervical intra-epithelial neoplasma to an invasive squamous cell carcinoma of the cervix, *J. Psychosom. Res.* 30:67.

Gottlieb, B.H., ed., 1981, Social networks and social support. Sage, Beverly Hills, CA.

Gottlieb, B.H., ed., 1983, Social support strategies, Sage, Beverly Hills, CA

Grossarth-Maticek, R., Eysenck, H.J., Vetter, H. and Schmidt, P., 1986, Results of the Heidelberg prospective psychomatic intervention study. Paper presented at the international conference on health psychology, Tilburg University, 3-5 July, 30.

Haynes, S.G., Feinleib, M. and Kannel, W.B., 1980, The relationship of psychosocial factors to coronary heart disease in The Framingham Study III. Eight year incidence of coronary heart disease, *Am. J. Epidemiol.* 111:37.

Haynes, S.G., Eaker, E.D. and Feinlieb, M., 1983, Spouse behavior and coronary heart disease in men: Prospective results from the Framingham heart study, *Am. J. Epidemiol.* 118:1.

Hinkle, L.E. and Wolff, H.G., 1958, Ecologic investigations of the relationship between illness, life experiences and the social environment, *Ann. Intern. Med* 49:1373.

Holmes, T.G., and Rahe, R.H., 1967, The social readjustment rating scale, *J. Psychosom. Res.*, 11:213.Holohan, C.J. and Moos, R.H., 1981, Social support and psychological distress: A longitudinal analysis, *J. Abnormal Psychol.* 49:365.

House, J.S., 1981, Work stress and social support, Addison-Wesley, Reading, MA.

House, J.S., Robbins, C. and Metzner, H., 1982, The association of social relationships and activities and mortality: Prospective evidence from the Tecumseh community health study, *Am. J. Epidemiol.* 116:123.

Ivancevich, J.M. and Matteson, M.T., 1988, Type A behavior and the healthy individual, *Br. J. Med. Psychol.* 61:37.

Jacob, R.G. and Chesney, M.A., 1986, in:Psychological and behavioral methods to reduce cardiovascular reactivity, in:Handbook of stress, reactivity, and cardiovascular disease; K.A. Matthews, S.M. Weiss, T. Detre, T.M. Dembrowski, B.F. Falkner, S.B. Manuck and R.B. Williams Jr., eds., Wiley, New York.

Jenkins, C.D., 1983, Psychosocial and behavioral factors, in: Prevention of coronary heart disease; N. Kaplan and J. Stamler, eds., Saunders, Philadelphia.

Kaplan, H.B., 1983, Psychosocial stress: Trends in theory and research, Academic Press, New York.

Kasl, S.V. and Cobbs, S., 1982, Variability of stress effects among men experiencing job loss: in Handbook of stress, L. Golderger and S. Breznitze, eds., Free Press, New York.

Kasl, S.V. and Wells, J.A., 1985, Social support and health in the middle years, in: Social support and health, S. Cohen and L. Syme, eds., Academic Press, New York.

Kessler, R.C. and Mcleod, J.D., 1985, Social support and mental health in community studies, in: Social support and health, S. Cohen and L. Syme, eds., Academic Press, New York.

Lazarus, R.S., 1966, Psychological stress and the coping process, McGraw-Hill, New York.

Maslow, A.H., 1954, Motivation and personality, 2nd edition, Harper and Row, New York.

Matthews, K.A. and Haynes, S.G., 1986, Type A behavior pattern and coronary artery disease: Update and critical evaluation, *Am. J. Epidemiol.* 123(6):923.

Medalie, J., Snyder, M., Groen, J.J. et al., 1973, Agnina pectoris among 10,000 men: Five year incidence and univariate analysis, *Am. J. Med.* 55:583.

Paulhus, D. and Christie, R., 1981, Spheres of control: An interactionist approach to assessment of perceived control, in: Research with the locus of control construct, H.M. Lefcourt, ed., Academic Press, New York.

Paykel, E.S., Myers, J.K., Dienelt, M.N., et al., 1969, Life events and depression: A controlled study, *Arch. Gen. Psychiatry.* 21:753.

Paykel, E.S., Prusoff, B.A. and Uhlenhuth, E.H., 1971, Scaling of life events, *Arch. Gen. Psychiatry.* 25:340.

Price, V.A., 1982, Type A behavior pattern, Academic Press, New York.

Rahe, R.H., 1968, Life-change measurement as a predictor of illness, *Proc. Roy. Med.* 61:1124.

Reed, D., McGee, D., Yano, K. and Feinleib, M., 1983, Social networks and coronary heart disease among Japanese men in Hawaii, *Am. J. Epidemiol.* 117:384.

Review Panel, 1981, Coronary-prone behavior and coronary heart disease: A critical review, *Circulation*, 63:1199.

Roos, P.E. and Cohen, L.H., 1987, Sex roles and social support as moderators of life stress adjustments, *J. Pers. Soc. Psychol.* 52:576.

Rosenman, R.H., Brand, R.J., Jenkins, C.D., et al., 1975, Coronary heart disease in the Western Collaborative Group Study: Final follow-up experience of 8-1/2 years, JAMA, 233:872.

Roskies, E., 1978, Considerations in developing a treatment program for the coronary-prone (Type A) behavior pattern, in: Behavior medicine. Changing health life styles, P. Davidson, Ed., Brunner Mazel, New York.

Roskies, E., 1983, Stress management for Type A individuals, in: Stress reduction and prevention. D. Melchenbaum and M. Jaremko, eds., New York.

Roskin, M., 1982, Coping with life changes - A preventive social work approach, *Am. J. Community Psychol.* 10:331.

Ruberman, W., Weinblatt, E., Goldberg, D.D. and Chandbury, B., 1986, Psychosocial influences on mortality after myocardial infarction, *N. Eng. J. Med.*, 311:552.

Selye, H., 1956, The stress of life. McGraw-Hill, New York.

Suinn, R. M., 1975, The cardiac stress management program for Type A patients, *Cardiac Rehabilitation*, 5:12.

Suinn, R.M., 1978, The coronary-prone behavior pattern: A behavioral approach to intervention, in: Coronary-prone behavior, T. Dembrowski et al, eds., Springer-Verlag, New York.

Suinn, R.M., 1982, Intervention with Type A behaviors, *J. Consulting Clin. Psychol.* 50:933.

Theorell, T. and Rahe, R.H., 1971, Psychosocial factors and myocardial infarction. An inpatient study in Sweden, *J. Psychosom. Res.* 15:25.

Theorell, T. and Rahe, R.H., 1972, Behavior and life satisfactions characteristic of Swedish subjects with myocardial infarction, *J. Chron. Dis.* 25:139.

Vachon, M.L.S., Lyall, W.A.L., Rogers, J., Freedman-Letofsky, K. and Freedman, S.J., 1980, A controlled study of self-help intervention for widows, *Am. J Psychiatry.* 137:1380.

Wells, J.A., 1985, Chronic life situations and life change events, in: Measuring psychosocial variables in epidemiologic studies of cardiovascular disease, N.I.H., Bethesda, MD.

Williams, A.W., Ware, J.E. and Donald, C.A., 1981, A model of mental health, life events and social support applicable to general populations, *J. Health Soc. Behav.* 22:324.

Wills, T.A., 1985, Supportive functions of interpersonal relations, in: Social Support and health, S. Cohen and L. Syme, eds., Academic Press, New York.

Wright, R.A., Contrada, R.J. and Glass, D.C., 1985, Psychophysiologic correlates of Type A behavior, in: Advances in behavioral medicine, E.S. Katkin and S.B. Manuck, eds., J.A.I., Greenwich, CT.

SPECIAL NEEDS IN STRESS COPING FOR THE CLERGY

Sarah Horsman

Society of Mary and Martha
Dunsford, Exeter, England

INTRODUCTION

The Society of Mary and Martha is a charity offering care to people in Christian ministry who are under stress. As we cover all the different Christian denominations I use "minister" as a generic term to cover anyone in full-time Christian ministry, whether male or female, ordained or lay.

Ministers are not generally perceived as a group under high pressure. It is a standard joke that they only work one day a week. In an *Observer* feature on stress earlier this year (1), Professor Cary Cooper included clergymen in the "very low stress" occupational group, using the basic model of "demand and control" as predictors of job stress. Unfortunately this model does not make allowance for the complexities of the problems people face.

I would like to take this opportunity to put forward some of the reasons why ministers are under stress, and explain what the Society of Mary and Martha is doing to help. We have not done epidemiological research to determine the prevalence of stress and burnout within the ministry, we are simply making ourselves available to meet the needs of the people we see in distress. We see evidence of stress in the full range of physical, mental, emotional, relationship and work-related problems.

Men and women who enter Christian ministry are generally highly motivated both in their faith and in their desire to be of service to others. They share many of the same problems as other "helping professionals" who are giving out in emotionally demanding situations. However, there are a number of additional features which can combine to make the job even more stressful.

JOB STRUCTURE

The job of a minister is never finished. This applies to many other over-stretched caring agencies, but even more so in ministry. The job itself is very broad and it is simply never possible to feel that everything is done. Very few people do have the satisfaction of being completely on top of their workload, but most can at least physically leave it behind when they go home at the end of the day. Most ministers work from home which means that they are often tempted to work far longer hours than is safe. Even if they are mentally able to switch off and not feel guilty about the work left undone, there is a good chance that the telephone or the doorbell will intrude.

The routine of the minister's day can mean that taking time off is difficult. It is not uncommon to have most evenings taken up with meetings, and of course Sundays are busy. This means taking time off during the day on weekdays when others are at work which can feel uncomfortable and also helps to perpetuate the "one day a week" myth.

Lack of a written job description can provide scope for the energetic and the visionary to function very well, but the range of possibilities combined with the lack of boundaries can prove overwhelming. Ministers frequently suffer with role overload, role conflict, and role ambiguity, being expected to be everything from a preacher and teacher to counselor, administrator, odd-job man and fountain of all goodness.

PERSONAL LIFE

People's expectations on a minister's behavior are very high both on and off duty. Most caring professionals do not live and socialize among the same people for whom they care. Ministers do, which makes them very exposed. Many put an enormous amount of effort into maintaining a good image.

Whether they like it or not, a minister's family is far more involved in his work than the family of any other caring professional, especially if he is working from home. They too have expectations to live up to and suffer invasion of their privacy. The marriage and family relationships are so much in the public eye that there is a temptation to maintain a good image even if this is at the cost of dealing with underlying problems. People often delay far too long in seeking the help they need.

Money can be an additional strain for families in ministry. Very roughly, an average salary is about 8,000 pounds a year, or 100 pounds a week after tax. A house is provided, which makes it look like a better deal, but they do not own the property and so have nothing for retirement, or to leave to their children. Additional extras such as car, administration expenses, heating allowance, etc. are very much up to the local church. Some provide very well for their minister, but some ministers effectively subsidize the church out of their own already low salaries.

PASTORAL CARE AND SPIRITUAL NEEDS

In the Anglican church, clergy are expected to receive pastoral care from their Bishops who also have authority and disciplinary powers over them. People do worry about getting a black mark in the big book, especially with more unacceptable problems such as marriage difficulties or alcohol abuse. We welcome the growth in counseling services which are independent of authority structures within the church.

Ministers rightly see themselves as representatives of a loving God, and seek to demonstrate that love to other people. Unfortunately, it is all too easy to fall into the subtle trap of trying to be God, rather than point people towards Him. An impossible reputation to live up to! Internal pressures such as these can be just as stressful as external ones. There is a strong tendency for ministers to feel they need to justify their existence to their church, themselves, and perhaps to God. This increases as the status of ministers is lowered and they become more marginalized in society, and seems to be a major reason for overworking.

The Society of Mary and Martha formally became a charity in 1987, although its founder, Carl Lee, has personally been engaged in this type of work for many years. It is currently based at the Church Army Sheldon Centre because it does not yet have the necessary finance to purchase a property for its home base. The staff of the Sheldon Centre live as a small, informal community, and this concept of community is central to the future plans of the Society of Mary and Martha for several reasons.

One reason is that people can be welcomed much more informally into a community than into a professional counseling setting. Human warmth and friendship, time, and space to just be are all important for people who are under stress, exhausted, or recovering from a personal crisis. Counseling is only one ingredient, and not always the most important. Within a community, people can contribute useful labor and feel a sense of purpose within the group rather than just be on the receiving end of therapy. It is a very valuable setting in which care for body, mind and soul can be offered.

The Society's "12,000-mile Service" weeks are an attempt to combine this all important care of body, mind and soul. The motoring analogy is to encourage people to see this as normal preventive work for everyone, rather than just for the weaker bretheren. Great care is taken over small details of hospitality to enable people to feel welcome and, yes, loved. The program for the week is unhurried to create an experience of space and relaxation which is totally unfamiliar to many people. With all the practical concerns taken care of, people are free to relax, sleep, read and enjoy the local countryside. For married couples it is a golden opportunity to spend time with each other.

However, we are offering far more than simply a health farm "fresh air and good food" approach. People need to know how to incorporate the benefits of the week into their daily lives back home. Each day there is a 2-hour workshop introducing skills broadly related to stress management. Christians are often wary of "alternative" approaches to health at least partly because the movement is associated with oriental culture and spirituality, and sometimes with the occult. In order to give people the confidence and security they need, we always ensure that our workshop leaders are themselves committed Christians. We are applying, in a broader context, the basic requirements for effective psychotherapeutic help:

1. a good rapport between client and therapist

2. a mutually acceptable technique

3. a "safe" place for both client and therapist

It is simply no use to tell people to change their attitudes or practice activities which they feel are in conflict with their religious beliefs. The setting needs to be "safe" if people are to be open enough to learn, and we are able to provide a safe environment for this group of people. Successful workshops so far have included relaxation, meditation, massage and movement, and we are keen to include others in the future.

All activities are completely optional for our guests to help them experience a freedom from the "I ought to" which rules so many lives. Other activities on offer include organized walks, good films and manual work such as gardening. People are also welcome to join the community for its regular worship each day. The spiritual side is not always very up front, but it underpins all that we do.

One problem of gathering a lot of helping professionals together in a group is that they all try to sort out each other's problems. This may be force of habit, but it is also a very good way of avoiding dealing with their own agenda. For this reason we always have people on the helping team who are available to listen and counsel when required. Guests are explicitly forbidden to counsel each other, which often has the paradoxical effect of allowing people to become more genuinely close to each other.

Both for the "12,000-mile Service" weeks, and in our other contacts, we try to avoid the formal "counseling" image. In the first place, the whole set up is much more informal. Because we live and work on the job, one of us is available on the telephone throughout the day. If someone needs to talk they can do so there and then, or arrange to meet later if they are local. As we are the only resource of our kind in the country, many calls do come from a distance, so much of our work is done on the telephone.

Being a broader organization than just a counseling service has other advantages. It is often a very big step for people to ask directly for counseling, but with the Society of Mary and Martha the initial request might be for information about resources, retreats, the Society itself, or events we are running. The contact is made over a more neutral issue which then gives the necessary confidence to take things further. We are not bound by an hourly-appointment system which is often not flexible enough to accommodate human needs. Casual conversations often give people opportunities to bring up issues of concern which can be followed up at once or later on.

Another unusual aspect of the way we work is a break away from the traditional roles of counselor and client. People coming to us for help on one day, might have something we can receive from them on another. Relationships with some people last for many years, and our work and social lives are so intimately related that some become genuine friends.

Although ministers are working closely with people all day, every day, it can be a lonely life because so many of the relationships are one-way. Professional and social isolation can be far greater than is immediately apparent. So often people just need someone who will listen and be willing to be there. As helpers, we have a great urge to do something helpful, but *being* who we are and *being* there is sometimes the most valuable thing we can offer. In a similar way, many ministers are helped simply by knowing that the Society of Mary and Martha is available should they need it.

Professional counselors may be envious of the freedom of the structures within which we work, but that freedom has both its costs and its risks. A group of people does not become a community without a good deal of commitment and sheer hard work. Being part of the Society of Mary and Martha is not just a job, but a complete way of life. Without our own individual Christian faith, and each continually seeking to be more spiritually and emotionally whole, our corporate work would certainly founder. Much of our personal "freedom" and spare time is sacrificed, but this is rewarded by the variety of our work and the mutual support of living in a group. We are as tempted to overwork as anyone else in Christian ministry, and have to work at creating a balanced lifestyle for ourselves. It is no bad thing that we are in many ways as vulnerable as those to whom we seek to minister, and exposed to some of the same pressures. Our own lives are far from stress free which means we need to put into practice every scrap of advice we presume to offer to others.

We often find that people know very little about basic stress symptoms and causes of stress. One of our functions is to educate ministers, and indeed the wider church, on this subject. I have found Dr. Peter Nixon's concept of human function curve (2) particularly useful in giving people guidelines on how to live within their resources. Massage, basic relaxation and breathing techniques are also important in dealing with some of the physical symptoms of stress. On a more fundamental level, we help people to explore their motivation and attitudes to their ministry, to pinpoint where the pressures are coming from, and enable people to develop more realistic expectations of themselves. Spiritual and emotional problems can be closely linked, in which case it is helpful to deal with the two together.

The Society aims to encourage ministers to be more open with each other about the joys and pitfalls of their chosen work, and to learn to offer one another more effective support. This could be classed as care which is truly preventive. We also realize that there are many practices and structures within the church which cause stress, and which the individual is powerless to change. We may well find ourselves developing work as a pressure group to try and effect change.

In conclusion, the Society of Mary and Martha is seeking to make good use of modern knowledge in the field of stress management. As Christians, we also have a rich tradition of caring which demands that we go beyond basic professional structures. We offer people our love as well as counsel and practical help. We are available to be of service to people rather than expect them to serve our timetable. We recognize our own needs to receive as well as give, and seek to develop reciprocal relationships. We recognize how central a person's spirituality is to their total functioning, and ensure that help and encouragement is available on this level as well. We hope that there can be a fruitful exchange between the church and secular professions to enable us all to care more effectively for people.

REFERENCES

(1) Cooper, C. *Observer Magazine*, 3 April (1988).

(2) Nixon, P. The human function curve. *The Practitioner* 217:765-769 and 935-944 (1976).

STRESS-COPING STRATEGIES IN BUSINESS AND INDUSTRY

COPING WITH OCCUPATIONAL STRESS AMONG PROFESSIONAL ENGINEERS

Tim Newton

University of Edinburgh
Edinburgh, Scotland

Introduction

The following research demonstrates how people cope with occupational stress. One way to do this is to compare traditional models of occupation stress with the model that guides this research. Figure 1 summarizes these simple models of occupational stress.

This figure is a crude but appropriate model of early occupational stress research. While it provides information about which job demands were associated with stress, it says little about why particular job demands appeared to be stressful (what factors moderate the relationship between job demands and whether or not individuals in the job feel stressed). To answer this question, researchers need to look more closely at the personal and environmental resources that can be used in coping with stress, since the extent to which individuals experience strain over time is likely to depend on the perceived and real consequences of how they cope with stress.

THE PEDR MODEL

The Person-Environment Demands and Resources (PEDR) model (illustrated in Figure 2) summarizes the key issues in the stress process. The unique aspects of this model are its attention to both personal and environmental resources and its focus on interactions between the elements of the model. According to the model, the way in which individuals appraise and cope with stress is a function of personal and environmental demands and resources.

```
Job            ------->-------------->     Psychological/
Demands            (Lead To)               Physiological
                                           Strain

E.G. ;                                     E.G. ;
Role Overload      ------->-------->       Anxiety
```

Figure l. A simple stress model

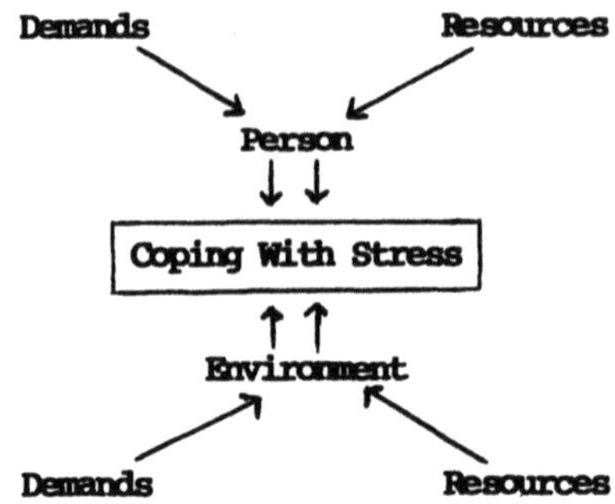

Figure 2. The Person-Environment Demands and Stress Model (PEDR)

In looking at occupational stress from the environmental side, there are a variety of job demands. In addition, however, there are also resources available, such as the opportunity to delegate some work to subordinates, or the existence of experienced and helpful secretarial support. Similarly, the individual has demands (needs in the work environment) and resources (skills, values and beliefs). Figure 3 illustrates the interaction of all elements of the model. For example, consider a sudden and potentially difficult increase in workload. If the environmental resource of a suitably skilled subordinate is available, new work may be delegated. However, the choice to delegate does not solely depend on the environmental opportunity to delegate to a skilled subordinate; it is also dependent on whether the individual possesses the leadership skills to be able to delegate. If the skills at leading and supervising others are poor, the effects of delegating may be of limited help or even counter- productive. In any case, if the personal demand of a strong need to maintain control is present, there may be an extreme resistance to delegate unless the need is absolute, since letting subordinates do the work creates uncertainty and less personal control. The interaction of both personal demands and personal environmental resources must be considered in understanding how someone appraises stress and copes with stress. (Further details of this model are provided in Newton, 1988a.)

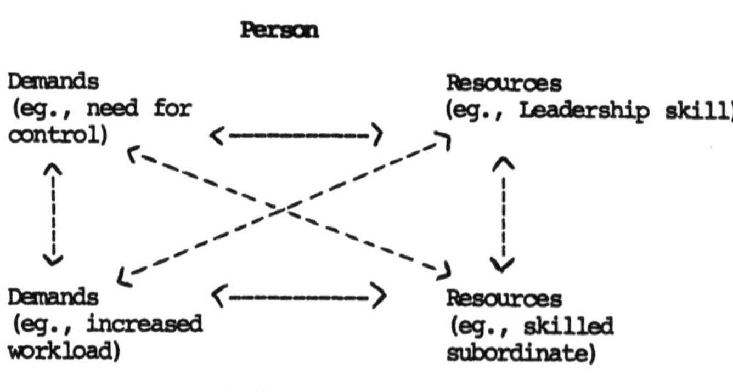

Figure 3. Illustrating the interaction of all elements of the model

THE RESEARCH

The "person side" of the PEDR model provides the focus for this research; specifically, research findings relating to the Type A Behavior Pattern (TABP). In the context of the PEDR model, Type A represents a particular type of personal demand, or need, which affects long-term coping style. This perspective on Type A derives from Glass's theory that the underlying motivation for the Type A behavior pattern is a need to maintain control (Glass, 1977).

As a prelude to this research, a brief background to the interest in TABP is appropriate. The concept of Type A has become somewhat unclear. It developed from the hypothesis of some U.S. medical researchers in the early fifties, who "did not believe that the striking 20th century increase of rates of CHD (Coronary Heart Disease) could be adequately explained by diet" or other known risk factors (Rosenman & Chesney, 1980). These researchers suspected that the then relative immunity of American women to CHD was not due to differences of diet or hormone, but rather was due to less exposure to the same socio-economic milieu and associated stress as their coronary-prone male counterpart. They also began to notice that many of their CHD patients under 60 exhibited a certain pattern of behavior (Rosenman & Chesney, 1980). This behavior was characterized by apparent impatience, aggressiveness, competitiveness, and a higher than average level of drive as well as a notable potential for hostility. In addition, these individuals tended to exhibit a rapidity of physical movement, a faster rate of speech and a higher than average level of muscle tension. Individuals who exhibited this pattern of behavior were subsequently termed "Type A's," with those showing fewer of these characteristics called "Type B's." Type A was frequently subtitled the "coronary-prone" behavior pattern because prospective studies which, after controlling for other known risk factors such as exercise, diet, smoking, etc. (e.g., Rosenman, Brand, Sholtz & Friedman, 1976; Haynes, Feinleib & Kannel, 1980) indicated that the TABP represented a CHD risk factor.

Two other points should be noted about TABP. First, and contrary to how it is often presented in the literature, Type A was conceived as a reaction to the environment which *any individual* might exhibit if placed in a sufficiently challenging environment and not as a simple personality trait(Rosenman and Chesney, 1980, p.4) At the right time, in the right place, it is theoretically possible that anyone can exhibit Type A behavior characteristics. Secondly, some studies have failed to replicate the link between TABP and CHD (e.g., Shekelle et al, 1985). However, I think that this controversy does not detract from the interest of understanding Type A as a means of coping with stress, because it is conceived of as a long-term style of coping. Perhaps even more significantly, a high volume of research effort has gone into defining Type A and examining its relationship to psychological and physical health. However, what is surprising about TABP research is that there have been few studies examining how TABP may moderate the relationship between job demands experienced at work and the psychological strain employees report. In the context of the PEDR model, the focus of this research is on the relationship between TABP (a personal demand) and job demand (an environmental demand) in terms of their impact on stress appraisal and psychological strain.

METHODOLOGY

This study, conducted with Tony Keenan, investigated the work experiences of young engineers who had been contacted in 1980 when they were in their final year of study at one of six British universities, three in Scotland and three in England. At that time they were asked to complete a short questionnaire. Follow- up occurred six months after they left the university and then at approximately yearly intervals. Each time they were mailed a questionnaire and asked to complete it.

As regards the measures employed, many of these were constructed and tested in the context of the research, though the nine-item Type A scale is very similar to that employed in the large scale stress study of researchers at the Institute for Social Research at the University of Michigan (French et al, 1982). The Type A scale was developed by Keenan and McBain (1979), who provide psychometric analyses employing the scale. Based on a slight adaptation of the scale, Orpen (1982) reports a $r=.44$ with the Bortner TABP scale, and a $r=.41$ with the Sales scale, as well as a $r_{bis}=.37$ with the observational assessment of a trained counselor. These validity correlations are comparable with those observed with other Type A scales (Bynre, Rosenman, Schiller, & Chesney, 1985). *Further details of all the measures employed in the study, together with relevant psychometric analyses, can be found in Keenan and Newton (1984 1987), Newton and Keenan (1985, 1987) and Newton (1987).*

A major question for research is whether TABP, as a personal demand, moderates the relationship between job (environmental) demands and the level of psychological strain reported. For instance, with increasing demands at work, Type A's might report higher levels of strain than Type B's. Certainly some authors argued that it would. Caplan and Jones (1975), for example, concluded: "Stress had its greatest effect on strain in the hard-driving, involved, Type A person."

Given the characteristics of Type A's (feeling time pressures, being competitive and aggressive, living life at a faster pace), such a conclusion seems intuitively appealing. However, the small amount of research in this area does not necessarily support this. There is a fair degree of uncertainty as to whether Type A's or Type B's would report more strain with increasing demands at work (Newton, 1987).

The analyses undertaken in the present research were designed to address precisely this issue. One difference between the present and previous research is that a longitudinal design was employed, with changes in reported levels of job demand related to changes in levels of psychological strain. The changes were observed over a two-year interval, from when the engineers had been working for a year after their graduation to when they had been working for three years. The interesting aspect of this design is that as Type A was being posited as a personal demand affecting longer-term coping style, it was appropriate to examine how it would moderate the relationship between job demands and strain over a lengthy interval, in this case two years.

Unlike most earlier research in this area, the analyses were based on moderated hierarchical regression rather than sub-group correlation analyses. The form of the moderator analysis is summarized below in algebraic form:

$$Y = a + b_1X_1 + b_2X_2 + b_3X_3 + b_4X_4 + b_5X_3.X_4$$

where Y = algebraic change in strain from T_1 to T_2, X_1 = strain at T_1, X_2 = job demands at T_1, X_3 = algebraic change in job demands from T_1 to T_2, X_4 = TABP.

This represents an adaptation of the conventional moderated regression procedure (Zedeck, 1971), applying it to the analysis of change data. Since change scores were employed here, there is a need to partial out the effect of T_1 scores, since the level of the T_1 score affects the meaning of any increase or decrease in demands or strain. (The simplest example here is that of salary increases: say individual A receives a salary increase from time 1 at £5000 to time 2 at £6000 , while B gets a rise from £50,000 to £51,000 over the same period. Both have the same salary increase, £1000, but the meaning is likely to be very different for the two individuals because of their different T1 scores. "A" has a salary increase of 20 percent, while "B" has an increase of only 2 percent).

While moderated regression analysis has greater validity than sub-group analysis (Zedeck, 1971; Arnold, 1982), it should be noted that it tends to be a very conservative approach; also, the analysis yields partial correlation coefficients or beta coefficients that are limited in strength. Therefore, in common with other researchers undertaking moderator analyses (e.g., Caplan & Jones, 1975), significance was set at $p < .10$, in order to guard against the probability of a Type II error.

Going straight to the heart of the results, consider the question of whether TABP moderates the relationship between job demand and strain. Five types of job demand were assessed, together with six forms of psychological strain. They are detailed in Table 1, which presents the critical results. While the size of these partial correlation coefficients in Table 1 is not very large compared with simple correlation coefficients, it should be kept in mind that these represent interaction effects, after the main effects have been controlled for. However, what is most interesting about these results is the pattern of the significant interaction effects. *All of the coefficients that are significant are negative in direction*, which suggests that where TABP moderates the relationship between job demands and psychological strain, it is Type B's, not A's, that will report less strain. That is to say, where TABP does moderate, increases in a job demand will be associated with greater increases in pyschological strain among Type B's than Type A's. This suggests that contrary to earlier conclusions, *stress has its greatest effect upon strain among Type B's, not A's.*

DISCUSSION

The question remains: why should Type A's report lower increases in strain, given that the characteristics of Type A behavior, such as aggressiveness, competitiveness, time-urgency, etc., might make them appear more likely to experience greater strain with increasing job demands? There are a number of possible answers to this question.

1. Type A's simply like their coping style; perhaps because they find it more exciting to be ambitious, aggressive, competitive, etc. More demanding environments may provide more opportunities to enact the TABP, with the result that Type A's may report greater satisfaction and less strain than Type B's. While Type A's may like their hard-driving coping style, this does not, of course, mean that it does not have potential negative health consequences.

2. The individual using the TABP may actually be more successful at dealing with job demands. Being ambitious, competitive, aggressive, etc., may have its pay-offs.

Table 1. Moderation of the relationship between changes in job demand and psychological strain by the TABP

Job Demands	Job Dis-satisfaction	Anxiety	Anger	Frustr-ation	Host-ility	Alien-ation
Role Conflict	-.04[a]	-.05	.01	-.12**	.01	.05
Role Ambiguity	-.02	-.14**	.07	-.10*	-.02	.05
Quantitative High-load	-.02	-.12**	-.08	-.09	-.06	-.05
Qualitative Low-load	-.10*	.05	.04	.01	.01	.04
Environmental Frustration	-.06	-.01	-.14**	-.19***	-.08	-.09*

[a]The figures represent the partial correlation coefficient when the interaction terms (job demands x TABP) were entered last into the regression equation.

*$p < .10$
**$p < .05$
***$p < .01$

3. Type A's may repress feelings of psychological strain more than Type B's, and therefore lower strain levels are observed. There is a problem, however, with this explanation. The simple product-moment correlations between Type A and strain indicate that overall Type A's report higher strain on a number of strain variables. This suggests that, at least for some forms of strain, Type A's do not repress more successfully than Type B's.

4. Type A's will only report lower strain than B's when there are low-to-moderate demand levels; where demand levels are high, however, Type A's may report higher strain. The present findings could result, therefore, from assessing a sample with low-to-moderate job demand levels. There is some support for this hypothesis in the laboratory work of Glass and his colleagues, who observed that while Type B's exhibited the worst task performance under conditions of moderate demand (e.g., completing tasks while subject to moderate noise levels), Type A's performed worst where demand levels were high (e.g., Glass, 1977).

This fourth explanation, like the third, is also not entirely supported by present research analyses. Looking at the moderator findings, there were two types of job demand where demand levels were fairly high among Type A's. These were environmental frustration and quantitative high-load. For example, with quantitative load, 52 percent of Type A's reported scores at or above point 4 on the 5-point Likert-type scales used. If the fourth explanation is valid, one would expect to observe higher strain scores among Type A's where there were increases in either environmental frustration or quantitative load. However, the results do not support this inference since, whether significant or not, all the partial correlations with quantitative high-load and environmental frustration are negative in direction (see Table 1).

Comparing the four explanations, explanations one and two emerge least unscathed, suggesting that the observed findings may result from the fact that Type A's essentially grow to like their particular style of behavior in the context of their work environment, and indeed their coping style may be more effective than that of Type B's. However, before finally backing this explanation, a word of caution is necessary. Other researchers (Newton and Keenan, 1985) have found that in coping with *short-term acute stress*, Type A's were associated with coping behavior which would appear to be neither particularly effective nor the kind of behavior in which people would necessarily like to be engaged. To provide an idea of these Type A coping behaviors, consider the following responses given by the engineers when asked to describe a stressful incident that had occurred at work within the previous two weeks. Coping behavior was assessed by asking, "How did you handle the stressful incident?"

This first category of Type A response relates to situations where Type A's ventilated their feelings towards others:

> "I let people know how I felt."
>
> "Badly, I allowed my frustration and disillusion to show and allowed my superior's annoyance to upset me."

The second association with Type A was that they were more likely to express helplessness when trying to cope:

> "Just left it, the people doing the assessment were particularly stubborn and it would not have been worth arguing."
>
> "Accept the situation and try to make the most of it as I didn't have much choice short of resigning."

At least with these situations of acute stress, Type A's do not look like archetypal successful copers. Why, then, do they report *less* strain than Type B's when there are increases in the level of job demand? It may appear that there are no valid explanations and hypotheses, but there is an escape in the theory of Glass (1977). He asserts that the underlying motivation of Type A behavior is a greater than average *need* to maintain control. Following Glass's theory, what the longitudinal results of this study may indicate is that *providing* Type A's generally stay in control of their jobs, they may experience the same or lower increases in strain than B's. However, in temporary situations of acute stress where Type A's lose control, they are likely to react with the type of behavior which Glass predicted: ventilation of feelings where control is severely threatened and the expression of total helplessness as soon as control is perceived as lost. However, this behavior may only apply to acute stress situations. Providing that there are not too many of these, Type A's may feel perfectly happy with the Type A style of coping and believe that it is generally effective. At a physiological level, however, the type of "fast-lane" life-style suggested by the TABP, may take its toll.

CONCLUSION

Combining these research findings with those linking Type A to CHD suggests an image of Type A's happily speeding along in the fast-lane at an aggressive, competitive pace, until their "vehicle" starts to either seriously deteriorate (e.g., very high blood pressure) or they crash (e.g., a coronary attack). Since their hard-driving style may seem generally enjoyable and successful to them (with the exception of control threatening acute stresses), Type A's may not feel or report greater psychological strain. However, at the physiological level, health problems may be accruing.

IMPLICATIONS FOR FUTURE RESEARCH

What has been presented here is a conjecture based on the analyses of current research. As usual, however, there is a need for further research. In particular, further research on the repression hypothesis is required. Although several writers have advanced it, there is little research directly examining it (Newton, 1988b). Research which focuses on how Type A's feel about and evaluate their own coping behavior would provide data on the hypotheses that Type A's are more effective copers who like the TABP and feel contented with their general style of coping. Finally, more studies which compare Type A's response to both acute and chronic stress are needed, since little information on the comparability of Type A's behavior across differing temporal forms of stress is currently available.

REFERENCES

Arnold, H.J. (1982). Moderator variables: A clarification of conceptual, analytic, and psychometric issues. *Organizational Behavior and Human Performance*, *29*, 143-174.

Caplan, R.D., & Jones, K.W. (1975). Effects of work load, role ambiguity, and Type A personality on anxiety, depression, and heart rate. *Journal of Applied Psychology*, *60*(6), 713-719.

Glass, D.C. (1977). *Behavior Patterns, Stress and Coronary Disease*. Hillsdale, New Jersey: Lawrence Erlbaum Assoicates.

Haynes, S., Feinleib, M., & Kannel, W.B. (1980). The relationship of psychosocial factors to coronary heart disease: III. Eight-year incidence of coronary heart disease. *American Journal of Epidemiology*, *111*, (1), 37-58.

Keenan, A., & McBain, G.D.M. (1979). Effects of Type A behaviour, intolerance of ambiguity, and locus of control on the relationship between role stress and work-related outcomes. *Journal of Occupational Psychology*, *52*, 1-9.

Keenan, A., & Newton, T.J. (1984). Frustration in organizations: Relationships to role stress, climate and psychological strain. *Journal of Occupational Psychology*, *57*, 57-65.

Keenan, A., & Newton, T.J. (1987). Work difficulties and stress in young professional engineers. *Journal of Occupational Psychology*, *60*, 133-145.

Newton, T.J., & Keenan, A. (1985). Coping with work-related stress. *Human Relations*, *38*(2), 107-126.

Newton, T.J. (1987). *Coping with Occupational Stress: An Investigation among Graduate Engineers*. Doctoral thesis, Heriot-Watt University, Edinburgh.

Newton, T.J., & Keenan, A. (1987). Role stress reexamined: An investigation of role stress predictors. *Organizational Behavior and Human Decision Processes*, *40*, 346-368.

Newton, T.J. (1988a). *Have We Really Considered the Person and the Environment in Models of Occupational Stress Processes: The Person-Environment Demands and Resources Model*. University of Edinburgh, Department of Business Studies, Working Paper.

Newton, T.J. (1988b). *Occupational Stress and Coping with Stress: A Critique*. University of Edinburgh, Department of Business Studies, Working Paper Series, 88/8.

Orpen, C. (1982). Type A personality as a moderator of the effects of role conflict, role ambiguity and role overload on individual strain. *Journal of Human Stress*, *8*, (2), 8-14.

Rosenman, R.H., Brand, R.J., Sholtz, R.I., & Friedman, M. (1976). Multivariate prediction of coronary heart disease during 8.5 year follow-up in the Western Collaborative Group Study. *American Journal of Cardiology*, *37*, 903-910.

Rosenman, R.H., & Chesney, M.A. (11980). The Relationship of Type A Behavior Pattern to Coronary Heart Disease. *Activitas Nervosa Superior*, *22*, (1), 1-45.

Shekelle, R., Hulley, S., Neaton, J., Billings, J., Borhani, N., Gerace, T., Jacobs, D., Lasser, N., Mittlemark, M., Stamler, J. and the MRFIT Research Group. The MRFIT behavior pattern study: II. Type A behavior pattern and incidence of coronary heart disease. *American Journal of Epidemiology*, *122*, 559-570.

Zedeck, S. (1971). Problems with the use of moderator variables. *Psychological Bulletin*, *76*, 295-310.

WORK-SITE STRESS AND CORONARY HEART DISEASE AMONG FOREMEN IN HEAVY INDUSTRY

Uwe Stocksmeier

Institut für Sozialmedizin,
Praevention und Rehabilitation
Haupstr, Tutzing
West-Germany

INTRODUCTION

The first phase of the project "Coronary Heart Diseases and Industrial Workshop Places" was aimed at defining, by means of two case control studies (n_{TG} = 299; n_{CG} = 216/n_{TG} = 912; n_{CG} = 180 males), and two clinical case studies (n = 13 and n = 18 male patients after cardiac infarction), those industrial work places where coronary heart diseases (CHD) and cardiac infarction (CI) are found most frequently.

In this phase of the project, two typical high risk occupations were defined. One of these involved professional drivers (taxi drivers, bus drivers, etc.). The other high risk professional endeavors consisted of foremen who were employed at industrial work places (group leaders, etc.). Importantly, the interpretation of these initial results led to the conclusion that the stress that foremen encounter could be considered as a paradigm for the stress causing CHD. Therefore, the second phase of the project involved an investigation of stress experienced by industrial foremen.

METHODS

In the Federal Republic of Germany, 151 foremen in nine enterprises were examined in two successive partial studies. Stress at the work place and coping behavior were registered by extensive standardized interviews and questionnaires.

The foremen were then further examined by an open interview before the other measurements were taken. The qualitative data from these interviews provide the focus of this article. Medical data (dependent variables), were registered with diverse methods (questionnaires, anamnestic interrogation by a medical doctor, determination of 31 blood parameters, ECG, blood pressure measurement, etc.). A case study of qualitative data produced the following definitions:

1) Typical stress constellations

2) Typical patterns of coping behavior

3) Functional interactions of objective stress and subjective coping behavior

On the other hand, quantitative data (standardized interrogation in writing, lab, medical data) were primarily used for answering the following questions:

1) Can qualitatively found constellations of stress and coping behaviors be confirmed by quantitative data, and if so how far?

2) Are there correlations between stress at work and coping behavior and impairments of health (especially CHD)?

TYPICAL STRESS FACTORS CONFRONTING FOREMEN

The most threatening stress for foremen was produced by time pressure and role pressure. Time pressure was found to be a characteristic of the daily encounters confronting foremen. This phenomenon is called "specific pathognomic time pressure." Not surprisingly, this type of time pressure and the situations where it is a negative factor are marked by a collapse of regulated working process and by a disappearance of an ordered regulation of action. In such situations the actions of foremen are characterized more as reactions than planned, self-regulated actions. Additional characteristics of such situations are:

- inconsistent demands (which are temporarily and/or factually incompatible)

- pressure for constant improvisation.

Unfortunately, some enterprises are hindered by the development of certain professional responsibilities that cause the development of time pressure. These occurrences are:

- areas and departments with little routine work (e.g., construction of prototypes, continually changing serial production, service departments);

- working domains where planning was inadequate, and the operational strategies did not wholly capture the interior structure of the work to be done. In these cases rationalization did not result in better chances to complete the work, but instead resulted in creating more intensive work and work related pressure;

- working domains with especially high responsibilities (e.g., "terminal stations" involving the final steps in production lines where time limits are to be kept). This is valid especially for "bottle neck domains," departments that depend on the continuity of production lines.

Also, management frequently fails to provide workers in such critical positions with sufficient resources, counting on the efforts and flexibility of the workers to overcome the lack.

For instance, the individuals exposed to substantial professional pressures are the foremen. The most frequently occurring example of increased work pressures involve time. As previously mentioned, management can impose unrealistic time expectations of the people most responsible for worker production, the foremen. There is one other type of conflict confronting foremen, and that involves role conflict. The role conflict unique to foremen results from two types of employer expectations:

- a foreman has to convey to his subordinates management's concerns, and communicate to management any worker's misconduct or inefficiency;

- at the same time he must promote the workers legitimate interests (protection function).

He is the classic shock absorber! Compared to the obligation intrinsic to the foreman's position to convey the pressure from above to his subordinates, there is no official regulation to motivate his protective function. It certainly exists, however, and it serves the functional interest of the enterprise. Importantly, it is evident that the foreman is dependent on the good will and cooperation of his subordinates if he wants to meet the demands of production.

These two expectations are clearly difficult to fulfill, and therefore become sources of conflict. If production quotas are not met, reprimanding action must follow. The foreman is forced to comply permanently with conflicting expectations (role pressure). It is because of role pressure that the foreman wishing to avoid losing the cooperation of his subordinates tries to minimize pressure originating from management creating a "buffer situation." In order for this buffer situation to exist, the foreman must provide emotional discipline and therein lies the real pathogenic potential of role pressure. Over time situations can arise that put the foreman in danger of being severely chastised if he does not meet everyone's expectations while at the same time he is unable to control the parameters of the situation.

TYPICAL STRESS PATTERNS AND RESULTANT HEALTH IMPAIRMENTS

The stress factors of time and role pressure are significantly correlated to CHD, especially with the variables "symptoms of coronary disturbances," "angina-pectoris symptoms," and "hints at CHD."

In the 40-50 age group, "hints at CHD" had a more significant correlation with stress factors than with risk factors. In the age group under 40, this pattern of correlation is inversed: risk factors are more highly correlated with "hints at CHD" than are stress factors. In the age group 50 and older correlations between stress factors and possible CHD no longer exist. This can be attributed to a certain "desensibilization" concerning stress factors. Also, there is a profound manifestation of CHD in this age group. Finally, research revealed a significant correlation between the stress level experienced at work and general physical and psychic impairment. A similar correlation involving poor worker efficiency and stress also existed. However, no readily evident relationship between organic diseases and stress was found.

TYPICAL PATTERNS OF COPING BEHAVIOR AND THEIR EFFECTS ON HEALTH

Factory foremen's patterns of coping behavior show considerable weaker correlations to CHD than do the corresponding stress factors. Highly significant correlations between singular characteristics of the coping behavior in buffer situations and "symptoms of coronary disturbances" were found only in part of the qualitative phase. Also, a correlation between disturbances of the gastrointestinal tract and the motoric apparatus with coping strategies was found. More correlations were found between stress and the impairment of general "physical" and "psychic" health, as well as distinct correlations between pathological patterns of coping behavior and disturbances of efficiency and sleep. Finally, the inability to settle conflicts in a resolute manner (emotional discipline), a base element of the pattern of coping behavior, was found to correlate with increased lipid levels (cholesterol, LDL-cholesterol, LDL/HDL-factor).

FUNCTIONAL INTERACTIONS OF STRESS AND COPING BEHAVIOR

This study showed that correlations between subjective coping behavior (pressure behavior, buffer behavior) and real stress at the work place (time pressure, role pressure) are systematic strategies (theorem of the "functional interaction"). Results supported, on several levels, the thesis that pressure situations can only be coped with by pathogenic behavior. Only the pressure and buffer behavior of the foremen keeps the working process consistent. Therefore, pathogenic patterns of coping behavior can be considered as making the objective working situation pliant with individuality. Although it is true that pressure and buffer behavior are manifested as maintaining objective stressor working conditions, the behaviors are also necessary subjective supplements to time and role pressure. A certain type of working condition demands the implementation of specific patterns of coping behavior. Strategies of selection and socialization processes are the mechanisms which cause this interaction.

MEDICAL INDICATORS OF STRESS

Foremen between 40 and 60 years of age answered affirmatively questions regarding stress and nervous strain caused by working conditions, in a manner similar to patients of the Bavarian cardiac infarction study. The inference here is that foremen are subjected to a high risk of cardiac infarction. Among the manifest diseases which the foremen saw as being correlated with their work, CHD were the most often mentioned, and psychic disturbances the next. Interestingly, an analysis of the index revealed highly significant correlations between validated variables of CHD and time and role pressure.

Additionally, documentation established a significant correlation between CHD and risk factors such as high blood pressure, hypercholesteraemia, hypertriglyceridaemia, diabetes, increased relative fluidity, smoking, weight problems, after Broca and lack of motion and impairments of physical and psychic health, and stress at work. Significant correlational data established a relationship between these listed variables and stress at work. Furthermore, these patterns of coping styles as indicated by the listed physical maladies are most evident in workers 40-50 years of age. It is here diseases develop but do not yet manifest themselves. Therefore, physical and psychic impairments of health in this age group can be considered to be more basic than CHD symptoms. Also, a comparison with other studies revealed that twice as many subjects showed high blood pressure as a risk factor. The realization must be made that blood pressure levels were independent of age, and that in the age group of 40-50 years no correlations with behavior risk factors could be found. The frequency among subjects of high blood pressure can be attributed to the high psychosocial stress in the work of foremen. A correlation between blood pressure and genetic disposition (high blood pressure of the mother) was found only in the group under 40. This observation is valid for the systolic as well as the diastolic blood pressure. Yet another important characteristic of this research is that the distribution of frequencies of the investigated risk factors were not at variance with other similar studies.

Compared with our 1979 study, this sample of foremen had a higher percentage of persons with increased hematocrite values and increased erythrocytes. When increased, these parameters lead to loss of fluidity, considered a risk factor for CHD. As an indicator for this loss of fluidity, the flowing speed of the blood (relative fluidity) was analyzed. Thus, a new risk factor in the risk-factor program was defined. The discovery that blood pressure, LDL-cholesterol and cholesterol were uncorrelated to behavior risk factors in the total sample was made. Therefore, these three risk factors were seen as being the more important indicators of psychosocial stress and resultant coping behavior than other risk factors. Triglyceride and uric acid were not as reliable in indicating stressors because they are highly correlated with other risk factors such as existing diseases, genetic dispositions and abuse of alcohol.

In conclusion, the study's results point to the possibility that connections between medical data and specific patterns of stress and coping behavior can be legitimately formulated.

FOREMEN IN THE INDUSTRY AS RISK GROUP FOR CHD

The first (retrospective) phase of the investigation, "Coronary Heart Diseases and Industrial Work Places," was to find those work places where CHD and CI were observed to be above the average. The research was also intended to investigate more closely those work environments with a "healthy" sample. This identification would allow the definiton of the potential mechanisms causing CHD and CI. It would then be possible to use this information in formulating preventive strategies. Possibly the reasons for foremen's work being prone to causing CI are the following:

1) Foremen are less physically mobile. Therefore, actual working conditions can be stressful.

2) More than other professions, a typical pattern of stress can be found with foremen in industry: stress confronting foremen is generated by general characteristics of industrial working structures.

3) The fact that an above average number of foremen are found in the CI-group in the first phase can be explained by the pathogenity of their work places.

MEDICAL RESULTS

The significant medical findings of the study include some of the following information. Sixty-seven percent of the foremen had heart disturbances. Furthermore, 30% were found to have CHD.

The strongest correlations of diverse variables of CHD were found to involve impairments of psychic and physical health. Also, several psychosocial stress and coping behavior indices characteristic of foremen (e.g., "time pressure" and "between two stools") were identified.

Data revealed psychosocial stress and coping behavior showed stronger correlations with impairments of well-feeling than with variables of CHD. Therefore, physical and psychic impairments can be considered to involve a definite connection between psychosocial stress and CHD. Variables of CHD showed no significant correlation between "family and private troubles" and "genetic disposition." Significant correlation, however, was found between psychic impairment of "well-feeling" and "family and private troubles." There is, accordingly, a causality between stress at work and psychic impairments of health. Mutual influences between family variables and psychic disturbances must be taken into account.

Surprisingly, nearly the same percentage of subjects from both groups studied, healthy as well as CI patients, complained of nervous strain and overtaxation at their work places. More CHD and physical impairments of health were found with increasing age, while psychic impairments of health counted heavily in the age group between 40 and 50. In this group there were the strongest correlations between impairment of well-feeling and psychosocial stress. Consequently prevention in this age groups would seem to be of the utmost importance.

CHD variables correlate to the number of risk factors more than to the sum score of the risk factors. As impairments of physical and psychic health show no correlations to risk factors, it is possible that CHD can be caused by risk factors as well as by feelings of well-being with or without risk factors. Unlike others, our study showed: The number of hypertonics was found to be twice that of what is considered to be normal. Also, there were more persons than usual with increased hematocrite values and erythrocytes. The high percentage of foremen with high blood pressure can be attributed , at least in the age group between 40 and 50, to stress at their work places. Furthermore, high blood pressure is uncorrelated to age and in the group of 40 to 50 years is uncorrelated to behavioral risk factors (smoking, overweight and lack of motion). Additionally, as compared with other studies, there is less of a correlation between cholesterol and CHD than with LDS-cholestrol and CHD. As LDL-cholestrol was uncorrelated to behavioral risk factors and cholesterol showed only a slight correlation to the number of risk factors, these parameters become good indications of psychosocial stress. Both parameters are correlated to indices of coping behavior. Correlations between HDL-cholesterol and CHD were not defined. A possible reason for this involves the consumption of alcohol (30% of the persons drank more than 20 glasses of beer, wine or liquor a week).

COPING BEHAVIOR AND IMPAIRMENT OF HEALTH

As mentioned in the discussion of pressure behavior and buffer behavior, both patterns of coping have a common base structure: there is an inability to limit others' expectations. There is also an inability to openly resolve conflicts. This subjective pattern of coping behavior and objective working conditions will likely cause health impairments. This fact is expressed in several ways:

- There is a considerable number of statistically significant correlations between emotional discipline, the inability to settle conflicts, an exaggerated feeling of duty, and the existence of diverse medical variables.

- Comparisons of health between foremen showing buffer behavior (specific manifestation of a pattern of coping behavior in situations with role pressure) were made with people not subjected to role pressure.

There is a loss of social and working coping resources caused by the foremen being removed from practical work and social networks. This leads to a decreasing ability to cope with stress.

SUMMARY

The intention of our investigation was to find those work places where coronary heart diseases and cardiac infarction are observed most often. Also, the research was conducted in order to identify relevant working conditions as possible causes in order to use these findings for the prevention of the aforementioned diseases.

Initially, an investigation of 920 myocardial-infarction patients was conducted. Another investigation of 43 normals provided sufficient results indicating the validity of the hypothesis that special groups in the hierarchy of management face an increased danger of suffering CHD. To measure the accuracy of the hypothesis, 151 foremen were examined using an extensive standardized interview which covered stress at the work place and the resultant coping behavior. Data were gleaned from written reports of the foremen, a conversation with a medical doctor and other examinations (lab, ECG, etc.)

These data provided the basis for defining the following:

1) typical stress constellations

2) typical patterns of coping behavior

3) functional interactions of objective stress and subjective coping behavior.

It was learned that the most important stress for foremen resulted from time pressure and role pressure. Also, coronary heart diseases were the most frequent diseases of foremen, with high blood pressure found twice as often as in the average population of West Germany. Increases in blood lipid values and increases in blood viscosity were also found.

Significantly, coronary diseases were correlated with stress at the work place, especially with foremen between forty and fifty years of age.

Finally, the results of the investigations showed that classical ergonomic measurements of foremen are less accurate in predicting coronary heart diseases. Better predictors are psychosocial stress and coping behavior.

COPING WITH DRIVER STRESS

Edith Gulian, Lorna M. Debney, A. Ian Glendon, D. Roy Davies, and Gerald Matthews

OS and AP Division
Aston University, Aston Triangle
Birmingham, England

INTRODUCTION

Driver stress and related issues influence a number of people and situational interactions. Indeed, in a review of the literature on driving stress, Gulian (1987) found a substantial body of research describing physiological modifications associated with various traffic incidents (e.g., increase in heart rate). Yet few investigations have addressed driver stress from a psychological viewpoint (but see: Stokols, Novaco, Stokols and Campbell, 1978; Hoyos and Kastner, 1987). There is apparently little information regarding coping strategies used by people to deal with driving-induced stress.

This article addresses the issue of driver stress and delineates some of the ways to successfully minimize its consequences. First, findings regarding the psychological structure of driver stress as determined by factor analyses are considered. Second, data on coping strategies from drivers' comments, reported behaviors and affective reactions in one of the most common stressful situations - traffic jams - are presented. Lazarus' transactional framework (Lazarus and Launier, 1978; Lazarus and Folkman, 1984) is used as a basis for analyzing these data. Finally, the possibility of reducing driver stress by implementing measures on an organizational as well as on an individual basis is discussed.

PSYCHOLOGICAL DIMENSIONS OF DRIVER STRESS

The issue of driver stress, like any other type of stress, is definitionally problematic. On the one hand driver stress can be described in terms of measurable reactions to specified traffic situations. Alternatively, driver stress may result from a more permanent aspect of a person's psychological make-up. Therefore, an initial research issue, and one which is addressed in this paper, is to determine the most useful way of defining the concept of driver stress. A second, no less important issue, mainly from the viewpoint of devising stress-reducing techniques, is to uncover the factors which contribute to maintaining, and perhaps exacerbating, driver stress.

An initial hypothesis for this article was that driver stress results from processes taking place on two distinct, though closely related, levels. One level is situational.

This type of stress would be elicited by particular traffic events evaluated by drivers as: a) taxing their abilities to the limit; b) involving events perceived to be relatively uncontrollable; and/or c) events considered to be threats to physical or mental well being. The other level at which driver stress manifests itself involves the crystallization of accumulated negative feelings and frustrations. There is a strong interdependence between these two levels of driver stress: an overall negative view of driving would bias and influence the driver's response to specific traffic events, and any unfortunate traffic incidents would reinforce the negative appraisal of driving in general.

It was also proposed that the level of driver stress would depend on stresses experienced outside the driving situation. Thus, domestic or work problems would contribute to an individual's stress level. The greater the extraneous stress, the more likely that it would influence the negative appraisal of traffic incidents and driving in general. However, it is far from clear whether this relationship is linear. There are numerous intervening factors, such as mood and motivation, which could shape it differently. While this study examined whether there is a relationship between driver stress and factors extraneous to driving, the exact form of the assessment remains a subject for future research.

These aforementioned assumptions were examined in two studies. Findings from one of the studies was reported earlier in part (Gulian, Glendon, Matthews, Davies and Debney, 1988).

METHOD

The investigation was based on the analysis of self-reported behaviors and affective reactions toward driving. Two self-report instruments were devised and completed by people who either commuted daily to work or travelled by car in a professional capacity. Some people fell into both categories.

Questionnaires

Drivers were asked to complete two questionnaires: 1) the General Driving Behavior Inventory (GDBI) which probed into people's general appraisal of driving, as well as associated events and feelings; and 2) a Diary, which examined the day-to-day behaviors and affects over a one-week period.

The GDBI consists of 97 questions covering: a) behaviors in traffic, attitudes toward driving and toward other road users; b) demographic, health and personal problems (domestic and occupational). Two types of scales were used. A four-point scale, ranging from "very much" to "not at all" was used for responses to questions such as "How much driving would you say your work involves?" For responses to questions which involved a higher degree of differentiation, such as "Do you find it difficult to control your temper when driving?" a visual analogue scale (VAS) 100 mm. long was used.

The Diary was a structured 30-item questionnaire divided into: a) a section requiring factual information about the journey (e.g., mileage, traffic conditions, etc.) and about respondents' own state (e.g., health, problems at home or at work); b) a section enquiring into the respondents' affective states while driving (e.g., annoyed, under pressure, etc.) before leaving home or when leaving work. Some respondents completed the diaries twice daily, morning and evening, while others completed them only at the end of the working day. The same type of scales were used in the Diary as in the GDBI.

Subjects

In all, 209 drivers from two multinational companies completed the GDBI, and between 140 and 209 completed the diaries (not all respondents completed diaries every day). Respondents were between 23 and 62 years of age, with educational background varying from having no formal education to those who earned a university degree. One sample consisted mainly of male drivers, the other was mainly female.

RESULTS

Respondents had been driving for an average of 20 years (range from 4 to 30 years). Over 90 percent reported that they currently drive every day, were commuter drivers and that they had driven over 10,000 miles in the past year. Eighty-nine respondents admitted to at least one conviction for speeding, 5 admitted to convictions for dangerous driving and 23 to other motoring traffic offences. One hundred and sixty-one respondents reported that they had been involved as a driver in a road accident, thirty-six during the last two years.

Factor analyses carried out separately on responses given by drivers in the two samples showed remarkable similarity. The Very Simple Structure Criterion (Revelle and Rocklin, 1979) indicated a single general factor solution, while on the basis of a screen test (Cattell, 1978), an alternative five factor solution was identified. The five driver stress factors and item exemplars are listed in Table 1.

Using items loading at 0.40 and above on any factor, six scales were constructed to yield aggregate measures of driver stress. Correlations were then calculated between these scales and a VAS question from the GDBI, the "Driving Stress Item:" "In general, based upon your entire driving experience, do you consider that driving is a stressful activity?" Most scales correlated significantly with the "Driving Stress Item."

It was also found that factors both intrinsic and extrinsic to driving contribute to driver stress and are predictive of it. Among the factors *associated with driving* are: being in a hurry; amount of time (too much) spent driving; worries about bad weather; being caught in a traffic jam. The main factors *external to driving* are: having problems at work; worries about redundancy; changes in responsibility at work; arguments at work/at home; health problems; sleeping badly.

Table 1. Labels of Driver Stress Factors and Item Exemplars

AGGRESSION	"when upset I drive aggressively"
IRRITATION WHEN OVERTAKEN	"I am angry when overtaken"
HIGH ALERTNESS/ANXIETY	"I feel tense when I have to negotiate a difficult stretch of road"
DISLIKE OF DRIVING	"too much driving is a waste of time"
FRUSTRATION AND TENSION RELATED TO OVERTAKING	"when I try but fail to overtake I am usually frustrated"

Finally, differences in the degree of driver stress depending on age were also brought to light: younger drivers (up to 35 years of age) were more stressed than drivers in other age brackets. Compared to older drivers, younger drivers when irritated drive more aggressively, are more irritated by a silly driver, are anxious when overtaken, find it difficult to control their temper and are impatient in the rush hour. Older drivers (over 46 years) also show signs of stress (for example, they mind being overtaken and are impatient when they cannot overtake).

COPING STRATEGIES

Lazarus contends that stress is explicitly cognitive-phenomenological, emphasizing how the person appraises what is being experienced and uses this information in coping, and ultimately, to shape the course of events. The effects of this strategy are, in turn, appraised and reacted to. Coyne and Lazarus (1980) stress the role of cognitive appraisal in the coping process: appraisal in this sense refers to the individual's judgment about demands and constraints in ongoing transactions with the environment and the resources or options available for managing them. *Primary appraisal* refers to the appraisal of a given situation in terms of the person's well-being: "Am I okay or in trouble in this situation?" *Secondary appraisal* refers to the person's ongoing judgments concerning coping options, and constraints encountered in the situation.

Coping is seen as having two major functions: 1) it is directed at managing or altering the source of stress itself, called *problem-focused coping*, a term that refers to one's efforts to deal with the source of stress, either by changing one's own behavior or by changing the environmental conditions; 2) it is directed at reducing emotional distress and maintaining an effective internal state for processing information and action. This reaction is called *emotion-focused coping*. Both forms of coping include both cognitive and behavioral strategies. Both are often employed simultaneously, with the possibility that one strategy may facilitate the other.

The implications of this model of coping are clearly important for driver stress, and analysis of the data was made within this framework.

The following is an examination of coping behaviors and emotions, first in a restricted domain such as in traffic jams, and next on a more general level. Most of the data presented originate from the diaries, although some of the data on attitudes and behaviors in traffic jams are findings from the GDBI.

A. Coping with Traffic Jams

Respondents were asked to reply to questions from the GDBI, choosing one or more alternatives as appropriate (Table 2). These were categorized as "inefficient" and "efficient" coping strategies. The inefficient coping strategies were the following (the digits in brackets indicate the questions' number): aggression (1,3), worry (4), and irritation (2,5). An example of an efficient coping strategy was shown by responses indicating the subject had a relaxed attitude (6,7).

Figure 1 shows that in traffic jams about 20% of respondents report aggressive behaviors, 50% are irritated and fed-up, while only about 10% experience anxiety. Together, these behaviors and associated affective reactions add up to inefficient coping styles, which characterize about 80% of the respondents. However, this should not be considered as being the only alternative, because respondents also report being able to relax in traffic jams and think of, or do, something else. Typical of this mixture is the comment of one female respondent: "I feel *relaxed while occupied* with make-up

Table 2. Questions Regarding Behaviors and Affective Reactions in Traffic Jams

When in a traffic jam do you usually:

1. Try to cut in front of other cars
2. Feel irritated even if you are not in a hurry
3. Take any opportunity to get out
4. Worry that somebody may bump into you
5. Feel that this comes on top of all other unpleasantness
6. Relax and wait patiently
7. Think of something else
8. Other (please specify)................................

or other distractions while waiting in traffic queues, but *stressed* because I would be *late* every time I drove up to yet another queue."

What is the likely relationship between levels of perceived driver stress and behavioral or emotional responses in traffic jams? Figure 2 shows that on a stress scale of 1-100 (the General Scale derived from the one-factor solution), there is a peak of adequate responses when stress is low and relatively moderate and a decrease

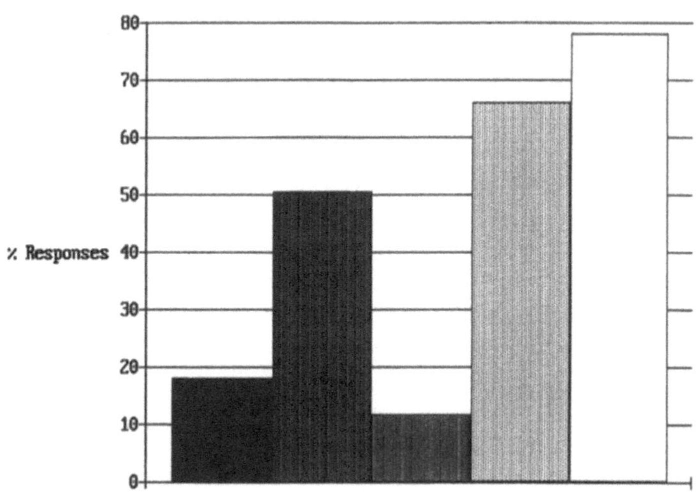

Figure 1. Reactions of respondents in traffic jams. Bars from left to right indicate percentage of reports of aggressive behaviors, irritation, anxiety respectively; the last two indicate total parameters.

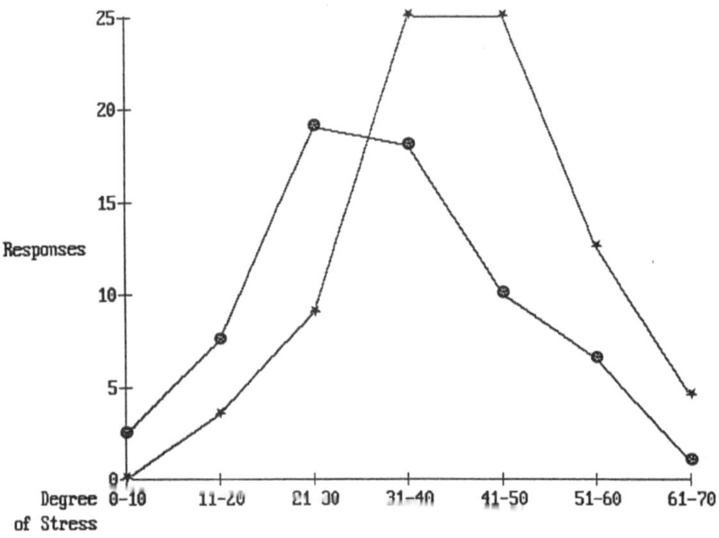

Figure 2. The percentage of adequate responses as a function of amount of stress.

in their frequency with an increase in stress. The inefficient coping responses are not found at all in the very low stress (i.e., the 1-10 range on the scale) group and their frequency clearly increases with increases in stress level.

Finally, we addressed the question: is there a relationship between driver's age, and feelings and behaviors in traffic jams? To answer this question the sample was divided along the median line into two age groups, under 44 years of age (n=57) and 44 years and older (n=55). Figure 3 shows that: a) drivers 44 years and over are more relaxed in traffic jams and have fewer inappropriate behaviors and emotions than younger drivers; b) there is no difference in the frequency of stress and positive responses in the younger age group; c) the 44 and above age group displays more efficient coping responses at the beginning of the week than at its end, and less stress on Mondays than on Fridays. As one respondent remarked: "I think with 'age' and the amount of driving done, I am much more tolerant now than years ago. When you sit in traffic jams most days you accept there is *nothing you can do but watch out and wait.*"

Certainly it is true that drivers employ a variety of coping strategies in traffic jams. Some of these coping methods are efficient while others are inefficient. Importantly, these categorizations are not mutually exclusive. It is likely that favoring one or the other type of coping depends to a great extent on the driver's mood, personality, motivation, the situation, or a combination of these. It is also apparent that age plays an important part in deciding to what extent traffic jams are perceived as stressful and how they will be reacted to.

B. Coping with Driving

What follows is a presentation of data gleaned from the analysis of respondents' comments, mainly in the diaries.

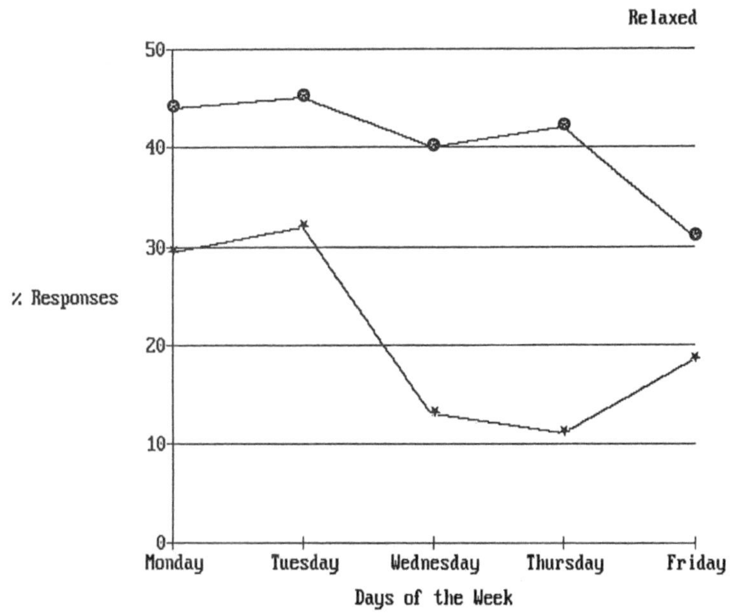

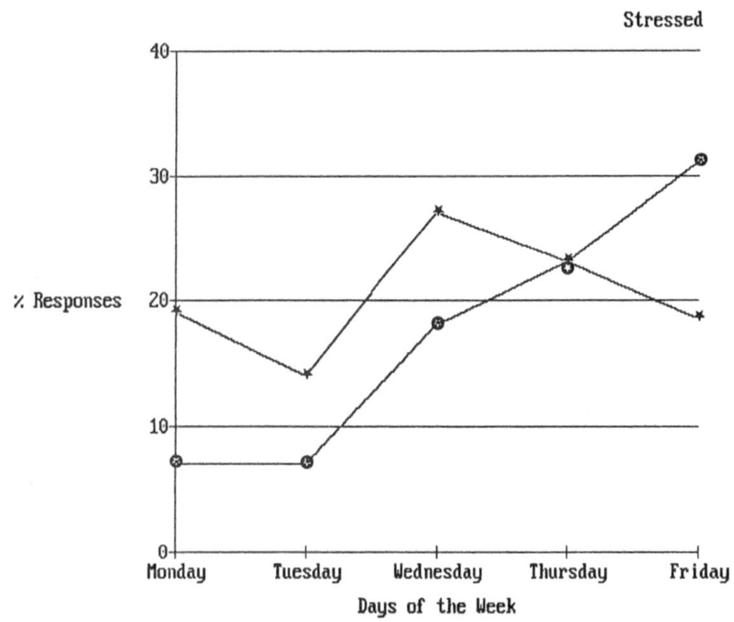

Figure 3. The percentage of relaxed responses (upper graph) and of stressed responses (lower graph) as a function of age.

Respondents' reported reactions toward traffic problems encountered while driving. Coping strategies included the subjects' methods of dealing with stressful situations. Responses were classified into three main categories as shown in Table 3: 1) sources of stress, which range from weather conditions to factors extraneous to driving (for example, having had arguments with a neighbor before leaving home); 2) affective and cognitive appraisal of the situation, which was found to vary from

Table 3. Classification of Respondents' Comments

Identified sources of stress	Appraisal (affective/cognitive)	Coping Strategies
1. Weather	1. Worry/concern	1. Planning
2. Traffic/road conditions	2. Negative (e.g., silly,stupid)	2. Alternative action
3. Car condition	3. Neutral	3. Precautionary measures
4. Near accident	4. Positive	4. Aggressive behavior/thoughts
5. Witnessing result of accident	5. Careful/cautious	5. Control
6. Other drivers' behavior (general)	6. Dangerous/ threatening	
7. Other drivers' behavior (specific)	7. Enhanced awareness	
8. Own behavior	8. Irritation	
9. Subjective condition (e.g., tired)	9. Annoyance	
10. Extraneous factors		

positive evaluation (usually of one's own driving behavior!) to annoyance and irritation; and 3) coping strategies used in a particular situation, including such behaviors as planning, or aggressive actions (e.g., flashing headlights) etc.

The first question asked concerns the existence of differences in the level of perceived driving stress between people who report traffic incidents and comment on other drivers' and their own driving behavior and those who refrain from reporting anything. Figure 4 shows that on a daily basis there are differences between drivers reporting traffic incidents, other problems or any other source of stress and those who do not make any comments. These differences are statistically significant for all days of the week, at least at $p = 0.01$. Drivers who comment have a consistently higher level of stress than those who do not report anything. Attributing the attitude toward traffic incidents and behavior on the road to higher stress is not supported by the data. Nor can an inference be made that noticing and commenting on occurrences necessarily increases the perceived stress. However, the data clearly indicate an association between perceived stress and problems in traffic. It is also possible that

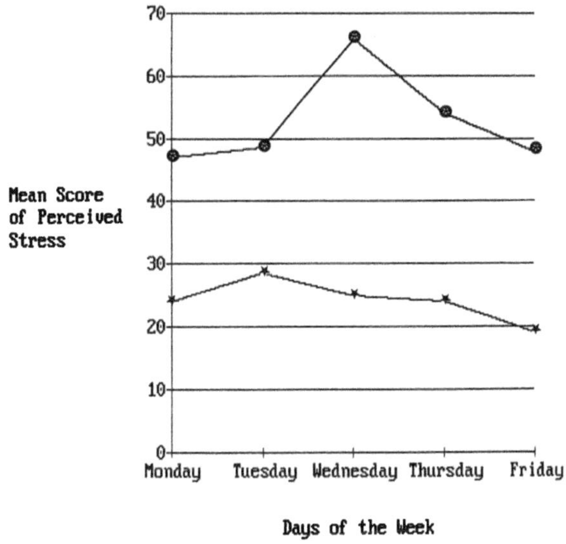

Figure 4. Perceived stress as a function of days of the week

the data are subject to a reporting effect which is independent (or only partly dependent) of subjective stress. Thus, there are several possibilities affecting research findings that should be considered. Drivers who report are actually more stressed than normal. Also, those who are stressed for various reasons may report more incidents. Finally, the non-reporters may either not be stressed or may not notice incidents. The data do not provide information allowing this issue to be analyzed correctly and thoroughly.

What are the main problems and events identified as eliciting stress? (See column 1 in Table 3.) The source of stress most frequently spontaneously mentioned is other drivers' behavior. Between 53 and 65 percent of all responses recognized this source of stress. This response is expressed in very general terms, as shown by one driver's comments: "I consider the present standard of driving is *pathetic* and getting worse all the time." Very specific answers were also formulated. For example, consider the following driver response, "On the motorway cars, and on one occasion an articulated lorry, were following my car far too closely and due to the weather and road conditions there was no way they could have stopped in the event of my having to stop."

Other sources of stress are weather and road/traffic conditions (between 9 and 25 percent of responses, depending on days), and very occasionally the person's subjective condition or driving behavior. An important source of stress mentioned by one particular category of drivers (service engineers) is the huge amount of driving (150-200 miles a day) on top of the normal work load expected to be carried out.

The next series of questions focused on the drivers' appraisal of the happenings they report and how they evaluate other people's and their own behavior on the road. The second column in Table 3 lists the various types of affective and cognitive appraisal derived from the respondents' comments. These were further classified into several subcategories describing degrees of tension and stress. For example, the 'negative' category subsumed such comments about other drivers as 'silly' and 'stupid' while the 'stress' category subsumed comments categorizing a behavior as 'dangerous' or 'annoying.'

Figure 5 shows that the highest proportion of responses indicated a stress reaction. The next most prominent response was negative evaluation. Few respondents expressed worry and even fewer had a good word about the driving situation, other drivers or even their own behavior. For example, one driver reported feeling, toward people trying to overtake him on a very crowded road, "a mixture of *intimidation* and *disgust* at the thoughtless and reckless driving of these people. This suggests that: 1) people tend to vent their disapproval; and 2) they react strongly and adversely to what happens on the road.

Adverse affective reactions showed a reported increase from Monday to Friday. On Mondays only one in five of the drivers exhibit such feelings, while on Fridays almost 80 percent of them admit to being fed-up (Figure 6).

The data also provided indications of how younger drivers differ from older drivers in their appraisal of traffic situations, weather and road conditions, and other drivers' behavior. Figure 7 presents the data. Again, reactions of people under the age of 44 years and over that age were examined. For each group, aggregated data over a 5-day period were considered. A kind of mirror effect may be seen from the graphical presentation of the data: compared with younger drivers, drivers aged 44 and over give more stress responses during the middle of the week. However, after the weekend and at the end of the week, older drivers make fewer stress responses compared with younger drivers. This might indicate that the weekend and the prospect of it plays a different role for older and younger drivers. One possibility is that it is more important for relaxation for older drivers because the days provide a chance to relax. For example, one respondent (aged 46 years) remarked: "Although drivers seemed aggressive this evening on my return journey, I did not feel irritated - perhaps because it was Friday!"

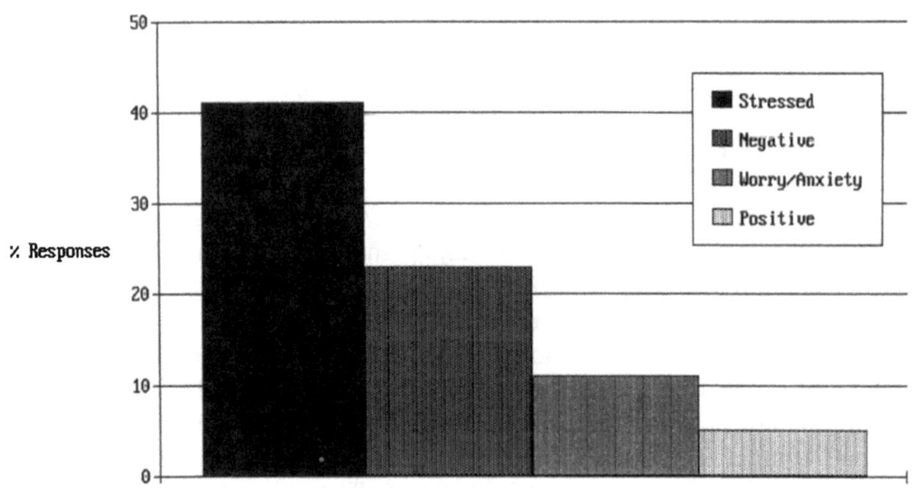

Figure 5. Percentage of responses indicating feelings from stressed to positive in driving situations

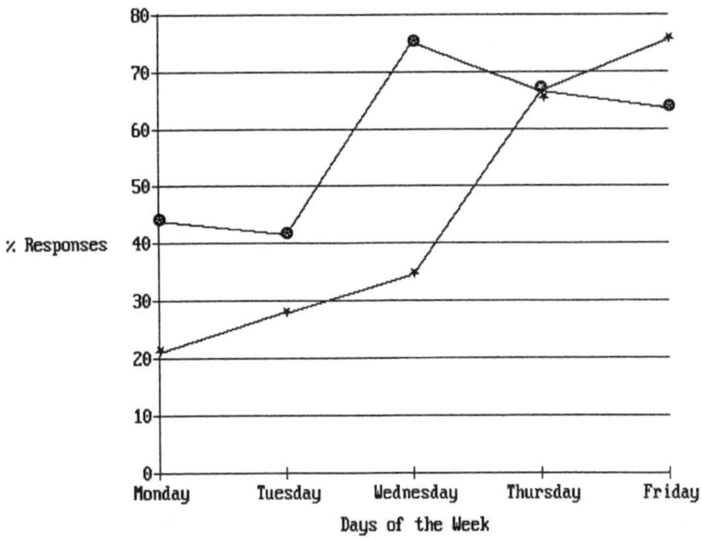

Figure 6. Frequency of stress responses and aggressive thoughts and behaviors over a five-day period. Aggressive thoughts and behaviors (circles), and feelings of irritation and annoyance (star).

Finally, types of strategies used by people when driving were examined and categorized, as shown in Table 3 (column 3). Examination of drivers' responses show that few cope with their driving problems in an adequate manner. For instance, rarely do drivers deal with stress by planning alternate courses of action. It was also found

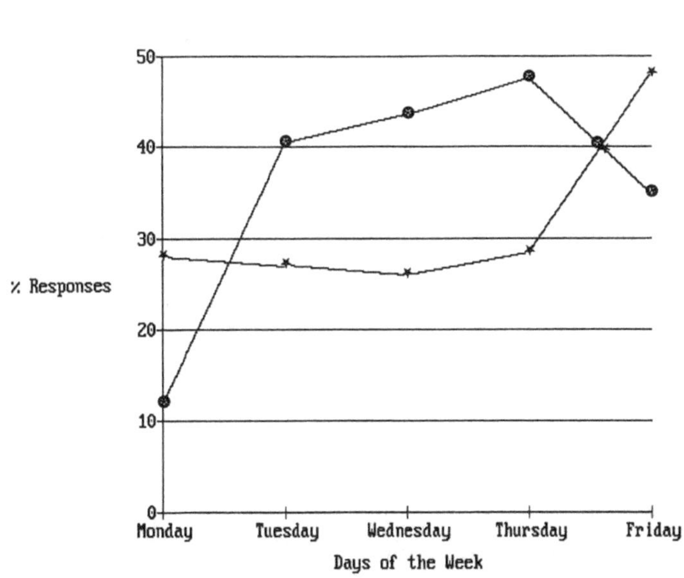

Figure 7. Differences between younger and older drivers in their appraisal of traffic situations over a five-day period. Respondents under 44 years (star), and over 44 years (circle).

that aggressive thoughts and behaviors are a very common mode of discharging tension. In fact, as can be seen from Figure 6, between 42 and 75 percent of responses are aggressive. Also, there are more aggressive responses in the second part of the week than in the first part. The beneficial effect of the weekend break disappears. For example, one respondent recorded the following: "A bad mannered idiot thoughtlessly pulled out in front of the car ahead of me, forcing a line of cars to brake suddenly. Classic case of the high risk of accidents within ten miles of home in the morning while the majority of drivers are still not awake; it woke me up!"

One potentially effective coping strategy used by a few respondents was 'enhanced awareness,' induced by the need to complete the GDBI and diaries. This issue is taken up in the Conclusions. To exemplify it, two quotes are presented. "Initial impulse was to blow horn at a guy who pulled out of side turn without looking, then remembered this exercise and saw the amusing side of the situation," and "I am coming to the conclusion that the need to fill this form in each day is having a positive effect on my driving. *I am resisting the temptation to display aggression.*"

In summary, an association was found between perceived driver stress level and the frequency and type of comments made by drivers. Respondents who made comments had a higher stress level and also a generally adverse attitude toward other drivers' behavior and toward driving conditions in general. Also documented was a clear age effect. Compared with older drivers, younger drivers more frequently used inefficient (e.g., aggressive) coping strategies. Moreover, there is a clear 'weekend effect,' with older drivers apparently relaxing and having a more positive attitude before and immediately after the weekend while younger drivers display the opposite trend.

CONCLUSIONS

The examination of drivers' behaviors and affective reactions has shown that they use a variety of coping strategies to come to terms with or to counter driver-induced stress. Some of these strategies are positive and efficient, in that they result in a reduction in stress level. Others, on the contrary, are inefficient and sometimes may fuel even higher levels of stress. For example, aggressive behaviors, even though apparently momentarily reducing tension, actually contribute to the maintenance of stress reactions. Inefficient coping strategies are generally more common than efficient ones, thus highlighting the need for possible intervention measures. The data presented also indicate two of the more vulnerable areas where such interventions may prove most profitable. One of these is linked with age, the other to attitude toward and ability to relax during the weekend. Evidently more research is needed on all aspects of coping with driver stress before producing a complete program for stress reduction. At this preliminary stage, on the basis of the available data, however, a few steps which could be taken are proposed:

A. Personal Strategies

People need to become *aware of the potential for substantial driver stress* which can have adverse effects on their health (resulting in heart problems, ulcer, etc.) (Netterstrom and Laursen, 1981; Holme and Helgeland, 1980). Performance and work capacity may be impaired (Brown, 1978; Treat, 1980). Finally, traffic safety is effected. Many more accidents involve people under stress (Isherwood, Adam and Hornblow, 1982; Brenner and Selzer, 1969).

Consequently, attempts must be made to warn people of the 'adaptation to pressure' syndrome. This means that people should be aware that although they feel they can and do cope with a lot of pressure (at work or otherwise), being under such stresses distorts their perception of what they really can achieve. Consequently, the likelihood of driving less safely is increased.

Drivers could also be advised to use simple, easy to learn *relaxation techniques* before leaving work and during traffic jams. Such techniques should be practiced. They would relieve tension and fatigue and make the journey home much safer. This point is important since the level of exhaustion in the evening is very high in practically all drivers.

B. Organizational Strategies

Flexible time management. This technique refers to the introduction of non-rigid appointment schedules (appointments could be made to be kept within a half-hour margin). This would prevent people getting worried because they failed to get to a certain place by a certain time and would help them avoid being in too much of a hurry, thus reducing anxiety.

Better planning of driving/work ratio. A recurrent complaint of long-distance drivers is that they have to complete a day's work *and* drive long distances. It should be possible, in some cases, to halve the distance driven (for example, by making overnight accommodation available). This would substantially diminish the exhaustion and pressure felt by drivers. Presumably, it would also decrease the speed with which some people drive when returning home after a long working day.

Finally, *counseling* sessions could be organized with interested people in which issues such as redundancy, retirement, or even domestic conflicts could be discussed and solutions sought, thus minimizing some of the causes of stress.

C. National Strategies

Under this heading are included strategies which would be the result of measures employed on a national basis by the Government. For example, it is known that younger drivers are the most likely to be involved in accidents. Research has shown that they do display more symptoms of driving stress than older drivers. An educational program emphasizing the reasons for their 'accident vulnerability' and also measures for lowering stress levels could be instituted.

ACKNOWLEDGEMENTS

The research described is sponsored by the Health Promotion Research Trust.

REFERENCES

Brenner, B. and Selzer, M.L. 1969, Risk of causing a fatal accident associated with alcoholism, psychopathology, and stress: further analysis of previous data, *Behav. Sci.*, 14:490-495.

Brown, I.D. 1978, Dual task methods of assessing work load, *Ergonomics*, 21:221-224.

Cattell, R.B. 1978, "The Scientific Use of Factor Analysis in Behavioral and Life Sciences," Plenum Press, New York.

Coyne, J.C. and Lazarus, R.S. 1980, Cognitive style, stress perception, and coping, *in*: "Handbook on Stress and Anxiety: Contemporary Knowledge, Theory and Treatment," I. L. Kutash and L.B. Schlesinger, eds., Jossey-Bass, San Francisco.

Gulian, E. 1987, Driver stress: a literature review, *CPERU Report 1*, Aston Business School, Aston University, Birmingham, U.K.

Gulian, E., Glendon, A.I., Matthews, G., Davies, D.R. and Debney, L.M. 1988, Exploration of driver stress using self-reported data, *in*: "Road User Behaviour: Theory and Research," T. Rothengatter and R. de Bruin, eds., Van Gorcum, Assen/Maastricht.

Holme, I., Helgeland, A., Hjermann, I., Leren, P. and Lund-Larsen, P.G. 1980, Four and two-thirds years incidence of coronary heart disease in middle-age men: the Oslo study, *Am J. Epidemiol.*, 12:149-160.

Isherwood, J., Adam, K.S. and Hornblower, A.R. 1982, Life event stress, psychosocial factors, suicide attempt and auto-accident proclivity, *J. Psychosom. Res.*, 26:371-383.

Lazarus, R.S. and Folkman, S. 1984, Coping and adaptation, *in*: "Handbook of Behavioral Medicine," W.D. Gentry, ed., The Guildford Press, New York.

Lazarus, R.S. and Launier, R. 1978, Stress-related transactions between person and environment, *in*: "Perspectives in Interactional Psychology," L.A. Pervin and M. Lewis, eds., Plenum Press, New York.

Netterstrom, B. and Laursen P. 1981, Incidence and prevalence of ischemic heart disease among urban bus drivers in Copenhagen, *Scand. J. Soc. Med.*, 9:75-79.

Revelle, W. and Rocklin, T. 1979, Very simple structure: an alternative procedure for estimating the optimal number of interpretable factors, *Multivar. Behav. Res.*, 14:403-414.

Stokols, D., Novaco, R.W., Stokols, J. and Campbell, J. 1978, Traffic congestion, type A behavior, and stress, *J. Appl. Psychol.*, 63:467-480.

Treat, J.R. 1980, A study of precrash factors involved in traffic accidents, *The Highw. Safety Res. Rev.*, 10:6-11.

STRESS-COPING STYLES AMONG SOUTH AFRICAN MANAGERS

Johann J. L. Coetzee

University of Potchefstroom
Graduate School of Business
Republic of South Africa

FOREWORD

The term "stress" has an unfortunate connotation among South African managers. It implies weakness, and the individual perceived to be "stressed" becomes vulnerable in the corporate and professional environments. However, the term "self-management" seems to serve as an acceptable alternative. It does not challenge and it de-stigmatizes the stressful state. Indeed, since 1985 the practice of self-management as a preventative and therapeutic intervention has been successfully practiced.

A Centre for Self Management was started in January, 1988 at Henley-on-Klip in South Africa. Executives attend this Centre for three days. During this time they are taught to incorporate into their lives practices that will allow them to successfully deal with stress. The managerial skills that have made the executive successful can be used as a means of achieving the aforementioned goals of the Centre's programs. Consequently, a balanced, integrated lifestyle can be created.

INTRODUCTION AND PERSPECTIVE

There is an unprecedented need and demand in the South African management community for self-management. The present rate at which managers are prepared to request professional aid in minimizing the negative effects of self-neglect, insufficient self-preservation and self-concept disintegration is unparalleled.

Unfortunately, participating in consultations with a psychologist has often been stigmatized. It is also believed that "managers don't cry" and that the facade of control, success and preservation has to be kept up at whatever cost.

The fact remains, however, that managers are ordinary people. They too struggle with emotional problems, stress, depression, despondency and self-neglect. Managers are not immune from the hurt meted out by modern society, nor can they constantly resist the hostile forces of their environment. Certainly, exposure to potential failure can create for the executive a perilous work place.

The South African professional culture is most unique. The present generation of managers is the first to intimately deal with advanced technology, conflict management, labor relations, trade-union negotiations, extraordinary interest rates and exceptional international pressure. They also have the responsibility for giving impetus to the industrial revolution in South Africa which only came into effect during the Second World War. In terms of this culture, these professionals are required to work extremely hard.

Furthermore, this generation of managers has been "bred" in a competitive world in which the prescriptions of the professional and working environment, and not the discretion of the individual, dictate the norm. Profession and business thus become all important. While the typical manager would never have confessed to trauma and afflictions, the contrary now holds true. Especially during the past five years, a dramatic change has occurred. Managers are beginning to realize that their preservation depends on consultation and counseling, and that rehabilitation frequently requires intensive therapy.

Another prominent, related concern is whether South Africa, with its limited management resources, can afford to neglect and overwork its managerial community through unusual job-related pressure and tension. Consequently, preventative strategies and structures to ensure the optimal functioning of managers should be considered and instituted.

Yet, to transform or drastically change the evolutionary model of the South African professional culture in the present political and economic environment is complicated. Expectations are for the manager to somehow uphold the impetus and drive of the economy. Also, the mounting threat of disinvestment and further isolation on the international economic scene will only produce more stress situations that the manager must overcome.

A balanced perspective is, in essence, a philosophical process. This requires consideration, meditation and constant evaluation eventually allowing for timely identification of areas of neglect. Such a strategy also allows for the development of a plan that deals with stress situations. Unfortunately, many professionals do not allow time for such activities. This approach is seen as not adhering to the image of a successful manager and is especially not the practice of the "macho manager."

Because a facade of pride, strength and survival must be constantly maintained, a great deal of energy is used up in disguising genuine emotions. However, in isolation, in the consulting room environment, professionals are frequently more willing to reveal their genuine emotions. This catharsis is dramatically and intensely experienced when the subversion of emotional reactions has occurred over a period of time. Such an individual has become an employer and manager first and then, only on rare occasions, a sincere human being. The world of the executive tends to be one where exactness dominates and where there is an avoidance of exposing genuine emotions.

This individual, because of professional training, naturally experiences a great deal of difficulty when attempting to accurately define the self. Consequently, the communication process is made more difficult.

THE PHILOSOPHY OF SELF-NEGLECT

It can be argued that certain philosophical aspects are difficult for managers to accept. It is also true that the average manager does not like to be confronted with language not related to the professional world. The purpose of this section is to put the condition and process of self-neglect in practical perspective. Of course, the viable alternative will also be delineated. Unfortunately, self-neglect has become an acute epidemic. A counter-argument supposes that self-neglect is the price that has to be paid for success and survival. It is also argued that self-neglect and loss of control, to a certain extent, are unavoidable for anyone who becomes preoccupied with career developments.

The process and impact of neglect among managers yields symptoms that can be used as an overview for self-evaluation. Consequently, critical areas of neglect can be identified and controlled. An outline for improved self-management is suggested as a strategy against continued self-neglect in the process of attempting to achieve managerial excellence.

Neglect is typically that process where a person fails to adequately define values, norms, principles and standards which are established as a framework for a personal lifestyle. Managers, in a neglected state, who report for counseling and therapy, experience conflict between that which they know and that which they do. In other words, the intellect is in conflict with action. It is admitted that certain practices of neglect are consciously being practiced. However, emotional strategies forcing behavioral change do not exist.

Many managers believe that the most serious aspect of neglect is not so much the physical damage done, but instead relates to resultant emotional complications. Consequently, it seems that a person who consciously neglects does not lack a normative infrastructure. Neglect actually takes place in the individual who understands the theory of self-management. It is these persons who experience the most intense form of emotional pain. Unfortunately, they typically are not equipped to stop the process of neglect and destruction. The processes of achievement, competition, career aspirations and personal disorientation take over in spite of the individual's realization that such behavioral patterns are destructive.

SELF-MANAGEMENT: PROBLEMATIC ISSUES AND CRITICAL CONFRONTATIONS

In this section the various contact areas triggering self-neglect are considered. The confrontations discussed are those which occur most frequently and are reported during counseling at the Centre for Self Management.

(1) The shortage of skilled manpower in South Africa and of managers in particular is acute and serious. The result is an increase in work load and pressure, a phenomenon which is frequently experienced. Consequently, the South African manager has attempted to resolve problems resulting from this dilemma.

Projections up to the year 2000 present a threatening scenario. By 1992 whites in South Africa will have a negative population growth. Consequently, the future availability of alternate managerial sources will be limited. Moreover, the rate at which black managers are being prepared for executive office is disappointing. Therefore, it is only realistic to assume that skilled people will have to work progressively more diligently in order to properly manage South African businesses.

(2) The political situation in South Africa, and the attendant unrest, cause extraordinary insecurity and stress. It is in the work environment that the black worker attempts to exercise political power. The sole concern of business may well have been profit and service with the industrial environment. However, as a result of this situation an additional political dimension must be dealt with.

In addition to the vertical political conflict that exists in the majority of business environments, lateral tension among managers also is evident. Party political differences at the managerial level emerge, thus creating among managers an implosive tension.

Encouraging the resolution of political differences and implementing, as part of management practice, the establishment of equal rights have become issues for theoretical debate. The impact of the inequities characteristic of the South African system force the international communities to denounce South Africa. As a result, traditional trading parties and former business associates are reluctant to deal with South African business. Consequently, South African managers have increased stress levels.

(3) Self-neglect has assumed epidemic proportions. The South African manager has one of the most threatening health records in the Western world, especially involving the following: cholesterol, hypertension, stress, obesity, divorce per capita, and alcohol and nicotine consumption. Achievers are confronted with a progressive physical deterioration that restrains psychological and physical energy. This occurrence serves to underscore the seriousness of self-neglect and the need for self-management. Certainly it is evident that there is an acute need for physical and mental health preservation and enrichment skills among South African management.

Unfortunately, South African managers' health and performance efficiency is negatively affected by the following:

(3.1) The consumption and abuse of alcohol and nicotine. While there is a strong claim for the continued health of the manager, the employer is frequently insensitive to the perils of alcohol and nicotine use. Furthermore, employers often unreasonably and inadvertently encourage and make possible alcohol and nicotine use. Merely relying on the sound judgment of the individual as regards the use of such substances has proven to be an inadequate means of regulation.

(3.2) The cholesterol count of the South African manager tends to be among the highest in Western economies. A result of this is obesity. Unfortunately, when management socializes, food and drink apparently must be present, thus allowing the proper completion of business transactions.

(3.3) Coronary heart problems are also a growing threat to the health of South African managers. The incidence of heart attacks among South African management, relative to the Western world, is significantly greater. It appears that the average manager's physical infrastructure is no match for his rate of physical activities and this consequently leads to a form of heart failure.

(4) The cultural superficiality among managers and the subsequent lack of moral depth are cause for grave concern. Many professional people characteristically devote little time to cultural enrichment. Managers have expressed their intense frustration at not having time to read periodicals, topical books and articles, or to attend stimulating presentations. Only matters which are directly related to their profession and which may have some bearing on profitability receive any consideration. Relaxing cultural experiences are believed to be a luxury and merely represent a further dimension of frustration.

Unfortunately, reading matter of the modern manager includes minutes of meetings, vocationally directed literature and computer print-outs. Business magazines are studied, replacing those that deal with cultural enrichment.

Obviously, there is a need for the recreative and the informal. Ideally, an increase in the choice of options for the family and the married couple could become the norm. The reality of the manager experiencing guilt when relaxing must be changed.

(5) Managers perceive spontaneous socializing as requiring too much time. According to managers, relaxed social interaction has become formalized and painful. For fear of being unwelcome and in the way, modern people now only visit by appointment or upon invitation. Moreover, they no longer call on friends or acquaintances in a discretionary manner, because they feel that they may be obligated to have their friends or acquaintances return their visit. Social interaction has thus become a matter of moral obligation more than social choice and preference. The tendency is for socializing to take place only among business associates.

(6) Normative decay has been noticeable in personal ideology, faith and religion. This process is most often the result of a sense of increasing independence, which is in direct proportion to an increase in the seniority and stature of professional people. Quite often managers are of the opinion that the ritual of divine worship provides a fine opportunity to be noticed and to display their excellence and merit by serving on the church council. However, genuinely sincere involvement is not present. Furthermore, religious virtues tend to be absent from the working environment. Thus, self-management also requires consistency in normative values and behavior.

Research confirms that the passage of time creates normative superficiality and distorts personal values. As professional obligations become more numerous, opportunities for the personally enriching acts of introspection and meditation are minimized.

Respondents to the research concerning this theme reiterate that the practice of continued neglect begins with the loosening of ties to the aforementioned higher order values which serve to enhance every human being.

(7) Marital disintegration and destabilization have reached epidemic proportions in South Africa. Current research shows that only 13 managers from a sample of 100 believe, without reservation, that they are happily married. In many cases, where the manager is of the opinion that he is happily married, the spouse's response is to the contrary.

A lack of common interests and true fellowship increases the likelihood of marital estrangement. An incomplete marriage in which the husband, characteristically, is either absent or late, has little hope of success or happiness.

Workaholic managers, however, have stated that they do not love their spouses less and are not consciously indifferent towards their marriage. Rather, they experience a sense of vulnerability due to the pressure of the working environment. This state of mind leads to a feeling of loss of control which in turn elicits feelings of guilt and, ultimately, remorse.

A disturbing situation is reflected in the trend that the spouse has to seek counseling on behalf of herself and her manager-husband; the workaholic, traditionally, is not prepared to seek help himself. The primary reasons for this managerial practice involve the perception that there is a danger of possible embarrassment in having to admit to an emotional incapacity to cope. Furthermore, the manager rationalizes that it is his spouse who is having a problem and therefore is in need of counseling.

(8) Poor self-management on the part of the manager often causes him to have a "schizophrenic" sense of existence. During the working day there is an experience of

success and progress, praise often being received when professional accomplishments are realized. However, in the marital and family environment the professional experiences quite the opposite: conflict and a continual sense of failure and inadequacy. Consequently, there begins to develop a preference for the uncomplicated company of colleagues or club members who tend to provide a sense of affiliation and comfort. Likewise, the manager begins to avoid the domestic environment where it is difficult to achieve a sense of happiness, and where professional successes are not recognized.

This conflicting existence eventually produces emotional development problems. The manager requires superhuman psychological energy in order to both distinguish between and reconcile his widely differing and conflicting roles, but the reality is that the manager becomes confused and disoriented. When the manager achieves insight and refuses to go on living a "lie," only then can a meaningful conversion take place. The need to engage in constructive life-and-work reconditioning manifests itself very prominently at the Centre for Self Management.

(9) Personal growth becomes superficial in favor of continued self-development (i.e., development happens to be at the expense of personal growth), while technological and managerial growth deepens. The average SA manager is successful and competent. However, this existence is characterized by a singularity that offers little variety. Existing processes and activities are repeated to the point of becoming stereotypical and conventional. The manager becomes someone who does not determine what his personal interests shall be. Instead, he is "made to live" in a certain manner as dictated by professional circumstances. A prescriptive lifestyle dominates, allowing minimal variety and alternatives.

(10) Successful and highly qualified people are guilty of ignoring the most fundamental principles upon which life is based. A lack of self-management causes them to acknowledge priorities only theoretically. Four primary factors demanding energy are self, spouse, family and work. The difference between the real and the ideal order of precedence confirms the sharp contrast mentioned above:

Real Order		Ideal Order
4	SELF	1
2	SPOUSE	2
3	FAMILY	3
1	WORK	4

The list of priorities thus clearly shows that self-management is replaced by self-neglect. Once again, the job becomes of primary importance to the detriment of the self.

Certainly hard work and dedication are not negatives. However, business professionals should prioritize so as to maintain values enabling them to work well and stay emotionally integrated. Drucker has rightly and eloquently suggested:

"Modern managers have to work smarter not harder." This implies a "smart" mentality in synchronization with all four factors.

(11) Strict conformity to prescriptions of the peer group is a weakness characteristic of many. With an achieving peer group it is difficult to advocate and pursue contrary ideals and values. In a specific social stratification there are "cruel" forces in operation which regulate membership and raise the group norm above individual choice.

To act contrary to the group norm could result in unpleasant repercussions. Those acting in such a manner often come to be classified as "drop-outs," "has-beens" and "occupational sissies." Those aspiring to be members of a group must uncompromisingly subscribe to the group's conduct code.

Further, the male ego often poses a real problem for certain managers. A distorted need to assert one's own means of action as being proper develops from the obsession with achievement and success. Such men are incapable of surviving without the regular applause of peers.

Ultimately, the group of equals not only takes possession of the values and norms of the individual but also starts to regulate and manipulate thoughts, behavior and aspirations. The manager performs in a manner undertaken to appease the group's expectations. Most managers who become a part of this process confess that they have to unwillingly participate in the prescriptions of the group in order to gain respect. Affiliation with the group necessitates conformity. The fear of rejection should the group's ideal not be adhered to represents, potentially, too much social and psychic pain.

When a manager must conform to both professional and social demands, and if these are in conflict with personal, real convictions, implosive stress is experienced. This implosive stress destroys the emotional infrastructure of the individual to such an extent that psychosomatic problems develop, leading to pathological behavior. Attempts to deal with this form of stress are seldom undertaken because the manager is reluctant to deal with subsequent social pressures.

To develop the courage to apply self-management in spite of peer group pressure is a tactical decision and one that ultimately serves to preserve one's health.

(12) Work is seen to create difficulties because the work load never diminishes and deadlines always inspire panic. The nobility of work and the cultural-historical ethics of labor are no longer given credence.

Critical youngsters contend that there is no joy in work and that the profits derived from work never seem to fulfill the parents' expectations. Working parents are perceived as always complaining, always being tired and criticizing the employer for exploiting and underpaying them. Working people, furthermore, speak deprecatingly of their chosen careers. These glimpses of working life give children a cynical perception of work. Instead, managers should give renewed consideration to the example set so as to enhance the credibility of vocational counseling.

It is important to note that the 21st century is precisely that phase in history which will be typified as the era when finite facts will replace abstract speculation as the foundation for formulating business decisions. Apart from a strong emphasis on human relationships, equal opportunities, negotiation and communication, business executives will continue to stress the importance of technology and other exact sciences. It has become necessary for the manager to understand confrontation not as a threat but rather as a potentially rewarding opportunity.

(13) The presented argument is not against success, prosperity and a passion for achievement. As a matter of fact, without these virtues there would be no economic growth, progress or survival. Also, as a result of the dramatic drop in the growth of the white population and hence the management community of South Africa, it will be necessary for managers to work much harder to give more impetus to the economy. It is disturbing, however, when the product of this process distorts the importance of certain human virtues and expectations.

The process of competition lies at the root of creating an obsession for material wealth. These symbols of success (cars, address, trips) must be exhibited in such a way that the stature of the manager is unconditionally recognized and recorded. The emphasis must be on achievement, and on the competition to achieve, rather than on the acquisition of material goods as symbols of that achievement. In any other way, values and norms are distorted and achievement becomes a disruptive obsession.

It is also true that an individual with ingenuity, initiative and vision will recognize and exploit opportunities not only in the interest of the organization, but also for the self. Yet, when the welfare of the self is neglected, the emphasis necessarily shifts from real growth to personal decay.

(14) While it can be argued that the vocational heritage of the present manager was dictated by the industrial pioneers of South Africa, it must, at the same time, be recognized that appropriate response mechanisms against professional pressure exist when work obsession is viewed reasonably and objectively. The self-neglecting manager is completely assimilated in the work situation, to the disadvantage of himself and his professional associates. Interestingly, the sensitive employer even expresses concern for the extent of devotedness required by his managers, yet the work load overcomes the power of conscience and the anxiety only exists in theory instead of becoming a preventative strategy.

Business ethics and morality tend to be irreconcilable with the forces generating and regulating profit. For that matter, the viability of business ethics is determined by the efficiency of business practices and the quality of the cash flow.

The cause of numerous stress related problems involves the emphasis placed on competition, optimal performance and success. Even at primary school level strong competition is established and elicited, setting aside such luxuries as discretionary time, informality and play. The ability to succeed becomes the criteria by which performances are judged. Those who succeed inevitably gain approval of adult society. However, one must question the extent to which such pressures can predict a successful future, and to what extent a fair perspective can be achieved at the school level.

It would seem that universities and colleges have a moral obligation to inform students about the dangers inherent in being obsessed with gaining professional success. It is necessary that the principles of balance and perspective, and the danger of poor self-management, be communicated. Research reveals that students have a real need for information concerning stress management.

(15) The gap that exists between management-ingenuity at work and the same process at home and in the area of personal life suggests the manager typically fails to transfer skills from the professional environment to the social arena. At work the process of strategic management may be brilliantly applied as follows:

(15.1) A mission is formulated which clearly outlines the organization's mandate.

(15.2) Hence, a definite philosophy is formulated which indicates how this goal can be achieved.

(15.3) Specific goals are set and a budget, which offers the infrastructure and logistics for achieving these goals, is established.

(15.4) Actions follow defining potential resources and also defining performance criteria.

(15.5) Finally, performance management is applied on a continued basis.

It is in these areas that the modern manager is most qualified. However, the issue here involves why similar talents and discretion are not applied to areas not related to professional involvement. There is a discrepancy between personal ingenuity at work and the total absence of this type of knowledge and skill at the personal level. Reiterated is the principle that the world of work is omnipotent at the expense of the personal environment.

(16)Characteristically, an ideal conversion is attempted after the fact. Only when confronted by traumatic experience does the manager show any willingness to acknowledge the benefit of self-management, but the price to be paid is then too high. Typically, the person engaging in poor self-management is immune to the logic of occupational conversion.

SELF-MANAGEMENT: PROCESS AND PERSPECTIVE

Before an active and constructive process of reconstruction and recovery can commence, there is a need to recognize and acknowledge the symptoms and conditions of poor self-management. The stressed manager has to be willing to recondition old ways.

Unfortunately, many managers believe that converting traditional behavioral patterns involves too great a sacrifice. Furthermore, there is a tendency to resist behavioral conversion because there is an unwillingness to risk appearing inept while learning new behavior patterns.

Personal lifestyles can be placed in perspective only through reflection. Managers tend to understand the necessity of undertaking this process. A reliable and credible role model facilitates the counseling process, making possible the communication of viable self-management skills. Such a person makes an acceptable counsellor because there is an understanding of the individual's trauma.

(1) Personal strategic management is the first step towards control and structure. It denotes much the same process that applies in business. To be meaningful, one's life must have some objectives, plans of action, achievement management and evaluation. Furthermore, it is necessary to seriously and regularly reflect on one's progress and to evaluate growth. Certainly it is also important to evaluate oneself in relation to achieving meaningful goals, and to allow others that opportunity. Through this process one is able to identify and remedy shortcomings and areas of neglect.

(2) Most people have ideals they define for themselves as being worthwhile. A problem arises, however, when these dimensions remain theoretical and are not realized in a meaningful way.

(3) Managers should guard against conforming to peer group pressure. To resist the expectations and the codes of conduct propounded by the peer group requires conviction and self-confidence. The professional culture is characterized by the desire to achieve professional goals at whatever cost. Unfortunately, disaffiliation can cause social anguish. It may also affect self-confidence in a totally negative manner. This would seem to discourage the dependent person who desires a change to a state of greater independence.

(4) Managers must create achievable expectations. Employers often erroneously encourage subordinates to formulate overly ambitious career goals. Consequently, it is necessary that individuals ask themselves if aspirations are commensurate with their real potential and ability.

The organizational structure in which promotion is symbolized only in terms of vertical mobility is erroneous. Lateral growth, whereby individuals are promoted at their level of competence, is preferable to promotion to a vertical level of incompetence. Knowledge of actual ambition and potential is only acquired through introspection and self-evaluation, an instrumental undertaking when attempting to understand the application of self-management.

(5) Ideally, the spouse can be included in all decisions regarding work and profession. An involvement in these matters allows the spouse to be meaningfully concerned in career management. Seemingly, it is a misconception that career decisions should be made in isolation Those affected family members obviously have the right to be equally involved in the decision process.

(6) Managers who have strong control systems at their disposal tend to be authoritarian. These people succeed in completing tasks and therefore frequently deal with a significant work load. This type of personality (A type) is easily irritated by non-achievers or malachievers and people who are under average. For this reason they frequently accept the majority of the work, even on behalf of others to whom it is delegated. The Type A personality believes that such an action is necessary in order to maintain standards and to meet deadlines.

(7) Being a manager does not require that one's unique identity be sacrificed. On the contrary, it signifies the right to be unconditionally unique and "different." Unfortunately, typical managers are people who totally conform to the system. Those who can rely on their own values, and are not hypersensitive to criticism, eventually experience a sense of psychological growth.

(8) South African managers tend to be confronted with significant work loads. Consequently, survival demands optimal effort. Ideally, the best resources should be used to alleviate the work load and to increase efficiency and productivity. The latter process demands critical evaluation on a regular basis.

(9) The ingredients of job quality consist of variety, balance, control, recognition and compensation. There should, however, be a balance between work and relaxation. When job routine is established as the norm, job performance can suffer significantly.

(10) Reconciliation of personal ideology with job and career expectations is the highest form of synchronizing these important factors. Normative differences involving these two areas may result in profound personal conflict. Self-management thus also implies that one should identify an environment where harmony between professional and personal expectations exists.

(11) One of the most important prerequisites for self-management is a sensitive employer, one who will allow such a phenomenon to take place. In much the same

way as people report for medical examination, they should be able to go for emotional counseling. Management should be sensitized to the idea and apply it conditionally to managers. An employer can make a meaningful investment by allowing preventative action to be undertaken, thus allowing the well being of managers to be insured.

FUTURE PERSPECTIVE

As involves the South African business environment, there must be an unprecedented development of regulations allowing effective self-management to exist. Historically, business managers encounter a significant amount of stress. This suggests a negative and compounding effect on both management and business. The work load will increase over the short term despite an attempt by the system to produce more managers to share the work load.

The challenge is to construct a new superstructure which will accommodate the unique variety of the South African business environment. Ideally, businesses and managers will be allowed to function optimally. Furthermore, the present system, especially among managers, induces distress. Certainly, the challenge facing South Africans is to allow the incorporation, within the professional community, of appropriate self-management skills.

STRESS AND RELAXATION IN EDUCATION

INTRODUCING RELAXATION METHODS TO YOUNG CHILDREN[1]

Jane Madders

Birmingham, England

INTRODUCTION

All children have to contend with stress: whether they are tough or timid, aggressive or withdrawn, intelligent or dull, they, like adults, have to meet stress head on every day (Varna, 1973). But because they are immature, have only limited experience, are passing through periods of rapid change and are very much at the mercy of adults, they are particularly vulnerable (Ollendick, 1985; Wolff, 1981). It is a myth that childhood is a carefree happy time (Pringle, 1974) for there is much to frighten and humiliate the growing child. Those who doubt whether children can suffer from the effects of stress must have forgotten their own childhood. Most adults bear scars from their earlier frustrations, fears and humiliations, and some of these will have lasting effects on personality and behavior. Many adults learning to relax remark how much they wished that they had learned these self-help, calming methods when they were at school. By introducing children to methods of stress control at an age when they are interested in acquiring physical skills and before they have learned bad habits of over-arousal and inappropriate muscle tension, they can be helped to acquire coping skills which will be of value throughout life.

THE POSITIVE ASPECTS OF STRESS

Stress for children can be fun and an exciting challenge. When it is well managed, it becomes the spur to action and is essential for success at work and sport. A measure of anxiety improves learning (Wankowski, 1969) and acceptable pressures can be creative, leading to excellent and original work. As they grow older, young people can learn to use manageable stress to their advantage. Shakespeare was aware of its value: "Sweet are the uses of adversity" (*As You Like It*). By taking some responsibility for their own well being, children can learn to enjoy the zest of life and experience positive stress without too much distress (Selye, 1974).

---

[1]This paper is based upon the author's work as a teacher of physical education in schools; with students at a teacher training college and at a university; with disturbed children at three Child Guidance clinics; as a physiotherapist at a Birmingham migraine clinic; and at a post natal Family Club for mothers with young children.

CHILDREN IN DISTRESS

Distress occurs when high levels of arousal and effort caused by anxiety, excitement or frustration are maintained for too long and become more than the child can manage (Wolff, 1981).

A long-term research study of thousands of children from birth to adulthood by the National Children's Bureau (Pringle et al, 1966; Davie, 1972) indicates that there is now plenty of evidence to show that a significant proportion of children suffer from behavioral and emotional problems in their early school years, and that many children suffer from stress disorders of sufficient severity to handicap them in their everyday life. There is no doubt that many young children maintain a high level of arousal much more often and for much longer than they should and some of them suffer intensely (McGee et al, 1984; Rutter, 1975).

THE CYCLE OF STRESS AND DISTRESS

Healthy functioning exists when arousal (effort) enhances performance. As Nixon (1976) has shown, increasing the effort beyond a certain point worsens the performance and can cause illness. Stress can affect learning. Over-anxiety acts as a block to understanding, disrupts efficient learning and the resultant failure may cause the child to lose all interest in academic work (Wankowski, 1969; Broadhurst, 1957). See Figure 1.

BREAKING THE CYCLE

There are inevitably some events that are so severely stressful that no child should be expected to cope alone and adult help will be required (Rutter, 1075). The cycle can be broken at several points:

A. It may be necessary to give the child a break, to change or avoid the situation.

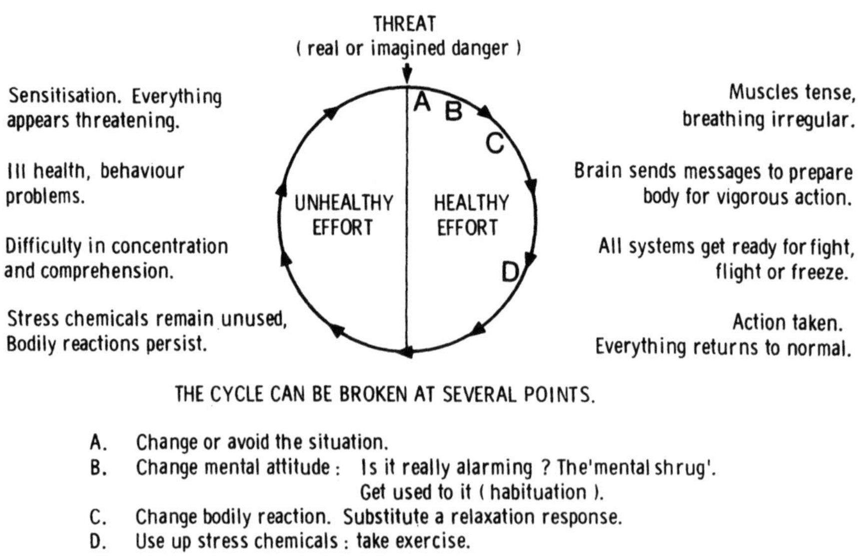

Figure 1. The cycle of stress and distress

B. Give help to change the mental attitude toward the threat. This may require adult help such as cognitive therapy, reassurance, habituation or hypnosis.

C. Change the bodily reaction by inducing relaxation. This is under the child's control.

D. Take vigorous but not exhausting exercise.

Laughter also can release tension and "fun" activities will help. (Bond, 1986; Madders, 1987).

PHYSICAL ACTIVITY AS AN AID TO RELAXATION

Vigorous physical activity is not only a good prelude to relaxation but is essential for the healthy growth of bones and muscles. Young children are skill-hungry and prowess in physical skills takes priority over most things. Upon their ability to climb, jump, kick a ball straight, wrestle, skip, hang upside down, dance ,will depend their acceptance by their peers. A boy or girl who is hopeless at games, is fearful of rough and tumble games, is clumsy and is always chosen last for the team will inevitably lose prestige in childhood; this may influence feelings of self esteem even into adulthood. Opportunities to become successful in a physical skill will help these young children. Porter and Omizo (1984) have found that large-muscle exercise and relaxation is helpful in treating hyperactive boys. Dance, especially expressive free dance, is an emotional experience and can relieve anxiety. Dance and drama have been found successful in helping abused children (Goodhill, 1987). Studies by Carter and Synolds (1976) have shown that relaxation can enhance handwriting.

INTRODUCING RELAXATION

There is no one particular coping method that is appropriate to all children, but muscle relaxation is easily learned when children are quite young (Frederick, 1980). This is especially the case when it is presented in the fun way (Koeppen, 1976; Madders, 1979, 1987). It is effective in coping with day-to-day stress (Jacobson, 1938) and can form the basis for a variety of quieting methods. I have used a multiplicity of methods and the training involves:

1. Recognizing tension by experiencing the contrast between tense and relaxed muscles in lively fun activities. Later there need be no preliminary tensing of muscles, the children start from where they are and then relax further.

2. A "calm down" quick relaxation technique which can be used anywhere without anyone noticing.

3. Guidance in how relaxation can be applied to everyday situations. Children share their successes.

4. Brief "time out" relaxation sitting in a chair. This is useful in the classroom. Relaxation of hands before writing.

5. Full relaxation lying on the floor.

6. Once relaxation has been learned, it is followed by Quieting.

QUIETING, A VISUALIZING METHOD

Many children have a remarkable eidetic memory: the ability to reproduce with almost photographic memory something they have seen. It would appear therefore that simple visualization is a good method for quieting a child's restless mind and cutting out unpleasant thoughts. There are a variety of quieting methods (Stroebel, 1983), but the one we have found most successful and interesting is: "My secret, happy picture." When they are relaxed, children visualize something that has given them pleasure, perhaps a place like the seaside, a pet, a favorite toy. The choice is theirs and the imagery is not guided by an adult, nor are they asked to tell anyone what they have chosen.

CLASSES WITH DISTURBED CHILDREN

Small groups of disturbed children were taught in Child Guidance clinics in Birmingham. One group was composed of withdrawn, fearful children, some of whom were suffering from school phobia. Another group was composed of stammerers, mostly boys because the incidence of stammering amongst boys is about five times as high as in girls (Jones, 1979). The third group was composed of hyperactive and disruptive children.

In all groups, vigorous activity and some coaching in certain physical skills was followed by calming, quiet movements requiring concentration and control. Some dance/drama gave opportunities for make-believe and emotional release. This was followed by relaxation on the floor, followed by visualization. A quick emergency technique was taught so that the children could use it at any time they felt over anxious.

With stammerers, no attention was paid to speech, but there were lively dance/drama activities (jabbering in a "foreign language"), followed by calm movements and relaxation. They went from this class to the speech therapists who reported that the children spoke more easily, were more receptive to training and spoke with less hesitation (Birmingham Education Committee, 1957). This assessment was supported by parents.

In the hyperactive group, many were normal, active children denied sufficient opportunities to relieve their tension and frustration by physical activity. They were encouraged to discover that they could enjoy vigorous and acceptable physical activity and then appreciate feelings of relaxation and calm. In all classes there was close cooperation with the psychiatrists, educational psychologists and speech therapists.

Relaxation with young children has also been found to be useful in the management of pain (McGrath, 1987), asthma (Dinnage, 1972; Sirot, 1974), migraine and other disorders. The above reports deal with sick or disturbed children. Preventative methods in school or at home may well be of greater importance.

RELAXATION IN THE PRIMARY SCHOOL CURRICULUM

An example of relaxation included as part of a physical education lesson for five to six year olds:

1. "Ogres" - Move around the room stamping vigorously, punching and looking angry.

2. "Escape from the ogre" - Creep around the room very softly and quietly.

3. "Free" - Stand still and relaxed, with a slight smile. Become aware of the pleasant feelings of relaxation.

4. Relaxation lying on the floor (only a very short spell) - When they have had some experience of relaxing, visualization is included ("My secret happy picture"). Children stretch and get up slowly.

Later, in the classroom, students are encouraged to discuss their experiences of relaxation and share ideas of when they could apply them. They also learn the quick emergency technique of calm breathing and relaxing hands.

Older children (9 to 10 years) enjoy games of strong, resisted tension followed by relaxation (DES 1953, 1972) and in testing each other for degrees of tension and relaxation.

RESULTS: COMMENTS BY CHILDREN

A group of children who had received six lessons in relaxation aided by a cassette and book were invited a year later to say how they had used the methods. They reported to an uninvolved adult:

Girl, 6 years: "I get frightened when the teacher shouts at the other children, so I say to myself: 'Relax, relax, relax' and it helps."

Girl, 8 years: "I climbed up a tree and no one knew where I was. I got stuck and couldn't get down. I was very scared, then I thought: 'STOP. Relax, and you will be able to think.' So I did. And I came down."

Girl, 8 years: "I get frightened by noises at night and can't sleep, so I relax and look at my secret happy picture."

Boy, 9 years: "I get worked up over my music exams and my fingers go stiff. Now I relax beforehand and it helps. I use the emergency trick."

Boy, 11 years: "I get aggressive when I play football, and when I was kicked on the ankle I was all ready to hit the boy. Then I relaxed my shoulders and calmed down. And I didn't get sent off as I was before."

REACTIONS BY TEACHERS

Comments by three school teachers (in three primary schools in the West Midlands) who introduced relaxation to 5- to 8-year-olds, either in physical education lessons or in the classroom.

"They enjoy it and are much quieter going in to lessons after P.E. It is diagnostic too: when they lie relaxing I notice those who are in difficulties and find problems I hadn't been aware of. They help me, too, because when I'm getting worked up they are likely to say, "Miss, you ought to relax."

"We found there was less nail biting and they were not so restless after a spell of relaxation."

"I usually give the children some hand relaxation exercises before they start writing. I find it helps the anxious ones who hold the pen too tightly. I sometimes have a brief spell of relaxing at their desks, looking at their "secret happy picture" when they are getting over-excited. I have introduced the ideas of tension and relaxation into English lessons: they try to find as many different words as they can to describe how they feel when they are tense and when they are relaxed. They have also used the ideas in art, painting things that have frightened them and also pictures that are calm and happy."

CONCLUSIONS

Although there is now ample, well-documented evidence for the positive effects of relaxation for adults, and some research into its value for sick or disturbed children, and growing interest and research into results of teaching relaxation to older school children (Setterlind, 1983), there is a paucity of serious study of the long-term effects of teaching simple relaxation and stress control methods to young children. It is difficult for adults to change long held habits of over reacting, high arousal and prolonged muscle tension. It is in early childhood that skills of relaxation can most easily be learned.

ACKNOWLEDGMENTS

The Cycle of Stress and Distress is reproduced for "*Relax and Be Happy: Techniques for 5 to 18 year olds,*" by permission of the publishers.

REFERENCES

Bond, T. (1986). "Games for Life and Social Skills," Hutchinson, London.

Broadhurst, P.L.(1957). Emotionality and the Yerkes-Dobson Law, *J. Exp. Psychol.* 54.

Carter, L., Synolds, D. (1974). Effects of Relaxation Training upon Handwriting Quaility, *J. of Learning Disabilities*, 7, 52:55.

Davie, R. (1972). "From Birth to Seven," Longman, in association with National Children's Bureau, London.

D.E.S. 1953 "Planning the Programme," H.M.S.O., London.

D.E.S. (1972). "Movement. Physical Education in the Primary Years," H.M.S.O., London.

Dinnage, R. (1972). "The Handicapped Child, Vol. 2," Longman in association with National Children's bureau, London.

Goodhill, S. (1987). Dance/Movement Therapy for Abused Children, *Arts in Psychotherapy*, Vol 14,(1) 59:68.

Jacobson, E. (1938). Progressive Relaxation, Chicago: University of Chicago Press.

Jones, M.V. (1979). "Speech and Language Problems," Charles C. Thomas, Springhill, USA.

Koeppen, A.S. (1974). Relaxation Training for Children, *Elem. Sch. Guid. & Couns.*, 9:14.

Madders, J. (1979). "Stress and Relaxation," Macdonald Optima, London.

Madders, J. (1987). "Relax and Be Happy. Techniques for 5 to 18 year olds," Unwin-Hyman, London.

McGee, R,, Silva, P.A. (1984). Behaviour problems in a population of 7 year old children, *J. of Ch. Psych. and Psychiat.*, vol 25, No.2.

McGrath, P.A. (1987). The multidimensional assessment and management of recurrent pain syndromes in children, *Behav. Res. Ther.*, vol 25, No 4, 21:263.

Nixon, P.G.F. The Human Function Curve, *The Practitioner*, 217, 765:769 and 935:944.

Ollendick, T.H., Matson, J.C. & Helsel, W.T. (1985). Fears in childhood and adolescence, *Behav. Res. Ther.*, Vol 23, No 4, 465:467.

Porter, S. (1984,Mar). The effect of relaxation training/large muscle exercise for hyperactive boys, *Exceptional Child*, vol 3(1), 54:64.

Pringle, K.M. (1974). "The Needs of Children," Hutchinson and Co., London.
Rutter, M. (1975). "Helping Troubled Children," Penguin Educational Books, London.
Selye, H. (1974). "Stress without Distress," Hodder and Stoughton, London.
Setterlind, S. (1978). Introducing Relaxation Training in Swedish Schools, Department for Sport Psychology, Orebro University, Sweden.
Siroto, A.D., Mahoney, M.J. (1974). Relaxing on cue: the self regulation of asthma, *J. Behav. Ther.*, 5, 65:66.
Stroebel, C.F. (1983). "Q.R. The Quieting Response," Berkeley Books, New York.
Varna, V.P. (ed) (1973). "Stresses in Children," Hodder and Stoughton, London.
Wolff, S. (1981). Children under Stress, Penguin Books, London.

HELPING YOUTH MANAGE STRESS: A CHALLENGE FOR EDUCATORS

Kathryn Raymer[1] and Wesley E. Sime[2]

[1]Lincoln High School
Lincoln Public Schools
Lincoln, Nebraska

[2]Biofeedback and Stress Management
University of Nebraska
Lincoln, Nebraska

...a high school student is absent every time a test is given in Biology...a sprinter gets butterflies in her stomach before every race...a twelve-year-old becomes embarrassed every time he is paired with a girl in social studies class...a six-year-old whose parents have been divorced recently complains of headaches everyday in school when he goes to his gifted reading class...

Each of these students is reacting to a stressful situation. Some students may adjust to these situations with little difficulty; others may feel considerable pressure. Regardless of how students perceive various stressors, these situations are examples of stress-related concerns which students bring to the school setting *and* which are created by the activities and challenges offered in the school setting. Many of these stress-related problems interfere with learning.

Statistics reported in a *U.S. News and World Report* article in 1986 indicated that: 1) three in five children born today will live with a single parent by age eighteen; 2) two of four children age thirteen and under live with parents who both work; 3) one child in six has tried marijuana and one in three has tried alcohol before ninth grade; 4) the number of girls who have had sexual intercourse before age fifteen has tripled in two decades; and 5) the suicide rate of youths under fifteen has tripled since 1960 ("Children Under Stress," 1986).

A study conducted by the American Council of Education and the University of California-Los Angeles of more than 300,000 university freshmen entering college in 1988 suggested that these freshmen were the "most anxious and emotionally unstable ever measured, according to their self-descriptions. More than 10 per cent reported depression, and 21.5 per cent said they felt 'overwhelmed' by their responsibilities, up from 8.2 and 16 per cent, respectively, in 1985." ("Signs of Stress," 1989).

Given these data, it is not surprising that *up to 35 per cent of American kids suffer stress-related health problems at some point* ("Children Under Stress," 1986). A recent Harris survey revealed that 35 per cent of students report they have not learned about personal feelings and 24 per cent of junior high school students have not learned about stress. According to the survey, eight million students--nearly one-quarter of the American school population--receive little or no health education. This study also showed that those students who do receive comprehensive health education are more apt to express a feeling of control over their own health and are more likely to follow more positive health practices ("Met Life," 1989).

Professor Lee Salk has considered the long-term effects of stress on tomorrow's adults, holding that they are yet to be determined, but he adds, there are some disturbing clues. Because studies show that children tend to repeat parental patterns with their own children, a self-perpetuating cycle of destructive behavior may already be in motion.

This notion of a self-perpetuating cycle is particularly significant given Louis Harris's (1987) report in *Inside America* that 89% of Americans feel "stressed out." Of these stressed-out individuals, approximately 36% do nothing to avoid or alleviate stress.

Within the school setting students experience various kinds of stressors, including: 1) being overloaded with material that is too difficult; 2) being punished for something they did not do; 3) being bored; 4) being embarrassed by having a low grade called out; 5) being afraid of being wrong; and 6) being the last one chosen for a team. Students respond to these stressors in very diverse ways. The responses of young people vary from totally passive acceptance to severe disruptive behaviors, such as deliberately getting into trouble, breaking school equipment and cheating. Some students respond in the first part of the classic flight/fight mode by simply dropping out of school (to flee).

In order to create a positive, stress-reducing school climate, teachers need to help students begin to feel a sense of personal identity. In the large school settings that exist for many students today, it becomes very easy for a student to feel like she/he is a number, one of numerous faces in an over-crowded classroom, a name on an attendance roster. In addition, students need to understand "why" they are doing what they are doing, i.e., why certain rules exist, why what they are learning is important, how what they are learning applies to real life, and why they have to take tests and complete certain assignments. Students also need to have a sense of group identity, a sense of belonging and a sense of control over some small part of their school or home experience.

In personal interviews conducted by the first author with over 100 young people, their major suggestion for reducing stress in the school setting was for teachers to be more understanding of their needs. These needs included being treated respectfully, being placed appropriately in classes, providing help when they are ill, and recognizing when they have personal problems which may be interfering with their performance in school. Students also want their teachers to be happier people themselves, to not let their personal problems interfere with the way they interact with students.

Schultz and Heuchert (1983) suggest the following prescription to help teachers create a classroom with low stress and high productivity:

1. Diminish the perceived threat to the student.

2. Increase student alertness through energizers.

3. Decrease tension through calming strategies.

4. Increase the variety of modes and topics of instruction.

5. Create a more liveable environment.

6. Re-discover your own creativity and delight in teaching.

They add that we must find helpful ways of breaking through this cycle of conflict; ways to divert child energy away from anxious feelings that accompany stressful school events and that lead to more problems; ways that help children to develop self-control, experience interpersonal success, master the school environment, and that establish the foundation for personal worth and dignity throughout their lives.

When children are coping successfully they are aware of their feelings and are able to express them. They value themselves as worthwhile individuals. They perform at expected achievement levels in school. They enjoy play, and they can develop and sustain friendships.

Today's children, however, are increasingly thrust into situations which require independence and self-reliance before they have developed the necessary coping skills. *If we are to make a major impact on the behavioral health of this nation, it is essential to educate our youth in stress management coping skills.* It is vitally important to help them establish these behavior patterns early in life. Obviously, it is much easier to help children learn new behavior patterns rather than help them "unlearn" ineffective habits later in life.

School-age children can be taught to identify situations in their own lives which are stressful. they can learn to predict when these event are likely to occur. They can learn ways to deal with stressors in their lives so that when they do experience stress, they know how to handle it. They can learn to improve their stress coping strategies by repeated practice, including reviewing their successes and failures.

Effective stress management education programs: 1) help young people understand stress and stressors; 2) teach appropriate coping and relaxation skills and when to use them; and 3) provide practice in non-threatening situations.

In order to provide educators the necessary knowledge to develop appropriate stress management education programs for their students, the authors initiated a graduate workshop in Stress Management for Educators at the University of Nebraska, Lincoln, Nebraska, in the summer of 1988. The course is scheduled to be repeated in the summer of 1989. The response to the course in 1988 was so overwhelming that the class size was eventually more than doubled in response to student demand. The enrollment consisted of full-time teachers, administrators and support personnel from the following areas (in descending order according to the number of students enrolled): Curriculum and Instruction; Health, Physical Education and Recreation; Educational Administration; and Special Education.

A complete description of the course follows.

A WORKSHOP IN STRESS MANAGEMENT FOR EDUCATORS

Course Description:

This workshop will help educators: 1) develop an academic understanding of basic concepts in stress management; 2) learn to recognize symptoms of stress; 3) understand the positive and negative impact of stress in educational settings; and 4) develop program skills in stress coping for the classroom. Simultaneously, participants will learn personal stress and tension control skills.

What is stress? What causes stress? How can stress be identified? How do people respond differently to potential stressful situations? What is the physiology of the stress response? What are the psychophysiological effects of excessive stress? How can stress be controlled? All of these questions will be major topics for consideration. Specific emphasis will be given to understanding how stress affects learning and ways of managing stress in various educational settings.

Participants will develop a blueprint for an effective stress management training program which can be adapted for use with children, youth, teachers, support staff and administrators.

Course Objectives: The participants will:

1. Gain a comprehensive understanding of stress and stress management techniques to facilitate the development of unit programming.

2. Develop basic skills in several personal stress and tension control strategies, including progress relaxation, autogenic training, etc.

3. Develop a blueprint knowledge base for minimum entry-level competency in effective stress management programming.

4. Understand how stress affects learning and develop strategies for managing stress in a variety of educational settings.

Course Content Overview:

1. Basic Concepts in Stress Management

    a. A Conceptual Understanding of Stressors (Eustress and Distress) and Stress Responses

    b. Personality, Perception and Sources of Stress

    c. The Physiology of Stress and Relaxation

    d. Stress Pathophysiology and Stress-Related Disorders

    e. The Relationship Between Lifestyle Behavior Patterns and Stressors/Stress Responses

2. Strategies for Enhancing Stress Management Skills

    a. Social and Environmental Change Strategies

    b. Cognitive and Behavioral Interventions

    c. Strategies to Achieve a Relaxation Response

3. Application of Learning Theory, Measurements and Ethics in Stress Management

a. Measurement of Stress Reactions and Relaxation Responses

b. Application of Learning Theory to the Teaching of Stress Management

c. Knowledge of Experimental Design and Research Related to Stress

d. Professional Conduct and Ethical Practices

Creative Ways to Teach Stress Management in Educational Settings:

Included in this section are several of the creative ways students in the class devised to teach stress management skills in a variety of educational settings. The lesson plans were developed for student populations spanning the range of pre-school to adult learners and public to private settings. They include unique ways of teaching students about stress and stress coping skills while at the same time teaching the curriculum unique to the content area (e.g., literature, social studies, health and music). Obviously, teaching stress management and relaxation skills as an independent class or as a unit in health or physical education is the more traditional mode of delivery.

However, the following examples illustrate several unusual ideas for teaching stress management and relaxation skills "across the curriculum."

Substitute Teaching: A series of one-day/one-class-period lessons which could be adapted to different grade levels when the classroom teacher did not leave plans for the class, when the class finished the assigned work early, or when the motivational and behavioral level of the class needed adjusting.

"Gear-shifting" in the Classroom: Relaxation strategies to help students quickly and calmly move from one instructional mode to another, e.g., moving from high intensity (excitement) in group work to lower intensity (relaxation) in working through individual class assignments.

Literature Class: Helping students understand stressors, stress reactions and the effectiveness of various coping skills as they analyze characters in literature selections.

Elementary Classrooms: Helping students understand their own feelings and reactions to stress through discussion of stories of children in distressing or exciting situations and subsequently teaching them a variety of stress coping strategies to use in similar "real-life" situations.

Typewriting/Computer Classes: Helping students to learn relaxation skills to help eliminate the muscle tension in arms, shoulders, neck and back which develops while working at a keyboard for extended periods of time.

Vocal/Instrumental Music Classes: Teaching students diaphragmatic breathing and progressive muscle relaxation techniques which can be used to enhance quality of performance, to minimize fatigue and to gain skills in efficiency during performances.

Athletic Teams: Helping athletes learn to recognize signs and symptoms of competitive stress and to learn relaxation to both calm them and to facilitate smooth, coordinated effort for peak performance during the intensity of competition.

It is our firm belief that in order to make a significant impact in developing stress coping strategies on a wide scale, instruction must be included in the school curricula for kids at an early age. Hopefully, teachers from numerous disciplines will be encouraged to seek training personally for the purpose of teaching and modeling stress coping strategies.

REFERENCES

Blom, G., Cheney, B., & Snoddy, J.(1986). Stress in childhood: An intervention model *for teachers and other professionals*. New York: Teachers College Press.

Brenner, A. (1984). *Helping children cope with stress.* Massachusetts: Lexington Books.

Chandler, L. (1985). *Assessing stress in children.* New York: Praeger.

Chandler, L. (1985). *Children under stress: Understanding emotional adjustment reactions.* Illinois: Thomas.

Children under stress. (1986, October 27). *U.S. News and World Report*, pp. 58-63.

Dreikurs, R., Grunwald, B., & Pepper, F. (1982). *Maintaining sanity in the classroom.* New York: Harper & Row.

Elkind, D. (1981). *The hurried child: Growing up too fast too soon.* Massachusetts. Addison-Wesley Publishing Company.

Garmezy, N. & Rutter, M. (Eds). (1983). *Stress, coping and development in children.* New York: McGraw-Hill.

Greenberg, S. (1984). *Stress and the teaching profession.* Baltimore: Paul H. Brookes Publishing Company.

Harris, L. (1987). *Inside America.* New York: Random House.

Hertzfeld, G. & Powel, R. (1986). *Coping for kids, a complete stress management control program.* New York: The Center for Applied Research in Education.

Humphrey, J. (1985). *Stress in childhood.* New York: AMS Press.

Humphrey, James & Humphrey, Joy (1985). *Controlling stress in children.* Illinois: Thomas.

Humphrey, James & Humphrey, Joy (1981). *Reducing stress in children through creative relaxation.* Illinois: Thomas.

Met Life Foundation/Louis Harris Survey. (1989, January). *Health-EXTRA,* 14 (2),p.8.

Schultz, E. & Heuchert, C. (1983). *Child Stress and the School Experience.* New York: Human Science Press.

Signs of stress in class of 1992. (1989). *Brain Mind Bulletin, 14*,(5), 1&6.

Student stress and suicide. *The Practitioner, 14*,(2), 1-12.

Wolff, S. (1981). *Children under stress*. Harmondsworth: Penguin.

STRESS RESPONSES AMONG MOTHERS DURING PREGNANCY, IN LABOR AND WITH INFANTS

STRESS AND PREGNANCY COMPLICATIONS: A PROSPECTIVE STUDY

Ellen Clifford[1], Susan M. Weaver[1] and Douglas M. Hay[2]

[1]University of Hull
Hull, England

[2]Hull Maternity Hospital
Hull, England

INTRODUCTION

Pregnancy is a major life event for most women and their families. Practical alterations in employment, financial status and living arrangements are likely to occur. In addition, roles, responsibilities and relationships with significant other people (principally the father) may be directly provoked by the impending birth of a child. The ease with which these adaptations can be achieved will be a function of many factors, including whether or not the pregnancy was planned or unwanted and also personal variables such as the woman's personality and coping skills.

In recent years there has been considerable interest in the influence of psychological factors on the course and outcome of pregnancy and labor (Morris, 1983). Interventions have been largely directed at the labor experience, developing psychologically based techniques for minimizing pain and facilitating the labor process (Dick-Read, 1933; Lamaze, 1956). Other work has evaluated the psychological impact of the contemporary medical management of pregnancy and childbirth (Oakley, 1983). The recent trend for a greater number of women to request home delivery and to seek the presence of the father or another supportive companion during labor and delivery attests to the importance they attribute to their psychological and emotional environment during childbirth.

That a woman's psychological and emotional state at the time of labor may affect her experience of that labor is uncontentious. Anxious women are more likely to label physical sensations as painful or threatening and their ability to respond appropriately to instructions given by medical staff may be reduced. Furthermore, evidence indicates that anxiety may reduce the tolerance of pain (Morris, Copstick and Taylor, 1986).

Labor, however, is only one part of the childbearing process. The focus of this article is the woman's psychosocial situation over the course of pregnancy and its impact on a wide range of medical conditions which may threaten the pregnancy or the normal development of the fetus. If psychosocial factors such as life events or lack of social support increase obstetric risk, then mechanisms other than purely psychological ones must be involved. At least three possible factors have been suggested in the stress-to-outcome sequence: 1) elevated levels of maternal stress hormones; 2) changes in maternal cardio-vascular functioning (especially raised blood pressure) and; 3) potentially damaging behavior provoked by the stressful situation, such as increased smoking, substance abuse, poor clinic attendance and poor self-care in general (including inadequate diet). In all three cases, anxiety is seen as central in precipitating these internal and behavioral changes (Reading, 1983).

Whatever the underlying mechanisms, popular wisdom has for centuries claimed that a woman's experiences, feelings and behavior during pregnancy can affect her health and that of her infant. An extreme example is the once widespread belief that the content of a woman's imaginings (in particular violent or horrific images) could directly impact on the infant, producing birthmarks or deformities which resembled the specific content of the image (Blondel, 1727). Medical opinion regarding the vulnerability of the embryo and fetus to external trauma has vacillated over the years. However, the prevailing medical view in the first half of this century of a fetus which was virtually invulnerable to such trauma has been revised. The documented effects of rubella, smoking and toxic substances such as lead have necessitated altering traditional beliefs.

The empirical work concerned with psychosocial trauma and obstetric outcome is more equivocal. Most recent research on this subject has employed the 'life events' model, using inventory measures similar to the Schedule of Recent Experiences developed by Holmes and Rahe (1967). Consequently, the methodological difficulties associated with this approach (e.g., Rabkin & Struening, 1976) also characterize the relevant data concerning pregnancy outcomes. The use of retrospective reporting, inadequacies in the assessment of life events and emotional state, and the neglect of temporal factors in the relationship between life events and poor pregnancy outcomes present difficult problems in the interpretation of the data (see Istvan, 1986 for a review).

However, the more proficient studies which have also used comparable measures suggest that stress during pregnancy (either life events or high anxiety) is prognostic of maternal complications, labor difficulties and suboptimal infant outcomes. Newton et al, (1979) showed higher life event scores late in pregnancy to be associated with pre-term delivery. Similarly, mothers of low birth weight babies reported a high incidence of life events (Newton and Hunt, 1984). Some work has examined life events or anxiety over the course of pregnancy, indicating a complex relationship between outcome and temporal factors. For example, Gorsuch and Key (1974) found that women with abnormal pregnancies characteristically experienced high state anxiety early in pregnancy and high life event scores in the final trimester. State anxiety scores occasioned by hospital admission have been shown to be predictive of length of labor (Beck, Siegel and Davidson, 1980). However, a differential and counter-intuitive pattern in state anxiety has been observed in the period preceding admission (Edwards and Jones, 1970). In this study, women with normal deliveries showed an increase in anxiety in the two weeks prior to delivery, while the anxiety scores of those having complicated deliveries declined.

These seemingly inconsistent findings on state anxiety may describe an inappropriate coping strategy in which defensive denial of the threat inherent in the impending birth leads to inefficient preparation and consequent high anxiety when confronted with actual labor. Similar paradoxical effects were noted by Janis (1958) in his original studies on pre-operative anxiety. The relative merits of preparation and denial prior to bereavement have also been discussed (Friedman, Mason and Hamburg, 1963; Parkes and Weiss, 1983).

Relatively little research has considered the combined contribution of psychosocial risk factors to pregnancy outcomes. Nuckolls, Cassel and Kaplan (1972) classified subjects according to both their life event scores and their psychosocial assets. Results indicated that only women with high life events scores in combination with low psychosocial assets were threatened with a great risk of poor outcomes. Psychosocial assets included, among other things, social support. A similar interaction between life events and social support was reported by Norbeck and Tilden (1983) in a more methodologically sophisticated study. Furthermore, both delivery and post partum complications have been shown to be predicted by high SRE scores and family dysfunction (Smilkstein et al, 1984).

This brief review indicates that life events, anxiety and social support are all factors affecting pregnancy outcome. The effects of these variables individually and in combination needs clarification. It also appears that monitoring psychosocial risk factors over the course of pregnancy is necessary in order to understand the complexity of their relationship to obstetric outcomes.

In the present study, women were assessed with respect to life events, anxiety (state and trait), and social support early in their pregnancies and again in the second and third trimesters. Following delivery, data were collated concerning maternal complications during pregnancy, labor difficulties, and infant outcomes. The study is prospective in that the medical outcomes were unknown to the researchers (and to the subjects in nearly all cases) when the psychological data were collected. Life events and their impact cannot, however, be reported until after they have happened. Therefore, such reports are inevitably retrospective. In this study the time interval over which subjects were asked to reflect was relatively short, compared to most life events studies. Also, the dates of events were documented in an effort to verify the event and minimize errors in recall.

A modified version of the Schedule of Recent Experiences, which attempted to take into account previous technical and theoretical criticisms, was used. For example, ambiguous items were clarified and those symptomatic of illness were omitted. Originally, the authors of the technique (Holmes and Rahe, 1967) believed that 'readjustment' was the key factor in precipitating health changes, a concept that has been the subject of widespread debate (Brown, 1986). Similarly, use of the standard Life Change Units in assessing event impact has been forcefully challenged (Craig and Brown, 1984) for not taking individual differences in meaning into account. As a consequence of this debate and the research addressing it, only potentially negative events were included in the life events list used in this study, and subjects' evaluations of the impact of events were evaluated (Sarason, Johnson and Siegel, 1978; Norbeck and Tilden, 1983).

It was expected that high life event scores, high state and trait anxiety and low social support would each be predictive of poor pregnancy outcome. It was also anticipated that women reporting more than one of these variables would be at increased risk. No specific predictions were made about trimester effects, but particular interest lay in the pattern of change in state anxiety over the course of pregnancy for women with normal and complicated outcomes.

METHOD

Subjects

One hundred volunteers were randomly recruited from the total population attending the Ante-natal Clinic at Hull Maternity Hospital (4000 births annually). The final sample consisted of 93 women, attrition resulting from (1) women changing clinics, (2) an inadvertent omission during repeat visits, or (3) the discovery that they were carrying twins (3 cases). The mean age of the resulting sample was 25.5 years, of which 43 were primiparus and 50 multiparus. Seventy-eight percent of the sample were from the Manual Worker social class or below, according to the husband's occupation.

Assessment Instruments

Three questionnaires were used which measured life events, social support and anxiety. A fourth 'information' sheet contained items concerning demographic features of the subjects. The measures of life events and social support were based on previously existing instruments, but were substantially modified for the particular purpose of this study. The instruments are described below:

Life Events List. This comprised a 26-item inventory adapted from the Schedule of Recent Experiences (Holmes and Rahe, 1967). Only major life events (those with more than 20 Life Change Units) and only those with potentially negative impact were included. All items which originally indicated 'change' only (e.g., change in financial situation) were rephrased to indicate a 'worsening' of the situation. Six items were added: death of a pet, trouble with children, burglary or robbery, car accident, physical assault, and a final open ended statement inviting subjects to list additional events which they felt to be important.

Subjects in the first instance were asked to report events over the period of time since they had become pregnant (about 16 weeks) and in the subsequent two interviews only events which had happened during the intervening period were recorded (about 12-week and 9-week intervals). Life Change Unit weightings were not used. Rather, subjects indicated, on a scale of -3 to +3, to what degree they found each event distressing or welcome. This enabled an evaluation of the impact of events for different individuals. Two scores were then available for analysis, that based on the simple frequency of life events (LEF) and the total of the Life Event Impact Scores (LEI).

Social Support Questionnaire. This consisted of 27 items based on Barrera, Sandler and Ramsay's (1982) Inventory of Social Supportive Behaviors (ISSB). In this instrument subjects indicate how frequently they have received specific supportive behaviors during the preceding month. This evaluation was made in four discrete areas: Directive Guidance, Non-directive Support, Positive Social Interaction and Tangible Assistance (Barrera and Ainlay, 1983). Eleven of the original items were omitted because it was felt that their apparent overlap with other items would confuse the subjects. Also, the original 5-point rating scale was shortened to 4 points (never, occasionally, quite often and very often).

Subjects were asked to answer each question and also to circle any item numbers for which they would have liked more of the particular type of help or support mentioned, thus yielding measures of both support received and satisfaction with support (number of items not circled).

State-Trait Anxiety Inventory. This is a 40-item self-report questionnaire, 20 items measuring trait (enduring) anxiety and 20 measuring state (transient) anxiety (Spielberger, 1983). For the Trait measure subjects were asked to reflect about how they usually felt 'before they were pregnant.'

Information Sheet. This was a record of: woman's age, number of weeks pregnant, number of children, living arrangements (with husband, boyfriend, parents, flatmate, on own), woman's occupation, husband/boyfriend's occupation, number of previous pregnancies and smoker or non-smoker.

Medical Outcomes

Following the delivery of all the subjects, information pertaining to complications of pregnancy, labor and delivery, and infant status were transcribed from the computerized hospital records which were routinely completed by hospital staff. These outcomes reflect prior decisions taken by hospital medical staff as to what are 'noteworthy' medical events. Some serious outcomes were not included because their cause is either known or believed to be unrelated to psychosocial stress (e.g., cord around the neck, injury incurred at birth, malpresentation). Also, not all of the outcomes monitored occurred in the sample. The complete list of complications which were potentially included is as follows: *Complications of Pregnancy*--miscarriage (spontaneous abortion); PET (hypertension); eclampsia; venous thrombosis, ante partum hemorrhage; threatened abortion; *Labor Difficulties*--emergency Caesarean Section; forceps delivery; venthouse delivery; post partum hemorrhage; ruptured uterus; manual removal of placenta; prolonged labor; *Infant Outcomes*--transfer to Special Care Baby Unit; fetal distress; small for gestational age; prematurity (less than 37 weeks); congenital malformation (presumed not to be genetically determined); Apgar Score less than 7; respiratory distress; stillbirth; neonatal death within first week, and; pyloric stenosis (within 6 weeks after birth).

Procedure

One thousand women due to come to the Ante-natal Clinic for a 16-week appointment were alerted by post that they might be asked to participate in a study concerned with "the things that happen to women during their pregnancies." Potential subjects were approached in the Ante-natal Clinic by the midwife and asked to participate in the study. Approximately 80 percent agreed, the most frequent reason for refusal being a reluctance to leave a companion who had accompanied them. The recruitment of subjects did not follow a prescribed schedule but depended on the simultaneous availability of the midwife (for recruiting) and the psychologist (for interviewing).

Interviews were conducted by the psychologist in a Mobile Assessment Unit adjacent to the Clinic. In the first session, a brief account of the procedure for that day and for the reexamining two assessments was given, followed by the questionnaires. All life events were briefly discussed with the subjects and then dated.

At the 16-week assessment, subjects completed first the Information Sheet, followed by the Trait Anxiety, State Anxiety, Life Event and Social Support questionnaires. All women were reassessed at 28 and 37 weeks of pregnancy under the same conditions, but only the State Anxiety Scale, Life Events List and Social Support questionnaires were readministered.

Treatment of Data

Because discrete medical outcomes occurred with insufficient frequency to permit analysis, all subjects were classified into one of two groups, Normal (N=49) or Complicated (N=44). Women in the Normal group had none of the outcomes listed above, while those in the Complicated group had at least one. Data were then subjected to Analysis of Variance and Multiple Regression Analysis. The latter included demographic variables tabulated from the Information Sheets.

As few subjects indicated dissatisfaction with their social support, data pertaining to this measure are not presented in the results. Furthermore, the separate subscales of the Social Support Questionnaire were highly correlated (r's ranging from .35 to .78) and hence only the total Social Support scores are subjected to analysis.

The Life Event Frequency scores and Life Event Impact scores for the second and third assessment interviews were corrected to account for the different time intervals over which subjects recalled their life events. A simple transformation was performed in which a weekly average for each subject was obtained, then multiplied by 16 (the time period of the first report) to produce 3 equivalent time intervals.

RESULTS

Two-way ANOVAS were used to explore the separate effects of Life Events, Anxiety and Social Support (Type of Outcome X Trimesters). Five subjects were randomly omitted from the Normal group to provide equal cell numbers. However, correlations and multi-variate analyses are conducted on the total sample of 93.

Life Events

Mean scores for Life Events Frequency (LEF) and Life Events Impact (LEI) over trimesters can be found in Table 1. The frequency and impact scores were highly correlated, r = -.79, -.44 and -.66 for the 3 trimesters (LEI scores are negative values). Hence, patterns in the data are similar for these two measures.

The means indicate that women with Complicated Outcomes report both a higher frequency of life events throughout pregnancy and give greater negative impact ratings to those life events than do women with Normal Outcomes. Normal Outcomes are associated with a progressive decline in both the Frequency and Impact scores, whereas with Complicated Outcomes this decline is less pronounced. In fact,

Table 1. Mean Life Events Frequency Scores and Life Events Impact Scores According to the Trimester of Pregnancy

	Life Events Frequency			Life Events Impact		
	Trimester			Trimester		
Type of Outcome	1st	2nd	3rd	1st	2nd	3rd
Normal	1.66	1.60	0.94	-2.80	-1.49	-0.85
Complicated	1.95	1.82	1.93	-3.84	-2.34	-3.80

N = 44 in each cell

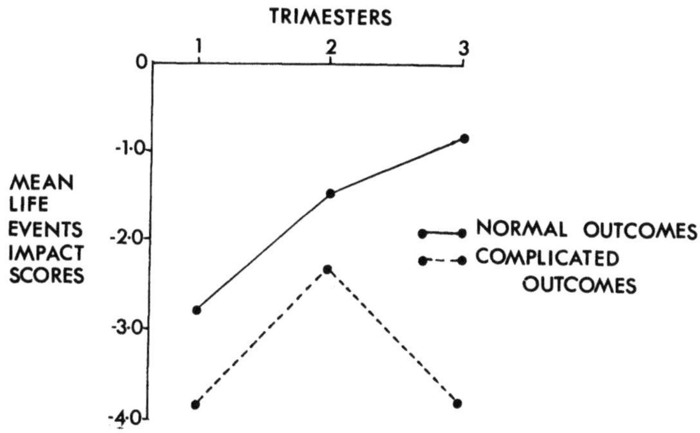

Figure 1. Mean life events impact scores for women with normal and complicated outcomes according to trimesters.

mean values in the first and third trimesters are equivalent. These observations are confirmed by Analysis of Variance, which for LEI scores shows a main effect for Type of Outcome ($F = 7.82$; df 1,86; $p < .001$) and a significant interaction of Type of Outcome with Trimesters ($F = 9.18$; df 2,172; $p < .001$). The latter is shown in Figure 1. Only the interaction reaches significance for the LEF scores ($F = 7.40$; df 2,172; $p < .001$).

Anxiety

Trait Anxiety means for Normal Outcomes ($M = 32.98$) and Complicated Outcomes ($M = 37.09$) are significantly different ($t = 2.15$, df 91; $p < .05$), with higher Trait Anxiety in the Complicated group.

The only significant effect for State Anxiety is the interaction between Type of Outcome and Trimesters ($F = 18.4$; df 2,172; $p < .001$). This is shown in Figure 2. Women with Complicated Outcomes report their highest State Anxiety in the first trimester. State Anxiety drops in the second and raises again only slightly in the third trimester. Women with Normal Outcomes, however, show lowest State Anxiety in the first trimester, with subsequent rises in the following trimesters. The difference between women with Normal and Complicated Outcomes is significant in the first trimester ($F = 6,83$; df 2,172, $p < .001$), and for women with Complicated Outcomes the drop in State Anxiety between the first and second trimesters is significant ($F = 3.80$; df 2,172; $p < .025$).

Social Support

Analysis of Variance conducted on the total Social Support scores (collapsed over the 4 subscales) shows only the interaction between Type of Outcome and Trimesters to be significant ($F = 5.11$; df 2,172; $p < .05$). Women with Normal Outcomes show very little change over the course of pregnancy, with highest Social Support scores in the second trimester (see Figure 3). Those with Complications report highest Social Support in the first trimester and this then diminishes. There are no significant differences between the two groups of women in any of the trimesters, but the decline in Social Support between the first and second trimester for Complicated women is significant ($F = 3.15$; df 2,172; $p < .05$).

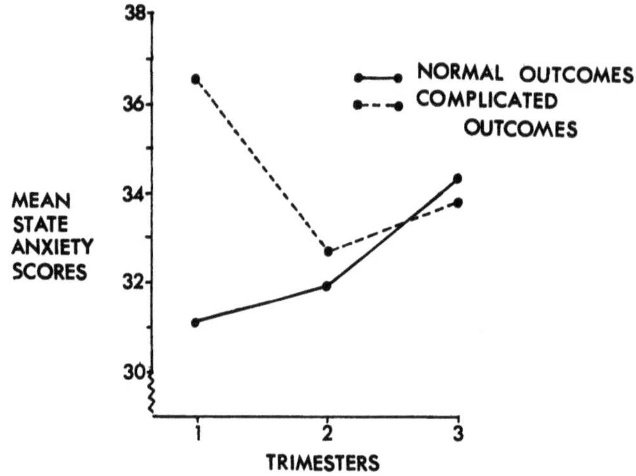

Figure 2. Mean state anxiety scores for women with normal and complicated outcomes according to trimesters.

Multi-variate Analysis

To assess the combined contribution of Life Events, Social Support and State and Trait Anxiety to complicated outcomes, the data were subjected to a Stepwise Multiple Regression Analysis (SPPS). Several analyses were completed using these four psychosocial risk factors in combination with other demographic variables believed to be associated with poor pregnancy outcomes. These latter included: age, social class, marital status, smoking, and previous problems (miscarriage, stillbirth, elective abortion). Given the high correlation between LEF and LEI scores, only the latter were included in regression analyses. Data pertaining to all trimesters were entered, and a total of fourteen variables were considered.

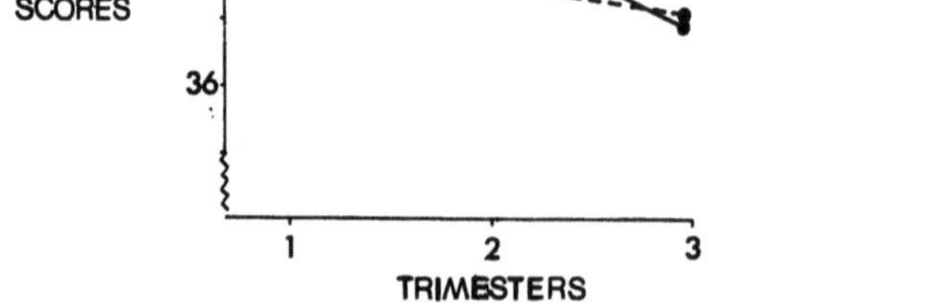

Figure 3. Mean social support scores for women with normal and complicated outcomes according to trimesters.

Table 2. Summary of Multiple Regression Analysis

Variable	t value	Probability level
Social Support (1)[a]	2.28	.025
State Anxiety (1)	1.97	.052
Life Events Impact (3)	-3.80	.0003
Trait Anxiety	1.90	.062
State Anxiety (3)	-3.00	.004

R Square = .253
F = 5.90, df 5;87; p < .0001, for the equation

N = 93

[a]numbers in brackets refer to the trimester of pregnancy

The best linear fit was achieved by the five following variables, arranged in order of the magnitude of the Beta Coefficient: LEI (trimester 3), State Anxiety (trimester 3). Social Support (trimester 1), State Anxiety (trimester 1) and Trait Anxiety. Details of this analysis are presented in Table 2. The best single predictor of complications is LEI (trimester 3), and these five variables together account for 25% of the variance in outcomes. All variables show a significant linear relationship to complications at conventional significance levels, although Trait Anxiety is only marginally significant (p = .062). None of the demographic variables considered make any additional contribution to the prediction of complications.

The results of the Multiple Regression Analysis are largely consistent with the finding of the Analyses of Variance, but not all findings are as expected. Contrary to predictions, high rather than low Social Support in early pregnancy predicts complications and so does low State Anxiety in the final trimester. The influence of the other variables is compatible with the hypotheses. Both high Trait Anxiety and high State Anxiety in the first trimester contribute to the prediction of complications, as does high LEI in the third trimester.

DISCUSSION

Analysis of Variance and Multiple Regression Analysis provide different perspectives on the data in this study, but both show that all the variables examined are related to poor pregnancy outcomes. Life Events in the third trimester is the most powerful predictor of complications, followed by State Anxiety (trimester 3), Social Support (trimester 1), State Anxiety (trimester 1) and Trait Anxiety.The impact of life events, stress and trait anxiety were as expected. High scores on these measures predicted complications. Several mechanisms have been suggested by which anxiety may impede the normal course of pregnancy. Changes in cardio-vascular function, which accompany anxiety, may restrict uterine blood flow, thus interfering with vital supplies to the fetus (Ascher, 1978; Hytten, 1984). Maternal stress-related hormones are believed to cross the placenta in small concentrations. In one dramatic case study (Pugh, Newton and Piercy, 1979), this possibility was cited as an explanation for an infant death due to gastric ulceration (hemorrhage) after only 21 hours of life. Subsequent inquiries revealed that the mother had suffered very severe life event stress in her final trimester. Possible mechanisms in the relationship between anxiety and labor problems have already been discussed in the Introduction, but biochemical mediators have also been implicated (Lederman et al, 1978; Crandon, 1979).

The data pertaining to life events in this study show interesting differences in the course of life events for women with normal and complicated pregnancies. Those with normal pregnancies indicated a progressive decline in the frequency and negative impact of life events. Women with complications had higher life events scores throughout their pregnancies and the difference between the two groups is greatest in the final trimester. This suggests possible coping differences in the two outcome groups. Women who have normal outcomes may be better able to plan and organize their lives early in pregnancy so as to avoid seriously disruptive life events later on when their activities may be more limited. Alternatively, the social environments of these two groups may be different, with poor outcomes being more likely in an unaccommodating social environment, one which fails to take account of the changing capacities and needs of the pregnant woman.

The role of social support and state anxiety in the prediction of outcomes is less clear, and findings in this study were not consistent with earlier work (e.g., Nuckolls et al, 1972). Women with normal and complicated outcomes did not significantly differ with respect to social support scores for any of the three assessments. Hence, women with complications did not lack social support initially in absolute terms, but their social support scores declined significantly after the first trimester. It would seem that fluctuations of this type in fundamental support systems (even relatively small ones) may be damaging to the course of pregnancy.

It is quite common for women to feel apprehensive at the prospect of their impending labor. In this context, the pattern of state anxiety over the trimesters of pregnancy for women with complications is puzzling. Unlike those with normal outcomes, complicated pregnancies are marked by highest state anxiety in the first trimester and a significant decline thereafter. State anxiety for the normal outcome group progressively increases over trimesters. Furthermore, the complicated outcome group report relatively high life event stress, increased trait anxiety, high state anxiety (in the first trimester) and diminished social support. This combination of conditions would arguably foster higher, not lower, state anxiety. While not wishing to over-interpret these data, the pattern observed here suggests a defensive coping strategy, with attendant poor psychological and practical preparation for labor, among women who ultimately experience complications.

Unfortunately, the number of discrete types of complications observed in this sample did not permit an analysis by type of complication. Grouping different types of complications is a common practice (e.g., Nukolls et al, 1972; Gorsuch and Key, 1974), although one has been criticized (Newton and Hunt, 1984). On the other hand, stress-related complications may be the result of one or a few related processes. Reading (1983) identifies this method of outcome classification as the most rigorous.

There is no doubt, however, that the effects of some variables were masked by the grouping together of all complications. For example, smoking did not appear as a predictor in the Multiple Regression Analysis. In fact a higher proportion of the Normal group were smokers (44%) compared with the Complications group (36%). In spite of this, three of the four mothers in the sample who delivered preterm babies were smokers, as were 75% of the women whose babies were small for gestational age (12 cases). Clearly, the effects of smoking, as a variable, have been obscured by the grouping together of different types of complications. It is likely that some complications of pregnancy and childbirth may be more influenced by psychosocial stress variables than are others, and while information on all complications is desirable, studies using sample sizes large enough to enable discrete types of outcome analysis would be more informative.

CONCLUSION

The data from this study indicate that psychosocial stress is a factor in poor pregnancy outcomes. Several avenues for useful stress management interventions are apparent. These may be aimed at 1) identifying women at risk, 2) assisting women and their families with planning and organizing life events during pregnancy, 3) providing women with anxiety management training, and 4) exploring and developing with pregnant women their coping strategies both with respect to life event management and preparation for labor.

SUMMARY

Ninety-three women were assessed at 16, 28 and 37 weeks of pregnancy with respect to Life Events, Social Support and State-Trait Anxiety. The medical outcomes included all major complications during pregnancy and labor, and also infant outcomes.

While Analysis of Variance and Multiple Regression Analysis show all three variables to be related to pregnancy outcomes, effects are specific to trimesters and not entirely consistent with expectations. In general, Life Events (the strongest predictor) is associated with poor outcomes, as are State and Trait anxiety. However, high Social Support in the first trimester and low State Anxiety in the third trimester are also associated with complications. These variables are better predictors of outcome than standard demographic characteristics such as age, marital status or social class. The results are explained by reference to the coping strategies that are likely to be employed in dealing with life events.

REFERENCES

Asher, B.H. (1978). Maternal anxiety in pregnancy and fetal homeostasis. *JOGN Nurs.*, May/June, 18.

Beck, N.C., Siegel, L.J., Davidson, N.P., Kormeier, S., Breitenstein, A., and Hall, D.G. (1980). The prediction of pregnancy outcome: Maternal preparation, anxiety and attitudinal sets, *J.Psychosom. Med.*, 42:429.

Blondel, J.A. (1727). *Imagination in Pregnant Women*, J. Peele, London.

Brown, R. (1986). *Social Psychology*, Free Press, New York.

Craig, T.K.J., and Brown, G.W. (1984). Life Events, Meaning and Physical Illness: A Review, *in*: *Health Care and Human Behaviour*, A. Steptoe and A. Mathews, (Eds.), Academic Press, London.

Crandon, A.J. ((1979). Maternal anxiety and obstetric complications. *J. Psychosom. Res.*, 23:113.

Dick-Read, G. (1933). *Natural Childbirth*, Heinemann, London.

Edwards, K.R., and Jones, M.R. (1970). Personality changes related to pregnancy and obstetric complications, *Proc. 76th Ann. Conven. Am. Psychol. Assoc.*, 341-3, as cited in A. Reading, *Psychological Aspects of Pregnancy*, Longman, London.

Friedman, S.B., Mason, J.W., and Hamburg, D.A. (1963) *Psychosom. Med.*, 25:364.

Gorsuch, R.L., and Key, M.K. (1974). Abnormalities of pregnancy as a function of anxiety and life stress, *Psychosom. Med.*, 36:352.

Hytten, F.E. (1984). The effect of work on placental function, *in: Pregnant Women at Work*, G. Chamberlain, RoyalSociety of Medicine and Macmillan Press Ltd., London.

Holmes, T.H., and Rahe, R.H. (1967). The social readjustment rating scale, *J. Psychosom. Res.*, 11:213.

Istvan, J. (1986). Stress, anxiety, and birth outcomes: a critical review of the evidence, *Psych. Bull.*, 100:331.

Janis, I.L. (1958). *Psychological Stress*, John Wiley and Sons Ltd., New York.

Lamaze, F. (1958). *Painless Childbirth* (L.B. Celestin, trans.), Burke Publishing Company,London.

Lederman, R.P., Lederman, E., Work, B.E., and McCann, D.S. (1978). *Am. J. Obstet. Gynecol.*, 132:495.

Morris, N. (1983). Labour, *in: Handbook of Psychosomatic Obstetrics and Gynaecology*, Dennerstein, L., and Burrows, G.D. (Eds.), Elsevier Biomedical Press, Oxford.

Morris N., Copstick, S.M., and Taylor, K.E. (1986). Contempory attitudes to care in labour, *in: The psychosomatic Approach:Contemporary Practice of Whole-person Care*. M.J. Christie and P. G. Mellet (Eds.), John Wiley and Sons Ltd., Chicester.

Newton, R.W., Webster, P.A.C., Binu, P.S., Maskrey, N., and Phillips, A.B. (1979). Psychosocial stress in pregnancy and its relation to the onset of premature labour, *Brit. Med. J.*, 2:411.

Newton, R.W., and Hunt, L.P. (1984). Psychosocial stress in pregnancy and its relation to low birth weight, *Brit. Med. J.*, 288:1191.

Norbeck, J.S., and Tilden, V.P. (1983). Life stress, social support, and emotional disequilibrium in complications of pregnancy: a prospective, multivariate study, *J. Health Soc. Beh.*, 24:30.

Nuckolls, K.B., Cassel, J., and Kaplan, B.H. (1972). Psychosocial assets, life crisis and the prognosis of pregnancy, *Am. J. Epid.*, 95:431.

Oakley, A. (1980). *Women Confined*, Martin Robertson, Oxford.

Parkes, C.M., and Weiss, R.S. (1983). *Recovery from Bereavement*, Basic Books, New York.

Pugh, R.J., Newton, R.W., and Piercy, D.M. (1979). Fatal bleeding from gastric ulceration during first day of life--possible association with social stress, *Arch. Dis. in Childhd.*, 54:146.

Rabkin, J.G., and Struening, E.L. (1976). Life events, stress and illnes, *Science*, 194:1013.

Reading, A. (1983). *Psychological Aspects of Pregnancy*, Longman, London.

Sarason, I.G., Johnson, J.H., and Siegel, J.M. (1978). Assessing the impact of life changes: development of the life experiences survey, *J. Consult and Clin. Psychol*, 46:932.

Smilkstein, G., Helsper-Lucas, A., Ashworth, C., Montano, D., and Pagel, M. (1984). Prediction of pregnancy complications: an application of the biopsychosocial model, *Soc. Sci. Med.*, 18:315.

DIFFERENTIAL STRESS RESPONSES IN MOTHERS AND NON-MOTHERS TO INFANT CRYING

A. E. Hall and G. Morsbach

Department of Psychology
University of Glasgow
Glasgow, Scotland

INTRODUCTION

Using psychophysiological measures as well as mental tests, a number of recent studies have examined the effect of infant crying on mothers and non-mothers. Early psychophysiological studies such as Donovan et al (1978) tended to use visual cues, presenting a 10-second silent videotape of a crying infant to subjects. In a similar study, Wiesenfeld and Klorman (1978) also used a visual presentation, but they included some pictures of the subjects' own infants. They found cardiac acceleration and increase in blood pressure in response to pictures of a familiar infant, but a slight cardiac deceleration and no increase in blood pressure to pictures of an unfamiliar infant.

Two studies by Frodi et al (1978 a,b) presented mother-father pairs with 2-minute video tapes, including sound, of unfamiliar crying and smiling infants. The researchers discovered in these two studies that crying infants produced greater autonomic arousal than smiling infants.

Later studies tended to use auditory cues instead of visual cues. Wiesenfeld et al (1981) presented mothers with 15-second audiotapes of familiar cries. Using heart rate as their measure, Wiesenfeld et al found a brief cardiac deceleration followed by a more sustained cardiac acceleration in mothers' response to the sound of their own infants. However, mothers reacting to the sound of an unfamiliar infant exhibited a slight cardiac deceleration. In another study Wiesenfeld and Malatesta (1982) report similar findings. Using heart rate as one of their measures they discovered the same biphasic response to familiar cries and deceleration to unfamiliar cries. In addition to heart rate, skin conductance was used as a measure of autonomic arousal. It was found that there were greater SCM responses to the cries of familiar infants than to the cries of unfamiliar infants.

Whereas most of these studies show greater autonomic arousal to the cries of familiar infants, not all studies document similar findings. For example, Bleichfeld and Moely (1984), using HR and SCM, reported autonomic arousal to the cries of unfamiliar infants. These findings are supported by Boukydis and Burgess (1982) who also used SCM.

The aims of this study were twofold. One purpose of the experiment was to investigate if mothers generally respond with arousal to infant crying, or if they differentiate in their physiological response to the cries of their own and unfamiliar infants. Also, research was conducted measuring mothers' performance on a mental test (concentration task) as conducted within the same paradigm.

Studies investigating infant crying have rarely looked into the effect of crying on mental performance by the listener. However, Morsbach and Stockbridge (1985) found that the concentration ability of midwives decreased to a significantly greater degree when exposed to the cries of a brain-damaged infant than to the cries of a full-term infant or a mechanical noise. In another study, Morsbach et al (1986) report that mothers not only experience a decrease in concentration ability in response to the cries of a brain-damaged child, but also in response to the cries of a full-term infant as compared to their performance in a machine noise condition.

Furthermore, the question can be raised as to whether the deterioration in performance is generally greater when infant crying is present, or whether there is a differential effect to the cry sounds of a familiar and an unfamiliar infant.

METHOD

Subjects

Eighteen mothers and eighteen non-mothers participated in the experiment. Three of the mothers were primiparous and the other fifteen were multiparous. Subject ages ranged from twenty-two years to thirty-four years, with the mean age being 28.15 years and the standard deviation 3.23 years. These individuals reacted to infants' cries that were recorded when they were between six and ten weeks old. Ten of the infants were female and eight were male. A final condition of the experiment involved non-mothers. The ages ranged from seventeen years to twenty-six years. The mean age was 20.25 years and the standard deviation was 2.28 years.

Procedure and Design

On two consecutive days, 6-10 weeks after childbirth, eighteen mothers recorded their babies' sounds for one hour after the morning, afternoon and evening feeding. From each six-hour set of recordings a 60-second episode of crying was prepared. Two to three weeks after making the recordings the mothers were visited individually in their homes. The experiment consisted of the following three conditions, each lasting for 60 seconds: Condition A involves subjects that were exposed to the cries of their own infant (as previously recorded); Condition B involved mothers' exposure to the cries of an unfamiliar infant; finally, Condition C consisted of not exposing mothers to cry sounds. Also, the mother was instructed to carry out a digit symbol test. At the same time her pulse-rate recordings were taken at 10-second intervals. The same procedure was carried out for Conditions A, B and C. The order of the presentation of the conditions was systematically varied. For each mother a non-mother was matched. The experimental procedure was identical to that of the mother group, with the exception that the experiment was not carried out at home, but in a quiet room at the subject's place of work.

RESULTS

Heart Rate Response

To test for differences in heart rate during stimulus presentation among the three experimental conditions, a 6 x 3 (heart rate readings x stimuli) analysis of variance was conducted separately for the two groups of subjects. In each group there were no significant differences between the six heart rate readings for mothers and non-mothers alike: $F(5,289) = 2.69$, $p > 0.05$, $F(5,289) = 1.80$, $p > 0.05$ respectively.

For non-mothers, ANOVA also yielded no significant effect in the experimental conditions: $F(2,289) = 1.45$, $p > 0.05$ ('familiar' infants' cries: $M = 81.62$; unfamiliar infants' cries : $M = 81.93$; silence: $M = 81.02$).

However, for the mothers a significant difference between the three experimental conditions was obtained: $F(2,289) = 24.25$, $p < 0.01$. Further analysis (t-test) showed that the mean heart rate was highest in response to their own infants' crying ($M = 90.95$), significantly higher ($p < 0.01$) than to the crying of an unfamiliar infant ($M = 88.52$) or to silence ($M = 88.00$). No significant difference was found between the latter two conditions.

Concentration Level

For both mothers and non-mothers an analysis of variance yielded a significant F = value: $F(2,38) = 3.35$, $p < 0.05$, $F(2.38) = 3.53$, $p < 0.05$, respectively.

Further analysis (using t-test) showed that non-mothers' concentration ability was significantly lower in both the unfamiliar and familiar infant crying conditions ($M = 39.55$, $M = 39.28$) than in the quiet condition, ($M = 41.72$, $p < 0.05$, $p < 0.05$ respectively). As expected, there was virtually no difference between the average score of the non-mothers for the familiar and the unfamiliar baby.

The lowest scores for mothers were obtained when they listened to their own babies ($M = 36.17$), which was significantly lower than those in the silent condition ($M = 40.33$, $p < 0.05$). The scores elicited by the unfamiliar baby ($M = 38.56$) did not differ significantly from those originated by the familiar baby or the silent condition.

DISCUSSION

The results produced by heart rate tests confirm, in general, Wiesenfeld and Malatesta's findings. They also reported cardiac acceleration (after an initial brief period of deceleration) in mothers as a response to their own infants' cry sounds. This response lasted for the first 15 seconds after the onset of crying. In our experiments we observed this phenomenon not only for the first 15 seconds, but throughout the entire 60 seconds of crying. The mothers did not seem to habituate to the crying sound as their heart rate values were as high during and at the end of the 60-second exposure as they were at the beginning. Thus, mothers seemed to be aroused for a considerable amount of time while their own infants were crying.

Like Wiesenfeld and Malatesta, we did not find this arousal phenomenon as extensive in response to the cries of unfamiliar infants. Mothers and non-mothers alike did not have a significantly higher heart rate when listening to an unknown infant than when they were situated in a silent environment. These results conflict with findings by other researchers. Bleichfeld and Moely (1984) observed heart rate increase in non-mothers in response to the 'pain' cries of an unfamiliar infant. Frodi et al (1978 a,b) reported autonomic arousal by mothers and fathers when listening to and seeing a crying infant at the same time. Boukydis and Burgess (1982) obtained similar results when they included the cries of an abnormal infant.

However, the difference in the results between Wiesenfeld and Malatesta and this study, and those reported by the latter three studies, lie in the difference of crying stimuli used. Whereas most studies used either 'hunger' or 'anger' cries, Bleichfeld and Moely used 'pain' cries. Wolff (1969) has investigated the effect of different cry types on mothers and non-mothers. He has reported that the pain cry is different in nature to other cry types. It has a sudden onset, and initial long cry and an extended period of breath-holding in expiration. Wolff argues that the pain cry can diminish differential responding by mothers and non-mothers. He also states that this is true of the cries of some abnormal infants, and it is noteworthy that Boukydis and Burgess included such cries in their study. Thus, Wolff's contention (that pain cries have, in general, a more arousing effect on the listener) may help to explain the findings of these two studies. On the other hand, it may be unreasonable to explain these findings in such a manner. For example, the two studies by Frodi et al (1978) did not employ pain cries, or cries of abnormal infants. However, Murray (1979) suggests that whereas mothers show arousal to the mere sound of their own infants' crying, non-mothers only experience such an effect to the simultaneous sight and sound of a crying infant (Murray's principle of heterogenous summation). This may explain the results obtained by Frodi et al

Murray argues that the response to crying depends on the presence of various crying cues, such as if the crying sound is unusual, e.g., as in 'pain' or 'abnormal' cries, and/or if the cries are visual and auditory at the same time, or only one or the other. It seems to be that mothers need fewer cues from their own infants to be aroused, whereas non-mothers need additional or more abnormal cues to experience a similar degree of arousal.

Our results on the concentration task show that mental performance is somewhat differently affected by infant crying than the physiological state. Although heart rate did not change significantly in non-mothers during the cry periods, concentration ability did. Non-mothers performed significantly worse in the two crying conditions than in the silent condition. On the other hand, mothers' ability to concentrate deteriorated mostly during the crying of their own infant, and less so during that of an unfamiliar infant. Although Morsbach et al (1986) found that mothers' concentration decreased significantly during exposure to an unfamiliar infant's cries, they used the 'pain' cries of the unknown infant. As argued before, the 'pain' cry of an unfamiliar infant seems to have a similar effect on the mother's concentration ability as the 'basic' cry of the familiar infant.

The most important finding of this study is that mothers respond to their own infants' crying, not only with increased heart rate, but also with a decrease in concentration ability on a non-infant-care related task. Further research is now in progress to investigate whether these responses, especially to prolonged episodes of crying, are associated with post-natal depression. In addition, it may prove worthwhile to investigate possible relationships between maternal responses to infant crying and such factors as domestic accidents and infant abuse.

SUMMARY

Pulse rate and concentration ability of eighteen mothers and eighteen matched females (non-mothers) were investigated under three conditions: (a) exposure to the cry sounds of the mothers' own infants, (b) exposure to the cry sounds of an unfamiliar infant and (c) no exposure to cry sounds. Using the Wechsler Digit Symbol Test (extended WISC) it was found that the concentration ability of both mothers and non-mothers deteriorated significantly when exposed to infant cries as opposed to silence. Mothers demonstrated no differential effect when exposed to their own infants' cries and the cries of an unfamiliar infant. Pulse rate recordings, on the other hand, increased significantly when mothers were exposed to the cry sounds of their own infants but not when exposed to those of an unfamiliar infant. Non-mothers demonstrated no significant changes in pulse rate in any of the three experimental conditions. These results indicate that mothers are particularly affected by the cry sounds of their own infants, not only in terms of psychophysiological arousal, but also in respect to their mental performance on a non-infant-care related task.

REFERENCES

Bleichfeld, B., and Moely, B.E. (1984). Psychophysiological responses to an infant cry: Comparison of groups of women in different phases of the maternal cycle, *Dev. Psychol.*, 20:1082.

Boukydis, C.F.Z., and Burgess, R.L. (1982). Adult physiological response to infant cries: Effects of temperament of infant, parental status, and gender, *Child Development*, 53:1291.

Donovan, W.L., Leavitt, L.A., and Balling, J.D. (1978). Maternal physiological response to infant signals, *Psychophysiology*, 15:68.

Frodi, A., Lamb, M., Leavitt, L.A., and Donovan, W.L. (1978a). Fathers' and mothers' responses to infant smiles and cries, *Inf. Beh. & Dev.*, 1:187.

Frodi, A., Lamb, M., Leavitt, L.A., Donovan, W.L., Neff, C., and Sherry, D. (1978b). Fathers' and mothers' responses to the faces and cries of normal and premature infants, *Dev. Psychol.*, 14:490.

Morsbach, G., and Stockbridge, C. (1985). Does infant crying affect concentration? *Midwife Health Visitor & Community Nurse*, May:170.

Morsbach, G., McCulloch, M., and Clark (1986). Infant crying as a potential stressor concerning mothers' concentration ability, *Psychologia*, 29:18.

Murray, A. (1979). Infant crying as an elicitor of parental behaviour: An examination of two models, *Psychol. Bull.*, 86:191.

Wiesenfeld, A., and Klorman, R. (1978). The mother's psychophysiological reactions to contrasting affective expressions by her own and unfamiliar infant, *Dev. Psychol.*, 14:294.

Wiesenfeld, A.R., Malatesta, C.Z., and DeLoach, L. (1981). Differential parental response to familiar and unfamiliar infant distress signals, *Inf. Beh. & Dev.*, 4:281.

Wiesenfeld, A.R., and Malatesta, C.Z. (1982). Infant distress: Variables affecting responses of caregivers and others, *in*: Parenting: Its causes and consequences. L.W. Hoffman, R. Gandelman, and H.R. Schiffman, eds., Erlbaum, Hillsdale, N.J.

Wolff, P.H. (1969). The natural history of crying and other vocalizations in early infancy, *in*: Determinants of infant behaviour. B.M. Foss, ed., Methuen, London.

THE EFFECT OF ANXIETY ON THE COURSE OF LABOR

Norman Morris[1] and Faith Haddad[2]

[1]Emeritus Professor of Obstetrics and Gynaecology
University of London

[2]Obstetrician and Gynaecologist
Garden Hospital, London

We report here briefly on three studies.

STUDY ONE

Influence of Induction

Fifty-five primiparous caucasian women completed the Spielberger State/Trait Anxiety Self Evaluation Inventory (Spielberger et al 1970). The State inventory was completed three times during labor and once 20 minutes after delivery. The Trait inventory was completed, also at the start of labor and again six weeks post partum. This study gave the following results:

1. During labor there is a steady increase in the degree of State anxiety (which is to be anticipated). (Figure 1)

2. There was no significant difference between the State anxiety in induced or normal patients. This may be because our 'induced' patients received very careful counseling and support. (Figure 2)

3. There was no significant difference in the levels of Trait anxiety in the two groups, suggesting that basic anxiety therefore probably does not play a part in the reason for induction.

4. There was a greater need for epidural anesthesia in women who at the start of labor exhibited higher levels of anxiety. This suggests a link between high anxiety and either greater intensity of uterine pain or a lesser ability to cope with or to tolerate uterine pain. (Figure 3)

5. There was no evidence that those patients who manifest high anxiety in early labor required more frequent interference by means of forceps delivery. (Figure 4)

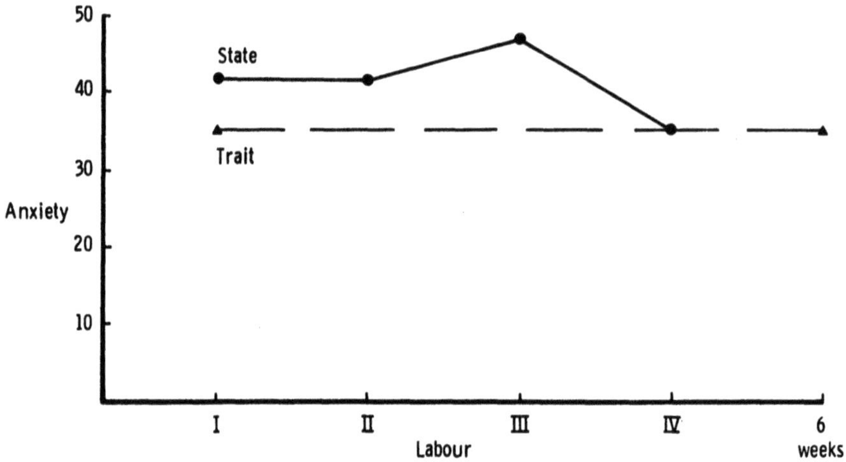

Figure 1. State/Trait anxiety levels-during labor and afterwards

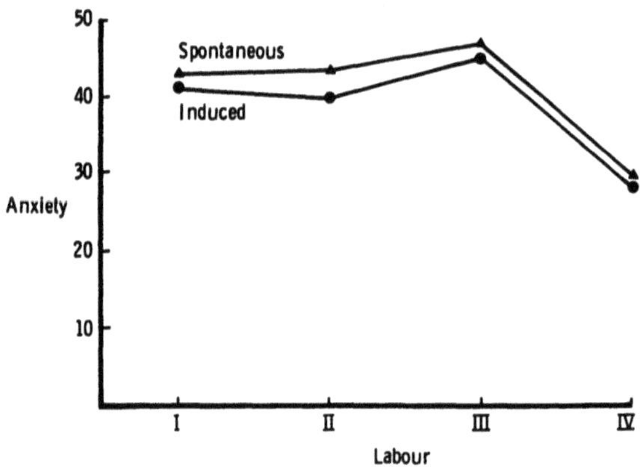

Figure 2. State anxiety levels in spontaneous/induced labor

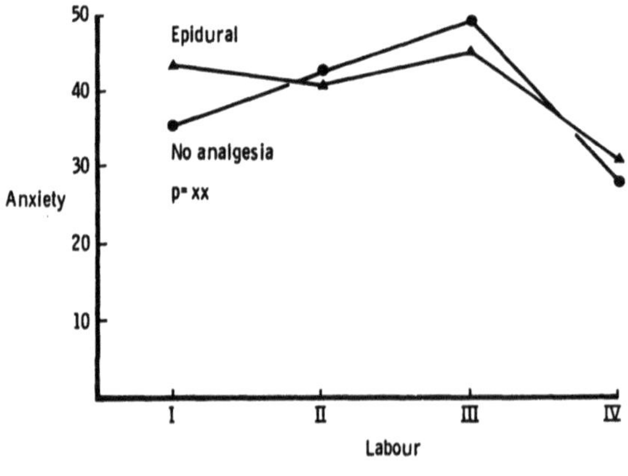

Figure 3. State anxiety levels in epidural/no analgesia

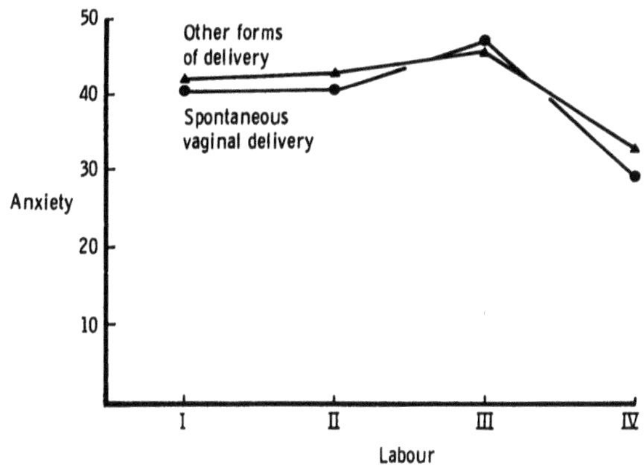

Figure 4. State anxiety in spontaneous/other forms of delivery

STUDY TWO

In this group, 249 primiparous caucasian women were studied during pregnancy. In this case they completed the Spielberger State/Trait Inventory once during each trimester. The subsequent behavior in labor was then also evaluated. The results in this study were as follows:

1. There was a fall in State anxiety in the mid-trimester. (Figure 5)

2. Those women who subsequently required augmentation for inadequate uterine action demonstrated higher levels of anxiety during pregnancy. (Figure 6)

3. Once again, those women who requested epidural anaesthesia in labor had higher levels of anxiety during pregnancy than those who did not require this form of pain relief. (Figure 7)

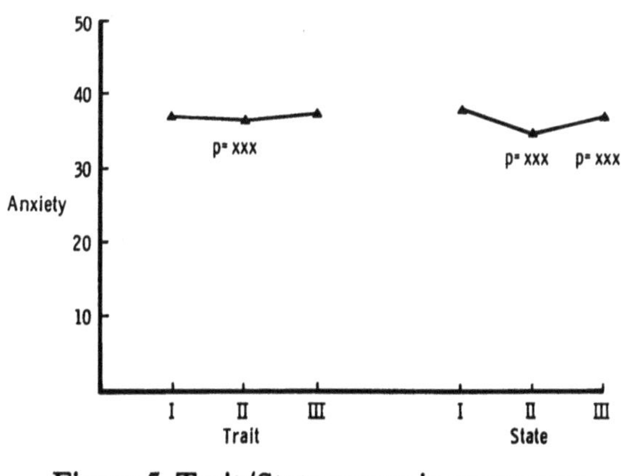

Figure 5. Trait/State scores in pregnancy

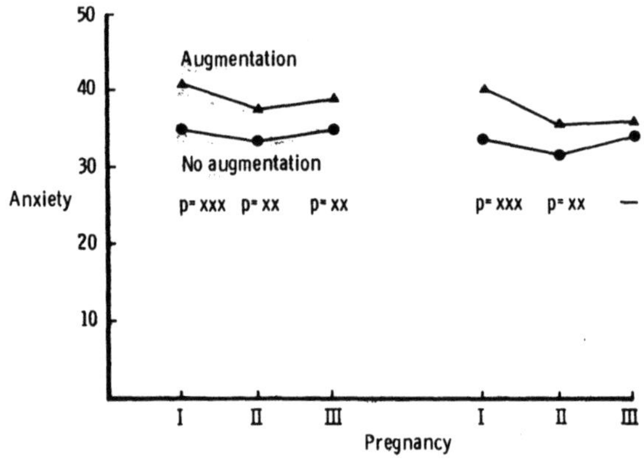

Figure 6. Trait/State scores in women in spontaneous labor with or without augmentation

These two studies suggest that there is a definite association between high anxiety in pregnancy and (1) being less able to cope with uterine pain unless this is relieved by epidural anaesthesia, and (2) inadequate uterine action which therefore requires more frequent use of oxytocin to achieve satisfactory augmentation.

Grantly Dick Read (1933) was the first to postulate that anxiety and fear could interfere with labor leading to less efficient and more painful uterine action. Our Studies therefore give some support to this hypothesis.

STUDY THREE

Hormone Levels in Labor

Serial levels of cortisol and prolactin serum levels have also been studied three times during labor in the same group of patients mentioned in Study One. As with

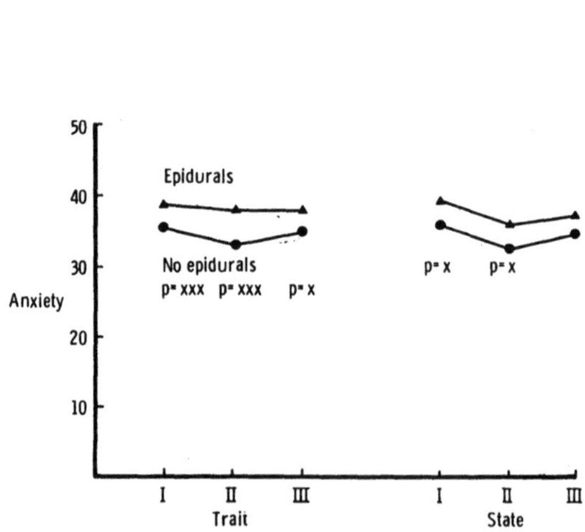

Figure 7. Trait/State scores-in women who selected epidural anaesthesia/no analgesia

Table 1. Cortisol levels in labor

I	1427	±	652	Labour
II	1616	±	576	
III	1775	±	686	
IV	2090	±	656	Post partum
V	658	±	374	Baby

other workers, we confirmed a regular increase in cortisol levels in labor (Table 1) but we could not identify an association between high cortisol levels and high anxiety.

Prolactin levels fall in labor. These findings accord with those reported by other workers (Table 2). However, here again we could find no correlation between anxiety and the prolactin levels. Prolactin levels were also high in umbilical cord serum. A.C.T.H. was also measured twice in labor. This confirmed that A.C.T.H. levels increase dramatically during labor except when an epidural is administered; there is then no increase at all in A.C.T.H. (Figures 8 and 9)

Table 2. Prolactin levels in labor

	Mean			
I	4892	±	2159	Labour
II	4307	±	2148	
III	3700	±	1862	
IV	2923	±	1562	Post partum
V	6879	±	2209	Baby

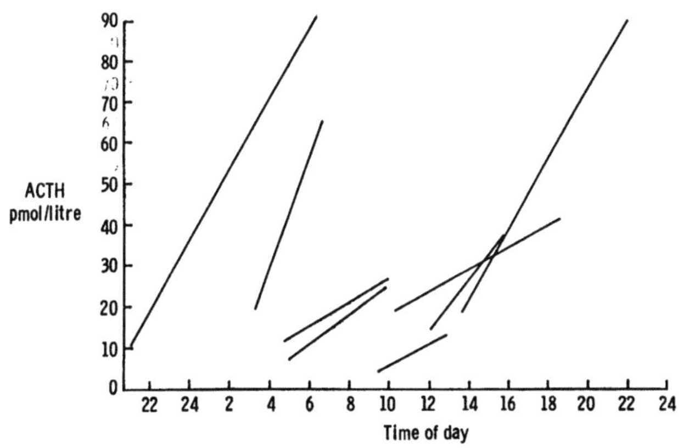

Figure 8. Pethidine analgesia

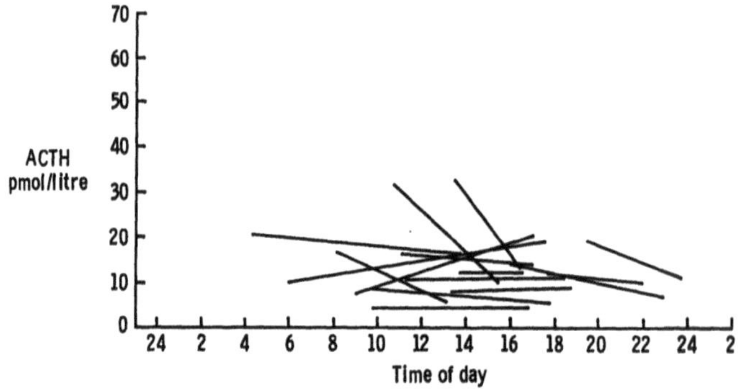

Figure 9. Epidural analgesia

CONCLUSION

Anxiety in pregnancy and labor has been studied by means of psychological questionnaires and hormone estimations. These studies suggest a definite relationship between high anxiety and (i) a greater need for epidural anaesthesia, as well as (ii) less efficient uterine action.

We hope we can encourage other workers to embark on similar studies that explore the relationship between emotional feelings (anxiety, etc.) on the one hand and performance in labor on the other.

REFERENCES

Dick-Read, G. (1933) Natural Childbirth. Heinemann, London.

Spielberger, C.D., Gorsuch, R.L., and Lushene, R.E. (1970) Manual for State Trait Anxiety Inventory (Self Evaluation Questionnaire). Palo Alto, California, Consulting Psychologists Press.

THE PHYSIOLOGY OF STRESS

OLIGOPEPTIDES IN THE BRAIN MECHANISMS OF RESISTANCE TO EMOTIONAL STRESS

K. V. Sudakov

P. K. Anokhin Institute of Normal Physiology
USSR Academy of Medical Sciences
Moscow, USSR

The problem of resistance to emotional stress in humans is of vital importance. Technological progress is the main reason for constantly increasing psychoemotional loads. People often have to work in extreme industrial, climatic, geographical or even cosmic conditions--environments also conducive to the promotion of psychoemotional stress. Indeed, numerous studies have documented the truth that emotional stress frequently results in psychosomatic disorders, namely neuroses and cardio-vascular diseases. Usually, conflict situations are the immediate causes of emotional stress, eventually resulting in the subject's restrained ability to satisfy social and biologic needs (1,2). That's why the problem of increasing human resistance to emotional stress is so urgent.

Natural history of psychosomatic disorders including arterial hypertension and gastrointestinal ulcers can be reproduced by simulating conflict situations in animals (2,6). Experiments have shown that in a population exposed to the same conflict situation inducing emotional stress there are individual animals with different stability of physiological functions (7,12).

Different resistance in rats is most vividly demonstrated under a conflict situation induced by immobilization, a state lasting for many hours (11). Wistar, Vag, August and unbred rats were immobilized in small-size cages for 30 h with their blood pressure (BP) and electrocardiograms (ECG) monitored. BP was recorded through a catheter implanted into the descending aorta via caudal artery. Standard ECG Lead II was recorded by means of needle electrodes.

Testing under the same conflict situation revealed several groups of animals each of which behaved differently. There were practically no changes in BP and heart rate (HR) throughout a 30 h immobilization in animals of the first group, called "resistant." Mean BP increases by 20-40 mm Hg with a subsequent decrease to and stabilization at the initial level was observed in animals of the second group during the first 5-6 h of immobilization. HR was relatively stable. Animals of this group were called "adapted." Animals of a third group responded to immobilization with a progressive BP fall and stable HR.

A fourth group displayed a rise, up to 140-160 mm Hg, in BP during 10-16 h of immobilization. Thereafter the distinct trend to lowering BP was evident, though it could eventually give an upsurge accompanied by increasing HR. Animals of this group died after different terms of immobilization while their HR slowed progressively. In a fifth group, immobilization caused both HR and BP to fall with fatal outcome within 13 to 17 hours. A sixth group manifested a sharp rise in BP (by 45-60 mm Hg) and HR (up to 600 bpm) after which both BP and HR fell abruptly and the animals died. Animals of groups 4 to 6 were termed "non-resistant" or "predisposed to stress."

The aforementioned reactions are produced in environments characterized by the existence of severe stress producing agents. For instance, by alternating electrical stimulation of ventromedial hypothalamus (HVM) defense centers and electric skin stimulation (12,13) rats react in a stressful manner. These responses were observed in other species as well (9).

Table 1 presents the distribution of the response patterns across different strains. These results show clearly different percentage of predisposed vs resistant animals under the stereotype stressor conditions. Wistar rats proved most resistant to immobilization stress, and August rats were the least resistant.

Under more acute emotional stress induced by immobilization combined with aperiodic electrical stimulation of the ventromedial hypothalamus alternating with electrocutaneous stimulation, resistant and predisposed animals demonstrated a different course of vascular response to HVM stimulation (13). Biphasic pressor-depressor response or even an absence of vascular response dominated in resistant animals. Prevalence of pressor responses to HVM stimulation was observed in predisposed rats. Pressor responses to emotional stimuli result in a steady BP rise that could partially account for the heart failure in these groups.

Stress-resistant and predisposed rats showed different catecholamine contents in brain structures (14,15), and different cyto- and histochemical changes in autonomic ganglia (16,17).

Characteristic of predisposed animals were substantially lower epinephrine levels in hypothalamus and increased dopamine levels in the midbrain reticular formation, as compared to resistant rats. In stress-resistant groups, dopamine content decreased in the medulla and increased in the brain isthmus in predisposed rats under the same conditions while hypothalamic norepinephrine level decreased.

Table 1. The distribution of the response patterns across different strains of rats

	resis-tant	adaptive		predisposed			total %	abs. N
	I	II	III	IV	V	VI		
Unbred	26.5	29.5	23.5	8.8	8.8	2.9	100	34
Wistar	50.0	26.9	15.5	3.8	3.8	-	100	26
Wag	33.3	25.0	33.3	4.2	4.2	-	100	24
August	14.8	13.1	50.8	9.8	8.2	3.3	100	61
								145

Special experiments showed that rats' resistance to acute emotional stress depended on the composition of protein in their daily diet (18). The decrease in the vascular tone and BP was found as a result of supplementing the animals' diet with low molecular weight peptides. This procedure took place while the rats were under acute emotional stress, thus suggesting the decrease in the tone of their sympathetic nervous system. The diets containing these peptides significantly decreased rats' resistance to emotional stress.

These experiments revealed the role of proteins in the mechanisms of animal resistance to stress. Besides, it is known that resistance to stress depends also on amino acid levels in the brain, namely of tyrosine and phenylalanine (19). So we have hypothesized that animal resistance to emotional stress is determined by protein-like endogenous substances.

Relevant to this hypothesis, we conducted a series of experiments (20,22). The content of oligopeptides in the blood and hypothalamus of animals with various degree of resistance to stress was analyzed by immunoenzyme technique. First, rat resistance to stress was determined in free behavior by the following: tail-flick test, general motor activity in the Warimex device, changes in ECG, impedance rheogram, BP, and respiration in response to orthostatic challenge (23).

There was a higher level of immunoreactive ß-endorphin-like substance in the blood and hypothalamus of resistant Wistar rats than in predisposed animals (20). During the first 1.5 h of acute emotional stress induced by immobilization combined with aperiodic electrical HVM stimulation alternating with electrocutaneous stimulation, the blood ß-endorphin level increased in both groups of animals. By the 3rd h of stress stimulation its content decreased in both groups compared to 1.5 h stress. Contrary to that, hypothalamic ß-endorphin content continued to increase by the 3rd h of stress. Thus, predisposed rats showed more intensive increase in ß-endorphin level in the blood while in resistant animals the increase was observed predominantly in the hypothalamus (Figure 1).

The content of immunoreactive delta-sleep inducing peptide (DSIP) was also measured in the blood and hypothalamus of animals with different resistance to emotional stress (22). Different baseline levels of the peptide in the blood and hypothalamus were characteristic of stress-resistant and stress-prone Wistar rats with a higher content found in the blood of resistant animals. A 1.5 h stress induced an increase of DSIP level in the blood and hypothalamus of both predisposed and resistant rats. A more pronounced increase was observed in the blood of resistant animals. By the 3rd h of stress stimulation the decrease in DSIP blood levels reached 50% in stress-resistant rats, far exceeding the strength of the response in stress-prone animals to a 1.5 h stress. Baseline DSIP level in the hypothalamus of stress-resistant Wistar rats was also high. By the 3rd h of stress stimulation the hypothalamic DSIP content continued to increase in both groups (Figure 2).

Comparative analysis of results on Wistar rats and data on August rats, a species less resistant to stress, is especially revealing (21). Different contents of immunoreactive ß-endorphin and DSIP-like substance were found in the blood and hypothalamus of both strains (Figure 3). Besides, in each of these strains consisting of two groups with individual resistance to stress, the content of ß-endorphin and DSIP was also different. The level of these peptides in the blood and hypothalamus was higher in both stress-resistant and predisposed Wistar rats compared to the same groups of August animals.

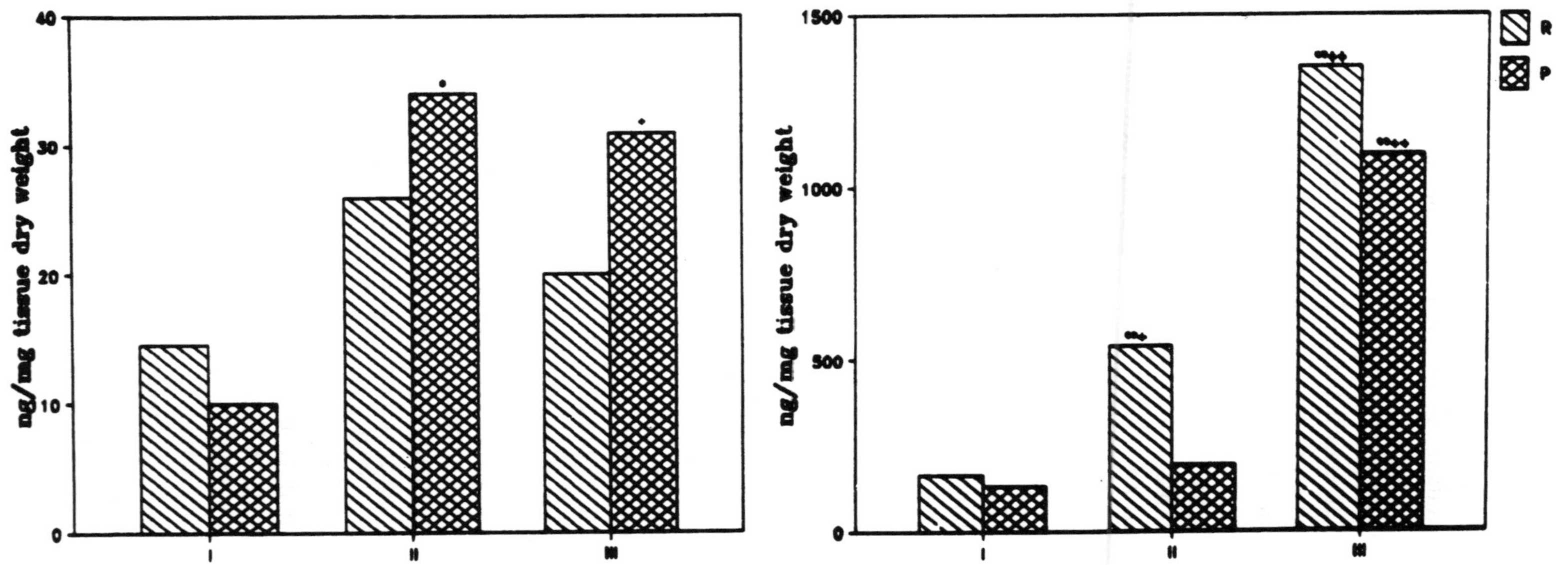

Figure 1. Blood (left panel) and hypothalamic (right panel) contents of ß-endorphin in control rats (I) and those subjected to 1.5 h (II) or 3 h (III) of emotional stress. R, resistant; P, predisposed animals. Control, resistant and predisposed groups contained 11, 12 and 11 rats respectively. Differences significance: * and **, $p < 0.05$ and $p < 0.01$ as compared to baseline; + and + +, $p < 0.05$ and $p < 0.01$ as compared to 1.5 h stress.

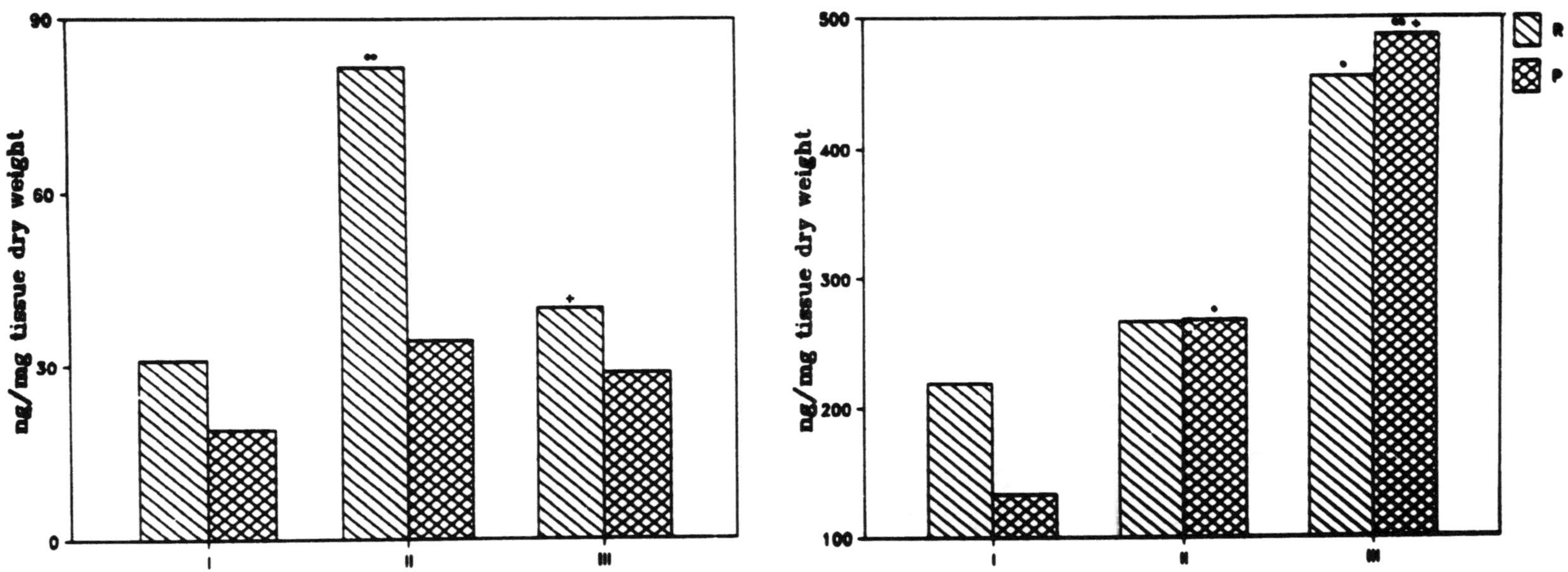

Figure 2. Blood (left panel) and hypothalamic (right panel) contents of delta-sleep inducing peptide in control rats (I) and those subjected to 1.5 h (II) or 3 h (III) of emotional stress. Control, resistant and predisposed groups contained 15, 13 and 11 rats respectively. See Figure 1 for designations.

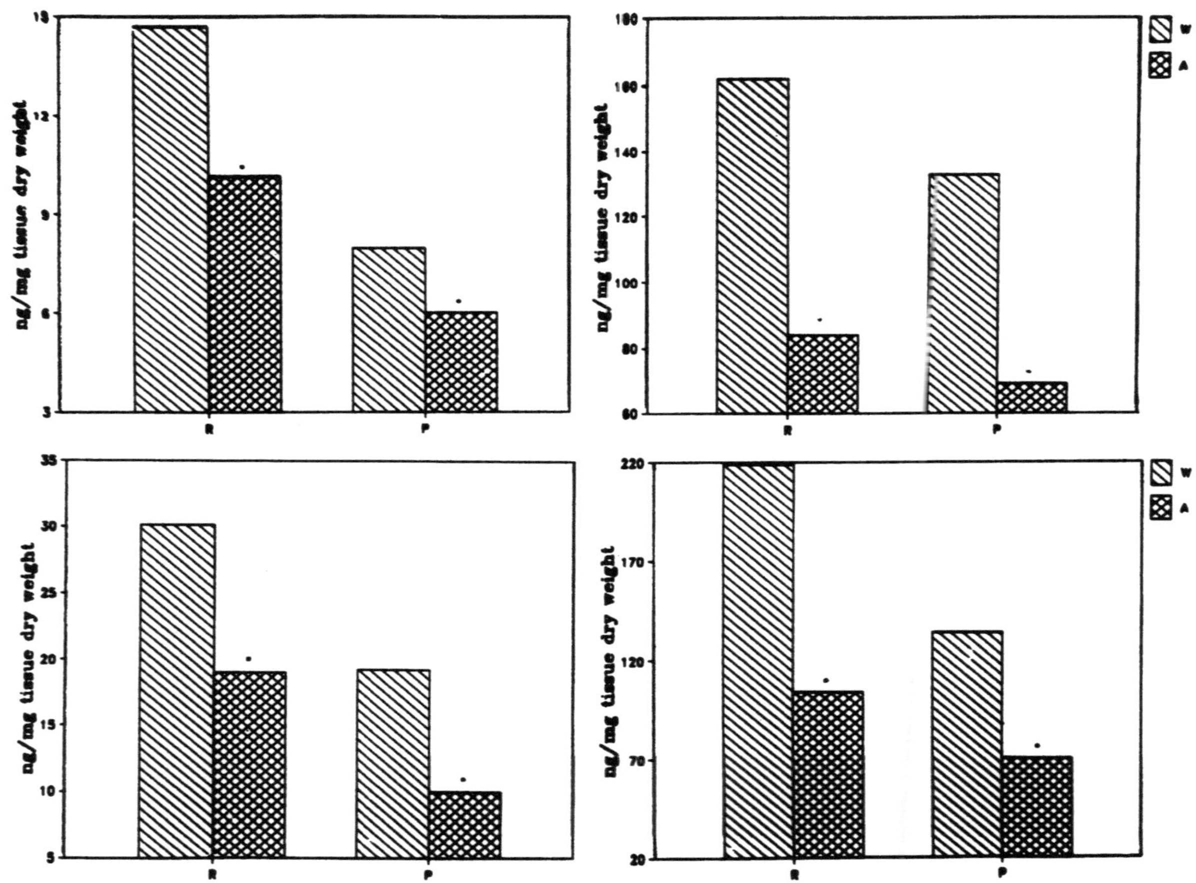

Figure 3. Comparison between Wistar and August rats in the blood (left panel) and hypothalamus (right panel) and August (A, N = 9) DSIP (bottom). R, stress-resistant Wistar (W, N = 13) contents of immunoreactive ß-endorphin (top) and rats; P, stress-prone Wistar (W, N = 11) and August (A, N = 16) rats. *, $p < 0.05$.

Therefore, it follows that there is a positive correlation between the content of ß-endorphin and DSIP-like substance in the blood and hypothalamus and the resistance to emotional stress in animals of various strains. Wistar rats are more resistant to stress. They have higher levels of these peptides compared to more stress-susceptible August animals. These data also show that there are animals, within one strain, with different resistance to stress. The content of DSIP and ß-endorphin in these animals was also different. Thus, in stress-resistant Wistar rats the level of DSIP and ß-endorphin was higher than in predisposed animals of the same strain. The same tendency could be observed in August rats.

Substance P (SP) content in the hypothalamus of Wistar and August rats with different resistance to stress was analyzed by radioimmunoassay (24). The difference in SP levels observed in animals of these strains was significant. More resistant to stress Wistar rats had higher levels of SP in the hypothalamus than August rats (Figure 4).

Thus, the experiments indicate that animal resistance to emotional stress depends considerably on the content of such oligopeptides as ß-endorphin, DSIP, and SP, particularly in the hypothalamus. The level of these oligopeptides in the hypothalamus of resistant to stress animals is much higher than in predisposed rats. These data suggest the possibility of increasing the resistance of predisposed animals by administering those oligopeptides of which they have a deficit.

These experiments on Wistar rats have shown that animal resistance to stress increased considerably after i.a. DSIP injection (25). Animals tested under acute emotional stress were classed into the following groups: "resistant," those that lived for 3 h; "adapted," those with increasing or decreasing mean BP; and "predisposed," those perishing at different terms of acute conflict situation. DSIP was administered in a

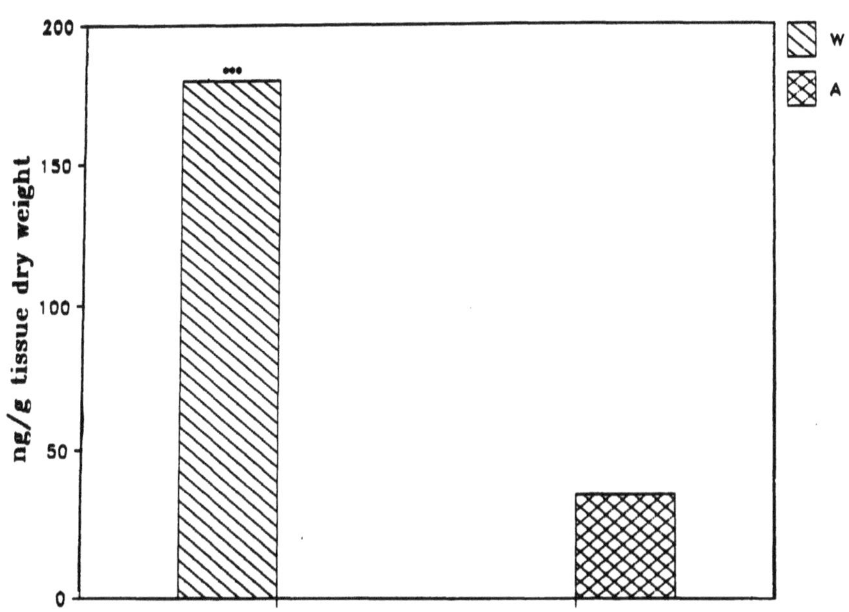

Figure 4. Hypothalamic substance P content (ng/g) in intact Wistar (W, N = 15) and August (A, N = 16) rats.

dose of 60 nM/kg into the tail artery, 10 min before exposing animals to a conflict situation.

Peptide increased the percentage of animals surviving the 3 h conflict situation. Under the effect of DSIP the percentage of stress-predisposed animals was reduced from 65% to 25%, and that of resistant animals increased from 14% to 60% (23). The same model of acute emotional stress was used to study the effect of DSIP on the intracellular messengers of the sympathetic and parasympathetic nervous system: cAMP and cGMP (26). Their contents were measured in medial hypothalamus, midbrain reticular formation and liver. The study demonstrated phasic changes in these messengers' activity in the brain and liver. By the 30th min of the emotional stress, the brain cAMP levels increased by a factor of 8 to 10 and those of cGMP of 6 to 8; liver cAMP was 11 times, and cGMP 2 times as high as before stimulation. By 60 min the brain cAMP and cGMP levels decreased, though remaining 4 to 5 times as high as their baseline levels. By that time the liver cAMP and cGMP contents also decreased to 3-4 times the control level.

DSIP preinjection influenced the course of biogenic amines and cyclic nucleotides contents in the medial hypothalamus and midbrain reticular formation under emotional stress (Table 2). The data indicate that in DSIP preinjected rats, as related to controls, the cAMP content in the medial hypothalamus was significantly reduced by 30 min. The histamine level increased and that of serotonin and norepinephrine decreased by 60 min. By 90 min histamine and serotonin levels increased and that of cAMP decreased. In the midbrain reticular formation, cGMP level rose by the 30th min of emotional stress; serotonin and dopamine levels decreased by 60 min. However, the cGMP level further increased by 90 min.

Other experiments have shown that DSIP injection into the brain lateral ventricles blocked behavioral and somatoautonomic manifestations of the avoidance response under direct electrical HVM stimulation.

Table 2. Influence of DSIP preinjection on biogenic amines and cyclic nucleotides contents in the medial hypothalamus and midbrain reticular formation under emotional stress.

Experimental conditions	Substances investigated	Histamine		Serotonin		Norepinephrine		Dopamine		cAMP		cGMP	
		1	2	1	2	1	2	1	2	1	2	1	2
stress	30	0.504 ±0.055	0.224 ±0.03	1.19 ±0.12	0.610 ±0.07	1.78 ±0.14	0.720 ±0.08	2.12 ±0.22	1.54 ±0.14	5.22 +0.70	3.40 ±0.50	0.29 ±0.03	0.23 ±0.035
	60	0.377 ±0.05	0.349 ±0.045	0.715 ±0.08	0.285 ±0.04	1.55 ±0.11	0.592 ±0.055	1.87 ±0.15	1.28 ±0.11	2.97 ±0.42	1.75 ±0.32	0.42 ±0.05	0.32 ±0.045
	90	0.317 ±0.04	0.244 ±0.03•	0.530 ±0.06	0.467 ±0.06	1.23 ±0.1	0.549 ±0.07	0.989 ±0.11	0.921 ±0.08	4.45 ±0.75	2.42 ±0.32	0.44 ±0.06	0.29 ±0.035
DSIP + stress	30	0.346 ±0.05	0.338 ±0.05	1.41 ±0.22	0.870 ±0.09	1.34 ±0.11	0.627 ±0.05	1.82 ±0.17	1.26 ±0.11	3.05x ±0.30	2.55 ±0.40	0.37 ±0.04	0.44x ±0.035
	60	0.644x ±0.08	0.439 ±0.05	1.58x ±0.18	1.15x ±0.12	1.15x ± 0.09	0.513 ±0.06	1.42 ±0.10	0.899x ±0.07	2.68 ±0.55	2.08 ±0.35	0.58 ±0.06	0.28 ±0.04
	90	0.752 ±0.075x	0.326 ±0.05	1.12 ±0.11	0.642 ±0.08	0.924 ±0.07	0.588 ±0.06	1.23 ±0.13	0.832 ±0.075	2.23 ±0.34x	3.12 ±0.40	0.52 ±0.05	0.46 ±0.05x

x- significance of DSIP effects, p 0.05

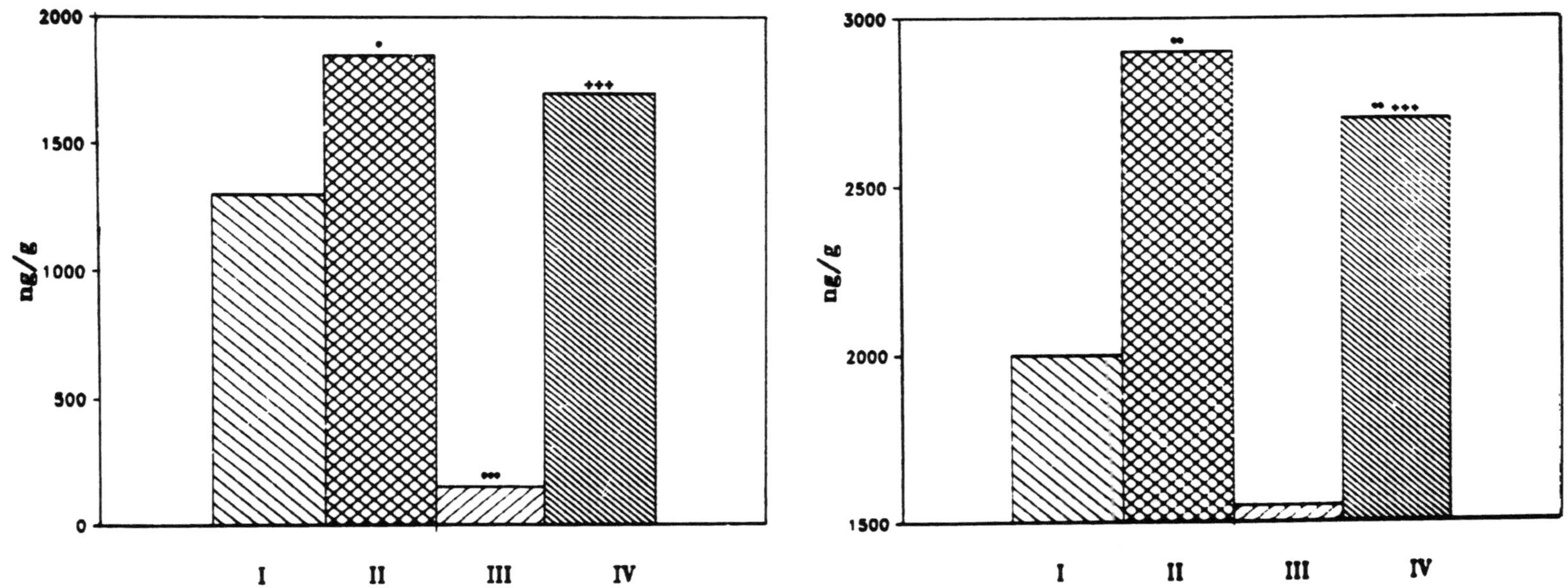

Figure 5. Hypothalamic norepinephrine (left panel) and dopamine (right panel) contents. Groups of rats: 1, controls (N = 12); 2, single SP administration (N = 11); 3, immobilization stress (N = 16); 4, immobilization stress after a single SP injection (N = 16). * and ***, $p < 0.05$ and $p < 0.001$ as compared to controls; + and + + +, $p < 0.05$ and $p < 0.001$ as compared to Group 3.

Interestingly, that block of somatoautonomic responses under electrical HVM stimulation was also observed after introducing certain doses of ß-endorphin into the lateral brain ventricles (27). DSIP was shown to block the ascending activating influences of the hypothalamic defense centers on the brain cortex, normalizing the cross-correlation between EEG rhythms on the right and left hemispheres (28). Thus it is clear that the increase of DSIP and ß-endorphin levels in the brain enhances the animals' resistance to emotional stress.

The experiments conducted by E. A. Yumatov et al (29) demonstrated that SP injected i.p. in a dose of 125 μg/kg, considerably increased the survival rate of August rats under emotional stress induced by isolation in small plastic boxes for 20 h every other day, over the course of 8 weeks. Under these conditions, up to 80% of August rats died, as a rule, from acute cardiac failure. SP injection resulted in a 50% survival of the rats by the 8th week while controls demonstrated a 25% survival rate.

Special experiments (30) have shown that SP returned to normal levels the hypothalamic content of dopamine and norepinephrine under emotional stress. A single (125 μg/kg) i.p. injection of the peptide prevented the immobilization to decrease the hypothalamic norepinephrine levels. A highly significant increase in the hypothalamic norepinephrine content was observed in these rats compared to controls matched in terms of immobilization (Figure 5). This effect clearly persisted, even 2 weeks after the injection.

Microiontophoretic application of norepinephrine and SP to single HVM neurons has essentially altered the animals' sensitivity to norepinephrine, irrespective of whether or not the peptide changed the neuron's baseline spike activity (31). In the course of acute emotional stress, the changes of HVM units' sensitivity to norepinephrine and SP run parallel.

Therefore, it appears that genetically determined individual resistance of animals to acute emotional stress depends on the baseline level of such oligopeptides as ß-endorphin SP, and DSIP in the blood and hypothalamus. Resistance to stress increases after additional administration of DSIP and SP resulting in the increase of these peptides' level in the brain structures and block of molecular changes in the brain induced by emotional stress. All this opens new perspectives in the use of oligopeptides for correcting (in animals and in future possibly in humans) resistance to extreme factors.

REFERENCES

1. Chirkov, A.M., Chirkova, S.K., and Startsev, V.G. *Emotional Stress in Primates*, Nauka, Moscow (1987).

2. Sudakov, K.V., "*Emotional Stress and Arterial Hypertension*," Amerinc Pub. Comp., New Delhi (1983).

3. Miminoshvili, D.I., and Magakyan, G.O., Experience in Experimental Modelling of Hypertension and Coronary Insufficiency in Primates, in: *Theoretical and Practical Aspects of Medicine and Biology in Experiments on Primates*, Meditsina, Moscow (1956) pp. 85-98.

4. Corson, S.A., and O'Leary Corson, E., Biopsychogenic Stress, in *Selye's Guide to Stress Research*, edited by Hans Selye, v.2, Van Nostrand Reinhold comp., New York (1983).

5. Sudakov, K.V., Badikov, V.I., Burchuladze, R.A., Gabunija, A.E., and Lomakina, E.A., Oligopeptides in Organization of Behavioral and Autonomic Responses Under Ventromedial Hypothalamic Stimulation, in: *IUPS Proc.*, V. XV., 32401, Sydney (1983) p. 250.

6. Weiss, J.M., Effects of Punishing the Coping Response (Conflict) on Stress Pathology in Rats, *J. Compar. Physiol. Psychol.*, 77:14 (1977).

7. Skotselyas, Yu. G., and Ymatov, E.A.: Correlations between Autonomic Parameters in Acute Emotional Stress, *Zh. Vissh. Nerv. Deyat.*, 33:146 (1983).

8. Sudakov, K.V., Emotional Stress in the Genesis of Cerebrovisceral Disorders, in: *Motivation and Emotional Stress Pt II*, Published by the USSR Council for Human and Animal Physiology, Moscow (1987).

9. Sudakov, S.K., The Course of Individual Cardiovascular Responses in Rabbits Under Acute Experimental Emotional Stress, *Byull. Eksper. Biol. Med.*, 89:662-664 (1980).

10. Yumatov, E.A., Cardiovascular Responses under Emotional Straining, *Fiziol. Cheloveka*, 6:893-905 (1980).

11. Yumatov, E.A., and Skotselyas, Yu.G., Comparative Analysis of Resistance of Cardiovascular Functions to Immobilization in Different Rat Strains, *Zh. Vissh. Nerv. Deyat.*, 29:345-352 (1979).

12. Vedyaev, D.F., and Koplik, E.V., Individual Course of Blood Pressure in Rats Under Actue Emotional Stress. in: *Proc. 2nd USSR Conference on Physiology of Cortico-Visceral Relations*, Leningrad (1981) pp. 114-115.

13. Vedyaev, D.F., and Sudakov, S.K., Animal Studies of Vascular Reactivity to Episodic Ventromedial Hypothalamus Stimulation under Acute Emotional Stress, *Fiziol. Zh. Ukr. SSR*, 1:(1983) (34-43).

14. Belova, T.I., and Kvetnansky, R., Brain catecholamines in experimental emotional strain, *Uspekhi Fiziol. nauk*, 12:67-90 (1981).

15. Ivanova, T.M., Skotselyas, Yu.G., and Bolyakin, V.I., Stability of Cardiovascular Functions in Different Rat Strains Under Emotional Stress, *Zh. Vissh. Nerv. Deyat.*, 29:1052-1060 (1979).

16. Gorbunova, A.V., Petrova, N.V., Portugalov, V.V., and Sudakov, S.K., Acute Emotional Stress in Rabbits (Physiologic and Cytochemic aspects), *Isvestiya AN SSSR Ser. Biologiya* . Nr 1:45 (1981).

17. Portugalov, V.V., and Goncharuk, V.D., Mechanism of Changes the Nervous Cells Undergo in Acute Emotional Stress, *Byull. Eksper. Biol. Med.*, 91:745-748 (1981).

18. Koplik, E.V., Dmitrieva, N.V., and Ioffe, M.L., On the Effect of Low-Molecular Peptides on Stress Responses, in: *Oligopeptides as Body Functions Regulators*, edited by V.N. Yarygin and E. I. Gusev, Moscow, (1987) pp. 65-68.

19. Wurtman, R.J., Reinstein, D., Lehnert, H. During, M., and Acworth, I., Effects of Tyrosine of Phenylalanine on Brain Catecholamine Synthesis: Implication for the Management of Stress, in: *Fourth Symp. of Catecholamines and Neurotransmitters in Stress*, Smolenice Castle, Chehoslov. (1987) p. 97.

20 Salieva, R.M., Koplik, E.V., Poletaev, A.B., Kamenov, Z.A., and Storozheva, Z.I., Beta-Endorphin in the Blood and Hypothalamus in Rats Under Acute Emotional Stress, *Byull. Eksper. Biol. Med* (1988) (in press).

21. Salieva, R.M., Koplik, E.V., Kamenov, Z.A., and Poletaev, A.B., Delta-Sleep Inducing Peptide in the Blood and Hypothalamus in Rats with Different Resistance to Emotional Stress, *Byull. Eksper. Biol. Med*, (1988) (in press).

22. Salieva, R.M., Koplik, E.V., and Kamenov, Z.A., Beta-Endorphin and Delta-Sleep Inducing Peptide in Mechanisms of Resistance to Emotional Stress, *Byull. Eksper. Biol. Med.*, (1988) (in press).

23. Koplik, E.V., Effect of Delta-Sleep Inducing Peptide on Changes of Vascular Reactiveness Under Acute Emotional Stress, in: *Problems of Physiology of Hypothalamus*, vol. 17, Kiev Univ. Press, Kiev (1983) pp. 45-50.

24. Yumatov, E.A., Kirillova, O.I., Poppai, M. and Ratsek, R., Substance P Hypothalamic Levels in Rats Resistant Or Predisposed to Emotional Stress, *Zh. Vissh. Nerv. Deyat.*, 37:371-372 (1987).

25. Sudakov, K.V., Ivanov, V.T., Koplik, E.V., Vedyaev, D.F., Mikhaleva, I.I., and Sargasyan, A.S., Delta-Sleep Inducing Peptide as a Factor Increasing Animals' Resistance to Emotional Stress, *Doklady AN SSSR*, 267:230-233 (1982).

26. Koplik, E.V., and Khovanskaya, T.P., Time Course of the Cyclase Systems under Acute Emotional Stress in Rats Injected With Delta-Sleep Inducing Peptide, in: *Neurophysiological Mechanisms of Motivations, Mechanisms of Emotional Stress, Abstracts of Papers. 1st Soviet-Indian Symposium*, Tsakhkadzor (1983) pp. 66-68.

27. Burchuladze, R.A., Analysis of Action of Increasing Electric Skin Stimulation in Rats Under Acute Emotional Stress, *Eksper Byull. Biol. Med.*, Nr 7:77-79 (1983).

28. Sukhbat, G., Interhemispheric Relations in Rabbits Under Effect of Delta-Sleep Inducing Peptide, *Fiziol.* Zh. *SSSR*, 72:729-735 (1986).

29. Yumatov, E.A., Hecht, K., and Skotselyas, Yu.G., Substance P As a Factor in Resistance to Emotional Stress, *Zh. Vissh. Nerv. Deyat.*, 34:771-777 (1984).

30. Yumatov, E.A., Anokhina, I.P., Mesentseva, L.N., and Skotselyas, Yu.G., The effects of Substance P on the Catecholamine Levels in Hypothalamus and Midbrain of Rats Subjected to Immobilization Stress, *Zh. Vissh. Nerv. Deyat.*, 35:570-574 (1985).

31. Yumatov, E.A., and Bykova, E.A., Microiontophoretic Studies of Chemical Sensitivity to Substance P on Medial Hypotalamic Neurons in Rats, *Fiziol. Zh. SSSR*, 73:1052-1056 (1987).

NEUROPHYSIOLOGICAL MECHANISMS OF BEHAVIORAL SELF-REGULATION DURING EMOTIONAL STRESS IN ANIMALS

M. M. Khananashvili

I. S. Beritashvili Institute of Physiology
Georgian Academy of Sciences
Tbilisi, USSR

From the moment a pathogenic agent starts to affect the brain higher function until the formation of a stable pathology of behavior, a certain time passes. During that time, in addition to the development of pathological processes, the defensive brain mechanisms, including the self-regulatory ones, become activated. Investigations have shown that both the former and the latter have a complex dynamics, develop in the time and space with different intensity and are characterized by definite external (behavioral), intracerebral and neurohumoral manifestations. Manifestation and correct interpretation of their bilogical value and the knowledge of their mechanisms greatly account for the strategy of treatment and prophylaxis of the behavioral pathology, including stress management. However, until recently various changes, arising in the animal's behavior shortly after it undergoes the influence of a pathogenic agent, were most frequently interpreted as the earliest symptoms of the pathology, and accordingly, measures were taken for their elimination (suppression). Though, as shown by our investigations, they must be enhanced and maintained, since they play an exclusively significant, bilogically positive role, e.e., they promote either the enhancement of the nervous system stability against a pathogenic agent or reduce its pathogenic influence upon the organism.

Therefore, it is important to study the external manifestations and brain processes that precede the formation of stable pathology of behavior and especially, to single out among them the phenomena having relations to self-regulation. In our experiments these phenomena were studied on dogs and cats subject to external influences, eventually resulting in the development of behavioral disturbances. The latter, according to I. P. Pavlov were termed as "experimental neuroses." Accordingly, the time interval from the beginning of the action of a pathogenic agent on the brain up to the formation of its stable pathology, we call "experimental preneurosis."

Since the study of preneurosis was carried out by us using a behavior pathology paradigm that will be referred to as informational, we shall briefly note that informational pathology of behavior implies pathological disorders in higher brain functions. There is also resulting impairments of functions in other systems of the organism, arising due to prolonged exposure of the brain to the conditions of unfavorable combination of the three following factors: a) a certain volume of information to be processed by the brain for making a decision; b) time allotted for such operations of the brain; c) the level of motivation determining the significance of information (i.e., the necessity of its processing and the importance of decision-taking). The combination of these three factors(they form an "informational triad") may prove to be unfavorable for the brain if: first, the animal has to process a vast body of information (including the stage of decision-making) in the conditions of a prolonged deficit of time allotted for such an activity of the brain, and a high level of motivation: or, second, if there is a deficit of information for a long time while the motivation (in particular, the necessity of decision-making) is very high. Thus, in both cases the unfavorably combined triad of factors affects the brain in terms of i) information volume (in the first case it is excessive, in the second case it is insufficient), ii) time (in the first case it is insufficient, in the second case it is excessive), and iii) motivation (in both cases it is very high). If the clinical picture of the disease caused by this triad of factors corresponds to neurosis, then we speak about the informational pathology of a corresponding nosology, thus emphasizing the term "informational pathology," which is determined by the etiological sign.

In terms of the conception of informational pathology of behavior the above-mentioned triad of factors is combined into a separate group (primary factors or factors of group I) thus emphasizing its pathogenic value. We attach great importance to this group because the persons of a variety of professions engaged in mental activity often have to work in the conditions of unfavorably combined triad of factors. On the other hand, animal experiments as well as observations of humans have demonstrated that hypodynamia, astenia of infectious, traumatic or genetic origin, including a weak type of nervous system and a number of other reasons, which ought to be included into another group of pathogenic factors (secondary factors or factors of group II), essentially contribute to the decrease of the nervous system resistance to the factors of the informational triad. Factors of group II appear to be the risk factors for the origin of informational pathology of behavior.

In reality, there often occurs the combination of group I and II factors, but each of these combinations is distinguished by the produced effect or the mechanisms of pathogenic action. In order to understand the forms of behavioral self-regulation used by animals when the unfavorably combined triad of factors affects the brain, it is reasonable to consider typical dog experiments.

The method of motor-alimentary conditional reflexes and delayed responses was applied. During intersignal intervals the animal was placed on a starting place (or in a cage) in a large experimental chamber with three feeders located at 4 m distance from the starting place and at 3 m distance from each other. After the elaboration of conditional reflexes, the animal's behavior was as follows: after the onset of a positive signal the animal ran to the signalled feeder and being reinforced (with a small piece of raw meat) it immediately returned to the starting place as the subsequent conditional stimulus was to be delivered only after its return. Generally, the intersignal interval was 2-3 min. and the animals accomplished the above-mentioned behavior for several months without any alterations. If one considers this behavior in terms of the theory of informational pathology of behavior, then it is evident that the volume of information in these experiments is determined by the number of conditional signals, delivered during a single experiment, the time factor of the experiment is determined by the intersignal intervals and the level of motivation by the level of hunger, which is permanent, since the food calorie content is also permanent, and the experiment is always carried out at the same time of day. Thus, in case of optimal combination of these factors, the performance of the conditional reflex activity takes place without any disturbances. With a view to producing informational pathology of behavior the correlation of the three factors was altered, for example, by means of a sharp decrease of intersignal intervals. This resulted immediately in a number of changes in behavior, and in a certain period of time in the development of experimental neurosis. This method of alteration of informational triad factors was applied to study behavioral self-regulation.

We shall consider the basic forms of behavioral self-regulation.

As mentioned above, after the food reinforcement the animal immediately runs back to the starting place expecting the subsequent signal. The shortening of intersignal intervals already after several presentations of stimuli resulted in the increase of return time to the starting place; at the same time the following regularity was observed: the shorter the intersignal interval (determined by an experimentater) the more time was spent to reach the starting place. We consider that such an increase of return time by the animals themselves is the manifestation of self-regulation; the animal itself regulated the correlation between the information volume to be processed for decision-making, the time factor during which such brain activity must be performed and the level of motivation. The fact that it is virtually a manifestation of self-regulation is well proved by the following: the better it manifests itself, the slower and easier is the pathology development and, on the other hand, if such self-regulation does not occur (and the animal does not use any other forms of self-regulation that will be mentioned below) then pathology develops rapidly and proceeds in severe forms.

Another manifestation of self-regulation in the conditions of unfavorable combination of triad factors is the cessation of reaction to a part of conditional stimuli. It means that if throughout one experiment the fixed number of positive conditional signals is always reinforced by food, then, after decreasing the intersignal intervals, the animal does not react to every signal by running up to feeders. Thus, though the total volume of food reinforcement is decreased (i.e., the animal receives less meat), the volume of analytical-synthetical activity is also decreased, and such correlation of informational triad factors is attained that does not appear to be pathogenic. With this behavior the animals increase the latent period of pathology development which, in this case, also proceeds more readily than in the animals not able to elaborate different forms of self-regulation.

One more manifestation of self-regulation consists in the alteration of behavior strategy. For instance, when the order of signal presentation is random and consequently the animal is not able to predict the possible significance of the subsequent signal (whether it is positive or negative) then, after the shortening of intersignal intervals stereotyed behavior may be observed. Thus the animal makes for the feeders not in accordance to the signalling value of stimuli, but responding only to every second one, e.e., according to a stereotype. It is known that such stereotyped behavior is not attended by the emotional tension as it is observed during the random reinforcement of signals, and appears to be an easier task for the nervous system.

One of the earliest symptoms of behavioral alterations observed after the impact of pathogenic factors on the organism is the increase of motor activity, i.e., animals move more than usual in the intersignal intervals, shake off more frequently, and the enhancement of some other signs of excitability also take place.

It has been experimentally established that the artificial prevention of possible manifestation of the increased motor activity results in the enhancement of emotional excitation and development of pathology, and therefore such a reaction of the organism to a pathogenic agent plays a biologically positive role and is also considered by us as a manifestation of self-regulation.

A vivid manifestation of brain self-regulation in the conditions of unfavorable combination of informational triad is the alteration of higher nervous activity levels, which is manifested especially by recurrent alteration of qualitative indices of conditional reflexes and delayed reactions.

Periods of high and low levels of the higher nervous activity vary from several days to several weeks. More often such alterations acquire a cyclic character, they become typical and promote the elimination of neuroses. The alteration in the functional state of the brain can be observed throughout one experiment. Thus, the animal in the conditions of sharp decrease of intersignal intervals, as well as after the above-mentioned types of behavioral changes (or independently of them), lies down on the floor and falls asleep. During this period of time it does not respond to any conditional stimuli, nor to any unusual stimuli, and soon, after some seconds or minutes, without any additional external stimuli, it wakes up and performs conditional reflex activity in a correct way.

The foregoing evidence indicates that the described types of animal behavior are directed toward the elimination of pathology or to the conditions leading to its development ent, and it enables us to consider them as the manifestation of brain self-regulatory activity. This is supported also by the fact that the development of pathology was much more rapid and severe when the conditions preventing such self-regulation were artificially created.

The types of self-regulation described in dogs' behaviors were observed in cats as well.

In cat and dog experiments some neurophysiological mechanisms responsible for the self-regulatory activity of the brain were also studied.

With this aim, stimulating electrodes were implanted in the limbic structures, thereby creating a biotechnical system due to which electrical stimulation of this or that structure depended on the location of the animal in the experimental chamber. For this reason the floor of the experimental chamber was divided into 9 sections and the animal's location in one of them served as a signal to the onset of electrical stimulation of a definite structure. Thus, the animal's movement on the floor enabled to stimulate different brain structures. As shown by earlier experiments, animals prefer self-stimulation only of a definite structure that is evidenced by their prolonged stay on the corresponding section of the floor. In the conditions of such a possibility to choose the brain structure for its electrical self-stimulation, formation of experimental informational neurosis was carried out by means of the above described method. It has been demonstrated that after the decrease of intersignal intervals, i.e., after creating a pathogenic situation, usually leading to experimental neurosis, animals, as a rule, self-stimulate the septum, i.e., they mainly stand on the section of the floor triggering the stimulation of this structure. It appeared that such a drive for septal stimulation caused delay in the development of experimental neurosis, i.e., it developed later and proceeded more readily than in the absence of such brain stimulation. The comparison of the results on the self-stimulation of different limbic structures enables us to single out a system of brain structures (septum, lateral hypothalamus, dorsal hippocampus) that, though to a different extent, has above-mentioned influence upon the development of experimental neurosis. We suppose that the mechanism of such an influence consists in the increased resistance of the nervous system against the pathogenic agents, in particular, against the informational triad, and points to the role of this system of brain structures in the behavioral self-regulation

The above-stated conclusions contribute to profound study of the theory of stress: thus it becomes possible to determine the bilogical meaning of separate manifestations of stress reactions - those, ensuring brain self-regulation and behavior optimization. On the other hand, the revealed system of brain structures increasing the resistance of the brain to informational loadings and psycho-emotional stress enables us to consider the possibility of using these data for the elaboration of new means (neurophysiological, pharmacological, etc.) for stress and tension management.

EXPERIMENTAL STRESS AND IMMUNITY: PAST, PRESENT AND FUTURE

G. Guencheva[1], P. Popova[1], F. J. McGuigan[2], and N. Nikolov[3]

[1]Institute for State Control of Drugs
Bulgarian Medical Academy

[2]Institute for Stress Management
United States International University, San Diego, USA

[3]Department of Pathophysiology
Scientific Medico-Biological Institute
Bulgarian Medical Academy

Emotional stress represents a human plague and has always been present from the beginning of mankind (Nikolov & Sudakov, 1985). Increasing scientific evidence supports age-old observations that stress is closely associated with changes in immunity. Naturally occurring life stress often correlates with immunosuppression.

PAST

Since antiquity, mankind has confronted a great number of problems, many of them not conducive to successful solution. Those problems critical for existence, such as for food and protection of life, when left unsolved, invariable give rise to emotional stress. Primitive people were conspicuous for great muscular force and resistance to infections because the unstable and nonresistant individuals usually perished. Nevertheless, life span was short owing to the helplessness of mankind in the struggle against infections, starvation and natural calamities. Those who survived possessed good immunity and physical strength.

The idea that health requires a maintenance of balances goes back to ancient China and to Greek medicine at the time of Hippocrates. According to the mythology of the ancient Greeks, Appollo was the symbol of beauty and harmony of the human body and human spirit. Most likely, he could also be the personification of a firm resistance to emotional stress. The ancient Greeks were endowed with the art of harmonic development insofar as the body and spirit are concerned. Ancient Sparta was the city where the weak people were thrown down from the rocks and killed.

Since the dawn of history, epidemic outbreaks have taken a great toll of human life. Plagues as well as wars belong to the oldest disasters of mankind. They are referred to in the earliest documents we know of - the Gilgamesch epos, the Bible, the Egyptian hieroglyphs, the Chinese scrolls. Their consequences were not merely disastrous for the individual, the family and the community, but often enough they led to important historical changes, decided the outcome of wars and destroyed civilizations.

Even before the infectious nature of such diseases was appreciated, incisive empirical observations linked dramatic emotions with a low resistance against illness. Historians have suggested that the spread of Europe's Black Death in the 14th century was facilitated by the stress of urban living and that its disappearance coincided with the improvement of the social conditions and of the living standard of ordinary people. In the past, emotional stress evoked long-standing adverse emotions which in turn induced a powerful mental strain. Whenever one lost hope of solving vitally important problems, diseases related to stress occurred. People living in the past centuries must have been highly susceptible to infectious diseases against which humanity was almost defenseless. Vaccination - the prevention of infections with safe preparations of different origin - as well as immunology, the medical science dealing with various processes of resistance or with the impairment of resistance to foreign bodies and to infectious agents, were both created by Eduard Genner, who introduced smallpox vaccination in 1796. However, a whole century passed until the first great microbiologists and immunologists, such as L. Pasteur, R. Koch, E. Behring, P. Ehrlich, laid the scientific basis for further development in this field and have given us safe and universally effective vaccines; those against diptheria, whooping cough, tetanus, etc. Later, immunity became a topic of numerous investigations and its basic features were successfully revealed. At that time, scientists were still far from being completely aware of the practical implications of the interactions between the two forms of immunity - humoral and cellular - and the effect of hormones and the nervous system on immunity. The immune system was considered to be a self-monitoring, autoregulated system, a notion which explains why, in the past, the struggle against infections was never associated with that against stress.

W. B. Cannon's basic idea, the wisdom of the body in maintaining homeostasis and emergency reactions, contributed to the study of adaptive functions and response to stress (Cannon, 1922, 1939). Selye (1952) was the one who developed the concept of stress and the study of the body's reactions to stressor situations, namely:

- adrenal cortex enlargement, increased level of glucocorticosteroid hormones (these hormones account for the compromised immune functions and their suppression);

- retrograde development (involution) of the thymo-lymphatic apparatus with ensuing impairment of the function of T and B lymphocytes.

The fact that the immune responses could be classically conditioned was first discovered by Metalnikov & Chlorine in 1926 and later was convincingly demonstrated by Ader & Cohens (1975) in immunopharmacological experiments. This fact implicated the central nervous system in the modification of immune reactions. By 1975, immunity could no longer be considered an "autonomous" area of defence, and we developed a new approach for investigating the different mechanisms of neural regulation of the immunologic functions. The notion that there could be neurological influence on host immunocompetence derived from reports showing immunosuppression associated with stress and emotions (Cullen & Van Belle, 1975; Berenbaum et al, 1973).

PRESENT

General Considerations

Considerable evidence has accumulated suggesting the possibility that the susceptibility to disease may be enhanced by emotional stress both in humans and animals (Levy, 1972; Sudakov, 1977; Sudakov et al, 1982; Wehrmacher & Randal, 1984; Nikolov & Sudakov, 1985). Recently there has been a significant increase in the study of the functions of the immune system. The popularity of this research is due to the awareness of scientists of the importance of immunity in the maintenance of a disease-free homeostasis, and to technical advances in the field of immunology. The growing role of this science in medicine opens new avenues to the understanding of stress and its immune consequences. Nowadays it has become apparent that the immune system interacts with all the body systems, especially with the endocrine and the nervous systems. A number of lines of evidence document the links between emotions, immunologic functions and subsequent illness. It is now accepted that psychoneuroendocrine responses to stress can influence immune competence and thus affect proneness to infections, autoimmune diseases and possibly even cancer both in humans and animals (Fox, 1984; Plotnikoff et al, 1986; Dorian & Garfinkel, 1987). Scientific research in animal studies;in vitro studies of the immunologic response; studies of immune reactions in healthy, bereaved and depressed populations, acute or chronically stressed; and studies on the timing of the onset of illness all report such an association. Animal studies demonstrate complex effects of stress on disease susceptibility.

Experimental Data

The evidence from experimental data document that stressor factors which tax the animal's adaptive capacity are associated with immune alterations which tend to be in the direction of immunosuppression. Multiple parameters of the immune system must be assessed in animal studies as there is no single index of immune competence, and it is known that the immune response is a phasic phenomenon regulated by complex interactions among different cell types, each of which may show alterations in response to a given stressor. One parameter of immune function may increase while another decreases. However, due to the various levels of regulation and integration of the immune system, the overall effect may be a reduction in immunocompetence or host defense.

There are many other critical factors altering the immune-stress relationship. Depending on the age of animals, the intensity, timing, and duration of stress, the type of stressor - such as physical restraint, overcrowding, electric shock, swimming, etc. - the immune system is capable of reacting immediately and specifically to the distinct stimulus. The exposure of rats to a mild emotional stress (a single electric footshock) induces an increase of immune response (Croiset et al, 1987). However, when the animal is confronted with a conflict situation, as tested by the retention of the avoidance response after a single learning trial, the initially enhanced reactivity of the immune system decreases. The long-term chronic stress (a signaled, escapable electric footshock stress for 2-4 h/day over a period of 6 months) causes pronounced immunosuppression in rats (Odio et al, 1986).

Models for Stress-Induced Immunosuppression

The interest in models for stress-induced impairment of immunity has promoted several investigations in our laboratory. Our aim is to evaluate the effects of restraint stress on different parameters of the immune system in more than one species of animals. The animals we used were male Wistar rats, 3-4 months old, weighing 170-250g, housed in groups of five with an adaptation period of 2 weeks before the experiment. We also used male ICR strain of mice, 6-8 weeks old, weighing 20-22g, housed in groups of ten under conventional conditions with free access to water and standard food.

To stress them, the animals were restrained in small wire cages for 24 hours. Control (non-stressed) rats and mice were handled in the same laboratory environment. We shall briefly summarize a sample of some of the results that have been obtained. Details of these experiments can be obtained by writing to the first author.

Effect of Stress on the Weight of Lymphoid Organs The indices of lymphoid organs (thymus and spleen) were determined by calculating the organ weight in relation to body weight. For better comparison between the experiments, the ratio of the mean organ index of the experimental group to the mean organ index of the control group was presented as a relative organ index. The exposure of mice and rats to stress induced significant reduction of the relative thymus and spleen indices, the atrophy of the thymus being more pronounced in both species (Figure 1).

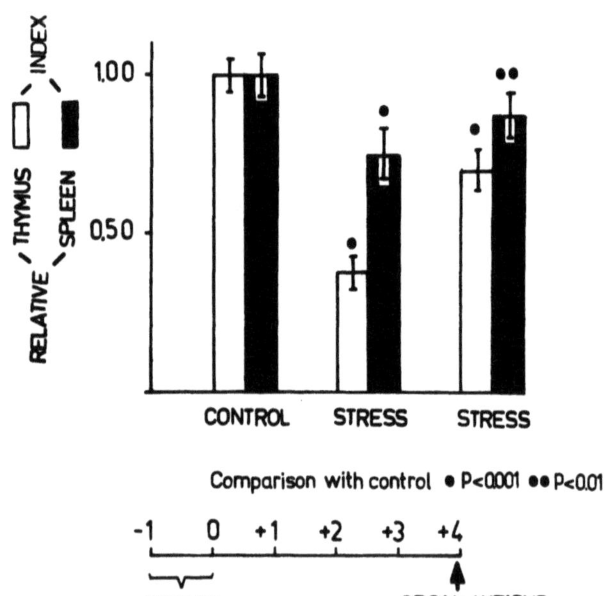

Figure 1. Effect of restraint stress on the weight of thymus and spleen in mice and rats. The animals were subjected to restraint stress for 24 hours. Four days afterwards they were sacrificed,their organs were removed and the organ indices were calculated. The values represent the mean ± SE of ten animals per group.

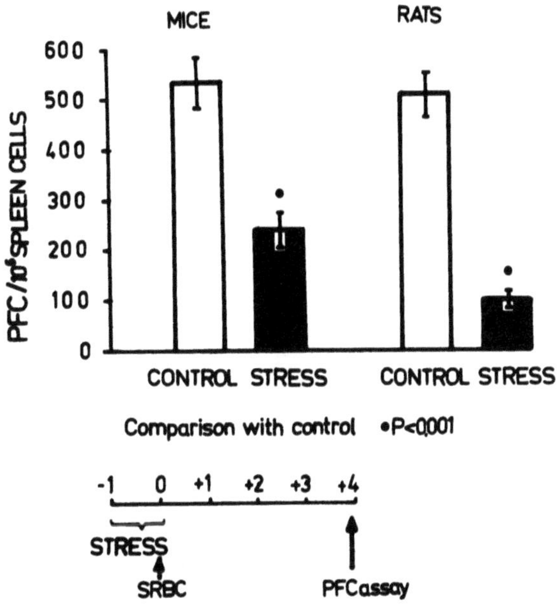

Figure 2. Effect of restraint stress on the plaque-forming cells (PFC) response to SRBC in mice and rats. Restraint stress was performed 24 hours before immunization. Stressed and control animals were immunized with 5×10^8 SRBC/0.5 cm^3 saline i.p. Four days afterwards they were sacrificed, the spleens of each group were removed and pooled, and the number of PFC was determined. Each value represents the mean ± SE of three determinations of 5 animals per group.

Effect of Stress on Humoral Immunity. This was evaluated by means of antibody-producing spleen cells (hemolytic plaque-forming cells)-(PFC) to sheep red blood cells (SRBC) according to Cunningham & Szenberg (1968). The restraint stress caused a marked suppression of the antibody production (Figure 2).

Effect of Stress on Cell-Mediated Immunity. This was evaluated by means of the delayed-type hypersensitivity (DTH) reaction to SRBC (Liew, 1982). Mice and rats exposed to stress demonstrated a significantly depressed ability to generate a DTH response. An approximately 40-50% reduction was observed (Figure 3).

Effect of Stress on Phagocytosis. This was determined by measuring the hagocytic activity of peritoneal macrophages, isolated from stressed and control mice and incubated with radiolabelled bacteria. This parameter was 50% decreased in restrained mice (Table 1).

Effect of Stress on Host Resistance to Experimental Infection. The stressed mice exhibited a higher mortality rate after infection with Klebsiella pneumoniae, strain 52145, obtained from "Pasteur Institute," Paris (Figure 4).

The results indicate that restraint stress decreases all the immunological parameters assessed. Humoral and cellular immune functions, phagocytosis and host resistance are suppressed in both mice and rats. The reported data may contribute to

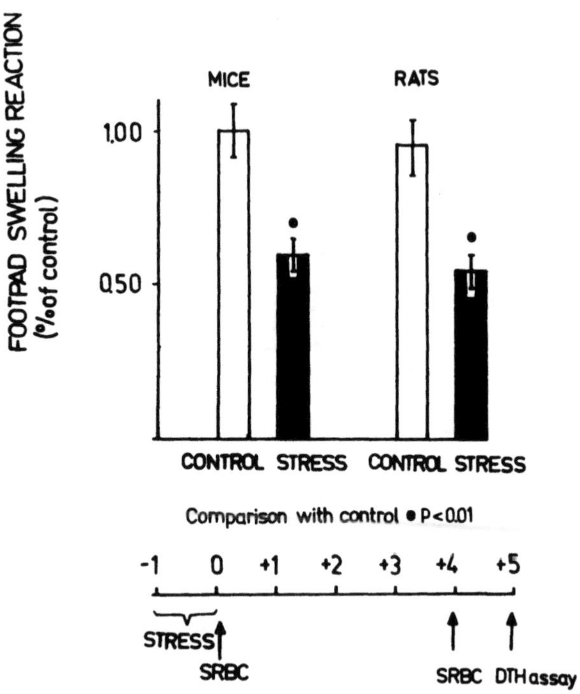

Figure 3. Influence of restraint stress on delayed-type hypersensitivity (DTS) reaction in mice and rats. Mice and rats were restraint-stressed for 24 hours before sensitization. Stressed and control animals were injected subcutaneously (s. c.) with 4×10^8 SRBC/0.5 cm^3 saline, and after 4 days were challenged with 1×10^8 SRBC/0.5 cm^3 saline s. c. in the right hind footpad. The left footpad was injected with the same volume saline only. Twenty-four hours after challenge the DTH reaction was measured as the difference in the swelling of the right and the left footpad. Each value represents the mean ± SE of 10 animals per group.

the analysis of the mechanisms of stress-induced immunosuppression and also to the search and evaluation of antistress and immunomodulating drugs.

Other models for stress-induced immunosuppression include the induction of a number of experimental animal tumors: Walker carcinoma, Ehrlich ascites virus and methylcholantrene induced tumors, spontaneous mammary tumors and leukemias. Glaser et al, (1985) have provided evidence for the influence of acute stress on tumor development at the level of DNA repair. There seem to be differences based on the chronicity of the exposure to stress. It has been found that an acute stress enhances the growth of syngeneic transplanted tumors; chronic exposure appears to produce a slight retardation of tumor growth (Sklar et al, 1979).

Experimental stress models also demonstrate the increased susceptibility to viral infections (Eduards & Dean, 1977; Rogers et al, 1979) and acceleration of the onset of autoimmune diseases such as diabetes (Huang et al., 1981; Carter et al, 1987) and arthritis (Rogers et al, 1980).

Animal experiments have thus demonstrated complex effects of stress on the immune system. These findings may contribute to a better understanding of the

Table 1. Effect of restraint stress on the phagocytic activity of peritoneal macrophages in mice[a]

groups	Number of animals	Phagocytosis (% of control)[b]	p (comparison with control)[c]
Control	5	100±9	< 0.002
Stress	5	50±4	

[a]Peritoneal macrophages were collected on the 5th day after stress and were incubated with the strain Escherichia coli C 600 K 12 labelled with ^{3}H-Thymidine (Amersham).

[b]Each result is the mean of three determinations ± SEM.

[c]Statistical analysis was done by Student's t-test.

suggested association between stressful life events and increased susceptibility to diseases in humans.

EMOTIONAL STRESS, IMMUNITY AND HEALTH CONSEQUENCES

There has long been an interest in the relationship between stress and immunity in humans. The studies demonstrating immune alterations due to stress encompass a number of variable findings, although most types of occurring stresses have been associated with immunosuppressive modulation. There is evidence to show consistent immunologic changes in people undergoing acute psychological stress such as bereavement or an important examination. In humans, the effects of chronic stress may be different from acute stress, corresponding to the studies in animals. Stress may enhance vulnerability to certain diseases by exerting immunosuppressive effects

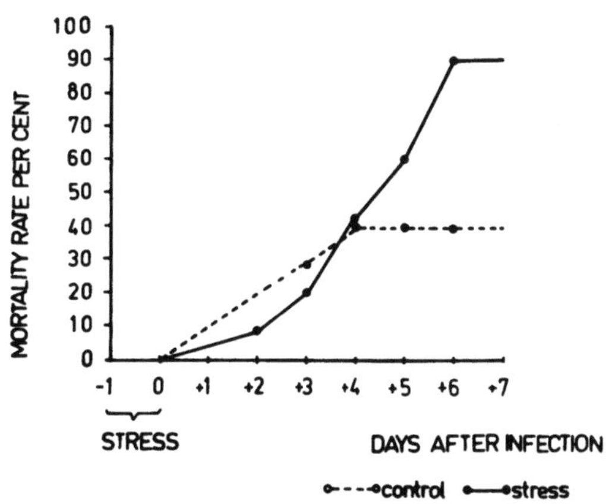

Figure 4. Influence of restraint stress on experimental infection with Klebsiella pneumoniae in mice. Mice were restrained for 24 hours before the infection. Klebsiella pneumoniae strain 52145 was suspended in saline at a concentration of $0.25x10^2$ microorganisms/cm^3. All groups of mice were injected i. p. with 0.1 cm^3/10g of body weight.

and especially to those diseases intimately connected with immunological mechanisms such as infection, malignancy and autoimmune diseases (Dorian & Garfinkel, 1987). Stress may also contribute to the increase in mortality and to aggravation of other situations accompanied by alterations in immunocompetence, such as surgical trauma (Linn & Jensen, 1983a) and anaesthesia, diabetes (Linn, 1983b) and cancer (Levy, 1987). Palmblad et al, (1981) and Locke (1982) demonstrate the critical role which timing and duration of stressor exposure play as factors affecting the immune reactions. Another critical factor in the relationship of stress to altered immunity in humans is the adaptive capacity of the individual.

Several studies examine the influence of bereavement stress on immune functions (Bartrop et al, 1977; Schleifer et al, 1983; Linn et al, 1982; Locke, 1982). These studies of bereavement stress constitute some of the strongest evidence of immunosuppressive changes during exposure to naturally occurring life stress and may provide preliminary evidence for a psychoimmunologic mediation of increased illness susceptibility among the bereaved.

Dorian et al (1982, 1986) study the relationship between examinations and immunological functioning. The immunosuppression found correlates more closely with the individual's perception of the stress than with the live event itself. Jemmott et al (1983); Kiecolt-Glaser et al (1984); Locke et al (1984); Glaser & Kiecolt-Glaser (1986) demonstrate the interactions between academic stress, power motivation and immune functions, Workman & La Via (1987) present results indicating a clear functional relationship between a high-stress condition during examinations and delayed decrements in T-lymphocyte polyclonal proliferation. Perhaps more importantly, their investigation demonstrates that there are significantly different lymphocyte response decrements across types of individuals grouped on the basis of how they are coping with stressors in life.

Poor marital quality and recent separation or divorce are associated with reduction in immune functions and, in turn, with a degree of consequent depression (Kiecolt-Glaser et al, 1987).

While most studies suggest alterations in the immune status after a relatively acute stress, a recent investigation of Dorian et al (1985) examines chronic stress situations and finds enhancement of immune response potential. However, an alternative explanation is that the effect of psychological distress is to impose a dysregulation of the immune system rather than specific changes. The result may be widely different at different points of time. Dorian et al (1985) are interested in whether chronic work stress may produce immune alterations. The accountants tended to display an increase in immunologic defence at the time of peak stress followed by a suppression during the post stress period.

Depression is the only psychiatric disorder which constantly demonstrates immunologic changes. For example, there are reports of an increase in the frequency of herpes simplex disease in depressed people (Rimon et al., 1971; Cappel et al, 1978). Recent carefully controlled studies of patients have shown an impairment in cell-mediated immunity (Kronfol et al, 1983; Schleifer et al, 1984, 1985). Exemplified by early reports of abnormalities of the immunoglobulin levels in schizophrenic patients, a variety of immune aberrations, including antibodies, are found in conjunction with mental diseases (Solomon, 1981).

In several instances, effects similar to those observed in rodents may happen in humans through emotional (occupational or social) stress exemplifying certain characteristics of secondary immunodeficiency diseases. Infectious diseases and neoplasia are a recurring consequence of chronic immunosuppression or of aberrant lymphoid cell differentiation in stressed organisms. For example, the morbidity and the mortality after Klebsiella pneumoniae infection is higher after stress. All these examples and our current knowledge about the pathogenesis of diseases support the possibility that stress-induced damage to the immune system may be associated with a wide spectrum of diverse pathologic conditions, some of which may only become detectable after long latency (Luster & Blanck, 1987).

*Stress and Infections.*The role of psychological distress is most convincing in this area of human illness. Cohen-Cole et al, (1981) show the inter-relationship between psychosocial, endocrine and immune variable in people with acute necrotizing ulcerative gingivitis ("trenchmouth"). Kasl et al (1979) prospectively study a large group of Cadets over four years in order to understand the relationship between academic stress, seroconversion to Epstein-Barr virus and susceptibility to infectious mononucleosis. Kiecolt-Glaser et al (1987) have demonstrated that women experiencing the stress of separation and divorce have higher antibody titres to Epstein-Barr virus, reflecting poor cellular immune control over the latent virus. Similarly, Glaser et al (1985) show that medical students display highest antibody titres to three herpes viruses at the time of peak stress, these changes being most pronounced in subjects who report high levels of loneliness. The development of acute respiratory infections can be influenced by psychosocial factors. Totman et al (1980) study volunteers inoculated with rhinoviruses; Dorian et al (1986) and Jemmott et al (1983) note an increase in respiratory infections in subjects who responded to examination stress with high levels of distress. Glaser et al (1986) document an association between periods of immunosuppression and acute infections prior to examinations in medical students. McClelland et al (1982) further relate the onset of upper respiratory infections to stress with high levels of Ig A in saliva. Herpes simplex virus can be reactivated by a number of factors: psychosocial stressors, colds, sunburns, fever and menstruation. the stress of "examination week" activates latent herpes simplex virus infection (under T-cell control) in the students, to a greater degree in lonely students (Glaser et al, 1985). Luborsky et al (1976) have demonstrated that the recurrences of cold sores in student nurses could be correlated with unhappiness on Clyde Mood Scale. Virus activation in AIDS also may be the consequence of stress. New results suggest that length of survival in AIDS can be correlated with psychosocial factors (Solomon, 1987).

Stress and Autoimmune Diseases. The evidence for linking psychosocial stress to autoimmune diseases is at least well documented (Dorian et al, 1987). The literature is suggestive of a role of stress in the onset and course of rheumatoid arthritis and should encourage future investigations of the nature of this relationship (Solomon, 1981; Meyerowitz et al, 1968' Feigenbaum et al, 1979; Koehler, 1983; Crosby, 1986). Wallace (1987) points out the role of stress in the development of two autoimmune diseases, rheumatoid arthritis and lupus erythematosus. According to Robinson & Fuller (1986), patients suffering from insulin-dependent diabetes mellitus, type I, often observe a correlation between some stressful episode in their life and the clinical manifestation of the disease.

*Stress and Malignancy.*The observations concerning the personality characteristics and the affective states of cancer patients date back 2000 years (Bahnson, 1980). Many studies provide some support for a role of psychosocial factors in the risk and in the initiation of malignancies. For more complete discussions of this, the reader is referred to the reviews of Bahnson (1980); Fox (1981); Borysenko (1982a); and Greer (1983).

Stress and Allergy. It is well known that the nervous system plays an important role in the pathogenesis of allergy (Takino, 1978; Goetzl, 1985). Sukovatykh & Zhernokek (1986) indicate the role of the stress-induced neuropsychological changes in the pathogenesis of bronchial asthma mainly in children.

The effects of psychological stress in vulnerable individuals may be manifested by a dysregulation of the immune system rather than by an absolute suppression in one aspect or another. The clinical significance of stress-induced alterations in immune functions need further research on the specific association between diminished immunocompetence and development of illness, the magnitude of this association, etc. More attention must be paid to these factors in human research and greater consideration given to disentangling the relative effects of physiological versus psychological factors in inducing immunosuppression.

BASIC MECHANISMS OF IMMUNOMODULATION BY EMOTIONAL STRESS

Currently there are increasing investigations of the hormonal and neurotransmitter mechanisms which modulate the immune responses. There is evidence for the complex regulation of the immune system by enkephalines, endorphines, corticosteroids, catecholamines (Axelford & Reisine, 1984; Grossman, 1986; McCain et al, 1987; Borysenko, 1982b; Maestroni, 1988). Immune deficiency may be associated with emotional stress by the following mechanisms:

- pituitary-adrenocortical hyperactivity,
- functional impairment of the limbic system, hypothalamus in particular,
- heightened level of catecholamines,
- homeostasis impairment by damage to the liver, etc.
- opioid peptides, melatonin, enzymes related to synthesis of neurotransmitters in the brain,
- activated sympathetic nervous system.

The existing evidence links stress and immunity beyond a reasonable doubt. The exponential growth of the field of psychoneuroimmunology and the consequent accretion of experimental data confirm the multifactoral nature of all diseases as the result of interactions among genetic, endocrine, nervous, immune, and behavioral-emotional factors. Such a concept of health and disease has been created by such pioneers George Engel (1960) and Jonas Salk (1962) and has also been sensed by wise clinicians since ancient times, from practitioners of Ayurveda in India two millenia ago to Hippocrates, Galen, and Osler (Solomon, 1987).

THERAPEUTICAL MODIFICATION OF STRESS-INDUCED IMMUNOSUPPRESSION

Attempts have been made, with various drugs, to restore the immune functions decreased due to stress.

Neurotropin (NSP) is a preparation consisting of non-protein bioactive substances isolated from the inflamed tissue of rabbits inoculated with vaccinia virus. Its intended pharmacological actions cover a broad range of effects such as action on autonomous nervous function, analgetic-sedative, antiallergic and immunonormalizing effects. The actions of neurotropin on the immune system have not yet found any clinical application. However, experimentally it has been shown that neurotropin exerts immunomodulating effects (Yanagihara et al, 1981; Yoshii et al., 1987). Moreover, NSP has been reported to restore impaired immune reactivity due to stress load in mice (Yamamoto, 1982).

The interest in drugs which might abolish the stress-induced impairment of immunity has promoted our present investigation. Its aim is to evaluate the effects of neurotropin in our model for suppressed immunity after restraint stress in mice and rats.

These experiments were performed using the same strains of animals, type of stress and methods for assessment of the immunological paramcters as described previously.

Neurotropin was kindly supplied by Nippon Zoki Pharmaceutical Co., Ltd., Japan. The drug was applied intraperitoneally (i.p.) in two doses (1 mg/kg and 20 mg/kg body weight) on 5 consecutive days. The neurotropin treatment of stressed animals started 24 hours following the restraint. Sodium chloride 0.9% (Saline) - Pharmachim, Bulgaria was used as vehicle control. The results of our research will be briefly summarized. As with the previous results, details can be obtained by writing the first author.

Effect of Neurotropin on the Weight of Lymphoid Organs. In a dose of 1 mg/kg body weight the drug restored the decrease of thymus and spleen weights in mice and rats under stress (Figure 5).

Effect of Neurotropin on Humoral Immunity. NSP in both doses tested restored the suppressed antibody-production due to stress and increased the number of plaque-forming cells in mice and rats (Figure 6).

Effect of Neurotropin on Cell-Mediated Immunity. Treatment with 1 mg/kg body weight NSP abolished the suppression of delayed-type hypersensitivity reaction in stressed mice (Table 2).

Effect of Neurotropin on Phagocytosis. NSP did not cause significant recovery of phagocytic function decreased in restrained mice (Table 3).

Effect of Neurotropin on Host Resistance to Experimental Infection. The five-day treatment with 1 mg/kg NSP increased the survival rate of the stressed mice after Klebsiella pneumoniae infection (Table 4).

On the basis of these observations it is evident that neurotropin exerts a restorative effect on most of the immune parameters decreased by restraint stress. Lymphoid organs' atrophy and the depression of humoral and cellular immunity are abolished by NSP treatment. The drug increases the resistance to bacterial infection. Briefly, NSP has the potential to reverse the immunosuppressive effects of restraint stress in animals.

FUTURE

In summary, despite some inconsistencies and methodological flaws, the bulk of evidence suggests a relationship between stress, altered immunity and illness. The complex interactions between physiological and social factors which may enhance or

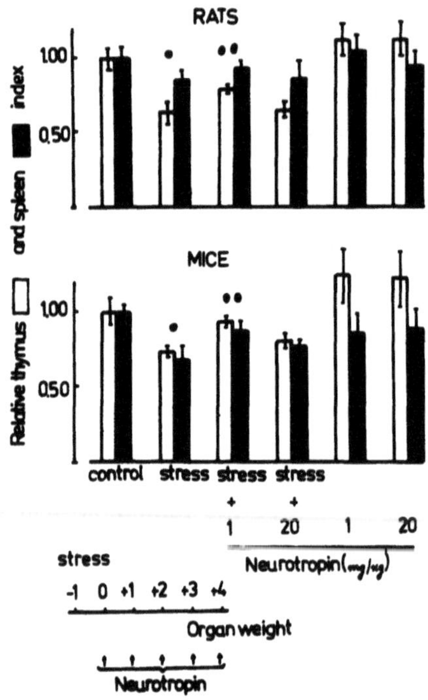

Figure 5. Effect of neurotropin (NSP) on the reduced thymus and spleen weights due to restraint stress in rats and mice. Animals were restrained for 24 hours. The 5-days treatment with NSP started immediately after their release. NSP was administered i. p. in doses of 1 mg/kg and 20 mg/kg of body weight. The organ indices were calculated at the end of NSP treatment. Each value represents the mean ± SE of 10 animals per group. *Comparison with control (not stressed) $p < 0.001$. ** Comparison with stress group (without NSP) $p < 0.05$.

diminish psychobiological adaptation and the physiological mediating mechanisms remain in the area for further research.

Could We Meet Eventual Dangerous Situations?

In the future, the struggle against emotional stress and immune deficiency should be conducted in a complex manner (Levi, 1981). The premise is that life changes require adaptation and it is the lack of adaptation that may promote immune alterations leading to the onset of disease. The focus on adaptation has led to a second stage in the evolution in this field which was the search for potent modifiers of the life change-illness-onset relationship. Research is actively pursuing the effects of social support and coping style, and empirical studies have confirmed that exposure to stressors of individuals receiving adequate support does not increase the risk of illness.

Emotional Stress, Immune Dysfunction and Prevention by Relaxation

No one is immune to the stress of life. Those individuals who are genetically predisposed to organismic breakdown should pay special attention to this point. People can act at least to prevent further damage. Some of our stresses are easy to handle, while others are more unmanageable and tragic in their consequences. We

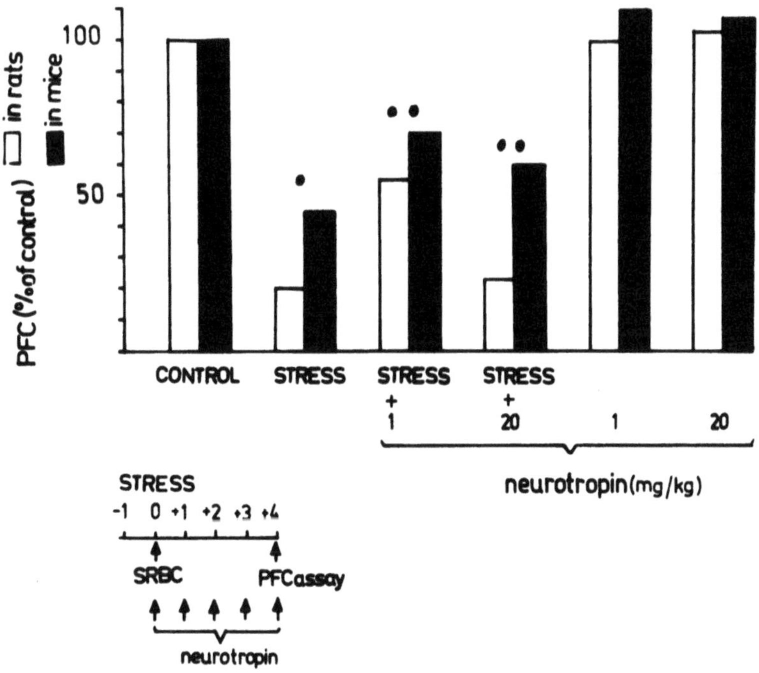

Figure 6. Effect of neurotropin (NSP) on the suppressed plaque-forming cells (PFC) response after stress loading in rats and mice. Animals were restraint-stressed for 24 hours. Immediatley after their release started the 5-days treatment with NSP. It was applied i. p. in doses of 1 mg/kg of body weight. All animals were immunized with $4x10^8$ SRBC/0.5 cm^3 saline i. p. together with the first administration of NSP. Four days after immunization the control and stressed animals were sacrificed, the slpeens of each group were removed and pooled, and the PFC response was measured. Each value represents the mean ± SE of three determinations of 5 animals per group. * Comparison with control (not-stressed) $p < 0.001$. ** Comparison with stress (without NSP) $p < 0.05$.

must work to adapt to the stressors in life, to be supportive of ourselves. We are adaptable and should consider ourselves thus.

Many techniques have been proposed for coping with stresses but Progressive Relaxation, the "grandfather" of them all, is the most thoroughly and carefully validated (McGuigan, 1981). Behavioral interventions should be able to enhance or to optimize immune function. Recovery from a major depressive illness is accompanied by reversal of associated immunosuppression (Stein et al, 1985). Longevity should correlate with superior immune function. An important question is whether behavioral intervention can enhance immunity. The research on the effects of such intervention on the immune response is just beginning. Are positive emotions such as relaxation, happiness, security and other accompanied by immune otpimization? It is this kind of research that remains to be done and it would certainly contribute to the therapeutic approaches in clinical medicine.

Table 2. Effect of neurotropin on delayed-type hypersensitivity[a] reaction of mice under restraint stress.

Groups	Number of animals	Footpad swelling (% of control: x ± SEM)[d]
Control (Saline)	10	100 ± 9
Stress + Saline	10	[b]24 ± 5
Stress + 1 mg/kg NSP	10	[b,c]70 ± 8

[a]Neurotropin treatment started 24 hours after the restraint. Mice were immunized with $5x10^8/0.5cm^3$ saline SRBC subcutaneously (s. c.) on the day of the first NSP injection, and were challenged with $1x10^6/0.05\ cm^3$ saline SRBC s. c. in the right footpad four days after sensitization. The left footpad was injected with the same volume saline. The reaction was measured 24 hours after challenge as the difference in the swelling of the right and left footpad.

[b]Comparison with the control: $p < 0.001$.

[c]Comparison with the group "stress + saline": $p < 0.001$.

[d]Statistical analysis was done by Student's t-test.

New Drugs Against the Stress-Induced Immunosuppression

The prevention of stress and immune deficiency is better but not always possible. The drugs against stress, especially the tranquilizers, can be quite helpful in moments of crisis but like the short-term value of tranquilizers for relaxing, these drugs provide no long-term solutions. Immunomodulators are among the perspective branches in medicine concerned with the management of immunosuppression. Clearly, there is a need for pharmacological agents to prevent the immune disorders and to restore the immune parameters decreased by stress.

New Sciences Appear and Discuss Interactions Between Stress and Immunity

It would be far beyond the scope of this paper to discuss the inter-relationships between the central nervous system and the immune system. Psychoneuroimmunology is concerned with the complex bidirectional interactions between these two systems. This field is subdivided into several disciplines: psychoimmunology, immunopsychiatry, immunoneurology, neuroimmunoregulation, etc. (Solomon, 1987; Jankovic, 1987). All these terms are used to indicate that the central nervous system and the immune system have multiple pathways of communication and that neuropsychological factors exert effects on the development of immunologically resisted and immunologically mediated diseases.

There are many complex levels of interactions which require further investigation in the infant area of psychoneuroimmunology. There is clearly a need for long-term prospective studies to identify individuals at risk for those numerous diseases in which psychosocial factors and impaired immune faction play a pathogenic role. It is necessary to delineate the role of psychosocial factors as the stimulus for and the response to the disease process. Can preventive measures be taken to reduce immunosuppression effects of anticipated stress? This approach to illness will alter the physician's approach to disease and to patients as they are evaluated and treated in the psychosocial context in which they live. As Hippocrates said, "It is more important to know what sort of a person has a disease than to know what sort of disease a person has," (Shindler, 1985).

Table 3. Effect of neurotropin on phagocytosis in mice under stress[a]

Groups	Number of animals	Phagocytosis (%of control)[b]	P (comparison with control)[e]
Control (Saline)	5	100±6	
Stress + Saline	5	55±3	<0.002
Stress + 1 mg/kg NSP	5	[c]64±5	<0.01
Stress + 20 mg/kg NSP	5	[c]67±5	<0.025
1 mg/kg NSP	5	85±9	NS
20 mg/kg NSP	5	83±8	NS

[a]Mice were treated i. p. for 5 days with neurotropin, starting 24 hours after the restraint stress. Peritoneal macrophages were collected on the day of the last NSP injection and were incubated with the strain Escherichia coli C 600 K labelled with ^{3}H-Thymidine (Amersham).

[b]Each result is the mean of three determinations ± SEM.

[c]Comparison with the group "stress + Saline": NS.

[d]NS = statistically non-significant.

[e]Statistics was performed by Student' s t-test.

Table 4. Protective effect of neurotropin on stressed mice, infected with Klebsiella pneumoniae.

Groups	Number of animals	Survival rate - % on day 7 after infection
Control (Saline)	10	70
Stress + Saline	10	10
Stress + 1 mg/kg NSP	10	60

Klebsiella pneumoniae strain 52145 was suspended in saline at a concentration of $0.25x10^2$ microorganisms/cm^3. All groups of mice were injected i. p. with 0.1cm^3/10g of body weight. The restraint stress was performed 24 hours before the injection. The 5-day treatment with neurotropin (saline in controls) started 24 hours after the restrain.

ACKNOWLEDGEMENTS

We are indebted to Mr. Jin-emon Konishi, President of Nippon Zoki Pharmaceutical Co., Ltd., Osaka, Japan for encouraging the work related to neurotropin.

REFERENCES

Ader, R., and Cohen, N. (1975). Behaviorally conditioned immunosuppression. *Psychosomatic Medicine*, 37, 333-340.

Axelford, J., and Reisine, T.D. (1984). Stress hormones: their interaction and regulation. Science, 224, 452-459.

Bahnson, C.B. (1980) Stress and cancer: the state of the art. *Psychosomatics*, 21, 975-981.

Bartrop, R.W., Luckhurst, E., Lazarus, L., Rilch, G., and Penny, R. (1977). Depressed lymphocyte function after bereavement. *Lancet*, i, 834-836.

Berenbaum, M.C., Fluck, P.A., and Hurst, N.P. (1973). Depression of lymphocyte response after surgical trauma. *British Journal of Experimental Pathology*, 54, 597-607.

Borysenko, J.Z. (1982a). Behavioural-physiological factors in the development and management of cancer. *General Hospital Psychiatry*, 4, 69-74.

Borysenko, M., and Borysenko, J. (1982b). Stress, behaviour, and immunity: animal models and mediating mechanisms. *General Hospital Psychiatry*, 4, 59-67.

Cannon, W.B. (1922). What strong emotions do to us. *Harper's Magazine*, 234-241.

Cannon, W.B. (1939). Law of denervation (Hughlings Jackson Memorial Lecture). *American Journal of Medical Science*, 198, 737-750.

Cappel, R., Gregoire, F., Thiry, L., and Sprecher, S. (1978). Antibody and cell mediated immunity to herpes simplex virus in psychotic depression. *Journal of Clinical Psychiatry*, 39, 266-268.

Carter, W.R., Herrman, J., Stokes, K., and Cox, D.J. (1987). Promotion of diabetes onset by stress in the BB rat. *Diabetologia*, 30, 674-675.

Cohen-Cole, S., Cogen, R., Stevens, A., Kirk, K., Gaitan, E., Hain, J., and Freeman, A. (1981). Psychological, endocrine and immune factors in acute necrotizing ulcerative gingivitis ("trenchmouth"). *Psychosomatic Medicine*, 43, 91-95.

Croiset, G., Heijnen, C.J., Veldhuis, H.D., de Wied, D., and Ballieux, R.E. (1987). Modulation of immune response by emotional stress. Life Sciences, 40, 775-782.

Crosby, L. (1986) Stress factors. Emotional stress and rheumatoid arthritis disease activity. *Arthritis and Rheumatology*, Suppl. 4, 29, s151-s156.

Cullen, B.F., and Van Belle, G. (1975). Lymphocyte transformation and changes in leukocyte counts - effect of anaesthesia and operation. *Anesthesiology*, 43, 563-569.

Cunningham, A.J., and Szenberg, A. (1968). Further improvements with plaque technique for detecting single antibody-forming cells. *Immunology*, 14, 599-600.

Dorian, B., Garfinkel, P., Brown, G., Shore, A., Gladman, D., and Keystone, E. (1982). Aberrations in lymphocyte subpopulations and functions during psychological stress. *Clinical and Experimental Immunology*, 50, 132-138.

Dorian, B., Garfinkel, P., Keystone, E., Groczynski, R., Garner, D., Darby, P., and Shore, A. (1985). Occupational stress and immunity. *Psychosomatic Medicine*, 47, 77-83.

Dorian, B., Garfinkel, P., Brown, G., Shore, A., Gladman, D., Keystone, E., and Darby, P. (1986). Stress, immunity and illness. *Psychosomatic Medicine*, 48, 304-311,

Dorian, B., and Garfinkel, P. (1987).. Stress, immunity and illness - a review. *Psychological Medicine*, 17, 393-407.

Eduards, E.A., and Dean, L.M. (1977). Effect of crowding of mice on humoral antibody formation and protection to lethal antigenic challenge. *Psychosomatic Medicine*, 39, 19-24.

Engel, G.L. (1960). A unified concept of health and disease. *Perspectives in Biology and Medicine*, 3, 459-485.

Feigenbaum, S.L., Masi, A.T., and Kaplan, S.B. (1979). Prognosis in rheumatoid arthritis: a longitudinal study of newly diagnosed young adult patients. *American Journal of Medicine*, 66, 377-384.

Fox, B.H. (1981). Psychological factors in the immune system in human cancer. In: R. Ader (Ed.), Psichoneuroimmunology, New York: Academic Press.

Glaser, R., Kiecolt-Glaser, J.K., Speicher, C.E., and Holliday, J.E. (1985). Stress, loneliness, and changes in herpes virus latency. *Journal of Behavioural Medicine*, 8, 249-260.

Glaser, R., and Kiecolt-Glaser, J.K. (1986). Stress and immune function. *Clinical Neuropharmacology*, Suppl. 4, 9, 485-487.

Goetzl, E.J. (1985). Neuromodulation of immunity and hypersensitivity. *Journal of Immunology*, 135, 739S-863S.

Greer, S. (1983). Cancer and the mind. *British Journal of Psychiatry*, 143, 535-543.

Grossmann, C.J., and Roselle, G.A. (1986). Regulation of the immune response by adrenal hormones. *Progress in Clinical Biochemistry and Medicine*, 4, 18-21.

Huang, S.W., Plant, S.M., Taylor, B., and Warenheim, A. (1981). Effect of stressful stimulation on the incidence of streptozotocin-induced diabetes in mice. *Psychosomatic Medicine*, 43, 431-437.

Jankovic, B.D. (1987). Neuroimmune interactions: experimental and clinical strategies. *Immunology Letters*, 16, 341-354.

Jemmott, J.B., Borysenko, J.Z., Borysenko, M.C., McClelland, D.C., Chapman, R., Meyer, D.J., and Benson, H. (1983). Academic stress, power motivation, and decrease in secretion rate of salivary immunoglobulin A. *Lancet*, i, 1400-1402.

Kasl, S.V., Evans, A.S., and Weidermann, J.C. (1979). Psychosocial risk factors in the development of infectious mononucleosis.*Psychosomatic Medicine*, 41, 445-466.

Kiecolt-Glaser, J.K., Speicher, C.E., Holliday, J.E., and Glaser, R. (1984). Stress and the transformation of lymphocytes by Epstein-Barr virus. *Journal of Behavioural Medicine*, 7, 1-12.

Koehler, T. (1985). Stress and rheumatoid arthritis. A survey of empirical evidence in human and animal studies. *Journal of Psychosomatic Research*, 29, 655-663.

Kronfol, Z., Silva, J., Greden, J., Dembinski, S., Gardner, R., and Carroll, B. (1983). Impared lymphocyte function in depressive illness. *Life Sciences*, 33, 241-247.

Levi, L. (1872). Prevention of stress related disorders on a population scale. *International Journal of Mental Health*, 9, 9-26.

Levy, S., Herberman, R., Lippman, M., and d'Angelo, T. (1987). Correlation of stress factors with sustained depression of natural killer cell activity and predicted prognosis in patients with breast cancer. *Journal of Clinical Oncology*, 5, 348-353.

Liew, F.J. (1982). Regulation of delayed-type hypersensitivity to pathogens and alloantigens. *Immunology Today*, 3, 18-23.

Linn, B.S., Linn, M.W., and Jensen, J. (1982). Degree of depression and immune responsiveness. *Psychosomatic Medicine*, 44, 128-129.

Linn, B.S., and Jensen, J. (1983a). Age and immune responses to a surgical stress. *Archives of Surgery*, 118, 405-409.

Linn, M.W., Linn, B.S., Skyler, J.S., and Jensen, J. (1983b). Stress and immune function in diabetes mellitus. *Clinical Immunology and Immunopathology*, 27, 223-233.

Locke, S.E. (1982). Stress, adaptation and immunity. Studies in humans. *General Hospital Psychiatry*, 4, 49-58.

Locke, S.E., Kraus, L., Leserman, J.M., Hurst, M.W., Heisel, S., and Williams, R.M. (1984). Life change stress, psychiatric symptoms and natural killer cell activity. *Psychosomatic Medicine*, 45, 441-453.

Luborsky, L., Minta, V.J., Brightman, V.J., and Katcher, A.h. (1976). Herpes simplex virus and moods: a longitudinal study. *Journal of Psychosomatic Research*, 20, 543-548.

Luster, M.I., and Blanck, J.A. (1987). Molecular and cellular basis of chemically induced immunotoxicity. *Annual Reviews in Toxicology*, 27, 23-49.

Maestroni, G.I.M., Conti, A., and Pierpaoli, W. (1988). Role of the pineal gland in immunity. III. Melatonin antagonizes the immunosuppressive effect of acute stress via an opiatergic mechanism. *Immunology*, 63, 465-469.

McCain, H.W., Bilotta, J., and Lamster, I.B. (1987). Endorphinergic modulation of immune function: potent action of the dipeptide glycyl-L-glutamine. *Life Sciences*, 41, 169-176.

McClelland, D.C., Alexander, C., and Marks, E. (1982). The need for power, stress, immune function and illness among male prisoners. *Journal of Abnormal Psychology*, 91, 61-70.

McGuigan F.J. (1981). Calm Down. A Guide to Stress and Tension Control. New Jersey, Prentice-Hall Inc.

Metalnikov, S., and Chorine, V. (1926). The role of conditioned reflexes in immunity. *Annals of Pasteur Institute*, 40, 893-900.

Meyerowitz, S., Jacox, R.F., and Hess, D.W. (1968). Monozygotic twins discordant for rheumatoid arthritis; a genetic, clinical and psychological study of 8 sets. *Arthritis and Rheumatology*, 11, 1-21.

Nikolov, N.A., and Sudakov, K.V. (1985). Emotional Stress. Sofia, Medizina and Fiskultura.

Odio, M., Golisek, A., and Ricardo, M.J.Jr. (1986). Impairment of immune function after cessation of long term chronic stress. *Immunology Letters*, 13, 25-31.

Plotnikoff, N.P., Faith, B.E., Murgo, A.J., and Good, R.A. (1986). Enkephalins and Endorphins: Stress and the Immune System. New York, Plenum Press.

Rimon, R., Haloneu, P., Anttineu, E., and Evola, E. (1971). Complement fixing antibody to herpes simplex virus in patients with psychotic depression. *Diseases of the Nervous System*, 32, 822-824.

Robinson, N., and Fuller, J.H. (1986). Severe life events and their relationship to the aetiology of insulin-dependent (Type I) diabetes mellitus. *Pediatric and Adolescence Endocrinology*, 15, 129-133.
Rogers, M.P., Dubey, D., and Reich, P. (1979). The influence of the psyche and the brain on immunity and disease susceptibility: a critical review. *Psychosomatic Medicine*, 41, 147-164.
Rogers, M.P., Trentham, D.E., McCune, W.J., Guisberg, B.I., Rennke, H.G., Reike, P., and David, J.R. (1980). Effect of psychological stress on the induction of arthritis in rats. *Arthritis and Rheumatology*, 23, 1337-1342.
Salk, J. (1962). Biological basis of disease and behaviour. *Perspectives in Biology and Medicine*, 5, 198-206.
Salo, M. (1982)..Effects of anaesthesia and surgery on the immune response. In: J. Watkins (Ed.), Trauma, Stress and Immunity in Anaesthesia and Surgery. London, Butterworth & Co., (Publishers) Ltd.
Schindler, B.A. (1985). Stress, affective disorders and immune function. *Medical Clinics of North America*, 69, 585-597.
Schleifer, S., Keller, S., Meyerson, A., Raskin, M.J., Davis, K.L., and Stein, M. (1984). Lymphocyte function in major depressive disorder. *Archives of General Psychiatry*, 41, 484-486.
Schleifer, S.J., Keller, S.E., Siris, S.G., Davis, K.L., and Stein, M. (1985). Depression and immunity. Lymphocyte function in ambulatory depressed patients, hospitalized schizophrenic patients hospitalized for herniorrahaphy. *Archives of General Psychiatry*, 42, 129-133.
Selye, H. (1952). The Story of the Adaptation Syndrome. Montreal, Acta Inc. Med. Publ.
Solomon, G.F. (1981). Emotional and personality factors in the onset and course of autoimmune disease, particularly rheumatoid arthritis. In: R. Ader (Ed.), Psychoneuroimmunology, New York, Academic Press.
Solomon, G.F. (1987). Psychoneuroimmunology: interaction between central nervous system and immune system. *Journal of Neuroscience Research*, 18, 1-9.
Stein, S.P., and Charles, E. (1971). Emotional factors in juvenile diabetes mellitus. *American Journal of Psychiatry*, 128, 56-60.
Stein, M., Keller, S.E., and Schleifer, S.J. (1985). Stress and immunomodulation; the role of depression and neuroendocrine function. *Journal of Immunology*, 135, 827-833.
Sudakov, K.V. (1977). Acute experimental emotional stress and natural history of arterial hypertension. *Physiology and Behaviour*, 19, 213-221.
Sudakov, K.V., Gantan, D., and Nikolov, N. (1982). Emotional stress and arterial hypertension. *Agressologie*, 23, 193-203.
Sukovatykh, T.N., and Zhernosek, V.F. (1986). Characteristics of the course of bronchial asthma with neuropsychological pathogenetic mechanism in children. *Zdravookhranenie Belorussia*, O: 14-17.
Takino, M. (1971). The role of the autonomic nervous system in pathogenesis of allergy. *Japanese Journal of Allergology*, 20, 637-652.
Totman, R., Kiff, J., Reed, S.E., and Graig, J.W. (1980). Predicting experimental colds in volunteers from different measures of recent life stress. *Journal of Psychosomatic Research*, 24, 155-163.

Wallace, D.J. (1987). The role of stress and trauma in rheumatoid arthritis and systemic lupus erythematosus. Seminars in Arthritis and Rheumatology, 16, 153-157.

Wehrmacher, W.H., and Randall, W.C. (1984). Performance of the heart in health and disease. In: W.C. Randall (Ed.), Nervous Control of Cardiovascular Function, Oxford, Oxford University Press.

Workman, E.A., and LaVia, M.F. (1987). T-lymphocyte polyclonal proliferation: effect of stress and stress response style on medical students taking national board examinations. *Clinical Immunology and Immunopathology*, 43, 308-313.

Yamamoto, K. (1982). Proceedings of the 60th Annual Meeting of Kinki District Division of the Japanese Pharmacological Society, 80-83.

Yanagihara, Y., Shida, T., and Yoshii, H. (1981). Immunopharmacological actions of neurotropin (1): immunostimulating actions of neurotropin. *Folia Pharmacologica Japonica*, 78, 439-449.

Yoshii, H., Suehiro, S., and Watanabe, K. (1987). Immunopharmacological actions of an extract isolated from inflamed skin of rabbits inoculated with vaccinia virus (neurotropin); enhancing effect on delayed type hypersensitivity response through the induction of Lyt-1^+2^-T cells. *International Journal of Immunopharmacology*, 9, 443-451.

STRESS NEUROPEPTIDES AND ADDICTION

Ann Karnitschnig

Eastern Virginia Medical School
Health America
Norfolk, Virginia, USA

When the first living organism appeared on earth it already possessed the ability to feed, reproduce and defend itself against the environment. More and more species appeared, so they had to develop methods of defense against each other. Antibiotics were probably the first weapons of defense, a capacity that was lost in the higher organisms. Poisons and plant movements helped survival, but fast motor reactions in the first animals were a quantum leap in the genesis of defense. With the development of emotions and memory, vertebrates were able to learn. Add to this human intelligence so that we talk to each other even over distances. In spite of all these wonderful developments we still puzzle over ESP and we do not understand how the salmon knows, from the genetic blueprint, how to return to its river of origin.

Answers probably lie in neuropeptides. In the genesis of defense, amines began to serve as the first method of intercellular communication. By clubbing together, these amines form peptides which become increasingly complex. The interesting thing is that all peptides are made from the amino acids. These peptides come directly from DNA without any enzyme link. The DNA is present in every single cell and stores information to make our brains and bodies. Beta-endorphin is created in nerve cells so it is a neuropeptide and has 30 amino acids. Widely scattered are so called receptors that are specific to certain neuropeptides. Opiate receptors, for example, have 20,000 amino acids and can not only be activated by Beta-endorphins, but also by opiate-like drugs such as morphine, codeine and heroin.

The body and mind are bound together by the neuropeptides, so to speak, talking to each other. The mind is the process that perceives, feels, reasons, thinks and judges. The conversation between the neuropeptides proceeds at a cellular level. Certain immune cells contain all the receptors identified so far. We must now consider the body-mind as a single entity communicating through the neuropeptides (Pert, 1986). Consider the incredible memory of the immune system which we have known about and accepted for years. An 80-year old will resist diptheria, 75 years after immunization.

All stresses are emotional and so are mediated by the limbic system of the brain including the hypothalamus, the pituitary and amygdela, focal points for receptors and for neuropeptides. A physical stress such as a broken leg will have an emotional component depending on perceptions and memories. We can consider all illnesses as a failure of the immune system to regulate the organism. The organism can be impacted by physical/emotional external stresses and external substances that are either ingested and absorbed by the gut, absorbed through the skin, or inhaled through the lungs or nasal mucosa. Add to this the hypodermic syringe injecting substances into our muscles and veins and you have the full spectrum. External substances, of course, include foodstuffs, toxins, drugs, bacteria and viruses. If a disease develops somehow, the immune system, memory, and neuropeptides have not been able to handle the stress or substance.

Robert Adler (1975) made a very important discovery. While working with rates he tried to instill in the animals an aversion to saccharin flavored water. He fed them saccharin, then injected them with cyclophosplamide which made them nauseated. Cyclophosplamide suppresses the immune system, but it quickly reverts to normal. Adler found that he conditioned the rats not only to avoid saccharin, but to suppress their immune system whenever they drank saccharin. Let us look at how all illnesses can be viewed as an over-reaction or under-reaction to an outside or inside antigen. If our bodies over-react to an outside antigen we get allergies or under-react, infections. Inside antigens emerging inside the body produce auto-immunity if over-reactive, or cancer if under-reactive. All diseases can be understood using these concepts.

Let us consider the developing child. During those nine months in utero the child is exposed to such external substances as alcohol, drugs and viruses through the placenta. The unborn child is also responding to the mother's stresses and neuropeptides--nonadrenaline, cortisone, gamma-aminobutyric acid and endorphins. The child will also be differentially developing his left brain with its reading, writing, mathematical and speech skills from the right brain with its skills in perception and recognition. The right brain is creative, artistic, and holistic. There is some evidence that marijuana and hallucinogens tend to make us use our right brains.

Hans Selye described the non-specific response of the body to any demand--the stress response, fight, flight or fright--with the classical sympathetic neuropeptide adrenaline. The sympathetic overflow is counterbalanced by the parasympathetic mediated by acetylcholine inhibited by atropine. The quick response to stress is adrenaline produced in the adrenal medulla and the locus ceruleus while the slower response is from the adrenal cortex producing cortisone. Beta-lipotrophin (a neuropeptide with 91 amino-acids) is the precurser for both cortisone and endorphins (30 amino-acids). Our own endogenous opiate blocked by nalloxone not only kills pain, but produces the calmness we need to overcome the crisis. I want you to imagine the brain as a bubbling laboratory with the DNA producing the 50-60 neuropeptides we have so far identified each with specific receptors. Sigmund Freud was right when he hypothesized that every mental event is traceable to a chemical reaction in the brain.

What is addiction? The old definition of substance abuse with withdrawal syndrome and tolerance is now replaced by a definition which includes compulsion, loss of control and continued use despite adverse consequences. It seems that the user needs the drug to feel normal and has a more or less irresistible urge to continue drug usage. The concept of a reinforcing drug must be understood. Cocaine is one of the best examples of a reinforcing drug, so given a choice a monkey will die from an overdose of cocaine. This is unlike other abusable drugs such as alcohol and opiates where the animal will continue eating, grooming and sleeping as the addiction continues.

Designer drugs are modifications of illicit drugs to circumvent the Controlled Substance's Act. Methylene dioxymethamphetamine (MDMA) or Ecstasy, acts like an amphetamine/hallucinogen. On the streets, a hit (150mg) will cost $8 - $20. It is a fairly short-acting drug that seems to promote trust and enhance insight, while promoting a feeling of well-being. Unfortunately, repeated use may alter the serotonin neurons. Another designer drug, a chemical analoge of demerol, MPPP (methylphenylparahydropyridine), may contain the impurity MPTP (methylphenyltetrahydropyridine). Young intravenous drug abusers have arrived in hospitals with severe catatonia. The so-called "frozen addict" is found to have severe and permanent Parkinsonism from MPTP, which destroys the neurons that reduce dopamine.

No discussion of addiction would be complete without ethyl alcohol. The normal breakdown of alcohol in every person is acetaldyde, acetic acid, then carbon-dioxide and water. It has been shown that sons of alcoholics have a four-times higher level of acetaldyde after a challenge, than controls. Genetically, they may be deficient in aldehydedehydrogenase. Aldehyde combines with brain amines to form hallucinogenic substances such as tetrahydroisoquinolines (TIQs). The makeup of TIQs may coincide with the advent of loss of control. Some people may never produce TIQs, even after years of heavy drinking, so they may genetically be somewhat immune from the disease, alcoholism. Others seem to make TIQs with their first drink. In the alcohol field, it's the so-called "X-factor." The first drink is remembered as extremely pleasant, but often associated with a blackout (amnesia) and followed by episodes of aberrant and excessive drinking. So, some children may be genetically predisposed to alcoholism by lack of aldehydedehydrogenase and the ability to produce TIQs, amongst other possible imbalances (endorphins, GABA, etc.).

Of course, alcoholism may have other genetic markers of biochemical consequences. Coffman and Pelty (1985) have looked at blood GABA levels (Gamma aminobutyrol acid) in chronic alcoholics and age-matched comparison individuals. The results are striking:

Chronic alcoholics	14.3 ± 7.3 mg/ml
Comparison groups	57.5 ± 12.0 mg/ml

Do these differences reflect a predisposition to develop alcoholism secondary to GABA deficiency? Or, are these results secondary to alcoholism?

The locus ceruleus, our pleasure and appetite center, is switched on by alcohol, opiates, benzodiazapines and noradrenaline. The drug withdrawal syndrome seems to be secondary to an over-activity of the chronically suppressed locus ceruleus. Endorphin boosters, such as acupuncture, exercise, biofeedback, certain foods, friends, or the placebo effect are natural ways of switching off the locus ceruleus.

The pain gate of Melczak and Wall depends on a critical balance between endorphins and substance P. Since pain is the major reason all people seek physicians' care, it is essential for everyone to understand substance P. Noxious stimuli (thermal chemical or chemical) in the periphery makes substance P travel up neurons to the dorsal horn (substantia gelatinosa-lamina II). If enough messages get to the dorsal horn, they are relayed to the brain and pain is perceived. Without substance P (familial dysautonomia), pain is absent. Another important action of substance P is the axon reflex or axon reflex stimulating the mast cells to produce histamine. The triple response described by Sir Thomas Lewis (calor, dolor, rubor - heat, pain and redness) is absent without substance P. Substance P is a very important neuropeptide acting often like acetylcholine increasing circulation to the gut. It has been shown to improve learning, enhance sleep and counteract excess adrenaline release in hemorrhegic shock.

Dr. Frederick Goodwin at the National Institute of Mental Health (NIMH) looked at the enlisted men who had troubles adjusting to military life. A questionnaire determined their aggressiveness. Cerebrospinal fluid levels of the aggressive men showed elevated naradrenaline and diminished serotonin (5-hydroxytryptamine) levels. Goodwin hypothesized that this is not genetic, but that early life experiences influence chemical balance. A child, repeatedly confronted with situations arousing aggressive behavior, learns to elevate noradrenaline and decrease serotonin levels. The pattern remains and makes them docile. It has been tried on aggressive prisoners, but again, ethical issues arise.

In summary, we might consider serotonin boosters as useful. Not only does serotonin reduce aggression, but it is well known to reduce depression. As so often happens in medicine, the old-wives tale of a cup of milk at bedtime being a good sedative is now explained: milk contains tryptophane (an essential amino acid) which is hydroxylated to a form 5-hydroxytryptamine (serotonin). Serotonin's third useful action is that it enhances sleep.

Let us consider the brain as an enchanted forest, remodeling and restructuring itself instant to instant, with neurotransmitters as chemical messengers. We are on the edge of a "choose your mood" society, since we can enhance or suppress specific moods or emotions. The real problem is not the creation of new drugs, but who makes the decisions when they should be used? On whom should they be used?

Hippocrates told us the body fights to restore normal conditions. Claude Bernard said, "One of the most characteristic features of all living beings is their ability to maintain the constancy of their interior milieu despite the change in surroundings." As physicians, we have challenging ethical questions. Should marijuana be available to patients with glaucoma, or as an appetite stimulant, mood-elevating substance for patients dying of cancer? Would it be appropriate to give patients with terminal illnesses Ecstasy to help them talk to their family and friends? It's sad that as physicians, we probably feel more comfortable prescribing sedatives.

We are always searching for the mystical substance, a miraculous drug that will deliver us instantly from a miserable state. Vitamins (vital amines), the first wild reactions to cortisone, or Freud's encounter with cocaine are examples of how drugs are perceived as elixirs. Our foodstuffs may contain neuropeptide replacements (L. DOPA for dopamine in Parkinsonism), and other "natural" remedies will probably always be best cures for addiction. The production of pleasure through the stimulation of loving friends, quite apart from mobilizing endorphins, will always be more effective than any chemical or drugs.

REFERENCES

Adler, Robert and Cohen, Nicholas. (1975). Behaviorally conditioned immunosuppression, *Psychosomatic Medicine*, 37, p. 338.

Coffman, J.A. and Pelty, I. (1985). Plasma levels in chronic alcoholics, *American Journal of Psychiatry*, 142, p. 1204-1205.

Pert, Candice B. (1986). The wisdom of the receptors advances. *Institute for the Advancement of Health*, 3, No. 3, p. 8-17.

INDEX

MIX
Papier aus verantwortungsvollen Quellen
Paper from responsible sources
FSC® C105338

If you have any concerns about our products,
you can contact us on
ProductSafety@springernature.com

In case Publisher is established outside the EU,
the EU authorized representative is:
Springer Nature Customer Service Center GmbH
Europaplatz 3, 69115 Heidelberg, Germany

Printed by Libri Plureos GmbH
in Hamburg, Germany